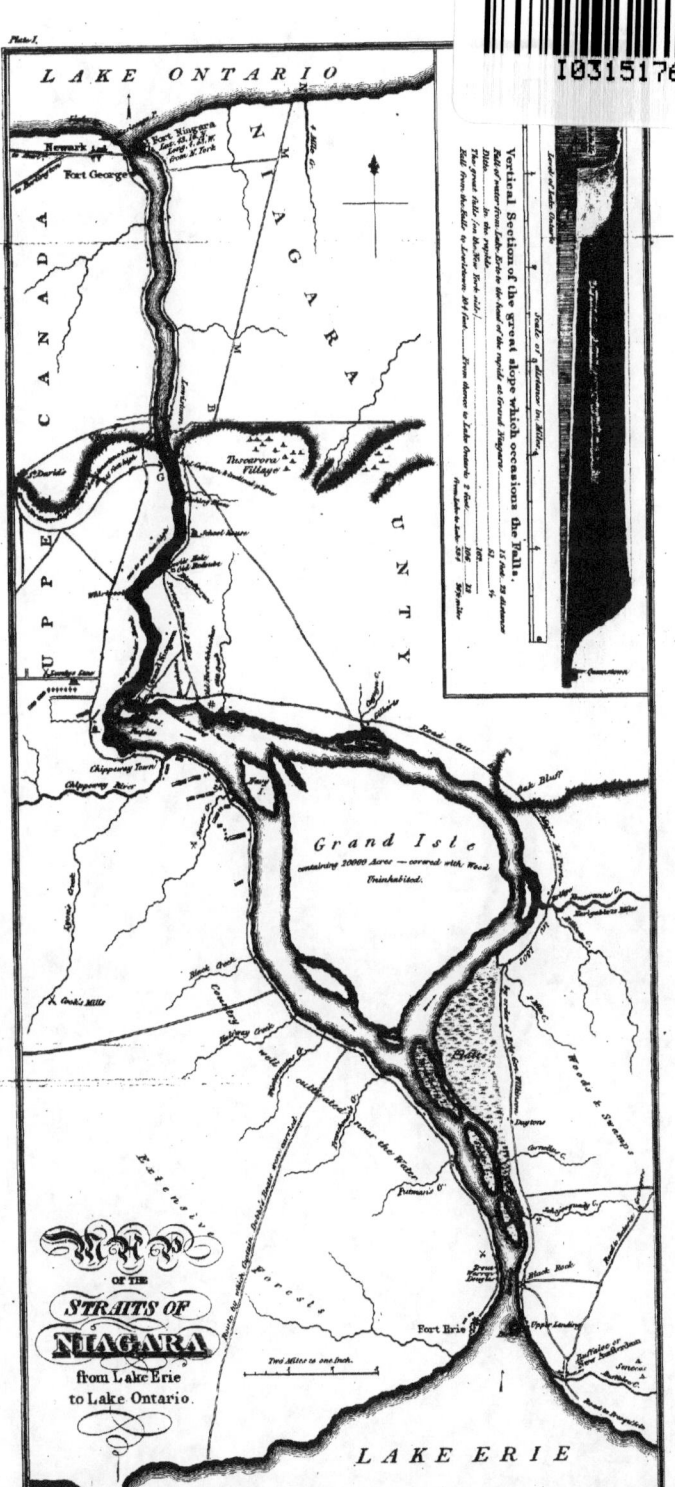

A

FULL AND CORRECT ACCOUNT

OF THE

MILITARY OCCURRENCES

OF

THE LATE WAR

BETWEEN

GREAT BRITAIN

AND

THE UNITED STATES OF AMERICA;

WITH

AN APPENDIX,

AND

PLATES.

By WILLIAM JAMES,

AUTHOR OF " A FULL AND CORRECT ACCOUNT OF THE CHIEF
NAVAL OCCURRENCES, &c."

Alterum alterius auxilio eget.
SALLUST.

IN TWO VOLUMES.

VOL. I.

London:

PRINTED FOR THE AUTHOR:
AND SOLD BY BLACK, KINGSBURY, PARBURY, AND ALLEN, LEADENHALL-STREET;
JAMES M. RICHARDSON, CORNHILL; JOHN BOOTH, DUKE-STREET,
PORTLAND-PLACE; AND ALL OTHER BOOKSELLERS.

1818.

Printed & bound by Antony Rowe Ltd, Eastbourne

TO
LIEUT.-COLONEL JOHN HARVEY, C.B.

DEPUTY-ADJUTANT-GENERAL OF HIS MAJESTY'S FORCES

IN THE CANADAS;

WHO,

BESIDES DISTINGUISHING HIMSELF ON SEVERAL

OTHER OCCASIONS,

DURING THE LATE AMERICAN WAR,

DID,

AT MIDNIGHT, ON THE FIFTH OF JUNE, 1813,

LEAD THE ADVANCE OF AN ATTACK,

PLANNED BY HIMSELF,

IN WHICH

SEVEN HUNDRED AND FOUR BRITISH

SURPRISED,

AND, AFTER A SHORT STRUGGLE,

DROVE FROM THEIR FORTIFIED ENCAMPMENT,

NEAR STONEY CREEK,

IN

UPPER CANADA,

THREE THOUSAND FIVE HUNDRED AMERICANS:

AN EXPLOIT

WHICH TENDED, IN A HIGH DEGREE, TO THE SAFETY OF TWO

VALUABLE BRITISH PROVINCES;

THIS WORK

IS

MOST RESPECTFULLY DEDICATED,

BY

THE AUTHOR.

SUBSCRIBERS' NAMES.

A.

Abbott, Wm. esq.
Adair, A. esq.
Adlington, Thomas, esq.
Admiralty, the hon. lords commissioners of the, 20 copies.
Allen, John, esq.
Anglesey, lieutenant-general the marquis of, G.C.B.
Arbuthnot, lieutenant-colonel the honorable Henry.
Arrowsmith, Aaron, esq.

B.

Baker, John, esq.
Banks, William, esq.
Barnes, William, esq.
———, Thomas, esq.
Bartholomew, D. E. esq. captain R.N. and C.B.
Bathurst, the right honorable earl, K.G. and F.A.S.
Beazley, Charles, esq.
Beresford, rear-admiral sir John Poo, bart.
Black, Kingsbury, Parbury, and Allen,   100 copies.
Blake, J. esq.
Booth, Mr. John,   20 copies.
Brisbane, major-general sir Thomas, K.C.B.

SUBSCRIBERS' NAMES.

Broke, sir Philip Bowes Vere, bart. captain R. N. and
    K.C.B.   3 copies.
——, lieutenant-colonel sir Charles, K.C.B.
——, major, 58th foot.
Brown, John, esq.
Bowdery and Kerby, Messrs.   6 copies.
Brace, Edward, esq. captain R.N. and C.B.

C.

Campbell, John, esq.
Canterbury, his grace, the lord archbishop of.
Carter, J. esq.
Chambers, S. esq.
Christie, captain Brath. 5th dragoons guards.
Cockburn, rear-admiral sir George, K.C.B.
Cole, sir Christopher, captain R.N. K.C.B. and M.P.
Collins, Enos, esq. Halifax, Nova Scotia.
——, and Allison, messrs. ditto.   30 copies.
Cradock, general sir John F. G.C.B. and K.C.
Clarke, Thomas, esq. Upper Canada.
Clinton, W. B. esq.

D.

Davis, Thomas, esq.
Dennis, major, 49th foot.
Digby, Stephen Thomas, esq. captain R.N.
Donaldson, J. esq.
Drummond, John, junior, esq.

E.

Eaton, Mr. George, Halifax, Nova Scotia.   25 copies.
Ellis, John, esq.
Eppes, William J. esq.

F.

Fisher, William, esq.
——, captain.
Fitton, Michael, esq.

SUBSCRIBERS' NAMES.

Forbes, John, esq.
Fraser, William, esq. Halifax, Nova Scotia.

G.

Gerrard, John, esq.
Gibson, John, esq.
Gordon, major-general, sir James Willoughby, K.C.B.
———, John, esq.
Grant, major-general sir Charles, K.C.B.
———, Alexander, esq. Jamaica.
Gray, the reverend Benjamin G. Halifax, Nova Scotia, 3 copies.
Green, John, esq.
Griffith, George Edward, esq.

H.

Hamilton, J. esq.
Hammond, James, esq.
Hanchett, J. M. esq. captain R.N. and C.B.
Hardy, ——— esq.
Harrison, Richard, esq.
Heath, J. esq.
Hill, James, esq.
Hooper, lieutenant-colonel Henry.
Hotham, rear-admiral sir Henry, K.C.B.
Hunter, vice-admiral.
Hurd, Thomas, esq. captain R.N.
Hutchinson, general lord, G.C.B. and K.C.

J.

Jackson, John, esq.
James, major Charles.
———, Thomas, esq. M.D.
Jennings, Mr. Robert,   12 copies.
Johnson, John, esq.
Jones, William, esq.

K.

Kemp, William, esq.
Kendall, Edward Augustus, esq. F.A.S.   2 copies.
Kenyon, the right honorable lord, F.S.A. and L.L.D.

SUBSCRIBERS' NAMES.

King, the reverend J. rector of Witnesham, Suffolk
———, John, esq.
Knowles, John, esq.

L.

Lambert, major-general sir John, K.C.B.
Larkins, captain, H. E. I. C. ship Warren Hastings.
———, J. P. esq. Calcutta.
Layman, William, esq. captain R.N.
Lemon, Charles, esq.
Lewis, John, esq.
Liverpool, the right honorable the earl of, K.G.
Lockwood, Anthony, esq. Halifax, Nova Scotia.

M.

Maberly, John, esq. M. P.
Macdonnell, lieutenant-colonel George.
Malcolm, rear-admiral sir Pultney, K.C.B.
Maples, John F. esq. captain R. N. and C.B.
Martin, H. esq.
Medley, William, esq.
Melville. the right honorable viscount.
Metcalfe, A. esq.
Middleton, sir William, baronet.
Miller, John, esq.
Morris, John, esq.
Mulgrave, general, the right honorable the earl of, F.S.A.
Mure, John, esq. Lower Canada.
Murray, lieutenant-general sir George, G.C.B.

N.

Nichol, Robert, esq. Upper Canada.
Nicolls, major Edward, R. M.
Niel, J. P. esq.

O.

Owen, John, esq.

P.

Pack, major-general sir Denis, K.C.B.

SUBSCRIBERS' NAMES.

Patterson, James, esq.
Parry, William, esq.
Pearson, J. esq.
Phillips, J. esq.
Plenderleath, lieutenant-colonel, C.B.
Powell, John, esq.
Pratt, William, esq.
Price, James, esq.
Pudner, captain.

R.

Reynolds, Mr. William, St. John's, New Brunswick, 5 copies.
————, lieutenant-general.
Richardson, John, esq. Lower Canada.
————, —— M., esq. 50 copies.
————, William, esq.
Robertson, William, esq.
Robinson, J. esq.
Rogers, Robert, esq.
Ross, William, esq.

S.

Saunders, John, esq.
Scott, John, esq.
Shaw, John, esq.
Sidmouth, the right honorable viscount.
Simpson, John, esq.
Sims, James, esq.
Skegg, W. H. esq.
Smith, Thomas, esq.
————, William, esq.
Souter, Mr. John, 12 copies.
Stewart, James, esq.

T.

Tate, ——, esq.
Taylor, William, esq.
Thompson, J. T. esq.

SUBSCRIBERS' NAMES.

Thompson, ——, esq. captain R. N.
Thurston, Thomas, esq.
Times newspaper, proprietors of the.
Torrens, major-general sir Henry, K.C.B.
Torrington, rear-admiral the right hon. viscount, D.C.L. F.R.S.

U.

Usborne, Henry, esq.

V.

Vincent, major-general.
Vivian, major-general, sir Hussey, K.C.B.

W.

Wakerbarth, ————, esq.
Walker, James, esq.
Warner, Edward, esq.
Warren, Frederick, esq. captain R.N.
Wellington, field-marshal his grace the duke of, K.G. and G.C.B.
Welsh, James, esq.
————, Thomas, esq.
Wright, lieutenant-colonel, royal engineers.

Y.

Yeo, sir James Lucas, captain R.N. and K.C.B.
York, field-marshal his royal highness the duke of, K.G. and G.C.B.

PREFACE.

THE length of time that has elapsed since the appearance of the work to which this bears so close a relation, has arisen out of the delays and difficulties experienced by the author in collecting materials; few of which were in his possession, when he promised the public to extend his labors, beyond the naval, to the military, occurrences of the late American war.

Immediately on the publication of his former volume, he transmitted copies to some of the principal reviewers in the United States; hoping to have it in his power, through the medium of the present work, to correct any mistatements that he may have made, upon a topic so interesting to the two nations. Beyond one or two newspaper paragraphs, first misnaming, and then calumniating, the author, nothing of the kind has yet reached him. He has, however, been favored with the sight of an American periodical work, entitled,—' Analectic Magazine and Naval Chronicle;' which contains, among its pages, some very copious remarks upon an article in the British ' Naval Chronicle,' headed— 'SYNOPSIS OF NAVAL ACTIONS BETWEEN THE SHIPS OF HIS BRITANNIC MAJESTY AND OF THE UNITED STATES, DURING THE LATE WAR; BY A BRITISH NAVAL OFFICER ON THE AMERICAN STATION:'— the latter consisting of *extracts* from a series of letters, signed ' Boxer,' forwarded by the author, (but who had neither designated himself as, nor can claim the honor to be, ' a British naval officer,') from Halifax, Nova Scotia; and becoming, afterwards, the groundwork of the author's pamphlet in Halifax,* and subsequent volume in this country.

As the present is a military work, the author, after bestowing a passing glance of admiration upon the flashy vignette of

* ' An Inquiry, &c.'

gamboling dolphins, tridents, wreaths of laurel, &c. displayed, as if *in terrorem*, at the commencement of every fresh quotation from the 'Synopsis,' will digress no further, than till he has exposed some half a dozen of the American reviewer's mis-statements; thence submitting, as a fair inference, what degree of credit is due to the remainder of that gentleman's assertions.

Not being a 'naval officer,' the author could have no *esprit de corps* to bias his judgment. All inuendoes on that head, and pretty numerous they are, may therefore be blotted out of the piece. The same fate, for (as one may suppose) the same reason, must attend the commencing charge, that the 'production came abroad under the sanction of the admiralty.'*

Any railing at the author's 'affected arithmetical precision'† can but create a smile, when the American reviewer is compelled,

* Analectic Mag. and Naval Chronicle, Vol VII. p. 295.
† Ibid. 302.

for lack of argument, to ' pass by the cyphering business.'* It is that ' cyphering business,' that ' debtor and creditor account,'† in the naval warfare between the two countries, that is fast withering the laurels, with which one of them has, of late, so strutted in *caricatura.*

Who it is that ' weighs balls with the most minute precision,'‡ let American naval officers and American naval histories tell.§

The author, although he is no ' naval officer,' would be ashamed to be convicted of having stated, that the loss of a ship's ' jib-boom' is equal, in point of importance, to the loss of a brig's ' main-yard.' ‖ But, in truth, was the Wasp without her jib-boom? If so, as she carried it away three days before the action,¶ her officers and crew must have been very negligent

* Analectic Mag. and Nav. Chron. Vol. VII. p. 307.
† Ibid. 302. ‡ Ibid. p. 304.
§ Naval History of the United States, Vol. I. p. 179—American Naval Monument, p. 141. 181.—James's Naval Occurrences, p. 10. 124. 365.
‖ Analectic Mag. and Naval Chron. Vol. VII. p. 388.
¶ Naval Monument, p. 13.

PREFACE. xv

in not having rigged a fresh one; and 'M. Corné,' the Boston painter, and his employer, 'A. Bowen,' the Boston engraver, are chargeable with unpardonable inaccuracy, for having given to the Wasp, in their representation of the Frolic's capture,* a 'jib-boom,' and no short one either. After stating that the Wasp's crew ' consisted, in reality, of only 110,'† the writer does not proceed far in his ' magazine of wonders,'‡ before he introduces the following paragraph: ' They (the American captain and one of his officers) testified, on oath, that the whole number of persons on board the Wasp, previous to the action, was 137;'§—actually within *one* of the author's statement.¶

In the very teeth of American official papers,‖ does this American writer allege, that ' no complaint' was made, ' when several

---

* Naval Monument, p. 13.
† Analectic Mag. and Nav. Chronicle, Vol. VII. p. 387.
‡ Ib. 382.   § Ib. 487.
¶ James's Naval Occurrences, p. 152.
‖ Nav. Monument, p. 63.—James's Nav. Occurr. p. 223.

of the crew of the Chesapeake were killed, by firing down the gangway.'*

To the ' fabulous account,' that the vessel said to have declined engaging the President off Sandy Hook, was not ' a small frigate,' the Loire,† but the ' Plantaganet 74,' nothing was wanted but ' the trial of her commanding officer.'‡ This trial our ' candid' reviewer is 'authorized to affirm' took place at Bermuda. By way of corroborating, what must appear to all but him and his party as, an ' absurd and ridiculous story,' he brings to his aid—' the express admission of an officer of marines, then in the squadron cruizing off New York, and now a consul in one of our ports.'‡ Who can this be but lieutenant Patrick Savage, at that time of the Narcissus frigate, and now, or lately, consul at Norfolk, Virginia?—It is to be hoped that the statement will meet his eye, if only to afford

---

* Analectic Mag. and Nav. Chron. Vol. VII. p. 388.
† James's Naval Occurrences, p. 324.
‡ Analectic Mag. and Nav. Chron. Vol. VIII. p. 136.

him an opportunity of doing justice to his brother-officers late of the Plantaganet.

After, in several instances, flatly contradicting his own official accounts, the American reviewer puts European gravity to the test, by declaring, first, that his government made war ' in defence of the universal rights of man,'* and next, that the ' modest,' or, as recently and more truly styled, ' arrogant,' commodore Perry, when he filched the commencing words of Nelson's letter, ‡ ' was paying his lordship a high compliment.'†

Had the writer in the American ' Naval Chronicle' employed less ' acrimony,' and more research, in his calling, he might have received the author's thanks for pointing out several real ' inaccuracies,' particularly as to the size and armaments of the American ships. But these ' inaccuracies,' along with the hated ' cyphering business,' he has let ' pass by,' to

* Analectic Mag. and Nav. Chron. vol. VIII. p. 185.
† Ib. 145.
‡ James's Nav. Occurr. p. 294.

be rectified by the author himself, in his two works, that followed, in quick succession, that little hastily-drawn sketch, which, the American reviewer, not having seen those works, is pleased to say, ' appears to contain all that has hitherto been urged, as well as every thing that can be urged, in extenuation of the numerous disasters of England during the last war;'* but, as he more truly than consistently adds, ' which is in reality an indifferent production.'† If so, therefore; and if the ' production' teems with ' admissions,' such as ' British officers' ought to ' feel mortified at,' why is the American reviewer, in his ' candid' examination of it, so extremely irritable? Even his own countrymen, the ' gentle' readers for whose entertainment he has labored and sweated so much, will attribute his anger to the dilemma into which he is placed, by the ' novel' way of ' weighing and measuring, by the pound and by the foot,'‡ ' battles' that have turned out so

* Analectic Mag. and Nav. Chron. Vol. VII. p. 289.
† Ib. p. 295.   ‡ Ib. Vol. VII. p. 307.

PREFACE. xix

lucrative to the American press, in general, and to the American 'Naval Chronicle,' in particular.

What language contained in the 'Synopsis,' written when the two countries were at war, equals, in falsehood, absurdity, or intended 'severity,' the assertion, made while the two countries are at peace, that 'American officers are more brave than their rivals'?*

How much moderation, 'candour,' and discernment, the writer of the American review can bring into discussion, when his country is a party, may be gathered from his comparing,—without meaning it in irony,—'the battle of New Orleans,' with 'the battles of Cressy and Agincourt.'†

This sudden change from naval to military warfare recalls the author's attention to the subject immediately before him. The first point he would press upon the reader's attention is, that the system of tactics adapted to the

* Analectic Mag. and Nav. Chron. Vol. VII. p. 306.
† Ib. p. 294.

b 2

cultivated plains of Europe cannot be practised amidst the wild regions of America. Woods, precipices, creeks, and morasses, are traversed with ease by native troops, while a body of the best disciplined foreigners is either opposed in its advance by insurmountable obstacles, or led into an ambush, where the more ardent the courage, the greater is the slaughter, the more certain the defeat.

The British soldier can seldom trace his acquaintance with fire-arms beyond the day of his enlistment; but the American soldier has been accustomed, from his infancy, to the free use of the most destructive of all fire-arms, the *rifle*. No laws have interfered to restrain him from amusing his fancy, or furnishing his table, with the game that so abundantly surrounds his home; and the daily toils of the huntsman, while they have fitted his body for enduring, without fatigue, the longest marches, have familiarized him to the intricacies of his native forests. Where bush-fighting can be practised, he is truly formidable: an open country, and a struggle with the bayonet, he alike avoids, as the bane of his hopes.

Nearly the whole of the military contests treated of in these volumes were carried on amidst the thinly inhabited, and, of course, but slightly cultivated, parts of North-America. The reader whose mind is filled with the justly celebrated fame of British troops must, therefore, be careful how he forms an opinion upon the merits of the combatants. He should recollect, that the American troops fought their battles upon their own ground; and obtained, in consequence, a decided local superiority over the British sent out against them. Viewed thus, it cannot be objected, if all estimates of relative force between British and American troops, other than where batteries are concerned, be founded upon the principle of—not a presumed inequality of powers, but—man for man, or unit for unit.

The historian may describe, in the most impassioned language, the meeting of two armies, their furious onset, and long and bloody conflict; how this side fled and that pursued; yet, if he fail to impress upon the reader's mind a clear conception of the quantum of force which each party brought into the field, he shall employ his labors to very little purpose. Of the many printed narratives of battles, by far the greater number are deficient in this important particular. With due acknowledgement to the American reviewer for the hint, the author produces, as a prominent example, the celebrated battle of Azincour. Hume gives no figures, but states that the ' enemy was four times more numerous.' * ' Monstrelet says six times.' † ' P. Daniel says three times.' † Different French writers make their own force ' 100000 ;' ' 140000 ;' ' 150000, the third part horse ;' ' 150000 horse.' † Other historians say, that ' the French amounted to 150000, and the English but to 9000 ;' † which is nearly 17, instead of ' six,' ' four,' or even

* Hume, Vol. III. p. 100.
† Rapin (folio edit.) Vol. I. p. 512.

'*three*,' to one,—of all, the most probable proportion.

In detailing the operations of the British and American armies, a clear and satisfactory account of the force engaged will, next to the immediate result of the battle, form the most important object. As the fairest means of ascertaining this, each party will be considered as unquestionable authority for the amount of his own numbers; unless an evident contradiction, or attempt to deceive, discovers itself. In that case, reliance will be placed upon the positive assertions of the opposite party.

A British official account of every military action has appeared in the Gazette; and copies of the whole, as well as of such American official accounts as have been published, or could be procured, are given in the Appendix. The deficiency on the American side is compensated by the ample details, and, upon some points, apparently authentic information, contained in three very recent American publications on the events of the late war. As these works are rarely to be met with in this country, and will be frequently quoted in the progress of our enquiries, the reader is here presented with their respective title-pages:

'Historical Sketches of the late War between the United States and Great Britain; blended with Anecdotes illustrative of the individual bravery of the American Sailors, Soldiers, and Citizens, embellished with Portraits of distinguished Naval and Military Officers; and accompanied by Views of several Sieges and Engagements. By John Lewis Thomson. Third Edition. Philadelphia: published by Thomas Desilver; 1816.'

'An Impartial and Correct History of the War between the United States of America and Great Britain; comprising a particular Detail of the Naval and Military Operations, and a faithful Record of the Events produced during the Contest, from its Commencement, June 18, 1812, to the Treaty of Peace, ratified at the City of Washington, February 17, 1815. By T. O'Connor. Fourth Edition, revised and corrected. Carefully compiled from Official Documents. New York: printed and published by John Low, No. 62, Vesey Street, 1817.'

'History of the United States, from their first Settlement as English Colonies, in 1607, to the Year 1808, or the Twenty-Third of their Sovereignty and Indepen-

J.B.White P.t   Gimbrede Sculp.t

DAVID RAMSAY M.D.

Engraved for the Analectic Magazine.   Published by M. Thomas.

dence. By David Ramsay, M.D. Continued to the Treaty of Ghent, by S. S. Smith, D.D. and LL.D. and other Literary Gentlemen; in Three Volumes. (8vo.) Philadelphia: published by M. Carey, 1817.'

The first of these books is dedicated 'to the Honorable James Munroe, secretary of state of the United States;' and the third edition was published a very short time before the writer's patron attained the honors of the president's chair. This work, therefore, may be regarded as a demi-official performance; and, in some cases, especially where the American official letters have not been obtained, or prove deficient in particulars, Mr. Thomson's very minute details may be profitably employed.

The 'History of the War,' till the third, if not the fourth edition, was an anonymous work. At last, the people of the United States gave so loud and unequivocal proofs of the value of the writer's zealous, if not 'impartial' labors, that Mr. O'Connor must have possessed a very blameable degree of modesty, indeed, not to have avowed himself the author. How far, in so doing, he has consulted his reputation, will appear in the sequel.

The 'History of the United States' bears, upon the face of the title-page, the stamp of respectability. An 'M.D.' a 'D.D. and LL.D.' 'and other literary gentlemen' as the authors, without 'James Munroe,' and 'The navy department,' among a numerous list of subscribers, afford reasonable grounds for hoping, that, at last, a candid history has appeared from the press of the United States.

That the author may not, as often as a battle occurs, have to repeat remarks upon, what, without reference to the fair promises just noticed, may be termed, the staple commodity of American historians, a few words on the subject will not be out of place here.

Our old enemy in Europe has at all times been ready to do justice to the valor of our troops. A Frenchman is contented to boast, that the best soldiers of his country have beaten an equal number of ours. But an American historian will gravely tell you, that ' about 200 raw, undisciplined, American militia, entirely routed 600 veteran British regulars;' aye, and that ' with the bayonet' too: or, if the Americans are described as the routed party, it is,—' after a desperate struggle with five times their number.' None of these gentlemen think it worth their while to advance any authority for even the most improbable fact. In despite of our reason we are to credit their naked assertions; and to confess, that the heroes of the new, are giants in prowess, compared to the heroes of the old world. Scarcely is a battle recorded, wherein the superiority of numbers was not on the British side; unless, indeed, an opposite statement would serve to heap disgrace upon a certain commander, because he happens to differ, in political tenets, from that party, to whose sinister purposes the writer has devoted his talents and his conscience.

When a national officer does, as he always should, explicitly state the amount and quality of his own force, no one has a right to dispute his word; but his assertions respecting the force of an enemy, unless nearly the whole number that engaged him became his prisoners, ought to be received with caution. A general may find it convenient to show an extended front, of only one or two files deep; and thus deceive his opponent. A few stragglers in a wood may be considered as part of a larger body; or a severe unexpected repulse may induce the retreating troops, from their fears alone, to magnify the number of their foes. For this reason chiefly it is, that the author has resolved to take each party's positive enumeration of his own force, in preference to the loose statements and vague conjectures, too often admitted into the opposite official accounts.

In a work of details like the present, many

PREFACE. xxix

facts must be admitted, having no official foundation on either side. Here the reader, beyond the rule of probability, has only the author's veracity to trust to. Upon that point, he deems it proper to state, that, in his military, as in his naval work, his unofficial facts are the result of direct applications to officers of rank and respectability; but whose names (as must be obvious) he is not, in all cases, at liberty to disclose. Should, however, any mistatement have incautiously crept into his narrative, military or naval, the author would be happy to receive, and, when an opportunity offers, to make public, an authenticated correction.

A woody battle-ground is not the best calculated for a display, even on paper, of military evolutions; the author, therefore, in selecting his plates, has, in most cases, preferred a sketch of the country traversed by the contending armies, to a plan of their fluctuating positions during an engagement. One important exception is the battle near New Orleans. Here, without a plan of the natural, as well as artificial, military obstacles, the most minute verbal description would fall short. Fortunately, he can present Plate VII, with confidence in its general correctness; not weakened, he trusts, by his having wholly framed it out of the engravings in two American publications on the subject*. For Plates I, III, V, and VI, he is indebted, also, (some slight alterations excepted,) to an American work, major-general James Wilkinson's 'Memoirs of my own Time,' published in 1816; a work that will be frequently consulted in the course of the investigation.

As Great Britain and the United States of America are now, happily, at peace, a strong motive exists for describing the events of the late war between them, in language, if not courteous, temperate at least; and this, without any reference to the notorious fact,

* Latour's War in Louisiana, and Eaton's Life of Jackson.

that all American histories, from general Wilkinson's huge 'Memoirs' down to the 'Grub-street'* 'Analectic,' pursue quite an opposite course. The author, much as he has, while scrutinizing the American accounts, endeavoured to command his feelings, may, upon unravelling any design of marked atrocity, have been betrayed into a warmth of expression below the dignity of an historical subject. To the general reader, in that case, some apology is due: as to the American, let him vent his rage upon those of his countrymen, who, disgracing the name of 'historians,' are the authors or abettors of all the calumnies which gave the provocation.

He who shall succeed in teaching American writers to venerate truth, as much as their readers idolize vain-glory, will have achieved, for the republic of America, a ten-fold greater service, than the whole pantheon of demi-gods,

* Analectic Magazine and Naval Chronicle, Vol. VII, p. 246.

xxxii   PREFACE.

whose 'romantic'* feats, instead of being allowed to shine forth, bedizened out as—' Sir Tristian,' ' Don Belianis,' ' the Peers of Charlemagne,' * or any other tale of ' fiction' or mock-heroic, are presented to the world under the specious garb of ' FAITHFUL HISTORY.'

* Analectic Magazine and Nav. Chron. Vol. VII. p. 296.

London, May 16*th,* 1818.

PAINTED BY STUART. ENGRAVED BY W. R. JONES.
PUBLISHED BY JOSEPH DELAPLAINE S.W. CORNER OF CHESNUT & SEVENTH S.T. PHILAD.A 1814.

JAMES MADISON ESQ.R

MILITARY OCCURRENCES,

&c. &c.

CHAPTER I.

Origin of the late war with the United States—President's message—American declaration of war—Pacific views of the British—Determined hostility of the Americans—Prince regent's manifesto in answer to the president's message—Impressed Americans—Native and naturalized citizens—Case of Elijah Clarke—A resident in the Canadas shot as a deserter by an American officer—Acquittal of the officer—An opposite principle afterwards broached by the American government—Cause of Indian hatred to the Americans.

THE defensive measures adopted by the British government, in contravention of the Berlin and Milan decrees, no longer permitting the subjects of the United States, under the disguise of neutrals, to be the carriers of France, the ablest politicians in the republic were engaged to prepare a specious manifesto, representing the United States as the aggrieved, and Great Britain as the aggressing party. A moment of continental pressure upon the latter was deemed the fittest for promulgating this angry state-paper. Accordingly, on the 1st of June, 1812, Mr. Madison, the American president, sent the following message to the two houses of congress:

"Without going back beyond the renewal, in 1803, of the war in which Great Britain is engaged, and omitting unrepaired wrongs of inferior magnitude, the conduct of her government presents a series of acts hostile to the United States, as an independent and neutral nation.

"British cruisers have been in the continued practice of violating the American flag on the great highway of nations, and of seizing and carrying off persons sailing under it; not in the exercise of a belligerent right, founded on the law of nations, against an enemy, but of a municipal prerogative over British subjects. British jurisdiction is thus extended to neutral vessels, in a situation where no laws can operate but the law of nations, and the laws of the country to which the vessels belong; and a self-redress is assumed, which, if British subjects were wrongfully detained and alone concerned, is that substitution of force for a resort to the responsible sovereign, which falls within the definition of war. Could the seizure of British subjects, in such cases, be regarded as within the exercise of a belligerent right, the acknowledged laws of wars, which forbid an article of captured property to be adjudged, without a regular investigation before a competent tribunal, would imperiously demand the fairest trial, where the sacred rights of persons were at issue. In place of such trial, these rights are subjected to the will of every petty commander.

"The practice, hence, is so far from affecting British subjects alone, that under the pretext of searching for these, thousands of American citizens, under the safeguard of public laws, and of their national flag, have been torn from their country, and from every thing dear to them; have been dragged on board ships of war of a foreign nation, and exposed under the severities of their discipline, to be exiled to the most distant and deadly climes, to risk their lives in the battles of their oppressors, and to be the melancholy instruments of taking away those of their own brethren.

"Against this crying enormity, which Great Britain would be so prompt to avenge, if committed against herself, the United States have in vain exhausted remonstrances and expostulations. And that no proof might be wanting of their conciliatory disposition, and no pretext left for a continuance of the practice, the British government was formally assured of the readiness of the United States to enter into arrangements, such as could not be rejected, if the recovery of British subjects were the real and the sole object. The communication passed without effect.

"British cruisers have also been in the practice of violating the rights and the peace of our coasts. They hover over and harass our entering and departing commerce. To the most insulting pretensions they have added the most lawless proceedings in our very harbours, and have wantonly spilt American blood within the sanctuary of our territorial jurisdiction. The principles and rules enforced by that nation, when a neutral nation, against armed vessels of belligerents hovering near her coasts, and disturbing her commerce, are well known. When called on, nevertheless, by the United States, to punish the greater offences committed by her own vessels, her government has bestowed on their commanders additional marks of honour and confidence.

"Under pretended blockades, without the presence of an adequate force, and sometimes without the practicability of applying one, our commerce has been plundered in every sea; the great staples of our country have been cut off from their legitimate markets; and a destructive blow aimed at our agricultural and maritime interests. In aggravation of these predatory measures, they have been considered as in force from the dates of their notification; a retrospective effect being thus added, as has been done in other important cases, to the unlawfulness of the course pursued. And to render the outrage the more signal, these mock blockades have been reiterated and enforced in the face of official communications from the British government, declaring, as the true definition of a legal blockade, ' that particular ports must be actually invested, and previous warning given to vessels bound to them, not to enter.'

"Not content with these occasional expedients for laying waste our neutral trade, the cabinet of Great Britain resorted, at length, to the sweeping system of blockades, under the name of orders in council, which has been moulded and managed as might best suit its political views, its commercial jealousies, or the avidity of British cruisers.

"To our remonstrances against the complicated and transcendent injustice of this innovation, the first reply was, that the orders were reluctantly adopted by Great Britain, as a necessary retaliation on the decrees of her enemy, proclaiming a general blockade of the British isles, at a time when the naval force of that enemy dared not to issue from his own ports. She was reminded, without effect, that her own prior blockades, unsupported by an adequate naval force, actually applied and continued, were a bar to this plea; that executed edicts against millions of our property could not be retaliation on edicts confessedly impossible to be executed; and that retaliation, to be just, should fall on the party setting the guilty example, not on an innocent party, which was not even chargeable with an acquiescence in it.

"When deprived of this flimsy veil for a prohibition of our trade with her enemy, by the repeal of his prohibition of our trade with Great Britain, her cabinet, instead of a corresponding repeal, or a practical discontinuance of its orders, formally avowed a determination to persist in them against the United States, until the markets of her enemy should be laid open to British products; thus asserting an obligation on a neutral power, to require one belligerent to encourage, by its internal regulations, the trade of another belligerent, contradicting her own practice towards all nations, in peace as well as in war; and betraying the insincerity of those professions which inculcated a belief, that, having resorted to her orders with regret, she was anxious to find an occasion for putting an end to them.

"Abandoning still more all respect for the

neutral rights of the United States, and for its own consistency, the British government now demands, as pre-requisites to a repeal of its orders, as they relate to the United States, that a formality should be observed in the repeal of the French decrees, nowise necessary to their termination, nor exemplified by British usage; and that the French repeal, besides including that portion of the decrees which operates within a territorial jurisdiction, as well as that which operates on the high seas, against the commerce of the United States, should not be a single special repeal, in relation to the United States, but should be extended to whatever other neutral nations, unconnected with them, may be affected by those decrees.

"And, as an additional insult, they are called on for a formal disavowal of conditions and pretensions advanced by the French government, for which the United States are so far from having made themselves responsible, that, in official explanations, which have been published to the world, and in a correspondence of the American minister at London with the British minister for foreign affairs, such a responsibility was explicitly and emphatically disclaimed.

"It has become, indeed, sufficiently certain, that the commerce of the United States is to be sacrificed, not as interfering with the belligerent rights of Great Britain, not as supplying the wants of their enemies, which she herself supplies, but as interfering with the monopoly which she covets for her own commerce and navigation. She carries on a war against the lawful commerce of a friend, that she may the better carry on a commerce with an enemy; a commerce polluted by the forgeries and perjuries which are, for the most part, the only passports by which it can succeed.

"Anxious to make every experiment, short of the last resort of injured nations, the United States have withheld from Great Britain, under successive modifications, the benefits of a free intercourse with their market, the loss of which could not but outweigh the profits accruing from her restrictions of our commerce with other nations. And to entitle these experiments to the more favourable consideration, they were so framed as to enable her to place her adversary under the exclusive operation of them. To these appeals her government has been equally inflexible, as if willing to make sacrifices of every sort, rather than yield to the claims of justice, or renounce the errors of a false pride. Nay, so far were the attempts carried to overcome the attachment of the British cabinet to its unjust edicts, that it received every encouragement within the competency of the executive branch of our government, to expect that a repeal of them would be followed by a war between the United States and France, unless the French edicts should also be repealed. Even this communication, although silencing for ever the plea of a disposition in the United States to acquiesce in those edicts, originally the sole plea for them, received no attention.

"If no other proof existed of a predetermination of the British government against a repeal of its orders, it might be found in the correspondence of the minister plenipotentiary of the United States at London, and the British secretary for foreign affairs, in 1810, on the question, whether the blockade of May 1806 was considered as in force or as not in force. It had been ascertained that the French government, which urged this blockade as the ground of its Berlin decree, was willing, in the event of its removal, to repeal that decree; which, being followed by alternate repeals of the other offensive edicts, might abolish the whole system on both sides. This inviting opportunity for accomplishing an object so important to the United States, and professed so often to be the desire of both the belligerents, was made known to the British government. As that government admits that an actual application of an adequate force is necessary to the existence of a legal blockade; and it was notorious, that if such a force had ever been applied, its long discontinuance had annulled the blockade in question, there could be no sufficient objection on the part of Great Britain to a formal revocation of it; and no imaginable objection to a declaration of the fact that the blockade did not exist. The declaration would have been consistent with her avowed principles of blockade, and would have enabled the United States to demand from France the pledged repeal of her decrees; either with success, in which case the way would have been opened for a general repeal of the belligerent edicts; or without success, in which case the United States would have been justified in turning their measures exclusively against France. The British government would, however, neither rescind the blockade, nor declare its non-existence, nor permit its non-existence to be inferred and affirmed by the American plenipotentiary. On the contrary, by representing the blockade to be comprehended in the orders in council, the United States were compelled so to regard it in their subsequent proceedings.

"There was a period when a favourable change in the policy of the British cabinet was justly considered as established. The minister plenipotentiary of his Britannic majesty here proposed an adjustment of the differences more immediately endangering the harmony of the two countries. The proposition was accepted with a promptitude and cordiality corresponding with the invariable professions of this government. A foundation appeard to be laid for a sincere and lasting reconciliation. The prospect, however, quickly vanished. The whole proceeding was disavowed by the British government, without any explanation which could at that time repress the belief that the disavowal proceeded from a spirit of hostility to the commercial rights and prosperity of the United States. And it has since come into proof that, at the very moment when the public minister was holding the language of friendship, and inspired confidence in the sincerity of the negociation with which he was charged, a secret agent of his government was employed in intrigues, having for their object a subversion of our government, and a dismemberment of our happy union.

"In reviewing the conduct of Great Britain towards the United States, our attention is necessarily drawn to the warfare just renewed by the savages on one of our extensive frontiers; a warfare which is known to spare neither age nor sex, and to be distinguished by features peculiarly shocking to humanity. It is difficult to account for the activity and combinations which have for some time been developing themselves among the tribes in constant intercourse with the British traders and garrisons, without connecting their hostility with that influence, and, without recollecting the authenticated examples of such interpositions heretofore furnished by the officers and agents of that government.

"Such is the spectacle of injuries and indignities which have been heaped on our country; and such the crisis which its unexampled forbearance and conciliatory efforts have not been able to avert. It might, at least, have been expected, that an enlightened nation, if less urged by moral obligations, or invited by friendly dispositions on the part of the United States, would have found in its true interest alone, a sufficient motive to respect their rights and their tranquillity on the high seas; that an enlarged policy would have favoured that free and general circulation of commerce, in which the British nation is at all times interested; and which, in times of war, is the best alleviation of its calamities to herself, as well as the other belligerents; and more especially, that the British cabinet would not, for the sake of a precarious and surreptitious intercourse with hostile markets, have persevered in a course of measures which necessarily put at hazard the invaluable market of a great and growing country, disposed to cultivate the mutual advantages of an active commerce.

"Other councils have prevailed. Our moderation and conciliation have had no other effect than to encourage perseverance, and to enlarge pretensions. We behold our seafaring citizens still the daily victims of lawless violence, committed on the great and common highway of nations, even within sight of the country which owes them protection. We behold our vessels freighted with the products of our soil and industry, or returning with the honest proceeds of them, wrested from their lawful destinations, confiscated by prize-courts, no longer the organs of public law, but the instruments of arbitrary edicts; and their unfortunate crews dispersed and lost, or forced, or inveigled, in British ports, into British fleets; whilst arguments are employed in support of these aggressions, which have no foundation but in a principle supporting equally a claim to regulate our external commerce in all cases whatsoever.

"We behold, in fine, on the side of Great Britain, a state of war against the United States; and on the side of the United States, a state of peace towards Great Britain.

"Whether the United States shall continue passive under these progressive usurpations, and these accumulating wrongs; or, opposing force to force, in defence of their natural rights, shall commit a just cause into the hands of the Almighty Disposer of events; avoiding all connections which might entangle it in the contests or views of other powers, and preserving a constant readiness to concur in an honourable re-establishment of peace and friendship, is a solemn question, which the constitution wisely confides to the legislative department of the government. In recommending it to their early deliberations, I am happy in the assurance that the decision will be worthy the enlightened and patriotic councils of a virtuous, a free, and a powerful nation.

"Having presented this view of the relations of the United States with Great Britain, and of the solemn alternative growing out of them, I proceed to remark, that the communications last made to congress, on the subject of our relations with France, will have shown that since the revocation of her decrees as they violated the neutral rights of the United States, her government has authorised illegal captures by its privateers and public ships, and that other outrages have been practised on our vessels and our citizens. It will have been seen also, that no indemnity had been provided, or satisfactorily pledged, for the extensive spoliations committed under the violent and retrospective order of the French government against the property of our citizens seized within the jurisdiction of France.

"I abstain at this time from recommending to the consideration of congress, definitive measures with respect to that nation, in the expectation that the result of unclosed discussions between our minister plenipotentiary at Paris and the French government, will speedily enable congress to decide with greater advantage on the course due to the rights, the interests, and the honour of our country."

In seventeen days after the date of this declamatory speech, the two houses of congress formally declared war against Great Britain, and empowered the president to issue letters of marque and general reprisal; and, on the very day on which this declaration arrived at New York, appeared in the London Gazette the prince regent's declaration, absolutely and unequivocally revoking the orders in council, so far as they related to American vessels. Nothing could better demonstrate to the world the different feelings which actuated the two governments.

The American declaration of war reached the British government on the 30th of July; but, in the firm reliance that the revocation of the orders in council would produce a pacific effect, no further steps were taken by the latter, than to direct that American ships and goods should be brought in and detained. It was not till the 13th of October, when the American government had disregarded the notified repeal of the orders in council, and refused to ratify the armistice agreed upon between Sir George Prevost and General Dearborn on the Canadian frontier, that the British government published an order for granting general reprisals against the ships, goods, and citizens of the United States; and even this order concluded with a declaration, that nothing therein was to annul the authority which had been given to his majesty's commanders upon the American station, to sign a convention for recalling all hostile orders issued by the respective governments, with a view of restoring the accustomed relations of amity and commerce between the two countries. That pacific attempt failing, also, the prince regent, on the 9th of January, 1813, issued the following manifesto in reply to Mr. Madison's:

" The earnest endeavours of the prince regent to preserve the relations of peace and amity with the United States of America having unfortunately failed, his royal highness, acting in the name and on the behalf of his majesty, deems it proper publicly to declare the causes and origin of the war, in which the government of the United States has compelled him to engage.

" No desire of conquest, or other ordinary motive of aggression, has been, or can be with any colour of reason, in this case, imputed to Great Britain. That her commercial interests were on the side of peace, if war could have been avoided without the sacrifice of her maritime rights, or without an injurious submission to France, is a truth which the American government will not deny.

"His royal highness does not, however, mean to rest on the favorable presumption to which he is entitled. He is prepared, by an exposition of the circumstances which have led to the present war, to show that Great Britain has throughout acted towards the United States of America with a spirit of amity, forbearance, and conciliation; and to demonstrate the inadmissible nature of those pretensions which have at length unhappily involved the two countries in war.

"It is well known to the world, that it has been the invariable object of the ruler of France to destroy the power and independence of the British empire, as the chief obstacle to the accomplishment of his ambitious designs.

"He first contemplated the possibility of assembling such a naval force in the channel as, combined with a numerous flotilla, should enable him to disembark in England an army sufficient, in his conception, to subjugate this country; and through the conquest of Great Britain he hoped to realize his project of universal empire.

"By the adoption of an enlarged and provident system of internal defence, and by the valour of his majesty's fleets and armies, this design was entirely frustrated; and the naval force of France, after the most signal defeats, was compelled to retire from the ocean.

"An attempt was then made to effectuate the same purpose by other means—a system was brought forward, by which the ruler of France hoped to annihilate the commerce of Great Britain, to shake her public credit, and to destroy her revenue; to render useless her maritime superiority, and so to avail himself of his continental ascendancy, as to constitute himself, in a great measure, the arbiter of the ocean, notwithstanding the destruction of his fleets.

"With this view, by the decree of Berlin, followed by that of Milan, he declared the British territories to be in a state of blockade; and that all commerce or even correspondence with Great Britain was prohibited. He decreed that every vessel and cargo, which had entered, or was found proceeding to a British port, or which, under any circumstances, had been visited by a British ship of war, should be lawful prize: he declared all British goods and produce, wherever found, and however acquired, whether coming from the mother-country or from her colonies, subject to confiscation; he further declared to be denationalized, the flag of all neutral ships that should be found offending against these his decrees: and he gave to this project of universal tyranny, the name of the continental system.

"For these attempts to ruin the commerce of Great Britain, by means subversive of the clearest rights of neutral nations, France endeavoured in vain to rest her justification upon the previous conduct of his majesty's government.

"Under circumstances of unparalleled provocation, his majesty had abstained from any measure which the ordinary rules of the law of nations did not fully warrant. Never was the maritime superiority of a belligerent over his enemy more complete and decided. Never was the opposite belligerent so formidably dangerous in his power, and in his policy, to the liberties of all other nations. France had already trampled so openly and systematically on the most sacred rights of neutral powers, as might well have justified the placing her out of the pale of civilized nations. Yet in this extreme case, Great Britain had so used her naval ascendancy, that her enemy could find no just cause of complaint: and, in order to give to these lawless decrees the appearance of retaliation, the ruler of France was obliged to advance principles of maritime law unsanctioned by any other authority than his own arbitrary will.

"The pretext for these decrees were, first, that Great Britain had exercised the rights of war against private persons, their ships and goods; as if the only object of legitimate hostility on the ocean were the public property of a state, or as if the edicts and the courts of France itself had not at all times enforced this right with peculiar rigour; secondly, that the

British orders of blockade, instead of being confined to fortified towns, had, as France asserted, been unlawfully extended to commercial towns and ports, and to the mouths of rivers; and, thirdly, that they had been applied to places, and to coasts which neither were, nor could be, actually blockaded. The last of these charges is not founded on fact; whilst the others, even by the admission of the American government, are utterly groundless in point of law.

"Against these decrees, his majesty protested and appealed—he called upon the United States to assert their own rights, and to vindicate their independence, thus menaced and attacked; and as France had declared, that she would confiscate every vessel which should touch in Great Britain, or be visited by British ships of war, his majesty, having previously issued the order of January 1807, as an act of mitigated retaliation, was at length compelled by the persevering violence of the enemy, and the continued acquiescence of neutral powers, to revisit upon France in a more effectual manner, the measure of her own injustice, by declaring, in an order in council, bearing date the 11th of November, 1807, that no neutral vessel should proceed to France or to any of the countries from which, in obedience to the dictates of France, British commerce was excluded, without first touching at a port in Great Britain, or her depencencies.

At the same time, his majesty intimated his readiness to repeal the orders in council, whenever France should rescind her decrees, and return to the accustomed principles of maritime warfare; and at a subsequent period, as a proof of his majesty's sincere desire to accommodate, as far as possible, his defensive measures to the convenience of neutral powers, the operation of the orders in council was, by an order issued in April, 1809, limited to a blockade of France, and of the countries subjected to her immediate dominion.

"Systems of violence, oppression, and tyranny, can never be suppressed, or even checked, if the power against which such injustice is exercised be debarred from the right of full and adequate retaliation: or, if the measures of the retaliating power are to be considered as matters of just offence to neutral nations, whilst the measure of original aggression and violence are to be tolerated with indifference, submission, or complacency.

"The government of the United States did not fail to remonstrate against the orders in council of Great Britain. Although they knew that these orders would be revoked, if the decrees of France, which had occasioned them, were repealed; they resolved at the same moment to resist the conduct of both belligerents, instead of requiring France, in the first instance, to rescind her decrees. Applying most unjustly the same measure of resentment to the aggressor and to the party aggrieved, they adopted measures of commercial resistance against both—a system of resistance which, however varied in the successive acts of embargo, non-intercourse, or non-importation, was evidently unequal in its operation, and principally levelled against the superior commerce, and maratime power of Great Britain.

"The same partiality towards France was observable in their negociations as in their measures of alleged resistance.

"Application was made to both belligerents for a revocation of their respective edicts; but the terms in which they were made were widely different.

"Of France was required a revocation only of the Berlin and Milan decrees, although many other edicts, grossly violating the neutral commerce of the United States, had been promulgated by that power. No security was demanded, that the Berlin and Milan decrees, even if revoked, should not under some other form be re-established: and a direct engagement was offered, that upon such revocation the American government would take part in the war against Great Britain, if Great Britain did not immediately rescind her orders. Whereas no corresponding engagement was offered to

Great Britain, of whom it was required, not only that the orders in council should be repealed, but that no others of a similar nature should be issued, and that the blockade of May, 1806, should be also abandoned. This blockade, established and enforced according to accustomed practice, had not been objected to by the United States at the time it was issued. Its provisions were on the contrary represented by the American minister, resident in London at the time, to have been so framed as to afford, in his judgment, a proof of the friendly disposition of the British cabinet towards the United States.

"Great Britain was thus called upon to abandon one of her most important maritime rights; by acknowledging the order of blockade in question to be one of the edicts which violated the commerce of the United States, although it had never been so considered in the previous negociations—and although the president of the United States had recently consented to abrogate the non-intercourse act, on the sole condition of the orders in council being revoked; thereby distinctly admitting these orders to be the only edicts which fell within the contemplation of the law under which he acted.

"A proposition so hostile to Great Britain, could not but be proportionably encouraging to the pretensions of the enemy. As, by their alleging that the blockade of May, 1806, was illegal, the American government virtually justified, so far as depended on them, the French decrees.

"After this proposition had been made, the French minister for foreign affairs, if not in concert with that government, at least in conformity with its views, in a dispatch, dated the 5th of August, 1810, and addressed to the American minister resident at Paris, stated, that the Berlin and Milan decrees were revoked, and that their operation would cease from the 1st day of November following, provided his majesty would revoke his orders in council, and renounce the new principles of blockade; or that the United States would cause their rights to be respected; meaning thereby, that they would resist the retaliatory measures of Great Britain.

"Although the repeal of the French decrees thus announced was evidently contingent, either on concessions to be made by Great Britain, (concessions to which it was obvious Great Britain could not submit), or on measures to be adopted by the United States of America; the American president at once considered the repeal as absolute. Under that pretence the non-importation act was strictly enforced against Great Britain, whilst the ships of war, and merchant-ships of the enemy, were received into the harbours of America.

"The American government, assuming the repeal of the French decrees to be absolute and effectual, most unjustly required Great Britain, in conformity to her declarations, to revoke her orders in council. The British government denied that the repeal, which was announced in the letter of the French minister for foreign affairs, was such as ought to satisfy Great Britain; and in order to ascertain the true character of the measure adopted by France, the government of the United States was called upon to produce the instrument, by which the alleged appeal of the French decrees had been effected. If these decrees were really revoked, such an instrument must exist, and no satisfactory reason could be given for withholding it.

"At length, on the 21st of May, 1812, and not before, the American minister in London did produce a copy, or at least what purported to be a copy, of such an instrument.

"It professed to bear date the 28th of April, 1811, long subsequent to the dispatch of the French minister of foreign affairs of the 5th of August, 1810, or even the day named therein; viz. the 1st of November following, when the operation of the French decrees was to cease. This instrument expressly declared that these French decrees were repealed in consequence of the American legislature having, by their act of the 1st of March, 1811, provided that British ships and merchandize should be excluded from the ports and harbours of the United States.

" By this instrument, the only document produced by America as a repeal of the French decrees, it appears, beyond a possibility of doubt or cavil, that the alleged repeal of the French decrees was conditional, as Great Britain had asserted, and not absolute or final, as had been maintained by America : that they were not repealed at the time they were stated to be repealed by the American government ; that they were not repealed in conformity with a propositition simultaneously made to both belligerents ; but that in consequence of a previous act on the part of the American government, they were repealed in favour of one belligerent, to the prejudice of the other ; that the American government having adopted measures restrictive upon the commerce of both belligerents, in consequence of edicts issued by both, rescinded these measures, as they affected that power which was the aggressor, whilst they put them in full operation against the party aggrieved, although the edicts of both powers continued in force ; and, lastly, that they excluded the ships of war belonging to one belligerent, whilst they admitted into their ports and harbours the ships of war belonging to the other, in violation of one of the plainest and most essential duties of a neutral nation.

"Although the instrument thus produced was by no means that general and unqualified revocation of the Berlin and Milan decrees which Great Britain had continually demanded, and had a full right to claim; and although this instrument, under all the circumstances of its appearance at that moment, for the first time, was open to the strongest suspicions of its authenticity; yet, as the minister of the United States produced it, as purporting to be a copy of the instrument of revocation, the government of Great Britain, desirous of reverting, if possible, to the ancient and accustomed principles of maritime war, determined upon revoking, conditionally, the orders in council. Accordingly, in the month of June last, his royal highness the prince regent was pleased to declare in council, in the name and on the behalf of his Majesty, that the orders in council should be revoked, as far as respected the ships and property of the United States, from the 1st of August following. This revocation was to continue in force, provided the government of the United States should, within a time to be limited, repeal their restrictive laws against British commerce. His majesty's minister in America was expressly ordered to declare to the government of the

United States, that ' this measure had been adopted by the prince regent in the earnest wish and hope, either that the government of France, by further relaxations of its system, might render perseverance on the part of Great Britain, in retaliatory measures, unnecessary; or, if this hope should prove delusive, that his majesty's government might be enabled, in the absence of all irritating and restrictive regulations on either side, to enter, with the government of the United States, into amicable explanations, for the purpose of ascertaining whether, if the necessity of retaliatory measures should unfortunately continue to operate, the particular measures to be acted upon by Great Britain could be rendered more acceptable to the American government than those hitherto pursued.'

" In order to provide for the contingency of a declaration of war on the part of the United States, previous to the arrival in America of the said order of revocation, instructions were sent to his majesty's minister plenipotentiary, accredited to the United States, (the execution of which instructions, in consequence of the discontinuance of Mr. Foster's functions, were, at a subsequent period, entrusted to admiral Sir John Borlase Warren,) directing him to propose a cessation of hostilities, should they have commenced; and, further, to offer a simultaneous repeal of the orders in council, on the one side, and of the restrictive laws on British ships and commerce, on the other.

"They were also respectively empowered to acquaint the American government, in reply to any inquiries with respect to the blockade of May, 1806, whilst the British government must continue to maintain its legality, 'that, in point of fact, this particular blockade had been discontinued for a length of time, having been merged in the general retaliatory blockade of the enemy's ports, under the orders in council; and that his majesty's government had no intention of recurring to this, or to any other of the blockades of the enemy's ports, founded upon the ordinary and accustomed principles of maritime law, which were in force previous to the orders in council, without a new notice to neutral powers, in the usual form.'

"The American government, before they received intimation of the course adopted by the British government, had, in fact, proceeded to the extreme measure of declaring war, and issuing 'letters of marque,' notwithstanding they were previously in possession of the report of the French minister for foreign affairs, of the 12th of March, 1812, promulgating anew the Berlin and Milan decrees as fundamental laws of the French empire, under the false and extravagant pretext, that the monstrous principles therein contained were to be found in the treaty of Utrecht, and were therefore binding upon all states. From the penalties of this code no nation was to be exempt which did not accept it, not only as the rule of its own conduct but as a law, the observance of which it was also required to enforce upon Great Britain.

"In a manifesto, accompanying their declaration of hostilities, in addition to the former complaints against the orders in council, a long list of grievances was brought forward; some trivial in themselves, others which had been mutually adjusted, but none of them such as were ever before alleged by the American government to be grounds for war.

"As if to throw additional obstacles in the way of peace, the American congress at the same time passed a law prohibiting all intercourse with Great Britain, of such a tenor as deprived the executive government, according to the president's own construction of that act, of all power of restoring the relations of friendly intercourse between the two states, so far, at least, as concerned their commercial intercourse, until congress should re-assemble.

"The president of the United States has, it is true, since proposed to Great Britain an armistice; not, however, on the admission that the cause of war, hitherto relied on, was removed, but on condition that Great Britain, as a preliminary step, should do away a cause of war, now brought forward as such, for the first time; namely, that she should abandon the exercise of her undoubted right of search, to take from American merchant-vessels British seamen, the natural-born subjects of his majesty; and this concession was required upon a mere assurance, that laws would be enacted by the legislature of the United States, to prevent such seamen from entering into their service; but, independent of the objection to an exclusive reliance on a foreign state, for the conservation of so vital an interest, no explanation was, or could be, afforded by the agent who was charged with this overture, either as to the main principles upon which such laws were to be founded, or as to the provisions which it was proposed they should contain.

"This proposition having been objected to, a second proposal was made, again offering an armistice, provided the British government would secretly stipulate to renounce the exercise of this right in a treaty of peace. An immediate and formal abandonment of its exercise, as a preliminary to a cessation of hostilities, was not demanded; but his royal highness the prince-regent was required, in the name and on the behalf of his majesty, secretly to abandon what the former overture had proposed to him publicly to concede.

"This most offensive proposition was also rejected, being accompanied, as the former had been, by other demands of the most exceptionable nature, and especially of indemnity for all American vessels detained and condemned under the orders in council, or under what were termed illegal blockades; a compliance with which demands, exclusive of all other objections, would have amounted to an absolute surrender of the rights on which those orders and blockades were founded.

" Had the American government been sincere in representing the orders in council as the only subject of difference between Great Britain and the United States, calculated to lead to hostilities, it might have been expected, so soon as the revocation of those orders had been officially made known to them, that they would have spontaneously recalled their ' letters of marque,' and manifested a disposition immediately to restore the relations of peace and amity between the two powers.

" But the conduct of the government of the United States by no means corresponded with such reasonable expectations.

" The orders in council of the 23d of June being officially communicated in America, the government of the United States saw nothing in the repeal of the orders in council which should of itself restore peace, unless Great Britain were prepared, in the first instance, substantially to relinquish the right of impressing her own seamen, when found on board American merchant ships.

"The proposal of an armistice, and of a simultaneous repeal of the restrictive measures on both sides subsequently made by the commanding officer of his majesty's naval forces on the American coast, were received in the same hostile spirit by the government of the United States. The suspension of the practice of impressment was insisted upon, in the correspondence which passed on that occasion, as a necessary preliminary to a cessation of hostilities: negociation, it was stated, might take place without any suspension of the exercise of this right, and also without any armistice being concluded; but Great Britain was required previously to agree, without any knowledge of the adequacy of the system which could be substituted, to negociate upon the basis of accepting the legislative regulations of a foreign state as the sole equivalent for the exercise of a right which she has felt to be essential to the support of her maritime power.

"If America, by demanding this preliminary concession, intends to deny the validity of that right, in that denial Great Britain cannot acquiesce; nor will she give countenance to such a pretension, by acceding to its suspension, much less to its abandonment, as a basis on which to treat. If the American government has devised, or conceives it can devise, regulations which may safely be accepted by Great Britain, as a substitute for the exercise of the right in question, it is for them to bring forward such a plan for consideration. The British government has never attempted to exclude this question from amongst those on which the two states might have to negociate: it has, on the contrary, uniformly professed its readiness to receive and discuss any proposition on this subject, coming from the American government: it has never asserted any exclusive right, as to the impressment of British seamen from American vessels, which it was not prepared to acknowledge, as appertaining equally to the government of the United States, with respect to American seamen when found on board British merchant ships. But it cannot by acceding to such a basis in the first instance, either assume, or admit that to be practicable, which, when attempted on former occasions, has always been found to be attended with great difficulties; such difficulties as the British commissioners, in 1806, expressly declared, after an attentive consideration of the suggestions brought forward by the commissioners on the part of America, they were unable to surmount.

"Whilst this proposition, transmitted through the British admiral, was pending in America, another communication, on the subject of an armistice, was unofficially made to the British government in this country. The agent from whom this proposition was received, acknowledged that he did not consider that he had any authority himself to sign an agreement on the part of his government. It was obvious that any stipulations entered into, in consequence of this overture, would have been binding on the British government, whilst the government of the United States would have been free to refuse or accept them, according to the circumstances of the moment. This proposition was, therefore, necessarily declined.

"After this exposition of the circumstances which preceded, and which have followed the declaration of war by the United States, his royal highness the prince regent, acting in the name and on the behalf of his majesty, feels himself called upon to declare the leading principles by which the conduct of Great Britain has been regulated in the transactions connected with these discussions.

" His royal highness can never acknowledge any blockade whatsoever to be illegal, which has been duly notified, and is supported by an adequate force, merely upon the ground of its extent, or because the port or coasts blockaded are not at the same time invested by land.

" His royal highness can never admit, that

neutral trade with Great Britain can be constituted a public crime, the commission of which can expose the ships of any power whatever to be denationalized.

" His royal highness can never admit, that Great Britain can be debarred of its right of just and necessary retaliation, through the fear of eventually affecting the interest of a neutral.

" His royal highness can never admit, that in the exercise of the undoubted, and hitherto undisputed, right of searching neutral merchant-vessels in time of war, the impressment of British seamen, when found therein, can be deemed any violation of a neutral flag. Neither can he admit, that the taking such seamen from on board such vessels, can be considered by any neutral state as a hostile measure, or a justifiable cause of war.

" There is no right more clearly established, than the right which a sovereign has to the allegiance of his subjects, more especially in time of war. Their allegiance is no optional duty, which they can decline and resume at pleasure. It is a call which they are bound to obey; it began with their birth, and can only terminate with their existence.

" If a similarity of language and manners may make the exercise of this right more liable to partial mistakes, and occasional abuse, when practised towards vessels of the United States, the same circumstances make it also a right with the exercise of which, in regard to such vessels, it is more difficult to dispense.

"But if to the practice of the United States to harbour British seamen, be added their assumed right to transfer the allegiance of British subjects, and thus to cancel the jurisdiction of their legitimate sovereign, by acts of naturalization and certificates of citizenship, which they pretend to be as valid out of their own territory as within it, it is obvious, that to abandon this ancient right of Great Britain, and to admit these novel pretensions of the United States, would be to expose to danger the very foundation of our maritime strength.

"Without entering minutely into the other topics which have been brought forward by the government of the United States, it may be proper to remark, that whatever the declaration of the United States may have asserted, Great Britain never did demand that they should force British manufactures into France: and she formerly declared her willingness entirely to forego, or modify, in concert with the United States, the system by which a commercial intercourse with the enemy had been allowed under the protection of licenses; provided the United States would act towards her, and towards France, with real impartiality.

"The government of America, if the difference between states are not interminable, has as little right to notice the affair of the Chesapeake. The aggression, in this instance, on the part of a British officer, was acknowledged; his conduct was disapproved; and a reparation was regularly tendered by Mr. Foster on the part of his majesty, and accepted by the government of the United States.

"It is not less unwarranted in its allusion to the mission of Mr. Henry; a mission undertaken, without the authority, or even knowledge, of his majesty's government, and which Mr. Foster was authorized formally and officially to disavow.

"The charge of exciting the Indians to offensive measures against the United States is equally void of foundation. Before the war began, a policy the most opposite had been uniformly pursued, and proof of this was tendered by Mr. Foster to the American government.

"Such are the causes of war which have been put forward by the government of the United States. But the real origin of the present contest will be found in that spirit which has long unhappily actuated the councils of the United States: their marked partiality in palliating and assisting the aggressive tyranny of France; their systematic endeavours to enflame the people against the defensive measures of Great Britain; their ungenerous conduct towards

Spain, the intimate ally of Great Britain; and their unworthy desertion of the cause of other neutral nations. It is through the prevalence of such councils that America has been associated in policy with France, and committed in war against Great Britain.

"And under what conduct, on the part of France, has the government of the United States thus lent itself to the enemy? The contemptuous violation of the commercial treaty of the year 1800 between France and the United States; the treacherous seizure of all American vessels and cargoes in every harbour subject to the controul of the French arms: the tyrannical principles of the Berlin and Milan decrees, and the confiscations under them; the subsequent confiscations under the Rambouillet decree, antedated or concealed to render it the more effectual; the French commercial regulations, which render the traffic of the United States with France almost illusory; the burning of their merchant-ships at sea, long after the alleged repeal of the French decrees—all these acts of violence, on the part of France, produce from the government of the United States, only such complaints as end in acquiescence and submission, or are accompanied by suggestions for enabling France to give the semblance of a legal form to her usurpations, by converting them into municipal regulations.

"This disposition of the government of the United States—this complete subserviency to the ruler of France—this hostile temper towards Great Britain—are evident in almost every page of the official correspondence of the American with the French government.

"Against this course of conduct, the real cause of the present war, the prince-regent solemnly protests. Whilst contending against France, in defence not only of the liberties of Great Britain but of the world, his royal highness was entitled to look for a far different result. From their common origin, from their common interest, from their professed principles of freedom and independence, the United States were the last power in which Great Britain could have expected to find a willing instrument and abettor of French tyranny.

"Disappointed in this, his just expectation, the prince regent will still pursue the policy which the British government has so long and invariably maintained, in repelling injustice, and in supporting the general rights of nations; and, under the favor of Providence, relying on the justice of his cause, and the tried loyalty and firmness of the British nation, his royal highness confidently looks forward to a successful issue to the contest in which he has thus been compelled most reluctantly to engage."

The temperate language, dignified style, and

fair and manly arguments, which distinguish this important document, afford a happy contrast to the petulant complaints and laboured sophisms to be found in Mr. Madison's message. One part of the latter, however, can be more satisfactorily answered now, than it could have been at the date of the regent's declaration. The president protests vehemently against the "crying enormity" of impressing "*thousands* of American citizens;" and the government-editors in the United States have long been in the practice of assuring their readers, that the *real* number of their fellow citizens impressed by the British was 6257. The following extract, taken from a Boston work entitled—"The Massachusetts' Manual, or Political and Historical Register; by William Burdick,"—will exhibit this matter in its true light:

"During the debate on the Loan Bill in the United States' house of representatives in March, 1814, Mr. Pickering, of Massachusetts remarked—"I wish, Mr. Chairman, to present one more view of this subject of impressments ; the result of an examination of the public documents, about a year ago, by one of my colleagues. By those documents, the grand total is the well known number, 6257
From which he deducted for the same name, and apparently the same person, twice, thrice, or more times repeated, 548
For an excess arising from some errors between the returns of 1805 and 1808, 757—1305

Leaving, 4952

Brought over		4952
From which he deducted acknowledged British subjects,	516	
those who had no protecting documents,	568	
those with insufficient documents,	664	
those who had entered voluntarily,	281	
those with fraudulent protections,	195	
deserters,	95	
those married in Great Britain,	42	
neutral aliens and natives of the West Ind.	50	
prisoners of war,	21—2432	
Leaving,		2520
From this number he deducted one-third, which appeared to him, from the documents, rather less than the full proportion of seamen impressed from British merchant vessels, in which, if not British subjects, the American flag could afford no pretence for protection,		840
Leaving,		1680
From the last number he deducted those who had been discharged, or had been ordered to be discharged,		1524
Leaving, unaccounted for,		156"

In all questions of impressment, the American government has appeared to consider, equally as its subjects, the native, and the naturalized citizen; and it is too notorious for what a paltry sum a British soldier or sailor can purchase every privilege of the latter, in pretended abrogation of the allegiance he owes to the country of his birth. It is, however, as a matter of convenience only, that the United States' government adopts this novel principle; for, when one Elijah Clarke, who had emigrated from the United States to the Canadas, and there taken the oath of allegiance to the British government, returned to his native country, and was, on the 20th of October, 1813, tried, and sentenced to be hung, as a British spy, the secretary of war, by direction of the president of the United States, ordered him to be discharged, on the principle—" that said Clarke, being considered a citizen of the United States, was not liable to be tried by a court-martial."*

The denial of a nation's right to take deserters is made equally subservient to the narrow policy of the moment; as appears from the following fact, published in most of the American newspapers of the day:

On the 1st June, 1809, an American vessel, bound from Ogdensburg, New York, to Oswego, anchored in a bay on the British side of the St. Lawrence, having on board capt. W. P. Bennet, of the 6th United States' Infantry, and some of his men. While lying there, capt. Bennet, hearing that a deserter by the name of Underhill was in that settlement teaching school, despatched a serjeant and two men to apprehend him. This they effected, tied his hands behind him, and at the point of the bayonet drove him some dis-

* Burdick's Pol. and Hist. Reg. p. 104.

tance, till the prisoner making an attempt to escape, the party fired at, and killed him: they then fled to their boat, and proceeded to the American side. Capt. Bennet was tried by a court-martial for this offence, and *acquitted.**

This forcible seizure of a deserter from out of the British territory by an American officer, happened just two years subsequent to the affair of the Leopard and Chesapeake; in which all that the British officer required was, to have certain deserters delivered up to him.† How are we to reconcile the acquittal of captain W. P. Bennet with the conduct of the American government, both at the period of the asserted outrage in the Chesapeake's case, and five years afterwards, when it was revived as one of the pretexts for declaring war against Great Britain?— Who can help admiring Mr. Madison's profitable versatility, when, in March, 1813, he could pronounce against us the following specific charge:—" They have refused to consider as prisoners of war, and threatened to punish as traitors and deserters, persons emigrating without restraint to the United States; incorporated by naturalization into our political family, and fighting under the authority of their adopted country, in open and honorable war, for the maintenance of its rights and safety"?

The charge of exciting the Indians to offensive

* Burdick's Regr, p. 168, † James's Naval Occurr. p. 67.

measures against the United States, would not have needed a disavowal, had the system of spoliation, so long practised towards those wretched people, been as well known in Europe as it is in the British parts of America. The Indians cannot exist without their hunting grounds: these are continually cut down, and encroached upon, by the white borderers. It is true, purchases are sometimes made; but it is not less true that, where one acre is held by right, ten acres have been extorted by force. An Indian,— no matter upon what provocation,—kills an American citizen; a thousand presses* lend their aid to spread the exaggerated tale, and the whole republic is up in arms against the savage and his tribe. An American citizen,— out of mere wantonness, and with as little remorse as if it were a wild turkey,—shoots a poor Indian: the yells of the widowed squaw and her children rend the air in vain; no publicity is given to the murder, unless the civilized barbarian may choose to disclose to his friends that which, he well knows, they will either treat as a jest, or view with indifference.

* Scarcely a village in the U. States is without one.

CHAPTER II.

Description of the Canadian lakes, and the chief military posts in their vicinity—Notice of the declaration of war—British regular force in the Canadas—Surrender of Fort Michilimacinac—Previous hostile preparations on the part of the American government—Invasion of Upper Canada by general Hull—Capture of the American Chicago packet—Skirmishes between the Americans and Indians—Anecdote of the American captain M'Culloch—General Hull's disappointment, and his return to the American territory—The first battle between the British and Americans—Scalps taken by the American militia—Abandonment of Fort Chicago—General Brock's advance to Detroit—The surrender of that important post, and the whole of the Michigan territory—General Hull's trial—Effects of the loss of Detroit on the cabinet at Washington—Sir George Prevost's impolitic armistice.

As our Canadian frontier was unfortunately destined to bear the brunt of the war declared against us by the United States, it will be assisting the reader to give a brief account of the towns and military posts distributed along the

extensive stream of water, through the middle of
which the boundary line runs.

The most remote piece of water on this frontier, worthy of notice, is Lake Superior; a collection of fresh water unequalled by any upon the face of the globe. Lake Superior is of a triangular form, in length 381, in breadth 161, and in circumference, 1152 miles. Among its several islands is one nearly two-thirds as large as the island of Jamaica; but neither its islands nor its shores can yet boast of inhabitants. Out of Lake Superior a very rapid current flows, over immense masses of rock, along a channel 27 miles in extent, called St. Mary's river, into Lake Huron; at the head of which is the British island of St. Joseph, containing a small garrison. This post is nearly 1700 miles from the lowest telegraph-station on the St. Lawrence, and about 2000 miles from its mouth.

Lake Huron is in length from west to east 218, in breadth 180, and in circumference, through its numerous curvatures, 812 miles. Except the island of St. Joseph, and one or two trading establishments belonging to the north-west company, the shores of this lake, also, are in a state of nature. Lake Michigan is connected with Lake Huron, at its western angle, by a short and wide strait; in the centre of which is the island of Michilimacinac, belonging to the United States. This island is about nine miles in circumference;

and, upon some very high ground, has a fort, in which a garrison is maintained. The distance from Michilimacinac to St. Joseph's is 47 miles.

Lake Michigan, which, in length from north to south, is 262, in breadth 55, and in circumference 731 miles, belongs wholly to the United States, the boundary line passing from Lake Superior, along the centre of Lake Huron, in a southerly direction, to the entrance of the river St. Clair. This river flows for 60 miles, till it expands into a small circular lake, about 30 miles in diameter, and named after itself. The beautiful river Thames, in Upper Canada, opens into Lake St. Clair; from which lake the stream, as the river Detroit, in width from one to three miles, and navigable for vessels drawing not more than 14 feet water, pursues a course of 40 miles into Lake Erie.

Upon the western side of the river Detroit, is situate the American town of that name; containing about 200 houses, and, among its public buildings, a strong fort and military works. About three miles below Fort-Detroit, upon the opposite side of the river, is the British village of Sandwich, containing about 40 houses; and, 16 miles lower, and within three of the mouth of the river, is the British village of Amherstburg, containing about 100 houses, and a fort, where a small garrison is usually stationed, and where our principal vessels for the service of Lake

Erie were built. The distance from Quebec to
Amherstburg, by the nearest rout, is 1207 miles.
The American village of Brownstown, stands
opposite to the latter.

Lake Erie, from its south-west end, is in length
231, in breadth 64, and in circumference 658
miles. Its greatest depth of water is between
40 and 45 fathoms; but a very rocky bottom
renders the anchorage unsafe in blowing weather. Except Amherstburg, the British have no
harbor or naval depôt upon Lake Erie; while
the Americans have two or three excellent ones.
Presqúile harbor is situate on the southern side
of the lake, not far from the entrance to the
Niagara. It is a safe station, but has a seven-
feet bar at its entrance; as, indeed, have all the
other harbors on this lake. The town, named Erie,
is situate on the south side of the harbor, and contains about 200 houses, besides several storehouses, and a dock-yard, at which the Americans
built their Lake Erie fleet. To the eastward
of the town stands a strong battery; and, on
the point of the peninsula forming the harbor, a block-house, for the protection of this
naval depôt. The Americans have also a strong
battery and a block-house at the mouth of
another harbor, named Put-in-Bay, situate at
the opposite end of the lake. Most of these
works have been constructed since the commencement of the war. The rivers Raisin,

Sandusky, and Miami, the scenes of important operations during the war, discharge themselves into Lake Erie.

On the north-western side of the entrance to the Niagara river, stands, at a distance of 565 miles from Quebec, the British Fort-Erie; when the war commenced, without a cannon mounted upon it, and, at best, a very inconsiderable work; as may be conceived, when an American general can declare that, in July 1814, it "was in a defenceless condition."* The word *fort*, is, indeed, very vaguely applied throughout the British provinces, the Canadians usually calling by that name any building surrounded by a palisade, as a protection from the Indians; although not a cannon, perhaps, was ever seen within miles of the spot. Near to the same outlet from Lake Erie is Buffaloe creek, on the border of which stands the American village of Buffaloe, and beyond it, about two miles, Black Rock, where there is a battery, and a ferry, about 800 yards across, to Bertie in Upper Canada.

The Niagara proceeds, at a quick rate, past several small, and one large island, called Grand isle, ten miles long; about two miles below which, on the American side, and distant two miles from the falls, is the site of Fort-Schlosser.† At about the same distance from the

* Wilkinson's Memoirs, Vol. I, p. 647. † See Plate I.

falls, on the opposite side, standing on the northern bank of the river Chippeway, is the British village of the same name, distant from Fort-Erie 17 miles. Chippeway consists chiefly of store-houses; and near it is a small stockaded work, called Fort-Chippeway. At the distance of 23 miles from the entrance to the Niagara, is Goat-island, about half a mile long; and which extends to the precipice that gives rise to the celebrated falls. The larger body of water flows between Upper Canada and Goat-island; at the upper end of which the broken water, or *rapids*, commence. Here the stream passes on both sides of the island, over a bed of rocks and precipices, with astonishing rapidity; till, having descended more than 50 feet, in the distance of half a mile, it falls, on the British side 157, and on the New York side 162, feet perpendicular.*

From the cataract the river is a continued rapid, half a mile in width, for about seven miles. At this point stand, opposite to each other, the villages of Queenstown and Lewistown.* The latter, situate upon the American side, contained, till destroyed as a retaliatory measure, between 40 and 50 houses; the former has still remaining about 15 houses, with stores for government, barracks, wharf, &c. About three miles from Queenstown, upon the banks of a

* See Plate F.

stream, called the Four-mile creek, where it crosses the road leading to the head of Lake Ontario, is the village of St. David's; which contains, or rather did contain till visited by the Americans, about 40 houses. At about six miles and a half from Queenstown, near to the river side, stands the British Fort-George,* constructed of earthern ramparts, and palisades of dry cedar, to which a lighted candle would set fire. It mounted, when the war commenced, no heavier metal than 9-pounders, and those condemned for being *honey-combed*. About half a mile below Fort-George, and close to the borders of Lake Ontario, is the site of the once beautiful, once flourishing village of Newark.*

Directly opposite to Newark, upon a neck of land projecting partly across the mouth of the river, which is here 875 yards in width, stands the American fort of Niagara.* It was built by the French in 1751; taken by us in 1759; and, along with several other frontier-posts, ceded to the United States in 1794: and, though again taken, has again been ceded to the same power. Fort-Niagara, unlike any of the Canadian forts along that frontier, is a regular fortification, built of stone, on the land-side, with breast-works, and every necessary appendage. It mounts between 20 and 30 heavy pieces of ordnance, and contains a furnace for heating shot.

* See Plate I.

The strait of Niagara is about 36 miles in length; and its shores, on both sides, were, more or less, the scenes of active warfare during the whole period of hostilities. Lake Ontario, to which the strait leads, is in length, from west to east, 171, in breadth 50, and in circumference 467 miles. The depth of water varies much; it being in some places three or four, in other 50 fathoms: towards the centre 300 fathoms of line have, it is said, not found the bottom. York harbor lies on the north-side of Lake Ontario; is nearly circular, of about a mile and a half in diameter, and formed by a narrow peninsula extending to Gibraltar-point, upon which a block-house has been erected. The town, which is the infant capital of Upper Canada, is in lat. 43° 30′ north, and long. 79° 20′ west, distant from Fort-Niagara, by water 30, and by land about 90 miles. The plot of ground marked out for it extends about a mile and a half along the north-side of the harbor; but, at present, the number of houses, a very few of which are of brick or stone, does not exceed 300. The public buildings consist of a government-house, the house of assembly, a church, court-house, and a gaol, with numerous stores belonging to government. The barracks are situate at the distance of two miles to the westward of the town, and are protected by a small battery and two block-houses; which also serve, aided by the block-house at

Gibraltar-point, to defend the entrance of the harbor.

Kingston-harbor is situate at the eastern extremity of Lake Ontario. It contains good anchorage in three fathoms water; and is defended by a small battery of 9-pounders on Mississaga-point, and another, of the same metal chiefly, on Point Frederick. The town, which is the largest and most populous in the upper province, contains about 370 houses; including several buildings and stores belonging to government. Its distance from York is 145, from Montreal, in an opposite direction, 198, and from Quebec 378 miles. Opposite to, and distant about half a mile from the town, is a long low peninsula, forming the west-side of Navy Bay, the principal naval depôt of the British on this lake, and where the ships of war were constructed.

Of the American military posts on Lake Ontario, the principal one is Sackett's-Harbor,* distant from Kingston, by the ship-channel, 35 miles. We shall defer any further description of this important post, as well as of several other American stations upon Lake Ontario, and along the frontier to the eastward, until some action or military event brings them into notice. The line of demarkation, travelling all the way from the upper lakes, enters the river Cataraqui,

* See Plate II.

Iroquois, or, as more commonly called, St. Lawrence; down whose course it proceeds as far as St. Regis, distant about 109 miles from Kingston, where it strikes, due east across the country, along the parallel of 45°, till it reaches, at a distance of 147 miles, the west bank of the river Connecticut in the United States.

The instant the war became known at New York, some British merchants of that city despatched expresses to Queenstown in Upper, and Montreal in Lower Canada. According to an American editor, the Queenstown messenger, described as a native of Albany, told his countrymen, on the way, that he was proceeding with the news to Fort Niagara; and obtained, in consequence, every facility that money and horses could afford him. Thus, through private channels, notice of the war reached Queenstown and Montreal in six, and Quebec in eight days after it had been declared; which was fortunate, as, by some unaccountable accident, the official notification from the British minister at Washington did not arrive at Quebec till some weeks had elapsed. At this time, the British regular force in the Canadas consisted of the 8th, 41st, 49th and 100th regiments, a small detachment of artillery, the 10th Royal Veteran Battalion, and the Canadian, Newfoundland, and Glengary Fencibles; amounting, in the whole, to 4,450 men.

These were distributed along the different posts from the telegraph station, about 250 miles below Quebec, to St. Joseph's, but so unequally divided, that, in the upper province, whose front extends to nearly 1300, out of the 1700 miles, there were but 1450 men; and the restricted navigation of the St. Lawrence, by the time any succours could arrive from England, left no hopes of a reinforcement previous to the ensuing summer.

Major-general Brock, the president of Upper Canada, was at York when the news of war reached him. He, with his accustomed alacrity, sent immediate notice of it to lieutenant-colonel St. George commanding a small detachment of troops at Amherstburg, and to captain Roberts commanding part of a company of the 10th R. V. Battalion at St. Joseph's. A second despatch to the last-named officer contained the major-general's orders, that he should adopt the most prudent measures, either for offence or defence. Captain Roberts, accordingly, on the day succeeding the arrival of his orders, embarked with 45 officers and men of the 10th Royal Veteran Battalion, about 180 Canadians, 393 Indians, and two iron 6-pounders, to attack the American fort of Michilimacinac. This force reached the island on the following morning. A summons was immediately sent in; and the fort of Michilimacinac, with seven pieces of ordnance, and

61 officers and privates of the United States army,*·surrendered, by capitulation, without a drop of blood having been spilt.

The editor of the " History of the War," while he admits that " every possible preparation was made by the garrison to resist an attack," describes the force under Captain Roberts as " regular troops 46; Canadian militia 260; Indians 715." Here the regulars are correctly enumerated; but their inconsiderable number taught Dr. Smith a preferable method of stating the British force. He lumps the whole together thus:—" regular troops, Canadian militia, and Indians, amounting to 1,000 men;" and omits not to add, that they were " furnished with every implement for the complete investment and siege of the place."†—Lieutenant Hanks states, that he " had anticipated" the declaration of war:‡ in fact, there is no doubt that he, in common with the other American commanders at the posts along the frontier, had been instructed to expect it.

The misunderstanding that had, for several years, subsisted between Great Britain and the United States, and the recent broils between the latter and the Indians on the Wabash, had occasioned a considerable augmentation of the mili-

* App. Nos. 1. 2. 3.
† Hist. of the United States, Vol. III. p. 177.
‡ App. No. 3.

tary force of the United States. Since early in the month of May, brigadier-general Hull had been despatched with a force to the north-west; and was invested with discretionary powers to invade Canada from Detroit, immediately on receiving intelligence of the war, then resolved to be declared against Great Britain. This army, 2,500 strong, arrived at Detroit on the 5th of July, to be in readiness for the contemplated invasion.

Every preparation having been made, not omitting a proclamation to the Canadians,* sent purposely from Washington, the embarkation of the troops took place on the 12th. The army landed on the opposite or Canadian side of the Detroit; and, after a short cannonade, took possession of the defenceless village of Sandwich, situate about two miles within the province. The few militia, there stationed, had previously retired, carrying with them the most valuable of the stores, to Amherstburg.†

Lieutenant-colonel St. George, inspecting field-officer of the district, commanded at this post; having under his orders a subaltern's detachment of artillery, about 100 of the 41st regiment, 300 militia, and about 150 Indians, under Tecumseh. The timely notice of the war, sent by major-general Brock, enabled the lieutenant-colonel, early in July, to intercept, as she was entering

* App. No. 4. † See p. 48.

Detroit river, the American Chicago packet, having on board the baggage and hospital stores, and an officer and 30 men, of general Hull's army. Instead of proceeding against Amherstburg, which would have fallen an easy prey to so powerful a force, and proved an important acquisition to the American cause, general Hull remained in the neighbourhood of Sandwich, carrying on an excursive war by detached parties, and, through them, occasionally reconnoitring the British outposts in the neighbourhood.

A company of the British 41st regiment, about 60 militia, and a party of Indians, being posted near a bridge, crossing the river *Aux Canards*, four miles from Amherstburg, an American reconnoitring party, consisting of about 300 men,* under colonel Cass, advanced, on the 15th of July, to a plane, distant about a mile from the bridge. To induce the Americans to approach the position occupied by the British regulars and militia, 150 Indians were sent across the bridge. A company of American riflemen, concealed in a wood that skirted the plane, immediately fired upon the Indians, killing one, and wounding two. After scalping the dead Indian, the American force was no more seen. Not a musket was fired by the Indians, nor were the regulars or militia in any way engaged; yet

* Hist of the War, p. 37.

an American editor trumps up a story of colonel Cass having " driven the 41st regiment and some Indians more than half a mile, when the darkness of the night made further progress hazardous;" and adds :—" The colonel was content to possess the bridge and some adjoining houses until morning, when, after reconnoitring the neighbourhood, and not finding the enemy, he commenced his return to the camp at Sandwich."*

On the 19th a second reconnoitring party, consisting of 150 men of the Ohio volunteers, and a detachment of artillery, with two pieces of cannon, under the command of colonel M'Arthur, returned to the ground abandoned by colonel Cass; but who, with 100 men, soon afterwards joined M'Arthur's detachment.* Of a small look-out party of the 41st regiment, sent across the very bridge, which colonel Cass had been " content to possess," but too much flurried to destroy, two privates, who behaved like noble fellows, were wounded and taken prisoners. Upon the bridge the British had two light field-pieces, with the fire from which they disabled one of the American guns, and drove the Americans into the plane; but were too inferior in force to pursue them. The American editor, concealing that any artillery was engaged on his side, has multiplied the British guns from

* Sketches of the War, p. 22.

two to six, and, in despite of distance and shoal water, brought to the spot the British ship "Queen Charlotte, of 20 guns."* After stating that "the chief, Tecumseh, celebrated for his dexterity with the tomahawk and rifle, was at the head of the Indians," Mr. Thomson gravely pronounces "the escape of M'Arthur and his companions" as "truly miraculous."*

The American general, in expectation that 150 Ohio volunteers, under the command of captain Brush, were waiting at the river Raisin, 36 miles off, with a quantity of provisions for the army, despatched major Vanhorne, with 200 men,† to meet and escort the reinforcement to its destination. Fortunately, the major encountered, on his second day's march, near Brownstown, 70 Indians, under the brave Tecumseh, in ambuscade. The latter fired, and, according to the American accounts, killed twenty men, including captains M'Culloch, Bostler, Gilcrease, and Ubry; and wounded nine. Tecumseh and his 70 Indians, with the loss of only one man killed, drove these 200 Americans before them, for seven miles, and took possession of the mail they were escorting. When the American force first appeared in sight, Tecumseh sent an express to the river *Aux Canards*, for captain Muir and his company. But captain Muir had been de-

* Sketches of the War, p. 23.   † Hist. of the War, p. 40.

tached, across the river, to a spot three miles beyond Amherstburg. Being relieved by captain Mockler of the Newfoundland Fencibles, captain Muir hastened back; and, re-crossing the river, arrived at Brownstown just as the affair ended. Not a white man was engaged; yet have the American editors magnified Tecumseh's little party into "a very superior force of *regulars and Indians*." One editor says, "The whole detachment retreated in great disorder, and could not, by any exertion of major Van Horn, be rallied;" another says, "they fled with precipitation;" and a third editor, and he who alone has, in direct contradiction to the official account,* ventured to reduce major Vanhorn's command to "150 men," says:—"To the Americans the odds were fearful, but, after an obstinate resistance, they succeeded in making an *orderly retreat.*"† Here is confusion!

Among the numerous anecdotes which contribute to fill the pages of the American histories, the following most authentic one no where appears.—In the pocket of captain M'Culloch, of the American army, killed in this affair with the Indians, was found a letter addressed to his wife, in which this humane individual, this officer of a nation vaunting itself to the world as a pattern of civilization, states that, on the 15th of July,

* App. No. 9. † Sketches of the War, p. 25.

he killed an Indian,* and had the pleasure of tearing the scalp from the head of the savage with his teeth!—We may presume that, had this exploit been performed in December instead of July, the bloody trophy itself would have been found in the other pocket, ready to accompany the letter, as a still more delectable present to the American lady.

The fall of Michilimacinac had, to use general Hull's language, "opened the northern hive of Indians" upon him; and he was induced, from his fears, greatly to magnify "the reinforcements from Niagara" that had been sent to colonel Proctor, who had succeeded lieutenant-colonel St. George, at Amherstburg. But the worst of all was, that the general's proclamation, "so well calculated to inspire confidence, and secure the friendship of the Canadians,"† no longer produced its effect. The promised "protection to persons, property, and rights," was fulfilled in a way that taught the subjects of Canada what reliance they could place upon republican faith. The inhabitants received from their "brethren" worse treatment than the most ferocious enemy could inflict. This, by degrees, opened their eyes; and, as the American general deplores, "the desertion of the (Canadian) militia ceased." Much of

* See p. 59.   † Hist. of the War, p. 86.

general Hull's disappointment, no doubt, arose from the salutary effects of the counter-proclamation*, which general Brock, on the 22d of July, issued at Fort-George. These "untoward" circumstances combined to relieve the upper province from the tread of the invaders. The general and his powerful army, except 250 infantry and a corps of artillerists, left in a small fortress on the banks a little below Detroit, re-crossed the river during the night of the 7th of August, and, by day-break next morning, were safely encamped at Detroit; thus "shamefully leaving to their fate," says Mr. O'Connor, in the height of his indignation against general Hull, "the Canadians who had joined the American standard."

The communication which had been opened by the American army, between Raisin and their present post, was shut up by the Indians. It was deemed indispensably requisite that it should be re-opened, or the provisions at that river could never reach the garrison; which, in a few days, would be in want of subsistence. Accordingly, 600 men,† under the command of lieutenant-colonel Miller, accompanied by a detachment of artillery with two six-pounders, were immediately sent upon that service. Upon the lieutenant-colonel's arrival at Maguaga,

* App. No. 5. † Sketches of the War, p. 40.

about 14 miles from Detroit, and four from Brownstown, he fell in with 75 men of the 41st regiment, 60 militia, 120 Indians under Tecumseh, stationed on the left of the militia, and 70 Indians from the lake, under Caldwell, on the right of the regulars: the whole under the command of captain Muir of the 41st. This force one American editor has augmented to 200 regulars and 500 Indians, in order that he might make it " more than one-third superior" to his own, which he has, in his old way, reduced below the number stated in the official account. Nor is there a word of the two 6-pounders.

Here the first trigger was pulled between the British and Americans in the late war. The firing commenced on our side; and, very soon afterwards, the whole of the lake Indians fled. This gave an opportunity to the American troops to outflank the British regulars; who, to prevent being surrounded by four times their number, retired, but, in such order, that the Americans did not attempt to follow, contenting themselves with firing a few distant shots. The British drew up again, at a narrow way, within half a mile of the scene of action, intending to dispute the enemy's passage, but he advanced no further. The British lost three men killed, captain Muir, lieutenant Sutherland, (since dead,) and 10 men wounded. The Americans have stated the Indian loss at 100 killed, and their own at 83 killed and wounded. Colonel Miller, completely frustrated in his design by the trifling force opposed to him, returned to Detroit the following night.

It is perfectly consistent, that the American editor who can make so free with his own official accounts when they are not sufficiently extravagant, should here boast of a victory; but who expected he would resort to the silly expedient of representing the British regulars as almost naked, and frightfully painted, sending forth such dreadful whoops and yells, as "might have appalled almost any other troops,"* than those, whom Mr. Thomson afterwards dignifies with the title of " heroes of Brownstown." This ridiculous stuff would excite our laughter, but that feelings of disgust and indignation are suddenly called forth by a paragraph in the "National Intelligencer", (the American government-paper,) stating that, "when the American militia returned to Detroit from the battle of Brownstown, they bore triumphantly on the points of their bayonets between 30 and 40 fresh scalps, which they had taken on the field."

The American captain Brush, who was still waiting at the river Raisin for an escort, received orders to remain, and defend himself at that place, or to proceed by an upper route, crossing the river Huron; whither the militia

* Sketches of the War, p. 27.

of Raisin had been ordered to attend him. On the evening of the 13th, general Hull despatched colonels M'Arthur and Cass, with 400* of their most effective men, by an upper route through the woods, to form a junction with captain Brush, and to assist in the transportation of the provisions.

On the same day that the battle of Maguaga took place, captain Heald, the American commander at Fort Chicago, near the head of Lake Michigan, received orders to abandon his position. Accordingly, on the 15th, after delivering to the friendly Indians, in conformity to his instructions, all the goods in the factory, and such provisions as could not be taken away, and destroying all the surplus arms and ammunition, he commenced his march, with 54 regulars and 12 militia, and was escorted by captain Wells, of Fort-Wayne, and a few Indians of the Miami tribe, sent thither for that purpose. The Americans were afterwards met by a hostile band of Indians, attacked, defeated with great slaughter, and made prisoners. Captain Heald and his lady fortunately effected their escape; and, says one American account, " procured a conveyance to Michilimacinac, where they were politely received by the commandant, captain Roberts." Mrs. Heald, it appears, was wounded by six, and her husband by two shots.

* App. No. 9.

General Brock had just arrived at Fort-George from York, when he heard of general Hull's invasion. It was his intention to attack, and there is no doubt he would have carried, Fort-Niagara; but, sir George Prevost not having sent him any official account of the war, nor any order to guide his proceedings, the general was restrained from acting according to the dictates of his judgment, and the natural energy of his mind. After issuing a proclamation, to defeat the object of that circulated by general Hull, general Brock returned to York, to meet the legislature of Upper Canada; which, on account of the war, he had called together for an extra-session. This session was short; and, on the 5th of August, the general again left York, for Fort-George, and for Long-point on Lake Erie. On the 8th he embarked at the latter place, with 40 rank and file of the 41st regiment, and 260 of the militia forces; leaving the important command on the Niagara frontier to his quarter-master-general, lieutenant-colonel Myers, an able and intelligent officer.

General Brock and his little party landed safe at Amherstburg on the evening of the 12th; when that enterprising officer lost not a moment; but, with the reinforcement he procured at this place, pushed on for Sandwich. Here he found that the Americans had evacuated and destroyed a small fort which they had constructed soon after their arrival. On the morning of the 15th general Brock sent across a flag of truce, with a summons, demanding the immediate surrender of the garrison: to which an answer was returned, that "the town and fort would be defended to the last extremity." That being the case, at four o'clock in the afternoon, the British batteries, which had been constructed for one 18-pounder, two 12-pounders, and two $5\frac{1}{2}$ inch howitzers, opened upon the enemy, and continued to throw their shells into the fort until midnight. One shell killed three or four officers, and produced great alarm in the garrison. The fire was returned by seven 24-pounders, but without the slightest effect.

At day-light the next morning the firing recommenced; and the major-general, taking with him 30 of the royal artillery, 250 of the 41st regiment, 50 of the Royal Newfoundland regiment, and 400 militia, crossed the river, and landed at Spring-well, a good position, three miles west of Detroit. The Indians, 600 in number, under the brave Tecumseh, had effected their landing two miles below; and they immediately occupied the woods about a mile and a half on the left of the army. The direction of the batteries on the opposite shore had, in the mean time, been left to an intelligent officer.

At about 10 o'clock the troops advanced, in a close column, 12 in front, along the bank of the river towards the fort, and halted at about a mile distant: by which time, the Indians had penetrated the enemy's camp. When the head of the British column had advanced to within a short distance of the American line, general Hull, and the troops under his command, retreated to the fort, without making any use of two 24-pounders, advantageously posted on an eminence, and loaded with grape-shot.

Just as the British were about to commence the attack, a white flag was seen suspended from the walls of the fort. So unexpected a measure caused general Brock to despatch an officer in front, to ascertain the fact. Shortly afterwards the capitulation* was signed; and the fort of Detroit, its ordnance and military stores, a fine vessel in the harbor, the whole north-western army, including the detached parties, also the immense territory of Michigan, its fortified posts, garrisons, and inhabitants, were surrendered to the British arms.

General Brock permitted the American volunteers and militia to return to their homes, but sent general Hull and the principal part of the American regulars to Montreal; whence they were afterwards removed to Quebec. After issuing a proclamation,† announcing to the inhabitants of Michigan, the cession of that territory to the arms of his Britannic majesty; and after

* App. Nos. 6 and 7. † Ibid. No. 8.

placing colonel Proctor in command of the fort at Detroit, general Brock hastened back to Fort George; which place he reached on the 24th of the same month.

The editor of the "Sketches of the War" states the force of general Hull to have been, at muster on the morning of the surrender, 1060 men, exclusive of the detachments of "350" regulars, and 300 Michigan militia then out on duty. Having already convicted Mr. Thomson of underrating the American force, even in the teeth of his own official accounts, it would be an overstrained concession to place implicit reliance upon the accuracy of his numbers. However, to do no more than add 50 to his "350 men," detached under colonels Cass and M'Arthur, and who, on the day of the surrender, had, in pursuance of fresh orders, returned in sight of the fort and "were accidentally thrown into a situation, the best for annoying and cutting off the retreat of the British army,"* the force under general Hull would amount to 1760 men; of whom 1060 at least, were entrenched in a superior position, under the protection of a fort, mounting 33 pieces of ordnance, including nine 24-pounders. General Hull, in his letter states, that the "whole effective force at his disposal did not exceed 800 men." But *effective* is a very vague term; it may include the not willing, as well as the not

* Sketches of the War, p. 31.

able to fight. Nor, is it probable, that his sick amounted to 260, or to half the number; otherwise the American historians would have taken advantage of the circumstance.

It was natural for general Hull to magnify the British force; which he did to an extent that enabled him, assisted by the previous diminution of his own, to urge to his government the " great inequality" between the two armies. Mr. Thomson, however, has exerted himself, as successfully in the one, as he had in the other case, to disprove the general's assertion. Without answering for the authenticity of the alleged document, or the purity of the channel through which it reached Mr. Thomson, here follows a statement, purporting to be taken from the return of major-general Brock's quarter-master-general:

British regulars, infantry and artillery,	382
Indians, principally Chippeways, Hurons, and Putawatamies,	650
Militia, "in regular uniform," or, rather, in coats and jackets of all colours and shapes,	362
Total,	1394*

The best evidence that these figures are correctly transcribed, is the trifling amount by which they exceed the round numbers stated in major-general Brock's despatch. Were it not for that, we should be warranted in relying upon

* Sketches of the War, p. 33.

the American colonel Cass's letter, published in the " National Intelligencer." He says :—" I have been informed by colonel Findlay, who saw the return of their quarter-master-general, the day after the surrender, that their whole force, of every description, white, red, and black, was 1080." In another part of his letter the colonel says:—" I was informed by general Hull, the morning after the capitulation, that the British forces consisted of 1800 regulars, and that he surrendered to prevent the effusion of human blood. That he magnified their regular force nearly *five-fold*, there can be no doubt."—Except to blame general Hull for " the folly and ruin of crowding 1100 men into a little work, which 300 could fully man," the editor of the " History of the United States" has not touched upon the force of either party, in his brief notice of the surrender of Detroit.

No account of ordnance-stores found in the fort appears in the British official returns, for which a reason is there assigned. The editor of the " Sketches of the War," satisfies us that there was no deficiency in this respect, by stating, that the American troops had, among their stores, " 400 rounds of 24-pound shot, already fixed ; about 100000 cartridges made up ; 40 barrels of powder ; and 2500 stands of arms."*

One reason for general Brock's marching so

* Sketches of the War, p. 30. 31.

comparatively small a force against Detroit, was a deficiency of arms wherewith to equip the Upper Canada militia. Many of the latter were obliged, in consequence, to remain behind; and even the arms that had been distributed among their companions, were of the very worst quality: so that general Hull's "2500 stands of arms," which were, indeed, of the very best quality, became a valuable acquisition. The success that attended this first enterprise in which the militia had been called upon to act, produced an electrical effect throughout the two provinces. It inspired the timid, settled the wavering, and awed the disaffected; of which latter there were many. It also induced the Six Nations of Indians, who had hitherto kept aloof, to take an active part in our favor.

So determined appears Mr. Thomson's hostility towards general Hull, that he declares the American commander surrendered "to a body of troops inferior in *quality* as well as number." Upon what ground that assertion is made, other than the superior gallantry displayed by the American troops in the few skirmishes already recorded, no where appears; and how widely different were the sentiments of the commander of those *inferior* troops, Mr. Thomson has made known to us in his preceding page. "When," says he, "general Brock said, that the force at his disposal authorized him to require the surrender, he must have had a very exalted opinion of the prowess of his own soldiers, or a very mistaken one of the ability of those, who were commanded by the American general."*

Brigadier-general Hull was afterwards exchanged for 30 British prisoners; and his trial commenced at Albany on the 5th of January, and ended on the 8th of March, 1814. The particulars may not be uninteresting, and are therefore extracted from the pages of Mr. O'Connor's book:

"Three charges were presented against him; to wit, *treason against the United States; cowardice; and neglect of duty, and unofficer-like conduct*—to all which he pleaded *Not Guilty*.— The general having protested against the competency of the court to try the first charge, the court declined making any formal decision on it; but yet gave an opinion that nothing appeared to them which could justify the charge.

"The court acquitted him of that part of the third specification, which charges him with having forbidden the American artillery to fire on the enemy, on their march towards the said Fort-Detroit, and found him guilty of the first, second part of the third, and the fourth specifications. On the third charge, the court found the accused guilty of neglect of duty, in omitting seasonably to inspect, train, exercise, and order the troops under his command, or cause

* Sketches of the War, p. 32.

the same to be done. They also found him guilty of part of the fourth and fifth specifications, and the whole of the sixth and seventh; and acquitted him of the second and third, and part of the fourth and fifth specifications.

"The court sentenced the said brigadier-general William Hull, to be shot to death, two-thirds of the court concurring in the sentence; but, in consideration of his revolutionary services, and his advanced age, recommended him to the mercy of the president of the United States. The president approved the sentence, remitted the execution, and ordered the name of general Hull to be erased from the list of the army.*—It is an undoubed fact, that most of general Hull's *lenient* judges had, during the war, either run from, or been beaten by, a British force, much inferior to theirs. As their best excuse, we can only suppose, that the sentence of death was understood to be a mere form to save appearances; in short, that the president of the United States had pledged himself not to confirm it.

The chagrin felt at Washington, when news arrived of the total failure of this the first attempt at invasion, was in proportion to the sanguine hopes entertained of its success. To what a pitch of extravagance those hopes had been carried, cannot better appear than in two speeches

* History of the War, page 215.

delivered upon the floor of congress, in the summer of 1812. Dr. Eustis, the secretary at war of the United States, said:—" We can take the Canadas without soldiers; we have only to send officers into the provinces, and the people, disaffected towards their own government, will rally round our standard." The honorable Henry Clay seconded his friend, thus:—" It is absurd to suppose we shall not succeed in our enterprize against the enemy's provinces. We have the Canadas as much under our command as she (Great Britain) has the ocean; and the way to conquer her on the ocean is to drive her from the land. I am not for stopping at Quebec, or any where else; but I would take the whole continent from them, and ask them no favors. Her fleets cannot then rendezvous at Halifax as now; and, having no place of resort in the north, cannot infest our coast as they have lately done. It is as easy to conquer them on the land, as their whole navy would conquer ours on the ocean. We must take the continent from them. *I wish never to see a peace till we do.* God has given us the power and the means: we are to blame if we do not use them. If we get the continent, she must allow us the freedom of the sea." This is the gentleman who, afterwards, in the character of a commissioner,—and it stands as a record of his unblushing apostacy,—signed the treaty of peace.

Upon major-general Brock's arrival at Fort-George, he first heard of that most impolitic armistice, which, grounded on a letter from sir George Prevost to major-general Dearborn, had been concluded between the latter and colonel Baynes, sir George's adjutant-general. It provided that neither party should act offensively before the decision of the American government was taken on the subject. To the circumstance of the despatch announcing the event, not having reached the gallant Brock, before he had finished the business at Detroit, may the safety of the Canadas, in a great measure, be attributed. The armistice was already sufficiently injurious. It paralized the efforts of that active officer; who had resolved, and would doubtless have succeeded, in sweeping the American forces from the whole Niagara line. It enabled the Americans to recover from their consternation, to fortify and strengthen their own, and to accumulate the means of annoyance along the whole of our frontier. It sent nearly 800 of our Indian allies, in disgust, to their homes. It admitted the free transport of the enemy's ordnance-stores and provisions, by Lake Ontario; which gave increased facility to all his subsequent operation in that quarter.

CHAPTER III.

Termination of sir G. Prevost's armistice—State of the American army on the Niagara-frontier—Capture of the Detroit and Caledonia—American plan of invasion developed—Its derangement—False intelligence of a deserter—Ardor of the American troops—Attack on Queenstown resolved upon—First attempt at crossing the river foiled—Success of second attempt—Gallant resistance of the British—Arrival of mutual reinforcements—Death of general Brock—Surrender of the American army—Altered behaviour of the American troops at Lewistown—American misrepresentation exposed—Bombardment between Fort-George and Fort-Niagara—Brief sketch of general Brock's life and character.

It is now time to attend to the operations of the British and American forces confronting each other along the Niagara-line. The president of the United States, as might have been expected, refused to ratify the armistice which had been agreed upon between sir George Prevost, through his adjutant-general colonel Baynes, and major-general Dearborn;

and directed six day's notice of the recommencement of hostilities to be given by the commanding generals. The American government had made a proper use of the short period of suspension; and, when the 8th of September, the day for active operations, arrived, a strong force, well supplied with provisions, and styled " the army of the centre," had assembled on the borders of the Niagara-river.

This army, commanded by major-general Van Rensselaer of the New York militia, consisted, according to American official returns, of 5206 men;* exclusive of 300 field and light-artillery, 800 of the 6th, 13th, and 23d regiments, at Fort-Niagara; making a total of 6300 men. Of this powerful force, 1650 regulars, under the command of brigadier-general Smyth, were at Black Rock;† 386 militia at the latter place and Buffaloe; and 900 regulars, and 2270 militia, at Lewistown, distant from Black Rock 28 miles. So that, including the 1100 men at Fort Niagara, the Americans had, along 36 miles of their frontier, a force of 6300 men; of whom nearly two thirds were regular troops; while the British, along their line from Fort-George, where major-general Sheaffe commanded, to Fort-Erie, whither major-general Brock had just proceeded, could not muster 1200 men; nearly half of whom were militia.

* Wilkinson's Mem. Vol. I. p. 580.   † See plate I.

Although not strictly a military enterprise, the capture, in ten minutes, of two British "brigs of war, well-armed, and anchored under the protection of Fort-Erie,"* by two American row-boats, without any artillery, is an event of too extraordinary a nature, not to require an investigation. At the surrender of Detroit, we got possession of the United States' brig Adams, of about 200 tons, and mounting six 6-pounders. The prize (afterwards named the Detroit) and the north-west company's brig Caledonia, of about 90 tons, and mounting two swivels, were required to convey some of the American prisoners to Fort-Erie. A party of militia and Canadian sailors, in number 50, embarked for that purpose on board the Detroit, having in charge 30 American prisoners. This vessel carried, also, well-packed in her hold, a considerable quantity of small-arms, part of the spoils taken with general Hull. The Caledonia had her own crew of 12 men; to whose care were entrusted 10 American prisoners. She had on board a valuable cargo of furs, valued by the American editors at about 150,000 dollars. The author of the "Sketches of the War," ludicrously enough, styles these two vessels "well-appointed," or, in other words, well-manned and officered. He, next, unpacking all the cases, and distributing the arms, declares that the ves-

* History of the United States, Vol. III. p. 191.

sels were "supplied with blunderbusses, pistols, cutlasses, boarding-pikes, and battle-axes."*

On the morning of the 8th of October, the two vessels approached, and anchored off Fort-Erie, the place of their destination; but which, being still without guns, could afford them no "protection" whatever. Lieutenant Jesse Elliott, of the United States' navy, was, at this time, at Black Rock, superintending the equipment of some schooners, lately purchased for the service of Lake Erie. Having just received a supply of 50 seamen from New York, he borrowed the same number of infantry and artillery from general Smyth;* and, embarking the whole in two large boats, was alongside of the British brigs at about three hours before daylight on the morning succeeding their arrival. Joined by the prisoners, the Americans numbered 140; their opponents 68. Yet doctor Smith calls the capture of these vessels "a very gallant achievement;" and he has taken care to make his account almost warrant the assertion. After the capture, lieutenant Elliott succeeded in getting the Caledonia close under the batteries at Black Rock; but was compelled, by a well-directed shot or two from the Canada-shore, to run the Detroit upon Squaw Island. Almost immediately afterwards, a detachment of the 2d United States' regiment of artillery, with four

* Sketches of the War, p. 43.

field-pieces, landed on the island; and a company of the 5th regiment soon followed. It was in vain for a subaltern's detachment of the 49th, which had been sent from Fort-Erie, to offer any resistance; although the British had contrived to set fire to the brig, previous to the arrival of the American troops. The latter completed the destruction, both of the vessel, and of the greater part of her stores. But for the *defensive* measures, to which sir George Prevost had limited major-general Brock, this active officer would have destroyed those very schooners, for whose equipment, as men of war, lieutenant Elliott and his men had been sent from below; and, by so doing, have brought about consequences, far more important than the safety of the two brigs.

With so many troops under his command, general Van Rensselaer very naturally felt anxious to give a brilliant close to the campaign; the rather, as the national character had been degraded, in the eyes of all, by the tame surrender of general Hull and his army. A second invasion of Canada was, therefore, resolved upon; and, if the reader will take the trouble to turn to Plate I, we will endeavour to explain the plan of attack, as since promulgated by an American general-officer. A road (M.M) had been cut, by general Van Rensselaer's orders, from his camp at Lewistown (B), six miles through a wood to (N), at Four-mile creek; where lay, ready for service, sixty batteaux. From this creek it is four miles and a half, by water, to Fort-George; the whole way under a high bank, which conceals the boats until they turn Niagara-point. The ground at Queenstown and Lewistown is so much elevated, that it may be called a mountain. It forms an immense platform, and overlooks every part of the plane below, to its termination at the banks of the Ontario. Consequently, every movement by major-general Sheaffe at Fort-George, and by the commanding officer at Fort-Niagara, would be under major-general Van Rensselaer's eye. It was the general's intention that brigadier-general Smyth, and his 1650 regulars, should march, by the road (M M), to the mouth of the Four-mile creek; there to wait in readiness for embarking at a moment's notice. Queenstown was then to be attacked by the troops under the immediate command of general Van Rensselaer; and, as the only force, there stationed, was known to be two companies of the 49th regiment, and a small detachment of militia, no doubt was entertained about the town's being immediately carried, as well as the small battery on the heights. These operations, within hearing of Fort-George, could not fail to draw forth the garrison to sustain the post of Queenstown, and, if possible, to repel the invaders. The instant the British column was observed to be in motion, general Smyth was to be signalled to embark at the creek; and, so soon as the British reached Queenstown, he was to be ordered, by a courier, to attack Fort-George; which, being deprived of its garrison, would, it was expected, make but a vain resistance.*

The American general Smyth's backwardness, or some other cause, not made public, deranged the above most excellent plan of attack. In the mean while, the capture of "the two British brigs of war" near Fort-Erie had spread an irresistible ardor for conquest throughout the American army. The troops declared they "must have orders to act, or, at all hazards, they would go home."† About this time, some wag of a deserter came running into the American camp, with information, that general Brock had suddenly proceeded to the westward with the greater part of his troops, to repel general Harrison's attempt at Detroit. The thing was credited; the troops were absolutely furious; and the general himself concluded he had just hit the nick of time for getting possession of the peninsula, by a more direct road than that he had cut through the woods,—a mere traverse across the river to Queenstown. Accordingly, at three o'clock on the morning of the 11th of October, his eager troops were gratified by advancing to the river-side. Experienced boatmen had been provided, and a skilful officer, lieutenant Sim,

* Wilkinson's Memoirs, Vol. I. p. 571.   † App. No. 11.

sent in a boat a-head; but the latter played his countrymen a trick, and ran away; exposing them to a tremendous north-east storm, which continued unabated for 28 hours, and deluged the whole camp.*

All this drenching contributed nothing to allay the ardor of American soldiers. Invade Canada they would; and general Van Rensselaer resolved to carry the British works at Queenstown, before day, on the morning of the 12th. Thirteen boats were provided, and the embarkation was to take place in the following order: —Colonel S. Van Rensselaer, the commanding officer, with 300 militia, and lieutenant-colonel Christie, with 300 regulars; lieutenant-colonel Fenwick and major Mullany, to follow, with about 550 regular troops, and some pieces of flying artillery; and then the militia. It was intended that the embarkation of the regulars and militia should be simultaneous, as far as the boats would suffice to receive them; but, having to descend the bank by a narrow path which had been cut out of it, the regular troops got possession of the boats to the exclusion of the militia; and the latter were ordered to follow in the return-boats.†

The only British batteries from which the troops could be annoyed in the passage, were one, mounting an 18-pounder, upon Queenstown-

* App. No. 11.   † Wilkinson's Memoirs, Vol. I. p. 578.

heights (G), and another, mounting a 24-pound carronade, situate a little below the town (L). The river at Queenstown is scarcely a quarter of a mile in width, and the point chosen for crossing (O) was not fully exposed to either of the British batteries; while the American batteries of two 18 and two 6-pounders (H), and the two 6-pounder field-pieces brought up by lieutenant-colonel Scott, completely commanded every part of the opposite shore, from which musketry could be effectual in opposing a landing. With these important advantages the troops embarked; but, a grape-shot striking the boat in which lieutenant-colonel Christie was, and wounding him in the hand, the pilot and boatmen became so alarmed, that they suffered the boat to fall below the point of landing, and were obliged, in consequence, to put back. Two other boats did the same. The remaining ten, with 225 regulars,* besides officers, including the commander of the expedition, colonel Van Rensselaer, struck the shore; and, after disembarking the men, returned for more troops.

The only force at Queenstown consisted of the two flank companies of the 49th regiment, and a small detachment of militia; amounting, in all, to about 300 rank and file. Of these about 60, taken from the 49th grenadiers and captain Hatt's company of militia, having in charge

* Wilkinson's Memoirs, Vol. I. p. 575.

a 3-pounder, advanced, at four o'clock in the morning, with captain Dennis of the 49th at their head, towards the river; near to which colonel Van Rensselaer had formed his men, to await the arrival of the next boats. A well-directed and warmly continued fire killed and wounded several American officers and privates, including, among the wounded, colonel Van Rensselaer and three captains; and drove the Americans behind a steep bank, close to the water's edge. In the meantime, a fresh supply of troops had effected a landing; and remained, with the others, sheltered behind the bank; whence they returned the fire of the British, killing one man, and wounded four. The remaining subdivisions of the 49th grenadiers and of the militia-company had now joined captain Dennis; and the 49th light infantry, under captain Williams, with captain Chisholm's company of militia, stationed on the brow of the hill, were firing down upon the invaders.

Of five or six boats that attempted to land a body of American regulars under major Mullany, one was destroyed by a shot from the hill-battery, commanded by lieutenant Crowther of the 41st regiment; two others were captured; and the remainder, foiled in their object, returned to the American side. Day-light appeared; and, at the same instant, general Brock arrived at the hill-battery from Fort-George. Observing the strong reinforcements that were crossing over, the general instantly ordered captain Williams to descend the hill, and support captain Dennis. No sooner were captain Williams and his men seen to depart, than the Americans formed the resolution of gaining the heights. Accordingly, 60 American regulars,* headed by captain Wool, and accompanied by major Lush, a volunteer, also by a captain, six lieutenants, and an ensign of the 13th regiment, ascended a fisherman's path up the rocks, which had been reported to general Brock as impassable, and therefore was not guarded. The Americans were thus enabled, unseen by our troops, to arrive at a brow, about 30 yards in the rear of the hill-battery. Reinforcements kept rapidly arriving by the concealed path; and the whole formed on the brow, with their front towards the village of Queenstown.

"The moment general Brock discovered the unexpected advance of the American troops, he, with the 12 men stationed at the battery, retired; and captain Wool, advancing from the rear with his more than ten-fold force, took it without much resistance."† Captain Williams, and his detachment of regulars and militia, were now recalled; and general Brock, putting himself at the head of this force, amounting, in all, to about 90 men, advanced to meet a detachment of 150

* Sketches of the War. p. 72.   † App. No. 12.

picked American regulars, which captain Wool had sent forward to attack him. The American captain says that, in consequence of the general's "superior force," his men retreated; adding: "I sent a reinforcement, notwithstanding which, the enemy drove us to the edge of the bank." While animating his little band of regulars and militia to a charge up the heights, general Brock received a mortal wound in the breast, and immediately fell.

At this moment, the two flank-companies of the York militia, with lieutenant-colonel M'Donnell, the general's provincial aide-de-camp, at their head, arrived from Brown's-point, three miles distant. By this time, also, captain Wool had sent additional reinforcements to captain Ogilvie; making the latter's force "320 regulars, supported by a few militia and volunteers,"* or, in the whole, full 500 men. Colonel M'Donnell and his 190 men,—more than two-thirds Canadian militia,—rushed boldly up the hill, in defiance of the continued stream of musketry pouring down upon them; compelled the Americans to spike the 18-pounder; and would have again driven them to the rocks, had not the colonel and captain Williams been wounded, almost at the same instant; the former mortally. The loss of their commanders created confusion among the men; and they again retreated.

* Wilkinson's Memoirs, Vol. I. p. 573.

Hearing of the fall of general Brock, captain Dennis proceeded from the valley, towards the foot of the heights; and, mounting the general's horse, rode up, and tried to rally the troops. He succeeded in forming a few; but the number was so inconsiderable that, to persist in a contest, would have been madness. A retreat was accordingly ordered, by the ground in the rear of the town; and the men of the 49th, accompanied by many of the militia, formed in front of Vromont's battery; there to await the expected reinforcement from Fort-George.

While we had, at this period, not above 200 unwounded men at Queenstown, the Americans, by their own account, had upwards of 800, and general Van Rensselaer tells us, that " a number of boats now crossed over, unannoyed, except by the one unsilenced gun,"* or that at Vromont's battery; consequently, more troops were hourly arriving. Brigadier-general Wadsworth was left as commanding officer of the Americans on the Queenstown hill; and general Van Rensselaer, considering the victory as complete, had himself crossed over, in order to give directions about fortifying the camp which he intended to occupy in the British territory.

As whatever brilliant deeds were achieved by the Americans on " this memorable day," confessedly form part of those events which have

* App. No. 11.

just been detailed, we will suspend our narrative awhile, till a few of the American statements on the subject have been exhibited for the reader's amusement.

One writer, and he a general too, says: "The names of the officers who accompanied colonel Van Rensselaer on this hardy enterprise, deserve to be engraven on the scroll of fame, for surmounting obstacles almost insuperable, in the face of a determined enemy, under a heavy fire; and dislodging and pursuing a superior force, composed of two (captain Wool says, "four"*) companies of the 49th British regiment, advantageously posted, with a body of auxiliary militia and Indians: it was indeed a display of intrepidity rarely exhibited, in which the conduct and the execution were equally conspicuous. Here true valor, so often mistaken for animal courage," (a note adds: "In the American service, temerity is too often taken for bravery, &c.") "was attested by an appeal to the bayonet, which decided the contest without a shot."—" Under all the circumstances, and on the scale of the operation, the impartial soldier and competent judge will name this brilliant affair a *chef d'œuvre* of the war."†

Mr. Thomson describes the affair with the 190 British regulars and militia upon the hill, thus: "At this moment a reinforcement arrived, which

* App. No. 12. † Wilkinson's Memoirs, Vol. I. p. 578.

augmented the detachment to 320 men, who
were led to the charge; and, making a forcible
appeal to the bayonet, entirely routed the British
49th regiment, of 600 men, and pursued them
up the height, until the ground was regained,
which the detachment had just before lost.
Part of the 41st" (one officer, lieutenant Crowther) " were acting with the 49th, both of which
regiments distinguished themselves, under the
same commander, in Europe; and the latter had
obtained the title of the Egyptian Invincibles,
because they had never, on any occasion before,
been known to give ground;"*—or, we may
surely subjoin, had such an unprincipled enemy
to deal with. Mr. O'Connor has inadvertently
prefixed " a part of " to " the 49th regiment";
which, in some degree, exculpates him; but Dr.
Smith, like his friend Mr. Thomson, introduces
the whole 49th "regiment of British regulars, 600
strong," adding :—" They mutually resorted to
the bayonet; and, after a bloody conflict, the
famous invincibles yielded to the superior energy
of their antagonists, although so far inferior in
numbers."†

Leaving these contemptible historians to the
reader's castigation, when he has leisure to inflict it, we have now to call his attention to the
finale of " this memorable day." Between two

* Sketches of the War, p. 75.
† Hist. of the United States, Vol. III. p. 201.

and three o'clock in the afternoon, about 50 Indians, led by the chief Norton, advanced through the woods and an orchard, towards the mountain. As they approached, the American troops, " not knowing their number, at first faltered."* After a sharp conflict, in which the Indians lost a few men killed and wounded, and one made prisoner, the latter very prudently retired towards the reinforcement of regulars and militia, under major-general Sheaffe, which had just arrived from Fort-George. This reinforcement, consisting of about 380 rank and file of the 41st regiment, under major Derenzy, and about 300 militia, accompanied by one 3-pounder, joined the remnant of the 49th flank companies; and the whole proceeded to the heights, by a route through the enclosures;† the Indians pointing out to the troops the best track for ascending the mountain. As soon as the British column had reached a field adjoining the road to the falls, about 60 of the 41st under captain Bullock, and a party of militia, arrived from Chippeway. The whole British and Indian force, thus assembled, did not amount to 1000 rank and file; of whom about 500 were regular troops. The artillery consisted of two 3-pounders, placed under the orders of lieutenant Crowther of the 41st.

The attack commenced by the light infantry

* Sketches of the War, p. 73. † See Plate I. q. q. q. q.

company of the 41st, under lieutenant M'Intyre, about 35 militia, and the same number of Indians, composing the left flank of the British line. After a single volley, lieutenant M'Intyre's company resorted to the bayonet; and soon drove the American right. The main body of the British now advanced, firing their two 3-pounders, with destructive effect. The Americans sustained but a short conflict, ere they fled with precipitation towards the point at which they had first landed. There they threw themselves over the precipice, as if heedless of the danger; and many must have perished in the flood. Others, no doubt, swam across; and some escaped in the few boats that remained entire, or whose crews could be persuaded to approach the Canadian shore. "In retiring," says an American author, "they received considerable aid from the American batteries, which kept up a brisk and well-directed fire on the enemy, as he pressed upon their rear."*

All, however, would not do. A flag of truce, begging for quarter, came from the American commander. Mr. Coffin, aide-de-camp to general Sheaffe, and lieutenant M'Intyre, accompanied the bearer of the flag, and received the sword of major-general Wadsworth, the American commanding officer. While Mr. Coffin was conducting the latter to major-general Sheaffe,

* Sketches of the War, p. 75.

lieutenant M'Intyre received, as prisoners of war, lieutenant-colonel Scott and 71 officers, together with 858 non-commissioned officers and privates, of the American army. These were exclusive of the two boat-loads of troops which had been captured in the morning.

If we consider Mr. Thomson's account of the number of Americans surrendered, to refer to the non-commissioned officers and privates only, and then add his loss in wounded, 82, we shall obtain 846; not far short of lieutenant M'Intyre's return. None of the other American historians seem desirous to be particular on this point. The above 82 wounded include such only as had not been brought to the American side in the course of the day. We may safely estimate such as had been brought over at as many more; and those that succeeded in re-crossing the river, either by boats or swimming, and others that were drowned in the attempt, must have amounted to one or two hundreds. Mr. Thomson states 90 as the number of Americans killed in action. That, added to the number of prisoners, makes, without reckoning those taken in the boats, 1021.—Dr. Smith says:—" In the course of the day about 1100 troops, regulars, volunteers, and militia, passed into Canada from Lewistown; very few of whom returned."* But the "Albany Gazette," (an American northern

* Hist. of the United States, Vol. III. p. 200.

newspaper,) at the conclusion of "a most accurate account" of the Queenstown battle, fixes the number of Americans that crossed the river at 1600; consisting of 900 regulars, and 700 militia.

The editor of the "Sketches of the War" says:—" The British force in the different battles, with the exception of the first, was at no time less than 1100; in the last and fourth engagement it was much greater."* Doctor Smith fixes the British force at 2200.† Mr. O'Connor estimates the prisoners at "about 700;" and then adds:—"This little band surrendered to about five times their number,"‡ or 3500 men. These are the delusions so industriously practised upon the American people: no wonder those among them who have never been beaten into a contrary opinion, still fancy they are possessed of the prowess of demi-gods.

The British loss in this decisive affair amounted to 11 killed and 60 wounded, of the regulars and militia, and to five killed and nine wounded, of the Indians. Although Mr. Thomson had stated the American loss at 90 killed, and 82 (another account says 100) wounded; and, in reference to us, had said: "Their loss is not known," he could not refrain from adding, with an air of triumphant pleasantry:—"With regard to close and courageous fighting, the

* Sketches of the War, p. 76.
† Hist. of the U. S. Vol. III. p. 200,   ‡ Hist. of the War, p. 50.

victory belonged to the Americans; but with regard to the loss which was sustained, it was exclusively yielded to the British."*

General Van Rensselaer's letter gives a ludicrous account of the behaviour of the American militia at Lewistown. These men, a day or two previous, were for invading Canada, without waiting for orders from their commanding officer. Now, all the exhortations of their general, of lieutenant-colonel Bloom, and even of the grave "Judge Peck," could not induce them to budge a step. A north-east storm for twenty-eight hours† was nothing, compared to what their wounded comrades had told them they must expect, if they came in contact with the brave 49th, " the green tygers," as they called them. " The ardor of the unengaged troops," says the general, " had entirely subsided."‡ By contrasting all this with the national feeling excited by such writings as it becomes our unpleasant task to investigate, the difference between reality and fiction strikes forcibly on the mind.

The number of American troops, whose discretion came so well to their aid, is stated at from 12 to 1500; and the number of regulars and militia at Lewistown, exclusive of the several detachments ordered from Black Rock, Buffaloe, and Fort-Niagara, and whose commanding

* Sketches of the War, p. 76.
† See p. 86   ‡ App. No. 11.

officers can boast of their names being " engraven on the scroll of fame" for having "done honor to their country upon this memorable day," amounted to 3170;* a tolerable proof that, at the lowest estimate, 1600 Americans crossed over to Queenstown, on the "memorable" 13th of October, 1812.

When general Wilkinson complains that the executive has not rendered " common justice to the principal actors in this gallant scene," not exhibited it to the country " in its true light, and shewn what deeds Americans are still capable of performing;"†—who among us can retain his gravity? " It is true," says the general, " complete success did not ultimately crown this enterprise; but two great ends were obtained for the country:— it re-established the character of the American arms;"—it did indeed!—" and deprived the enemy, by the death of general Brock, of the best officer that has headed their troops in Canada throughout the war;"—truth undeniable!—" and, with his loss, put an end to their then brilliant career;" —yet the capture of general Wadsworth took place in less than five hours afterwards.

The instant we know what the Americans expected to gain, a tolerable idea may be formed of what they actually lost, by the attack upon Queenstown. General Van Rensselaer, in a letter

* See p. 80 † Sketches of the War, p. 76.

to major-general Dearborn, written five days previously, says thus :—"Should we succeed, we shall effect a great discomfiture of the enemy, by breaking their line of communication, driving their shipping from the mouth of this river, leaving them no rallying point in this part of the country, appalling the minds of the Canadians, and opening a wide and safe communication for our supplies; we shall save our own land,—wipe away part of the score of our past disgrace,—get excellent barracks and winter quarters, and at least be prepared for an early campaign another year."—Who could believe that this very letter is given at length in general Wilkinson's book, and precedes, but a few pages, those ridiculous remarks into which an excess of patriotism had betrayed him.

It is often said, that we throw away by the pen, what we gain by the sword. Had general Brock been less prodigal of his valuable life, and survived the Queenstown battle, he would have made the 13th of October a still more "memorable" day, by crossing the river, and carrying Fort-Niagara; which, at that precise time, was nearly stripped of its garrison. Instead of doing this, and thus putting an end to the campaign upon the Niagara-frontier, major-general Sheaffe, general Brock's successor, allowed himself to be persuaded to sign an armistice; the very thing general Van Rensselaer wanted. The latter, of course, assured his panic-struck militia, that the British general had sent to implore this of him; and that he, general Van Rensselaer, had consented, merely to gain time to make some necessary arrangements. Such of the militia as had not already scampered off, now agreed to suspend their journey homewards, and try another experiment at invasion.

On the 15th, all the militia who had been made prisoners, including the wounded regulars, were sent across the river, upon their parole: so were the whole of the American officers; not excepting major Mullany, and several others, known to be British subjects: nay, even their sidearms were restored to them. The non-commissioned officers and privates of the regulars were marched to Montreal, to await their exchange. The American editors acknowledge that the prisoners were treated with uncommon kindness by " the victorious enemy;" yet one editor adds: " For want of *will* or power, they put no restraint upon their Indian allies, who were stripping and scalping not only the slain, but the dying that remained on the field of battle."* Doctor Smith says: " No restraint, however, was imposed upon the Indians by general Sheaffe, a native of Boston." He then, to prove that the Indians " stripped and scalped the slain, and even the wounded and dying

* Sketches of the War, p. 76.

Americans," says:—"Captain Ogilvie saw the corpse of ensign Morris stripped even of his shirt, and the scull of a soldier who had been wounded, cloven by a tomahawk:"* but, whether the ensign's shirt had not been stolen by one of his own men, or the hole in the soldier's scull was not a wound he had received in the battle, is deemed a needless inquiry.

While the British and Americans were engaging at Queenstown, the batteries at Fort-George, under the direction of brigade-major Evans, opened a fire upon those at Fort-Niagara; which was returned with hot shot, and continued during several hours. The spirited cannonade on the part of the British compelled the American garrison, commanded by captain N. Leonard, to retreat, with the loss of two men killed by the bursting of a 12-pounder, and several men wounded by shot. The American account says, hot shots were used on both sides. On the contrary, none were, or could be fired from Fort-George; and the effects of such as were fired from Fort-Niagara are thus described in the American account:—" From the south block-house of the American fort, the shot was principally directed against the village of Newark, and several houses were set on fire, one or two of which were entirely consumed."†

* Hist. of the United States, Vol. III. p. 201.
† Sketches of the War, p. 77.

Considering the character of the distinguished chief who fell on the British side at the Queenstown battle,—of him who, undoubtedly, was " the best officer that headed their troops throughout the war,"—it will surely be deemed a pardonable digression to give a brief sketch of the more prominent features of his life and character.

Sir Isaac Brock was born at Guernsey, in October 1769; consequently, was but 43 when he received the fatal bullet. He had entered the army at the age of 16, and been lieutenant-colonel of the 49th regiment since 1797. During the campaign in Holland in 1799, he distinguished himself at the head of his regiment, and was second in command of the land forces at the battle of Copenhagen. He was gallant and undaunted, yet prudent and calculating; devoted to his sovereign, and romantically fond of his country; but gentle and persuasive to those whose feelings were less ardent than his own. Elevated to the government of Upper Canada, he reclaimed the disaffected by mildness, and fixed the wavering by argument: all hearts were conciliated; and, in the trying moment of invasion, the whole province displayed a zealous, and an enthusiastic loyalty.

Over the minds of the Indians general Brock had acquired an ascendancy, which he judiciously exercised, for purposes conducive no less to the cause of humanity, than to the interests of his country. He engaged them to throw aside the scalping knife; endeavoured to implant in their breasts the virtues of clemency and forbearance; and taught them to feel pleasure and pride, in the compassion extended to a vanquished enemy. Circumscribed in his means of repelling invasion, he studied to fix the attachment of that rude and wavering people; and, by reducing their military operations to the known rules of war and discipline, to improve the value of their alliance.

His strong attachment to the service, and particularly to his regiment, formed a distinguishing feature in his character. There was a correspondence of regard between him and his officers, and even the non-commissioned officers and privates, with an addition of reverence on the part of the latter, that produced the picture of a happy family. Those movements of feeling which the exertions of discipline will sometimes occasion, rarely reached his men. He governed them by a sentiment of esteem which he himself had created; and the consolation was given him, to terminate a useful and brilliant course in the midst of his professional family.

CHAPTER IV.

Bombardment between the batteries at Fort-Erie and Black Rock—Capture of some Canadian voyageurs—General Van Rensselaer's secession from the command—Appointment of general Smyth—The latter's plan for invading Canada—Re-commencement of hostilities after general Sheaffe's armistice—General Smyth's proclamation—Preparations for the invasion—General Porter's address to his countrymen—The landing of the advance of the American army—Its proceedings detailed—Summons to Fort-Erie—Attempt at invasion given up—State of the American army at Buffaloe—Commodore Chauncey's arrival at Lake Ontario—State of the two hostile fleets—Attack upon the Royal George—Midnight incursion into Gananoque from Ogdensburg—State of the British works at Fort-Wellington—Unsuccessful attack upon Ogdensburg—Mutual advance of the American northern army and the British troops at Montreal—American reonnoissance—Retreat of the American army, and termination of the campaign.

ABOUT the middle of October, the batteries at Fort-Erie, under the direction of lieutenant-colonel Myers, opened upon the opposite fort of Black Rock. The latter returned only a few shots; but not, as the Americans allege, on account of there being no heavier cannon mounted than 6-pounders; for, not many months afterwards, we spiked, upon the same battery, two 12, and two 9-pounders, and brought away one 12, and three 6-pounders. Several shots, it is stated, struck the Black Rock battery, and two or three passed through the upper loft of the west-barracks. The east-barracks were destroyed by a bomb, which blew up the magazine, and burnt a quantity of furs, the late cargo of the north-west company's brig Caledonia, whose capture, as a British man of war brig, we have already noticed.

On the 21st of October, 44 Canadian voyageurs, under the command of captain M'Donnel, were surprised, and, after losing four killed and four wounded, captured, by a body of Americans, under a major Young. The major's force is not stated; but, as the Americans proceeded to the attack in expectation of meeting " from one to three hundred British," we may conjecture that their numbers fully equalled the latter amount. Forty prisoners, (one having escaped,) along with their baggage, and some immaterial despatches, fell into the hands of the Americans; who, ingeniously enough, converted a large pocket-handkerchief which they found among the spoils, into " a stand of colours:" and Mr. O'Connor exultingly tells us, that major Young had the honor of taking the first standard from the enemy in the present war;" following it up with,—" The movements of the enemy, during these times, were not to them equally honorable or important."

Since the day succeeding the "brilliant" affair at Queenstown, major-general Van Rensselaer had resigned the command of the Niagara-frontier to brigadier-general Smyth. This officer, confident in the success of *his* plan of invasion, already felt upon his brow the gentle pressure of those laurels, so vainly sought after by his two predecessors. The information which the general had gained respecting the distribution of the British forces, and the superior facility, as he conceived, of disembarking troops above the falls, induced him to fix, for the invading point, some part of the shore between Fort-Erie and Chippeway. As the first step in the business, general Smyth was bound to give 30 hours' notice of his intention to break off the armistice, which had been so good-naturedly concluded by major-general Sheaffe with general Van Rensselaer. This the American general did, at three o'clock on the afternoon of the 19th of November; not, however, as he ought to have done, at general Sheaffe's head-quarters at Fort-George, but, with all the craftiness of his nation, to the commanding-officer at Fort-Erie, the extreme right of the British line; in full hopes, no doubt, that he should be able to make the attack, before succours could arrive from Fort-George, distant 36 miles.

Early on the morning of the 21st, by way perhaps of announcing the renewal of hostilities, the batteries at Fort-George, and those at Fort-Niagara, commenced a mutual bombardment, the latter with hot shot, and continued it throughout the day. The town of Newark was slightly injured; and several buildings in and near to Fort-Niagara were set on fire. Mr. Thomson celebrates, on this occasion, " the courageous fortitude" of the wife of one Doyle, a private in the United States' artillery, who had been taken at Queenstown. After stating that she assisted in supplying one of the guns at Fort-Niagara, he, in the true hyperbolic style, declares she " was surpassed, neither by Joan, maid of Orleans, nor the heroine of Saragossa."* We suspect that " the refusal of the British to parole her husband" arose from his being an Irishman; and that, had the lady herself not been his countrywoman, her birth-place would have been vauntingly set forth in the history. The British lost, by the cannonade, one man killed, and one wounded; the Americans, four men killed, (two by the bursting of a gun,) and four wounded.

General Smyth, in order that he might visit the Canadian shore, with a force competent to retain the posts he should capture, was desirous to encrease his numbers, by such

* Sketches of the War, p. 80.

volunteers, as would be willing to perform one month's service; to submit to the rigid discipline of a camp; and to encounter the British on their own soil. This zealous officer had already made known his wishes, by a pompous proclamation, dated on the 10th of November.* It fully answered his purpose; and, by the 27th of that month, the force collected at his station amounted to 4500 men.†

The whole of this army, properly drilled, equipped, and organized, was to embark, on the morning of the 28th, from the navy-yard at Black Rock. No possible preparation had been omitted. At the navy-yard there were lying, for the purpose of transporting the troops across the river, 70 public boats, calculated to carry 40 men each; 5 large private boats, to carry 100 men each; and 10 scows, for the artillery, to carry 25 men each; which, together with a number of small boats, were to convey the whole across, to effect the third invasion, and, it was more than hoped, the complete subjugation of Upper Canada.†

So easy was the task considered, that general Porter, of the New York militia, published an address to the people of Ontario and Gennessee; in which he assured them, that the American army would, in a few days, occupy all the British fortresses on the Niagara; restore peace to the whole of that section of the country; and redeem the tarnished reputation of the nation.

* Appendix, No. 14.   † Sketches of the War, p. 81.

Between one and two o'clock on the morning of the 28th of November, the advance of general Smyth's army, composed of detachments of picked men from the 12th, 13th, 14th, and 15th, United States' regiments of infantry, under the command of colonel Winder of the 14th, accompanied by a party of naval officers and seamen lately arrived from one of the Atlantic ports, embarked at Buffaloe in ten boats, to carry the British batteries on the opposite shore, and, by that means, facilitate the passage of the main body of the army.

At Fort-Erie the British force consisted of a detachment of 80 men of the 49th, under major Ormsby, and about 50 of the Newfoundland regiment, under captain Whelan. The ferry, opposite Black Rock, was occupied by two companies of militia, under captain Bostwick. At a house on the Chippeway-road, called the Red House, distant about two miles and a half from Fort-Erie, was stationed lieutenant Lamont, of the 49th, having under his orders two serjeants and 35 rank and file; also, lieutenant King, of the royal artillery, with two field-pieces, a three and 6-pounder, worked by a few militia-artillerymen. In the vicinity of the Red House were two batteries, one mounting a 24, the other an 18-pounder; and which were also under the charge of lieutenant Lamont. At the distance of about a mile further along the road, lieutenant Bartley, of the 49th, with two serjeants and 35 rank and file, occupied a post; and so did lieutenant M'Intyre, with the 41st light infantry, about 70 strong, upon the road-side, not far from Frenchman's creek; which is distant about four miles and a half from Fort-Erie. The headquarters of lieutenant-colonel Bisshopp, the commanding officer on that line, were at Chippeway. He had under his immediate command, a battalion-company of the 41st regiment, a company of militia, and a small detachment of militia-artillery, with a light 6-pounder; also, at no great distance, a detachment of militia under major Hatt.

The ten American boats had scarcely proceeded half the way across the river, when a smart fire from captain Bostwick's men compelled them to drop down opposite to the Red House. Here they met with a similar reception from lieutenant Lamont's party. Owing, however, to the extreme darkness, it was deemed useless to fire more than one or two rounds from the guns; but, as alarm-guns, they produced an unexpected effect, that of scaring away five of the boats, including the boat in which was colonel Winder.*

The division that effected a landing consisted of about 190 regular troops, under the command of lieutenant-colonel Boerstler, of the 14th, and captain King of the 15th, United States' regiment; and of about 60 seamen, under the orders of lieutenant-commandant Angus ; assisted by sailing-master Watts, lieutenant Dudley, and nine other naval officers.* Captain King, taking with him 60 regulars, also 40 seamen, armed with boarding-pikes and cutlasses, and headed by lieutenant Angus, proceeded to the Red House, about 50 yards from the beach, and whither lieutenant Lamont and his little detachment had just retired. The Americans charged, and received a volley from the British, succeeded by a charge, which drove the Americans towards their boats. Here they rallied, and re-advanced to the charge; but were received and repulsed as before. A third attempt to subdue this little band was equally unsuccessful; and the Americans retired to their boats, apparently to await a fresh reinforcement. Ashamed, however, to be thus beaten by a handful of men ; captain King, at the head of his regulars, again advanced, by a circuitous route, upon the left of lieutenant Lamont's position. In momentary expectation of reinforcements from Chippeway, lieutenant Lamont, in the dark, mistook Captain King's party for Canadian militia; until a most destructive volley, which killed seven, and wounded eight of his men, as well as lieutenant King, of the artillery, dangerously, and himself in five places, convinced him, too late, of his error. Being now without a commander, the few gallant fellows

* Sketches of the War, p. 83.

who had not been wounded, except three who were taken prisoners, dispersed, and effected their escape. On getting possession of the Red House, the Americans set fire to it; and spiked the two field-pieces. They then proceeded to the batteries, and dismounted the 24 and 18-pounder, the former of which had been previously spiked by one of the British officers. Having performed this " brilliant service,"* the Americans carried to their boats the three unwounded, along with several of the wounded prisoners, including lieutenant King of the artillery; whose death, a week or two afterwards, was no doubt occasioned by this inhuman act. Lieutenant Lamont was dragged a short distance; but, fortunately for him, the enemy considered that a dead prisoner would be a poor trophy, and therefore left him on the ground; where, already lay, 12 of their own killed, and the same number of their wounded. The sailors had, in the mean time, been amusing themselves with pillaging, and setting fire to the few private dwellings scattered along the beach.

It is now time to attend to the exploits of the remaining sub-division of the American force, and which had landed a mile or two below the Red House. This party consisted of about 130 regulars, under lieutenant-colonel Bærstler, and 20 seamen, led by sailing-master Watts. These

* History of the United States, Vol. III. p. 205.

were attacked, at the moment of landing, by the subaltern's detachment of the 49th under lieutenant Bartley; and kept greatly in check, till a very severe loss in killed, wounded, or missing, and the near approach of another part of the enemy's force, which, owing to the darkness, had been mistaken for militia, compelled lieutenant Bartley to retreat. Soon afterwards, the Americans again encountered captain Bostwick with his detachment of militia; and, after a few rounds, in which the latter lost three killed, 15 wounded, and six prisoners, compelled him also to retreat.

The whole of this warfare was conducted amidst darkness; and the fears of the American commanding-officer induced him to adopt a stratagem, that caused additional perplexity to the trebly inferior force opposed to him. "Lieutenant-colonel Bærstler," says the American editor, " exerting a Stentorian voice, roared in various directions, as though he commanded thousands, and created such a panic in the enemy, that they fled before him wherever he moved."*

It was still dark when major Ormsby, with his 80 men, arrived at the mill on Frenchman's creek. A few shots were there exchanged; and the major, after proceeding a short distance further, very properly halted; intending to remain till day-light, which was then fast approaching,

* Hist. of the United States, Vol. III. p. 204.

should discover to him the number and movements of the enemy. While here he was joined by the 41st light infantry, which had also been partially engaged; and, at day-light, lieutenant-colonel Bisshopp arrived on the ground with the expected reinforcement. His whole force, when first drawn up, did not exceed 250 regulars and 300 militia, aided by a light 6-pounder; but, by 11 o'clock in the forenoon, the number of regular troops became nearly doubled.

The expected day-light had not only stilled colonel Bærstler's "Stentorian voice," but driven him and his party to the safe side of the river; in such haste too, that captain King and about 30 of his men were left " in possession of the conquered ground,"* and became, in consequence, prisoners to the British. Just as day dawned, colonel Winder, with his five boats, containing 250 men,* was again on the river; but two or three well-directed shots from the 6-pounder, and a few rounds of musketry, made this division, as it approached the Canada-side, again wheel about, and retire, for the last time, under the shelter of Squaw Island, to the American shore.

The circumstances attending this predatory excursion having been as much exaggerated as the affair at Queenstown, it may be worth our while to bestow a glance at some of the more

* Sketches of the War, p. 84.

prominent mistatements. Mr. O'Connor has, strange enough, not thought this " brilliant service" deserving a place in his book; but Mr. Thomson has devoted four or five pages to it, and doctor Smith, in his usual way, has borrowed his account from the latter; first taking care, by transposing the words, and embellishing the style, not to be guilty of plagiarism.

Both of our zealous historians describe lieutenant Lamont's force as " 250 men;" and aver that captain King made from this party alone " about 50 prisoners." The dismounting of the two heavy guns, spiking of the two field-pieces, and the burning and destroying of private property for a few miles along the beach, are represented thus:—" Every battery, between Chippeway and Fort-Erie, was now carried; the cannon spiked or destroyed, and 16 miles of the Canadian frontier laid waste and deserted." Doctor Smith, having been informed that the guns were not " destroyed," and justly considering that " laid waste" might imply what, along an extent of a few miles, actually happened, to the disgrace of the invading force, states thus:—
" Every battery, between Chippeway and Fort-Erie, was carried, the cannon spiked, and a frontier of 16 miles entirely cleared." Captain King's stay on the Canadian shore, or, as Mr. Thomson happily expresses it, his " remaining in possession of the conquered ground, until the

main body of the army should cross over the strait, and march to the assault of the British forts," was because he and his " 12," not 30, men " were anxious to complete the destruction of every breast-work and barrack of the enemy."* The flight of colonel Bærstler and the remainder of the American regulars and sailors is denominated, returning " from their successful enterprise,"* " as soon as the ends of this daring and well executed adventure had been completely accomplished."†

The loss of the British, on this occasion, was in proportion to the strenuous exertions they had made to repulse an enemy, whose numbers were so superior. By the returns there were 17 killed, 47 wounded, and 35 missing.‡ And yet, according to the American accounts, besides the " 50 prisoners" taken at the Red House, colonel Bærstler made " several" in his excursion. The loss of the Americans, except as to officers, no where appears. Mr. Thomson names, among the killed, sailing-master Watts, and, among the wounded, a midshipman, and three captains and a lieutenant of infantry; adding, that seven out of 12 of the navy-officers were wounded.

In expectation, no doubt, that " this gallant and successful enterprize," seconded by four or

* Sketches of the War, p. 84.
† Hist. of the United States, Vol. III. p. 204   ‡ App. No. 13.

five hours' bombardment by the batteries at Black Rock, had inspired the British with dread of the American arms, general Smyth, about one o'clock in the day, sent across a flag of truce, to demand the surrender of Fort-Erie to the American army. To this ridiculous demand,* colonel Bisshopp sent a very proper reply, which may be summed up in these words: —" Come and take it." Captain Fitzgerald carried the return-message ; and general Smyth, displaying before him his numerous force, tried every means in his power to frighten the British commander into a bloodless surrender of his post.

The morning's success was to have been followed up by the embarkation of the whole 4000 men. One half of this force, it appears, had actually embarked ; " and," says Mr. Thomson, "about 500 British troops had been drawn up in line, about half a mile from the river, sounding their trumpets and bugles, and indicating their readiness to receive the Americans."† The American troops, however, after being allowed to enjoy this scene till late in the afternoon, were ordered to disembark, with " an assurance, that the expedition was only postponed until the boats should be put in a state of better preparation."†

On Sunday the 29th, the troops received orders to prepare for embarkation on the following

* App. No. 15. † Sketches of the War, p. 85.

morning, at nine o'clock. After a squabble among the general officers about the proper time for embarking, and the proper point for disembarking, the troops, the expedition was ordered to be ready by three o'clock on Tuesday morning. The men were ready, and partly in the boats; when general Porter received orders from general Smyth, to disembark immediately. " He was at the same time informed," says the American account, " that the invasion of Canada was abandoned, for the season ; that the regulars were ordered into winter quarters; and that, as the services of the volunteers could now be dispensed with, they might stack their arms, and return to their homes. The scene of discontent which followed was without a parallel; 4000 men, without order or restraint, indignantly discharged their muskets in every direction; and the person of the commanding-officer was threatened." Two or three pages more of Mr. Thomson's book are filled with complaints against general Smyth, for his behaviour on this occasion. To all of which he answers, that he " had called together a council of his officers, and they decided against the contemplated operations, upon the ground of the insufficiency of force; and that, circumstanced as he was, he thought it his duty to follow the cautious counsels of experience, and not, by precipitation, to add to the list of defeats."

Comparing the bombastic language of general Smyth's proclamation, wherein he had invited his countrymen to partake with him in the plunder of the Canadas, with the desponding tone he assumed when he ordered his troops, just at the crisis of their hopes, to retire to their huts for the winter, we cannot be surprised at their contemptuous indignation, so fully expressed in the nick-name they gave him of, ' general *Van Bladder;*' nor at the grief and perplexity of the Washington patriots, whose ardor for invasion a third discomfiture contributed nothing to allay.

We know not which to applaud most, the gallantry displayed by the few regulars and militia that defeated the enemy's plan of invasion, on the morning of the 28th of November; or the firmness of the field-officers of the line and of the militia, who, sitting in council, as they had been ordered, on the 1st of December, unanimously declared, that they did *not* consider a retreat to be at all necessary, nor a measure to be looked forward to; and that a small reinforcement would enable them to gain a most decisive advantage over any force which the bragging Mr. Smyth might have it in his power to send against them.

Disappointed in the expectation of gaining the command of the lakes by the invasion of Upper Canada, the American goverment adopted immediate measures to provide on those inland seas, a naval force superior to that of the British. As the first step, commodore Isaac Chauncey, one of the oldest captains in the American service, was appointed to the command. This officer arrived at Sackett's Harbor, in October, 1812; invested with full powers to buy, build, and equip, till his force should attain the requisite superiority. Some schooners were purchased; and a ship of 590 tons laid on the stocks. Previous to the end of the month, two detachments of seamen, one of 400, from the United States' frigate John Adams, (then about to be reduced to a corvette,) the other of 100, selected from the different ships on the seaboard, along with a number of active officers, arrived at Sackett's Harbor.

At this time, the British fleet consisted of the Royal George, a ship of 340 tons, and of three smaller vessels, that averaged about 150 tons; mounting, altogether, 50 guns; chiefly carronades and long sixes. These vessels were wholly manned by Canadians; and even commodore Earle, their commander, was not an officer of the royal navy. He had proved his incompetency, by not capturing the Oneida brig, lieutenant Woolsey, at the commencement of the war.

With so ample means in his power, commodore Chauncey had, by the 6th of November, equipped a fleet, composed of the brig Oneida, and six fine schooners, of the united burthen of

830 tons. The total number of guns in his fleet did not exceed 48; but several of these were long 32 and 24-pounders, and the greater part mounted upon traversing carriages, by which their effect was doubled.* When we consider that these seven vessels were manned with upwards of 500 experienced seamen, it will not be too much to say, that commodore Chauncey could appear on the lake with a force doubly superior to that of his adversary.

Accordingly, having ascertained that the Royal George and two of the schooners were hourly expected back from Fort-George, whither they had been carrying a small detachment of troops, the commodore sailed out upon the lake; and, on the afternoon of the 8th, to his great joy, fell in with the Royal George alone. Chase was given, but she was lost sight of in the night. On the next morning, however, she was discovered in Kingston channel, and again chased by the whole American squadron. "By the alternate prevalence of squalls and calms," says an American naval editor, "the squadron was led in close pursuit into the harbor of the enemy at Kingston." A mutual cannonading took place, and the Royal George was compelled to run further up the bay. The American editors all concur in celebrating the event, as a presage of the commodore's future fame. One

* See James's Naval Occurrences, p. 298.

of the American officers concludes a flaming account of the " bombardment of the town" thus: " Our sailors had no grog; they want no stimulus of that kind: they seem to have no fear of death." The reader's surprise will cease, when he learns that, during the whole of this two hours' appalling " cross-fire of five batteries of flying artillery, in all about 40 guns,"* so well-managed was the distance, that no one was hurt on shore, and only one man killed, and three wounded, on board the American squadron. It was not the "heavy showers of round and grape," but of *snow*, that compelled the commodore to haul off, and return to Sackett's Harbor. According to sir George Prevost's letter, the American squadron had sailed out " for the purpose of carrying the port of Kingston by surprise;" but no such intention was evinced on the part of the American commander. It is not improbable, however, that the latter's exaggerated account of his reception, tended, in no small degree, to the security of Kingston during the remainder of the war.

Our vicinity to the St. Lawrence reminds us, that we have to correct the mistatements of the Americans, respecting two otherwise unimportant operations in this quarter. In the autumn of 1812, about 600 American troops, under general Brown, of the New York militia, were garrisoned

* Sketches of the War, p. 93.

at Ogdensburg, a village of about 70 houses and some very strong works, situate on the river-side, and distant about 60 miles from Sackett's Harbor.* The first of these operations was a " daring exploit" performed by the Americans, on the morning of the 21st of September. To understand the thing properly, the American account must precede ours. " Captain Forsythe," says Mr. Thomson, " of the rifle-regiment, being at the garrison of Ogdensburg, projected an expedition against a small village in the town of Leeds, in Canada, called Gananoque. In this village was the king's store-house, containing immense quantities of arms and ammunition; and captain Forsythe was resolved on its destruction. In the night of the 20th instant, therefore, a number of boats being provided, he embarked with 70 of his own men, and 34 militia-men. Before day-light of the 21st, they reached the Canadian shore, and landed, unobserved, at a little distance from the village. The enemy soon after discovered them; and they were fired on by a party of 125 regulars and militia. Forsythe drew up his men, and returned their fire with such effect, that the British retreated in disorder; and were pursued to the village, where they rallied and resolved on making a stand, and disputing the passage of a bridge. An action took place here, which

* See Plate II.

resulted in the same manner as the former. The enemy again fled, making his escape over the bridge, and leaving 10 of his number killed, eight regulars and several militia-men prisoners, and the village and storehouse in possession of the American party. Captain Forsythe lost one in killed, and one wounded. After releasing the militia-prisoners on their parole, and taking out a quantity of arms, fixed ammunition, powder, flints, and other articles of public property, and setting fire to the store-house, he returned to Cape Vincent with these, and the eight regulars prisoners."*

The " village" of Gananoque consisted, at this time, of a public-house and a saw-mill, also a small hut, inhabited by colonel Stone of the militia; in whose possession were two kegs of fixed ammunition, and a chest containing about 30 muskets. The Americans landed, in the dead of the night, by the aid of a traitor; and entered the " village " while the inhabitants were asleep. On arriving opposite to colonel Stone's house, some villain of the American party fired into the window, and wounded Mrs. Stone, most dangerously, as she lay in her bed. When the commander of these midnight prowlers afterwards came into the house, the poor woman, sitting up in her bed, expostulated freely with him upon the dastardly attack which he and his followers had

* Sketches of the War, p. 67.

made ; and she actually possessed **magnanimity** enough to conceal from his knowledge, the dreadful wound she had received in the body. The noise of the firing had brought up between 30 and 40 militia-men ; but, as for " regulars," there was not one within 20 miles of the spot. Of the militia-men not more than six or eight came with arms in their hands ; and it was they, and not " 125 regulars and militia," that inflicted the small loss sustained by the Americans. Instead of " 10," we had only one killed. The other incidents mentioned in Mr. Thomson's account are, we presume, embellishments of his own ; not omitting the dignified appellation of " king's store-house" conferred upon Mr. Stone's hut, and of " village" upon that hut, a public-house, and a saw-mill.

Opposite to Ogdensburg, where the St. Lawrence is just 1800 yards across, is situate the British village of Prescott, or, as since called, Fort-Wellington ; distant 68 miles from Kingston, and 130, in an opposite direction, from Montreal. In 1809 or 10, sir James Craig, then governor of Lower Canada, sent parties of men upon several of the little islands in the St. Lawrence, to blow up or otherwise destroy a quantity of old French guns, that had been lying there, probably since the days of Wolfe. No sooner did news of the late war reach Prescott, than 13 of these guns, *honey-combed*, and without trunnions, were fished up from the bottom of the river. The loss of trunnions was attempted to be supplied by substitutes of wood, with iron hoops; and carriages for the guns were constructed by the Canadian carpenters.—These fine pieces of artillery were then mounted upon an open sea-battery, formed chiefly of mud; but yet denominated by Mr. Thomson, "a strong line of breastworks." With an old farmer for an engineer, the people of Prescott, on the 2d of October, opened a fire upon Ogdensburg; and, by the bursting of one of the guns, inflicted upon themselves the only loss that was sustained. A few months afterwards, an officer of the engineers, who had been sent from head-quarters to inspect the guns at this "strong breastwork," condemned the whole of them.

On the second day from that on which the "heavy cannonading" took place, colonel Lethbridge, who commanded at Fort-Wellington, determined to assault the fort of Ogdensburg. He took with him eight artillerymen, two companies of the Canadian fencibles, about 40 of the Newfoundland regiment, under captain Skinner, and 150 Highland militia, who, after travelling the whole night, had just arrived in carts, from Cornwall, distant 48 miles. There were several other militia-men at the post; but the Highlanders, fatigued as they necessarily must have been, were all that would consent to accompany the regulars across to the attack. Colonel Lethbridge, with his few men, advanced towards Ogdensburg; and captain Skinner, having his small detachment on board two gun-boats, attacked and silenced the American battery upon the point below the town. The small force that had embarked could make little or no impression upon so strong a position: the boats therefore returned, with a trifling loss. It was afterwards ascertained, that general Brown was preparing to abandon the fort; a clear proof that, had all the men embarked, the enterprise would have been successful. Mr. Thomson, after exaggerating the British force to the usual extent, confers ridicule upon the whole affair, by saying:—" There has been no engagement, perhaps, in which more gallantry was exhibited on both sides."*—Mr. O'Connor equally contributes to raise a smile. " By this action," says he, " the British are taught, that 400 Yankees will not decline a combat, when attacked by 1000 of their troops."†

The hopes of the war-party now rested upon the northern army, or " army of Canada," stationed at Plattsburg, in the state of New York. This army, which, according to Mr. Thomson's computation, consisted of 5737 men, or, according to other American accounts, of that number of regulars only, besides 2 or 3000 militia, was

* Sketches of the War, p. 68.   † History of the War, p. 61.

under the command of major-general Dearborn; who is stated to have received positive orders to winter in Montreal. As if determined to make the attempt, the whole army, divided into two brigades, under major-generals Bloomfield and Chandler, marched, on the 15th of November, to the American village of Champlain, situate about six miles from the boundary-line between Lower Canada and the United States.

The instant this was known at Montreal, the brigade of British regulars and militia stationed there, consisting of about 600 of the latter, and the 8th and Glengary regiments, in all about 1900 men, crossed the St. Lawrence, and marched for La Prairie, distant about nine miles. Here the men arrived at midnight, and were distributed into quarters.

The two armies, one of invasion, the other of defence, being now within a few miles of each other, about 300 of the 15th United States' regiment, under the command of lieutenant-colonel Pike, accompanied by a detachment of cavalry and some militia, were, at two o'clock on the morning of the 19th, despatched across the lines, upon a reconnoissance. Being unexpectedly fired upon by a party of 40 Indians and voyageurs, or north-west company's armed men, stationed as an advanced picket near the river La Cole, the American regulars were thrown into confusion, and fired upon each other; by which they wounded five of their own men. In the mean time, the British advanced party made good their retreat, unmolested, and without a man having been hurt. A wounded prisoner, brought in by the Indians, as well as some deserters, estimated the American loss at between 30 and 40. Mr. Thomson, without stating his own, describes our force, as " a large body of British and Indians;" and then boasts, that the Americans " burned a block-house, and put the garrison to flight." Not a word is there about the men, in their confusion, wounding each other, or about any loss whatever sustained by the American party.

After performing this gallant achievement, the American army hurried back, in full retreat, to Plattsburg and Burlington. Here the regulars prepared to winter; but the cavalry and flying artillery proceeded to the southward, in search of more comfortable quarters. General Dearborn's promised visit to Montreal being now put off *sine die*, the British troops re-crossed the St. Lawrence; the militia, who formed the chief part of the force, retired to their homes; the few regulars into winter-quarters; and thus ended the campaign of 1812.

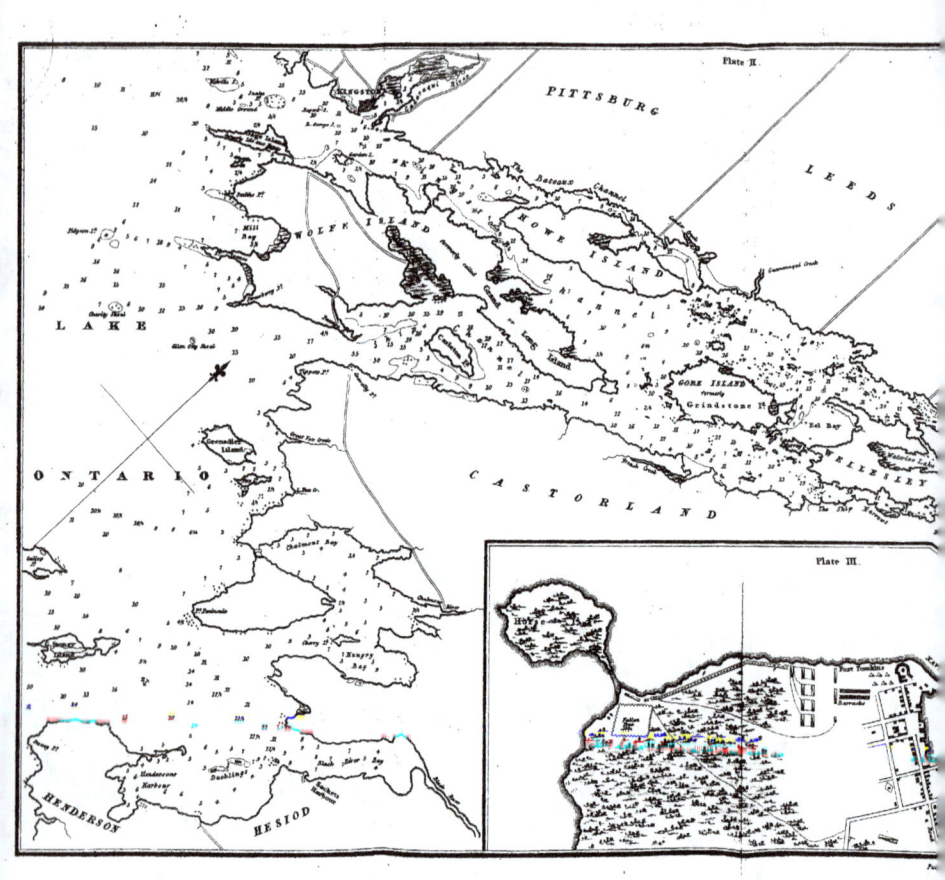

PART
of
LAKE ONTARIO
and of the
RIVER St LAWRENCE
from an actual Survey
by
Captn. W.F.W. Owen R.N.
1816

CHAPTER V.

Opening of the campaign of 1813—American plan of operations developed—British regulars in Upper Canada—Predatory excursions of the Americans on the St. Lawrence—Retaliatory attack on Ogdensburg, and capture of eleven pieces of ordnance—Unparalleled heroism of captain Jenkins—Alteration of an official letter—Capture of York in Upper Canada—Destruction of the public buildings—Remarks on the defenceless state of that post—Attack upon, and capture of Fort-George—Retreat of major-general Vincent—Capture of Fort-Erie—Arrival at Kingston of sir James L. Yeo—Sir George Prevost's attack upon Sackett's Harbor—His abandonment of possession—Remarks on the important consequences that would have ensued from an opposite proceeding—American strictures on sir George's despatches.

VIGOROUS preparations had been making by the American government, to open, with some *eclât*, the campain of 1813. Reinforcements of troops from most of the recruiting districts, together with the necessary supplies of provisions and military equipments, had been forwarded with the utmost celerity; and every thing promised a successful issue to the contemplated operations against the British North-American provinces. According to an important state-paper, dated on the 10th of February, 1813, and signed by the American secretary at war, the American government was now willing, or, in other words, compelled, to suspend, for a while, " the main attack;" that is, as we presume, the attack which was to result in finally expelling us from " the continent" of America.*

This friendly moderation is thus made known:—" It then remains to choose," says Mr. Armstrong, " between a course of entire inaction, because incompetent to the main attack, or one secondary, but still an important object. Such would be the reduction of that part of Upper Canada, lying between the town of Prescott on the St. Lawrence and Lake Erie, including the towns of Kingston and York, and the forts George and Erie. On this line of frontier the enemy have, at Prescott 300, at Kingston 600, at George and Erie 1200, making a total of regular troops of 2100. Kingston and Prescott, and the destruction of the British ships at the former, would present the first object; York, and the frigates said to be building there, the second; George and Erie the third. The force

* See p. 77.

to be employed on this service should not be less than 6000, because, in this first enterprise of a second campaign, nothing must, if possible, be left to chance."*

We have here, from the fountain-head of authority, a clear view of the intended operations against the upper province; and shall see, as we proceed, to what extent these *reduced* expectations became realized. It is gratifying to receive from the mouth of our enemy, so accurate an account of the British regular force in this quarter; nor is it less so, to observe the respect paid to that regular force, in the high odds that are required, to place the issue of a struggle beyond the reach of " chance."

The river St. Lawrence is seldom open for the purposes of navigation before the middle of May. Its frozen state, in the months of January and February, had enabled captain Forsythe, who still commanded a detachment of United States' riflemen at Ogdensburg, to send frequent parties across, not only to attack the few Canadian militia that occupied posts of communication along the British shore; but, as he had done in the preceding fall, to commit depredations upon the persons and properties of the unarmed inhabitants. A second of these nocturnal excursions † has been thought

* Wilkinson's Mem. Vol. III. his App. No. 26. † See p. 124.

deserving a place among the brilliant achievements of the American troops. Mr. Thomson tells us that, on the night of the 6th of February, captain Forsythe, with " 200 men, besides colonel Benedict and several private gentlemen,"* crossed over upon the ice to Elizabethtown, or, as now called, Brockville, distant about 10 miles from Fort-Wellington. After wounding a militia-sentry, the *gentlemen* broke into the few houses in the village, not omitting the gaol, and carried off the male-inhabitants, to the number of 52. Some of these, like many blacksmiths and tavern-keepers in the United States, held commissions in the militia. Nothing could happen better. The American public was, a day or two afterwards, officially told of the capture, in a very gallant manner, of a British guard, consisting of 52 men, including two majors, three captains, and two lieutenants.—"Of the militia," was left out; also, that the " 120 muskets and 20 rifles"* were not taken, as the intended inference is, upon the men's shoulders, but (except about half a dozen) packed up in cases. These arms were, indeed, the only " public property" at the place; although, under that denomination, the poor people's horses, pigs, and poultry, were carried off by the American regulars and private *gentlemen.*

On the 19th of the same month, lieutenant-

* Sketches of the War, p. 118.

colonel Pearson, who commanded at Fort-Wellington, despatched major Macdonnell, of the Glengarry fencibles, a corps raised wholly in the Canadas, with a flag of truce, across to Ogdensburg, to remonstrate with the American commanding officer, about sending over parties to commit such depredations as that we have just recorded. The American officers were very insolent to major Macdonnell, notwithstanding his flag; and disgusted him with their taunts and boastings. One of captain Forsythe's lieutenants was recognized as a fellow who had been a menial servant on the Canadian side. The American commanding officer expressed a wish to meet lieutenant-colonel Pearson and his men upon the ice; and, what was rather extraordinary, wanted major Macdonnell to pledge himself to that effect. The latter replied, that, in two days, the command at Fort-Wellington would devolve upon him; when he would have no objection to indulge captain Forsythe in the manner he wished.

On the day mentioned major Macdonnell succeeded to the command; and, on the same evening, sir George Prevost arrived at the post, on his way to Kingston. Major Macdonnell informed his excellency of the recent proceedings of the American soldiery, and of many particulars respecting the state of the garrison at Ogdensburg. He further apprized sir George, of the facility with which the Americans from Ogdensburg might cut him off in his route to Kingston; unless, by way of escort, a small party of the Newfoundland regiment should be sent a-head, in carriages, as well as a few Indian warriors to occupy the woods that skirted the road. This was immediately done; and then the major strongly urged sir George to allow him, in case the American troops should quit Ogdensburg for the purpose of seizing his person, to walk into the enemy's empty barracks. Sir George, however, would not listen to his making an attack; assigning as a reason, that he did not wish, by any offensive acts of the sort, to keep alive a spirit of hostility. At last, when getting into his sleigh, a little before day-light on the morning of the 22d, sir George most reluctantly consented, that major Macdonnell might, in order to discover if the garrison had abandoned Ogdensburg, make a *demonstration* before it, upon the ice; but, on no account, was a real attack to be made.

No sooner had sir George departed, than major Macdonnell commenced his arrangements for giving the promised meeting upon the ice, to his friend captain Forsythe. The militia *nominally* at the post amounted to about 700; but a muster would produce scarcely half of the number. These people ought, in fact, to be called *armed peasantry;* and, as such, were much more likely to be found earning their bread at their homes, than idling away their time at the place of rendezvous. By seven o'clock, major Macdonnell had collected about 300 of his militia-forces. Leaving a part of these to man the *honey-combed* guns, in case of a retreat being necessary, the major commenced his march on the ice, at half-past seven in the morning, with about 230 militia, and 250 regulars; including 11 artillerymen, along with three field-pieces, one 6 and two 3-pounders. The distance across the river, in the direction of the point of attack, was about a mile and a half. Owing to the caution requisite in marching over ice with 480 men, and at a place, too, which had never before been crossed in the same manner, the troops and militia were divided into two columns, and formed in extended order. The right column, commanded by captain Jenkins, of the Glengarry's, and consisting of his own flank company, and about 70 militia, was ordered to check the enemy's left, and intercept his retreat; while the left column, under the command of major Macdonnell himself, and consisting of the remainder of the regulars and militia, marched towards the town of Ogdensburg, where some heavy field-artillery was posted.

The drift of snow, on the American side of the St. Lawrence, was much deeper than had been expected, and retarded the troops considerably. All this while they were sustaining, particularly the men of the right column, a heavy cross-fire of round, grape, and canister from the American batteries; but the troops marched resolutely on. The details of this very gallant exploit, performed by men who had never before been in action, are fully given in major Macdonnell's letter.* During the warmest of the fire upon the right column, captain Jenkins ordered his men to fix bayonets, and charge the American troops that were firing down upon them from the bank. While wading through the deep snow, to get in contact with his enemy, the captain received a grape-shot in the left arm, which shivered the bones, from the wrist nearly up to the shoulder. He, however, marched on at the head of his company, heedless of the acute pain caused by the splintered bones rubbing, at every step, against his sword-belt. Not many minutes afterwards, a case-shot tore most of the flesh from his right arm; and down it dropped by his side. Still did this heroic young officer run on with his men, cheering them to the assault, till, almost maddened with pain, he staggered on one side; and, after making several turns, evidently unconscious of what he was doing, fell from the loss of blood.

The only American account of the capture of Ogdensburg which has been published, does not give numbers on their own side, but states,

* App. No. 16.

that colonel Benedict's regiment of militia had joined captain Forsythe's detachment. Consequently, major Macdonnel's estimate of "500 men under arms" cannot be overrated. Though unwilling, or perhaps unable, to state the amount of the American force, Mr. Thomson has not hesitated to fix that of the British, at two columns of "600 men each."* He admits the American troops were compelled to abandon the town and batteries, after losing 20 men in killed and wounded. Our loss, owing to the enemy's artillery, his secure position behind the houses of the town, and the delay caused by the depth of snow, amounted to eight killed and 52 wounded.

This action, in spite of captain Forsythe's declaration that he would *whip*† the British, with the greatest ease, did not continue beyond an hour; and yet resulted in the capture of 11 pieces of ordnance, among them two 12-pounders surrendered by general Burgoyne in October 1777; also a quantity of ordnance, marine, commissariat, and quarter-master-general's stores; together with four officers, and 70 privates. The British burnt two barracks; and, on account of their immoveable state in the ice, two armed schooners, and two large gun-boats. Mr. Thomson says, we " claimed the capture of immense stores, none of

* Sketches of the War, p. 110. † A favorite American word.

which had ever been deposited there." Of course, then, he pretends to be ignorant about the prisoners, cannon, armed vessels, and barracks. Still, the total silence of all the other American historians entitles Mr. Thomson to some credit, for the scanty account he has given of the capture of Ogdensburg.

It will be gratifying to the reader to be informed, that captain Jenkins, notwithstanding his desperate wounds, survives; although no higher in rank. His left arm was amputated close to the shoulder, and of his right arm he can now make some trifling use. He is a native of the province of New Brunswick; where his father, an American loyalist, and a brave old soldier, was, by the last accounts, living.

Previously to dismissing the affair at Ogdensburg, it may be right to mention, that sir George Prevost's secretary, or some person who had the transcribing of major Macdonnell's official letter, must have inserted, by mistake, the words: " In consequence of the commands of his excellency."* Of this there needs no stronger proof, than that major Macdonnell, while he was in the heat of the battle, received a private note from sir George, dated from " Flint's Inn,† at 9 o'clock," repeating his orders not to make the attack: and even, in the first private letter which sir George

* App. No. 16. † Nine miles from Fort-Wellington.

wrote to major Macdonnell, after being informed of his success, he could not help qualifying his admiration of the exploit, with a remark, that the latter had *rather* exceeded his instructions.*

About the middle of April, a powerful American force, for the invasion of Upper Canada, had concentrated at Sackett's Harbor, where lay commodore Chauncey, with 1900 tons of shipping, besides several small schooners and boats, ready to transport the troops across the lake; and, by 86 pieces of heavy cannon, to second their efforts at landing on the opposite shore. Our Lake Ontario vessels were lying *unmanned* in Kingston-harbor; and indeed, had their crews been on board, were scarcely strong enough to cope with the Madison, commodore Chauncey's flag-ship.

Having received information of the weak garrisons at York and Fort-George, major-general Dearborn determined, with the co-operation of the fleet, to attempt carrying into effect a part of Mr. Secretary Armstrong's plan. Accordingly, a body of troops, with some field-artillery, having embarked on board commodore Chauncey's vessels, the whole set sail, on the 25th of April, bound directly to York, the capital of Upper Canada.† It is not easy to get at the exact number of troops sent upon this

* Both of these letters the author has seen.   † See p. 53.

expedition. General Dearborn, in his letter, does not enumerate them. Commodore Chauncey says, that he "took on board the general and suite, and about 1700 men ;"* and this number has satisfied the three American historians. But major-general Sheaffe says: "The accounts of the number of the enemy vary from 1890 to 3000;"† and an Albany paper actually states the number at " about 5000." At the lowest estimate, therefore, the American troops must have amounted to 2000; which, added to the united crews of the armed vessels, make an aggregate force of 2790 men.

The guns upon the batteries at York, being without trunnions, were mounted upon wooden stocks, with iron hoops; and therefore became of very little use. Others of the guns belonged to the ship that was building, and lay on the ground, partly covered with snow and frozen mud. The accidental circumstance of the Duke of Gloucester brig being in the port, undergoing repairs, had enabled the garrison to mount, on temporary field-works, a few 6-pounders. The troops stationed there were commanded by major-general Sheaffe; and consisted of two companies of the 8th, or King's regiment, one company of the Glengarry fencibles, about a company of the royal Newfoundland regiment, a small detachment of the royal artillery, and a

* App. No. 20.   † App. No. 17.

General Pike.

gang of naval artificers; all of whom, together with the militia stationed at the post, amounted to no more than 600 men. There were, also, between 40 and 50 Indians, led by major Givens.

At seven o'clock on the morning of the 27th of April, the American squadron, with the troops on board, arrived, and took a good position about two miles and a half to the westward of the town. At eight o'clock the debarkation commenced; and the advance, consisting of major Forsythe and about 260 riflemen, pushed for the shore. Here they were unexpectedly assailed by major Givens and his Indians; who, after skirmishing for a short time, retired, and were joined by 60 of the Glengarry fencibles. This small force Mr. Thomson, taking general Dearborn for his authority, calls " the principal part of the British and Indians, under the immediate command of general Sheaffe."* In the mean time, general Pike had effected a landing, with, says the American official account, but not Mr. Thomson, " 7 or 800 men."† The whole of the American troops, at this time on shore, amounted, by their own accounts, to upwards of 1000. These were met by 210 men of the 8th and Newfoundland regiments, and about 220 militia-men; who " made a formidable charge upon the

* Sketches of the War, p. 122.   † App. No. 19.

American column, and partially compelled it to retire. But," continues Mr. Thomson, " the officers instantly rallied the troops, who returned to the ground, and" (gallant soldiers!) " impetuously charged upon, and routed the grenadiers."* The fact is, the remaining 1000 Americans had now landed, and were rapidly advancing to support their faltering companions. Then, and not till then, did the British regulars and militia retire, under cover of their insignificant batteries. The latter had, in the meanwhile, been engaging the whole of commodore Chauncey's schooners; which, from their light draught of water, had approached within gunshot.

The commodore's letter states, that the debarkation commenced at eight, and finished at 10 o'clock; therefore, the whole 2000 American troops, with general Pike at their head, accompanied by the artillery, were on shore at that hour. Yet this contest, with 650 British regulars, militia, and Indians, and in which the grenadier-company of the 8th suffered itself to be almost cut to pieces, did not terminate till 2 o'clock in the afternoon: a sufficient proof that the most determined bravery had been exerted, to defend the town of York against the combined attack of the American fleet and army.

After the British had been repulsed, according

* Sketches of the War, p. 122.

to Mr. O'Connor, " by a number far inferior to theirs,"* general Pike and his men, formed in platoons, marched towards the redoubts; at which the few cannon had been previously spiked. On arriving near the second redoubt, general Pike halted, to await the return of a strong corps of observation, under lieutenant Riddle, which had been sent forward to ascertain the strength of the garrison. While the general was sitting upon an old stump, examining, or, to use a homely but expressive phrase, *pumping*, a wounded British serjeant who had been taken in the woods, the stone powder-magazine, situate outside the barrack-yard, and to which a train had been laid, blew up, with a tremendous explosion, and killed or wounded 260 of the invading troops, along with their general.

The American historians, improving upon the statements in their own official letters, accuse general Sheaffe of *treacherously* ordering the train to be laid, and of artfully placing several cart-loads of stone to increase the effect. Mr. Thompson adds:—" Had not general Pike halted the troops at the enemy's second battery, the British plan would have attained its consummation, and the destruction of the whole column would have been the natural consequence."†
He who reflects that this was an invading army,

* Hist. of the War, p. 83.   † Sketches of the War, p. 126.

will be inclined to admit, that, even had the whole column been destroyed, the Americans would have met their deserts; or, if disposed to commiserate the poor soldiers, to wish that their places had been filled by the American president, and the 98 members of the legislature who voted for the war.

The chief part of the British troops had been withdrawn to the town, which was about three quarters of a mile from the scene of explosion. After ordering the destruction of the ammunition, naval stores, and the new ship that was building, general Sheaffe left directions with a lieutenant-colonel and major of militia, who were residents in the town, to treat with the American commander, for terms; and then, with the regulars and such of the militia as were not residents, retreated across the river Don, in the direction of Kingston.

According to the last article of the capitulation, the whole number of prisoners delivered up amounted to 293; yet one American editor has made the number of prisoners " 750," and his two contemporaries " 920;" and this, although the whole amount to which general Dearborn could swell the British force opposed to him, was " 700 regulars and militia, and 100 Indians." Our loss in killed and wounded is stated by the Americans at " 250;" no doubt an exaggeration; as the loss of the regulars, according to the official returns, scarcely exceeds half that amount; and 40 of these were killed or wounded by the accidental explosion of a wooden powder-magazine, the head of which had been carelessly left open. Mr. Thompson says, the British wounded were left in the houses, and " attended to by the American army and navy surgeons;"* but this is extremely doubtful, because the fifth article of the capitulation expressly provides, " that such surgeons as may be procured to attend the wounded of the British regulars and Canadian militia, shall not be considered as prisoners of war.†

The Americans state their own loss at 14 killed, and 32 wounded in battle, and 38 killed, and 222 wounded by the explosion; making a total loss, on shore, of 52 killed, and 254 wounded. Among those who fell by the explosion were general Pike, seven captains, seven subalterns, two aides-de-camp, and one volunteer. The squadron lost three killed, and 11 wounded; which makes the aggregate American loss, at the capture of York, amount to 334 men.

General Pike's behaviour, previous to his death, is thus recorded by Mr. Thomson:—" As they conveyed him to the water's edge, a sudden exclamation was heard from the troops, which informed him of the American, having supplanted the British, standard in the garrison. He ex-

* Sketches of the War, p. 43. † App. No. 18.

pressed his satisfaction by a feeble sigh, and after being transferred from the Pert schooner to the commodore's ship, he made a sign for the British flag, which had then been brought to him, to be placed under his head, and expired without a groan."* Considering the immense superiority of numbers, by which, after a long and desperate struggle, the feat of supplanting the flag was achieved, the officiousness of the American editor has conferred more of ridicule, than of honor, upon the last moments of his hero.

It was fortunate that the British brig Prince Regent had departed from the harbor, about three days previous to the attack. As it was, the Americans got possession of a small brig-hulk, the Duke of Gloucester; without very large repairs, unseaworthy. A considerable quantity of naval stores and provisions, which had not been destroyed, also fell into the enemy's hands. The American editors are loud in boasting of the lenient conduct of the troops towards the inhabitants and their houses; when, in fact, they set fire, not only to the public buildings, civil as well as military, but to a tavern at some distance from York; and were proceeding upon the same charitable errand to Hatt's mills, had they not been deterred by information of Indians being in the neighbourhood. It has never been sufficiently explained, why the British com-

* Sketches of the War, p. 125.

mander-in-chief had not ordered the fortifications to be put in order, and an adequate garrison stationed, at a post where, not only a considerable quantity of naval and military stores was deposited, but a comparatively large ship of war building for the lake. Even the two companies, or 180 men, of the 8th, had merely halted at York, on their way from Kingston to Fort-George; and, had the Americans delayed the attack one day, the latter would have had a still smaller force to contend with. The capture or destruction of " the frigates said to be building there,"* was the very purpose that carried the Americans to York ; otherwise, they would, no doubt, have proceeded direct to Fort-George; that being considered as the great bulwark of Upper Canada.

On the 1st of May the Canadian territory in the neighbourhood of York was entirely evacuated. To carry away the prisoners being found inconvenient, the latter were paroled and left behind; and a small schooner was despatched to Niagara, to apprize general Lewis, then in command at that place, of the result of the expedition against " the capital of Upper Canada," and of the intended approach of the troops towards the Four-mile creek. The prevalence of contrary winds detained commodore Chauncey and the fleet in York harbor, till the

* See p. 132.

8th; when they set sail, and arrived at the creek late on the same afternoon.

After disembarking the troops, the commodore proceeded, with the wounded men, to Sackett's Harbor; there to obtain reinforcements. Between the 11th and 22d of May, the vessels of the fleet made frequent trips between Sackett's Harbor and Niagara, each time loaded with troops; and, on the 25th, the commodore, in the Madison, with 350 artillerymen and a number of heavy pieces of ordnance on board, arrived at the latter place; having left the Pert and Fair American schooners, to watch the movements of the British at Kingston. The latter, however, as was well known to the Americans, could not leave port with their ships, till a supply of seamen arrived from Quebec.

On the 26th commodore Chauncey reconnoitred the intended point of landing on the Canada-side; and, at night, sounded the shore, and placed buoys to point out the stations of the different vessels of his fleet. The whole of this service the commodore performed, to his surprise no doubt, without the slightest molestation; owing, it seems, to a scarcity of ammunition at Fort-George, as well as to an apprehension, that a fire from that fort might bring on a return from the shipping, and from Fort-Niagara, to the destruction of Newark. A considerable number of new boats had recently been lauched at the Five-mile meadows, on the American shore; and several others had been provided, and were in readiness to receive the troops.

The British force upon the Niagara-line now amounted, sick and well, to about 1800 regulars, and 500 militia. The former consisted of the 49th regiment, and of detachments from the 8th, 41st, Glengarry, and Newfoundland regiments, and royal artillery; the whole under the command of brigadier-general Vincent, major-general Sheaffe's successor. Of this force, eight companies of the 49th, five companies of the 8th, three companies of the Glengarry, and two of the Newfoundland regiment; also a few additional gunners from the 41st regiment, and about 30 royal artillery, with two 3, and five 6-pounders, and a $5\frac{1}{2}$ inch howitzer; the whole amounting to less than 1000 rank and file; were stationed at Fort-George. At the same post, also, were about 300 militia, and 40 Indians.

Since the surrender of general Hull, five 24-pounders had been brought from Detroit; four of which were mounted on the three bastions at Fort-George, and the fifth on a battery, *en barbette*, about half a mile below Newark. On the afternoon of the 26th a few shots were fired from some field-pieces at the American newly-launched boats, as they were leaving the

Five-mile meadows to proceed to the rendezvous. This brought on a cannonade from Fort-Niagara; which did considerable injury to the block-houses and wooden buildings near Fort-George, as well as to the fort itself. If the guns at Fort-George were compelled, owing to a scarcity of powder, to remain silent, while commodore Chauncey, on the same evening, was sounding the shore, within half-gunshot, the American editors may well boast that Fort-Niagara sustained no injury whatever.

During the same night the American troops embarked in the vessels of the squadron, and in the numerous flat-bottomed boats and scows prepared for the occasion. At four o'clock on the morning of the 27th, major-generals Dearborn and Lewis, with their suites, went on board the Madison; and, " by that time, all the troops were afloat." The number is stated, by one American editor, at " more than 4000;"* by another, at " from 6 to 7000;" consisting of three brigades of infantry, under brigadier-generals Boyd, Winder, and Chandler, strong detachments of heavy, and of light artillery, and a corps of reserve, under colonel M‘Comb; exclusive of the marines of the fleet, under captain Smith, and of 250 dragoons, under colonel Burn, which crossed a little higher up the river. On referring to an American official return of

* Sketches of the War, p. 131.

troops at Fort-George in the succeeding July, we find the number stated at 6635;* and this does not include " M'Clure's Baltimore and Albany volunteers,"† mentioned as forming part of general Dearborn's force on the present occasion. We cannot, therefore, overrate the American force, now advancing to the attack of Fort-George, by fixing it at 6000 men.

Intelligence of the enemy's intention to attack Fort-George had been previously communicated by deserters; and, at day-light on the morning of the 27th, the American fleet, accompanied by boat-loads of troops, was seen advancing, with a light air from the eastward, towards the light-house on Mississaga-point. ‡ The batteries at Fort-Niagara now commenced a heavy cannonade upon Fort-George and Newark; but ceased firing, soon afterwards, on account of a very heavy fog that intercepted the view. In the mean time, two schooners, by the use of their sweeps, had reached their stations at the mouth of the river, in order to silence the 24-pounder, and a 9-pounder, also planted *en barbette*, close to Newark. Another schooner stationed herself to the northward of the light-house, and so close to the shore as to enfilade the first-named battery, and cross the fire of the two other schooners; and the remaining five schooners

---

* Wilkinson's Mem. Vol. III. his App. No. 5.
† Sketches of the War, p. 131. ‡ See Plate I.

anchored near to the latter, that they might cover the landing of the troops, and scour the adjacent plane and woods. The ship Madison, brig Oneida, and schooner Lady of the Lake, also placed themselves, so as to give the best effect to their cannon. These eleven American vessels fought 51 guns in broadside; including nine long 32 and 18-pounders.

When the fog dispersed, which was not till nearly eight o'clock, the American boats, in three lines, were discovered approaching towards the One-mile creek; close to which was the 9-pounder battery. The British advance, stationed in a ravine and copse-wood near this point, consisted of the Glengarry and Newfoundland detachments, numbering about 200 rank and file, under captain Winter of the latter regiment, and 40 Indians, led by their chief Norton. While the American schooners, with their heavy guns, were engaging the 9 and 24-pounder batteries, the British advance fired upon the boats, and compelled the troops in them to lie down for their better security. The fire from the American shipping now committed dreadful havoc among the British, and rendered their efforts to oppose the landing of the enemy's advanced corps of infantry and artillery, under lieutenant-colonel Scott, quite ineffectual. The Glengarry and Newfoundland detachments were, in consequence, obliged to fall back upon the left column, stationed in another ravine, about a quarter of a mile in their rear. It is but fair to mention, that the 9-pounder battery, although worked by militia-men, assisted by one gunner of the royal artillery, was most ably served, during the whole period of the enemy's first attempt to land; nor was the gun abandoned, till nearly all the men stationed at it had been killed or wounded. On the other hand, the 24-pounder, manned also by militia-artillery, and which ought to have sunk one or two of the enemy's schooners, was spiked and totally abandoned, almost at the commencement of the attack.

Let us see how the American editors describe the onset. Mr. Thomson, who is the most diffuse, says:—" When the advance, which consisted of 500 men, was approaching the point of landing, successive volleys of musketry were poured upon it by 1200 regulars, stationed in a ravine. A brisk exchange of shot was kept up for 15 minutes; the advance, nevertheless, continued to approach the enemy without faltering. Such, indeed, was the eagerness of the troops, that officers and men jumped into the lake and waded to the shore. Captain Hindman of the 2d artillery, was the first man upon the enemy's territory."* Were this our novitiate in American history, we might suppose the " 1" in " 1200" to have been a typographical surplus-

* Sketches of the War, p. 132.

age ; but, being skilled in such matters, we freely exonerate the American printer.

The remainder of brigadier-general Vincent's force at Fort-George had been divided into two columns; the left, consisting of 320 of the 8th regiment, and 150 militia, and protected by two or three light field-pieces, with a suitable detachment of royal artillery, assisted by a few additional gunners of the 41st, was commanded by colonel Myers, deputy-quarter-master-general. This column had been posted in a ravine not far from the point of landing. The right column, consisting of about 450 of the 49th regiment, and 150 militia, under the command of lieutenant-colonel Harvey, deputy-adjutant-general, was drawn up between Newark and Fort-George ; excepting about 50 of the 49th, and 80 of the militia, who were stationed within the fort itself.

The column under colonel Myers immediately advanced, in support of the Glengarry and Newfoundland detachments ; which augmented his force to about 600 men, including Norton and his Indians. About five minutes after the American advance had effected a landing, the boats containing general Boyd's brigade struck the shore. The American troops, now on the beach, amounted to " *only* 1800 men,"* accompanied by several pieces of artillery. As fast as these men attempted to ascend the bank, they were

* Hist of the War, p. 86.

driven back at the point of the bayonet; till the American ships, with their heavy discharges of round and grape, had too well succeeded in thinning the British ranks. One American editor describes, in a very handsome style, the landing of general Boyd's brigade.—" Thrice," says he, " with the most persevering courage, was the attempt made, and thrice were they repelled by an enemy more than five times their number."* General Dearborn in his letter tells us, that the brigades of general Winder and Chandler followed the first brigade " in quick succession."† The arrival of this reinforcement enabled the Americans, assisted by the contiued fire from their shipping, to drive the British left column; now considerably reduced in numbers. The loss sustained by the detachment of the 8th, under the gallant lieutenant-colonel Ogilvie, amounted to six officers and 198 privates, killed or wounded; nearly two-thirds of its original number; and of the 150 militia engaged, there were five officers, and 80 privates, killed or wounded: a sufficient proof that they had emulated the brave 8th. Every mounted officer in the field but one was wounded; and that one had his horse shot under him. Colonel Myers had fallen from several severe wounds. His place was taken by lieutenant-colonel Harvey, who had left his column under the charge of lieutenant-colonel Plenderleath, with directions

* Hist. of the War, p. 86.   † App. No. 22.

to move it forward. This order that gallant officer lost no time in obeying, and meeting the remnant of the left column in its retreat, the whole drew up on the plane.

After the whole of the enemy's force had landed, and formed, a strong detachment of American light troops and riflemen was sent in advance, to cut off the retreat of the British by the two roads leading to Burlington Heights. The main body of the American troops was now seen to move forward, in two columns; strongly protected by artillery. To attempt a further struggle with such overwhelming numbers would have been the height of rashness; therefore brigadier-general Vincent, first despatching orders to lieutenant-colonel Bisshopp at Fort-Erie, and to major Ormsby at Chippeway, to evacuate their respective posts, and to move, without delay, by Lundy's-lane, to the Beaver Dam, distant about 16 miles from Fort-George, directed the magazines at the latter to be exploded, and the fort, which had already been rendered untenable by the fire from Fort-Niagara, to be evacuated. Unfortunately, the 50 regulars in Fort-George, either less prompt in retreating, than they would have been in attacking, or mistaking the American riflemen for the detachment of the Glengarry regiment, (the two wearing nearly the same uniform,) fell into the enemy's hands. The remainder of the unwounded regulars and militia marched, without the slightest molestation, to the Beaver Dam; which place they reached about eight o'clock on the same evening, and were there joined by the garrisons of Fort-Erie and Chippeway.

At about 12 o'clock at noon, the American troops took quiet possession of Fort-George, and the village of Newark. Mr. Thomson describes the ceremony thus:—" General Boyd and colonel Scott mounted the parapet, and cut away the staff; whilst captain Hindman *succeeded* in taking the flag which the enemy had left flying, and which he forwarded to general Dearborn." This editor states, also, that, during the action, " few shots were fired from Fort-George, the panic being communicated to the garrison."* The fact is, Mr. Thomson's countrymen took care to land, where the shot from Fort-George could not reach them, without first passing through the houses of Newark.

According to the return of loss annexed to general Vincent's letter,† the Glengarry and Newfoundland detachments lost 48 officers and privates killed, and 66 wounded; which is upwards of half their united force. The dreadful state of the 8th regiment, has already been noticed. ‡ The loss sustained by the militia does not appear in the official returns: it was, however, as we have stated, 85 in killed and wounded. The total British loss, therefore,

* Sketches of the War, p. 132. † App. No. 21. ‡ See p. 157.

amounted to 445. Except the men accidentally taken in Fort-George, none of the British unwounded regulars fell into the enemy's hands; although Mr. Thomson has found it convenient to make a contrary assertion. He says:—" He (the enemy) had in killed 108, in wounded 163; 115 regulars were taken prisoners, exclusive of his wounded, all of whom fell into the hands of the Americans;" and then adds:—" The militia-prisoners, who were paroled to the number of 507, being added to their loss, makes a total of 893." * This nice calculator does not inform his readers, how the above 507 paroled " militia-prisoners" were obtained. We will do it for him. No sooner had the American army got possession of the Niagara-frontier, than officers and parties were sent to every farm-house and hovel in the neighbourhood, to exact a parole from the male-inhabitants, of almost every age. The disaffected were glad of this excuse for remaining peaceably at their homes; and those who made any opposition were threatened to be carried across the river, and thrown into a noithsome prison. We cannot wonder, then, that, by these industrious, though certainly unauthorized means, the names of as many as 507 Canadians were got ready to be forwarded to the secretary at war; so as, not only to swell the amount of the loss sustained, but, by a fair

* Sketches of the War, p. 133.

inference, of the force employed, on the part of the British, in resisting the attack. The Americans state their own loss before Fort-George, at 39 killed, and 111 wounded; which is not a little creditable to the few regular troops and Canadians, by whom the post was defended.

The extraordinary circumstance of general Dearborn's not stating, in his official letter, that the British were superior in force, would entitle him to praise, had he not, or some clerk at the war-office for him, made a boast of " the advantages the enemy's position afforded him."*—A plane, entirely exposed to a cross-fire of shot and shells, was an advantageous position, truly! —Even Mr. O'Connor, so dexterous at making " advantages," knew better. He prefers telling his readers of the " host" of British, against which the American troops had to contend; and, when disposed to enter more into detail, adopts his favorite expression,—" an enemy more than five times their number." Mr. Thomson, rather more modestly, says :—" The action was fought by inferior numbers on the American side:" but doctor Smith gives no numbers at all; leaving his readers to draw their own inference from the lavish encomiums he bestows upon " the firmness and gallantry" of the American troops.

When any extravagant statement connected

* App. No. 22.

with the war appears in an American newspaper, the credit of inventing it generally falls upon the cabinet at Washington; but we never expected to have the thing so completely confirmed, as it is by a paragraph in a "confidential" letter from general Wilkinson to the American secretary at war. "To secure," says the general, "a favourable issue to these enterprises without much loss of blood, the demonstrations of fear and alarm on our part will be continued, by more than the ordinary means of military deception, *in which you may be able to assist me, powerfully, through the medium of the prints known to be friendly to the war.*" This peep behind the state-curtain enables us to trace the authors of a piece of "military deception," extracted by Mr. O'Connor, along with other garbage, from one "of the prints known to be friendly to the war," in order to grace the pages of his "*Impartial* History." "Prior to the taking of Fort-George," says this "faithful" historian, "three Americans in the camp who refused to bear arms, were, by order of colonel Clark, taken out, and without ceremony *shot!* This infernal scoundrel met his deserts soon after:—he was killed at the time of the surprise of generals Winder and Chandler."*—The fact is, the only "colonel Clark," was Thomas Clark, a lieutenant-colonel of the 2d

* History of the War, p. 88.

Lincoln militia; who was not, and, if he were, could not "order," at Fort-George. Instead, too, of having been "killed at Stoney creek," he is, or, at the date of the last accounts, was, still living in Upper Canada. The officer referred to as subsequently "killed," was major Alexander Clerk, then of the 49th, and now alive. It remains only to add, that this officer was not present at the taking of Fort-George.

On arriving at the Beaver Dam, general Vincent was joined, not only by the remainder of his command from Chippeway and Fort-Erie, but by one flank and one battalion company of the 8th, and by captain Barclay, of the royal navy, and 19 seamen, on their way to Lake Erie. Thus reinforced, the major-general had with him about 1600 rank and file. With the view of cutting off this force, general Dearborn despatched forward major-general Lewis, at the head of two brigades of infantry, the whole of the light artillery and riflemen, and 250 dragoons; making a total of nearly 4000 men. These arrived at the dam too late, general Vincent being then far advanced on his way to the head of Lake Ontario; where he intended, if possible, to make a stand. The arrival of intelligence, on the night of the 28th, that the enemy was approaching in force, occasioned the destruction of a further quantity of ammunition and provisions; and the troops had to continue their retreat towards Burlington Heights, with only 90 rounds of ammunition per gun. Foiled in their purpose, the American troops advanced along the river-road, and took possession of the already abandoned post of Fort-Erie. Leaving a small garrison there, under lieutenant-colonel Preston, of the 12th United States' infantry, general Lewis, with the remainder of his army, returned to Fort-George. Thus we have the fulfilment of the "third object" in the American plan of operations exhibited at a preceding page.*

It is now time to draw the reader's attention to the opposite end of Lake Ontario; where, by the strenuous exertions of sir James Lucas Yeo and a party of officers and seamen, who had just arrived from England, our vessels in Kingston were manned and equipped, in a sufficient manner to enable them, led by so able a commander, once more to appear on the lake. If any thing could add to the general joy upon this occasion, it was sir George Prevost's consent to a proposition for employing this acquisition of naval strength in a combined attack upon the important post of Sackett's Harbor; now considerably weakened in its defences, by the absence of commodore Chauncey's fleet, and of the numerous army which had recently been stationed there.

Early on the morning of the 27th of May,

* See p. 132.

every arrangement being complete, the vessels of sir James Yeo's fleet, having on board the troops for the expedition, consisting of the grenadier-company of the 100th regiment, a section of the Royal Scots, two companies of the 8th, four companies of the 104th, one company of the Glengarry's, and two companies of the Canadian Voltigeurs; also, a small detachment of the Newfoundland regiment, along with two 6-pounders and their gunners, numbering altogether less than 750 rank and file, left the harbor of Kingston, and arrived off Sackett's Harbor at about noon on the same day. The weather was extremely fine, and the wind was a moderate breeze, calculated for carrying the vessels, either towards or from the shore. The squadron, with the Wolfe, having sir George Prevost on board, as the leading ship, stood in about two miles, to reconnoitre the enemy's position. While the squadron was lying to, the troops were embarked in the boats, and every one was anxious for the signal to pull towards the shore. After waiting in this state of suspense for about half an hour, orders were given for the troops to return on board the fleet. This done, the fleet wore, and, with a light wind, stood out on its return to Kingston.

About 40 Indians, in their canoes, had accompanied the expedition. Dissatisfied at being called back without effecting any thing, particularly as their unsophisticated minds could devise no reason for abandoning the enterprize, they steered round Stoney-point, and, discovering a party of troops on the American shore, fearlessly paddled in to attack them. These consisted of about 70 dismounted dragoons, who had just landed from 12 boats, which, along with seven others that had pulled past the point and escaped, were on their way to Sackett's Harbor. As soon as the American troops saw the Indians advancing, they hoisted a white flag, as a signal to our ships for protection. The latter immediately hove to; and lieutenant Dobbs, first of the Wolfe, stood in with the ship's boats, and brought off the American dragoons, along with their 12 batteaux.

This fortuitous capture was deemed an auspicious omen; and sir George Prevost determined to stand back to Sackett's Harbor. What little wind there was had now veered more towards the land; so that, with all their exertions, the larger vessels of the squadron were unable to get within eight miles of the point of attack, or six of their station in the forenoon. The troops were, however, again placed in the boats; and, before day on the morning of the 29th, the latter advanced towards the shore, covered by the gun-boats, under the orders of captain Mulcaster.

As none of the preceding facts are stated

in colonel Baynes's letter,* some doubts may be entertained of their authenticity. We have only to assure the reader that, not only every officer on board the fleet knows the account, as we have given it, to be true in the main; but all the American accounts concur in stating, that the British appeared off the port on two successive days. One editor remarks, indeed, that the delay and indecision on our part brought in from the neighbouring counties a considerable number of militia; and who, naturally thinking we were afraid, " betrayed great eagerness to engage in the contest."

Sackett's Harbor bears from Kingston, on Lake Ontario, south by east; distant in a straight course, 25, but, by a ship's course, 35 miles. It stands on the south-east side of an expansion of the Black River, near to where it flows into Hungry Bay. The harbor is small, but well sheltered. From the north-west runs out a low point of land, upon which is the dock-yard, with large store-houses, and all the buildings requisite for such an establishment. Upon this point there is a strong work, called Fort-Tompkins;† having within it a block-house, two stories high: on the land-side it is covered by a strong picketing, in which there are embrasures. At the bottom of the harbor is the village, containing from 60 to 70 houses: to

* App. No. 23. † See Plate III.

the southward of it is a barrack, capable of containing 2000 men, and generally used for the marines belonging to the fleet. On a point eastward of the harbor, stands Fort-Pike,* surrounded by a ditch, in advance of which there is a strong line of picketing. About 100 yards from the village, and a little to the westward of Fort-Tompkins, is Smith's cantonment, or barracks, capable of containing 2500 men: it is strongly built of logs, forming a square, with a block-house at each corner, and is loopholed on every side. This was the state of Sackett's Harbor at the date of the attack; at which time, also, many of the guns belonging to the works had been conveyed to the other end of the lake. Towards the middle of 1814, there were three additional works, Fort-Virginia, Fort-Chauncey, and Fort-Kentucky; as well as several new block-houses; and the guns then mounted upon the different forts exceeded 60.

Being without proper guides for the coast, the troops disembarked, by mistake, upon Horse Island;* where the grenadier-company of the 100th, which formed the advance, meeting with some slight opposition from a 6-pounder, mounted *en barbette*, as well as from 3 or 400 militia, stationed at that point, carried the 6-pounder before a second discharge could be fired from it, and drove the American militia with precipi-

* See Plate III.

tation into the woods. The whole of the British now quickly landed, although completely enfiladed by a heavy gun upon Fort-Tompkins.* The captured 6-pounder was unfortunately of no use, as the British artillery-men were still with their two field-pieces, in a merchant-vessel, which had not yet been able to reach the point of landing.

The behaviour of the American militia seems to have provoked Mr. Thomson's ire. " Though they were well protected by the breastwork," says he, " they rose from behind it, and, abandoning the honorable promises of noble daring, which they had made but a litle while before, fled with equal precipitation and disorder. A strange and unaccountable panic seized the whole line; and, with the exception of a very few, terror and dismay were depictured in every countenance."† This forms a cheering contrast to the behaviour of the Canadian militia at Fort-George. Of the volunteers who had been associated with the Sackett's Harbor militia, about 80 halted to fire a volley or two from behind a large fallen tree,* and then nimbly followed their companions.

Colonel Young, of the 8th regiment, taking with him about half the troops that had landed, penetrated the wood to the left, while major Drummond, with the remainder of the troops,

* See Plate III. † Sketches of the War, p. 143.

proceeded by the path to the right, through which the Americans had fled. Colonel Young and his men, who could not have amounted to more than 380, soon found themselves in a narrow road, flanked on the right by a thick wood, and on the left by a perpendicular bank of ten or fifteen feet.* Here they were engaged by such of the volunteers as had rallied, the dismounted dragoons amounting to 313, and a part of the regular troops; † making a total of at least 500 men. After a slight skirmish, these fell back to the main body of the American troops, stationed upon the open ground, near the barracks. Major Drummond, who had met with little or no opposition in scouring the wood, now formed a junction with colonel Young; and soon compelled the whole of the American regulars, volunteers, and militia, to abandon one of their guns, and to retreat into the log-barrack and stockaded fort. A force of at least 1000 men, thus favourably posted, and assisted by the heavy guns upon the batteries, could do no less than cause severe destruction in the British column, which had no artillery whatever. But these obstacles were nothing to British troops; and, so hopeless did the Americans consider their case, that lieutenant Chauncey had already set fire to the navy-barracks, the prize-schooner duke of Glo'ster, and the ship General

* See f. f. Plate III.   † Wilkinson's Memoirs, Vol. I. p. 584.

MAJOR GEN^L. BROWN, U.S. Army.

Engraved for the Analectic Magazine

Philadelphia, Published by M. Thomas.
1815.

Pike, and had completely destroyed the naval stores and provisions which had been captured at York.

The American editors say, that general Brown, who commanded at Sackett's Harbor, adopted the following stratagem to deceive the British general. Silently passing through the wood which led towards the point of landing, he evinced an intention to gain the rear of the British forces, to take possession of the boats, and effectually to cut off their retreat. This, the Americans say, convinced sir George Prevost of the vast superiority of the American force, and induced him to give the order to retreat; and general Wilkinson adds: "I have understood from good authority, that lieutenant-colonel at this time major Drummond, of the 104th, who was afterwards killed at Fort-Erie, stepped up to him, and observed,—'*Allow me a few minutes, sir, and I will put you in possession of the place.*' To which sir George replied,—'*Obey your orders, sir, and learn the first duty of a soldier.*' Sir James Yeo was also averse to the retreat, and the occasion gave rise to the animosity which afterwards existed between those officers, and drew on sir George the contempt of the army."*

The American force at Sackett's Harbor when the British landed, and which force was actually brought into action in defending the post,

* Wilkinson's Mem. Vol. I. p. 585.

amounted, by general Wilkinson's account, to 787 regular troops, and 500 militia and volunteers.* As soon after the reluctant British troops had turned round to obey their general's order, as the Americans could assure themselves that they were not in a dream, the latter hastened to repair the mischief which their rational fears had set them to committing. Lieutenant Chauncey extinguished the fire in the prize-vessel and the new ship. In the Pike, indeed, owing to her being built of green wood, the fire had made very little progress; and, had we *kept* possession of the place, that fine ship might have been launched by ourselves : for which express purpose sir James Yeo had actually embarked a number of shipwrights and artificers.

Soon after the British troops had retired to their boats, a reinforcement of 600 Americans arrived at the post, and other troops were every instant expected; but still our occupation of the forts, Tompkins and Pike, would have enabled us to resist every effort of the Americans, till our fleet had anchored in the harbor. The Americans say that, in the course of the morning, we "sent in a flag, with a peremptory demand for the surrender of the post, but which,"—as might indeed be supposed,—" was as peremptorily refused."†

* Wilkinson's Memoirs, Vol. I. p. 585.
† Sketches of the War, p. 145.

Our loss in this unfortunate expedition was no slight aggravation. We had 50 men killed, and 211 wounded; and the British official returns* expose us, very fairly, to the following observation by an American editor:—" The precipitation of his flight was such, that he left, not only the wounded bodies of his ordinary men upon the field, but those of the dead and wounded of the most distinguished of his officers." The Americans acknowledge to have had a loss of 20 regulars and two volunteers killed, 84 regulars wounded, and 26 missing; which, added to 25 militia killed or wounded, makes a total loss of 157.†

To the great mortification of the inhabitants of Kingston, they saw their fleet return into port on the morning of the 30th, with, instead of the whole garrison of Sackett's Harbor, and its immense naval and military stores, about 100 American officers and privates, including the 70 who had surrendered themselves the day previous. Out of the columns of strictures which one set of colonial newspapers devoted to the investigation of this disgraceful failure, not the slightest imputation is attempted to be thrown upon the behaviour of the troops concerned in it. They rushed eagerly on shore, drove the American militia like sheep, compelled the enemy to destroy his navy-bar-

* App. No. 23.   † Sketches of the War, p. 145.

racks, stores, and provisions; and, in ten minutes more, would have been in quiet possession of the town; but instead of that, to the indignation of the British, joy of the Americans, and surprise of both, the bugle sounded a *retreat.*   *   *   *   *   *   *

What should we have gained by even the temporary possession of Sackett's Harbor? The American fleet, having no port to which it could retire, would have been compelled to fight, and sir James Yeo, having the Pike to add to his squadron, or even without her assistance, would have conquered with ease. The British Ontario fleet no longer wanted, its officers, seamen, and stores, would have passed over to Lake Erie, and averted the calamity there: that done, they would have repaired to Lake Champlain, and prevented the *Saranac* that flows into it, from becoming so famous. The least benefit of all would have been, the saving to the nation of the incalculable sums expended in the building of ships, and the transportation of ordnance-stores.* Some will *feel* that the national pride would have been no loser; and able politicians could, perhaps, expatiate upon fifty other advantages that would have accrued to us, had we retained, for a few days only, the possession of Sackett's Harbor.

The sentiments of the Americans themselves

* See James's Naval Occurr. p. 285.

upon the subject may be taken from the pages of one of our three historians. " After being compelled," says Mr. Thomson, " to relinquish the further prosecution of an expedition, having for its primary object the capture and destruction of a post, the permanent possession of which only could give to the Americans any hope of a superiority on Lake Ontario; after having succeeded in his enterprise, in a degree which scarcely deserves to be termed partial; and after being obliged, by the predominance of his apprehension over his bravery and foresight, to retire from the assault, and precipitately to leave his dead and wounded to the mercy of his enemy; general sir George Prevost issued an official account to the people of Canada, and forwarded despatches to his government, in each of which he laid claim to a brilliant and unparalleled victory;* and alleged, that he had reluctantly ordered his troops to leave a beaten enemy, whom he had driven before him for three hours, because the co-operation of the fleet and army could not be effected. General Brown's stratagem had so far succeeded in deceiving him, that he reported the woods to have been filled with infantry and field-pieces, from which an incessant, heavy, and destructive fire had been kept up, by a numerous and

* This assertion is not warranted by colonel Baynes's official letter. See App. No. 23.

almost invisible foe, more than quadruple in numbers* to the detachments which had been taken from the garrison of Kingston; and that his loss was, nevertheless, very far inferior to that of his antagonist. Had the result of the expedition against Sackett's Harbor been of that character of unparalleled brilliancy, which would have entitled it to the encomiums of its commander, and to the warmest admiration of the British nation, its effects would have been long and deplorably felt by the American government. Immense quantities of naval and military stores, which had, from time to time, been collected at that depôt; the frames and timbers which had been prepared for the construction of vessels of war, and the rigging and armaments which had been forwarded thither for their final equipment; as well as all the army-clothing, camp-equipage, provisions, ammunition, and implements of war, which had been previously captured from the enemy† would have fallen into his hands. The destruction of the batteries, the ship then on the stocks, the extensive cantonments, and the public arsenal, would have retarded the building of another naval force; and that which was already on the lake in separate detachments, could have been intercepted, in its attempt to return, and might

* Sir George's General Order, dated Kingston, May 30th.
† These were destroyed by lieutenant Chauncey.

have been captured in detail. The prize-vessel which was then lying in the harbor, and which had been taken by the Americans, and the two United States' schooners, would have been certainly re-captured, and the whole energies of the American government, added to their most vigorous and unwearied struggles, might never again have attained any prospect of an ascendancy on the lake. As it proved, however, all these impending evils were averted, and the wisdom of the commanding officer, and the invincible firmness of those of his troops, who withstood the brunt of the action, converted that event into a splendid victory, which would otherwise have been an irretrievable disaster."*

So, it was not the imbecility of the British, but the " wisdom" of the American, " commanding officer," that saved Sackett's Harbor; not the orders of sir George Prevost, but the " invincible firmness" of American soldiers, that compelled the gallant colonel Young and major Drummond to retreat, with their men, to the boats.—We have no right, however, to find fault with the Americans, for considering as glorious to themselves, an event which it would be idle to say was not, in a high degree, disgraceful to us.

* Sketches of the War, p. 147.

CHAPTER VI.

Renewal of the American north-western army—Alliance in this quarter between the Americans and Indians—Advantages reaped by the enemy from sir George Prevost's armistice—Destruction of Indian towns—Scalping anecdote—Character of the Kentuckians—Skirmish at Frenchtown—Colonel Proctor's arrival from Detroit—Battle of the river Raisin—Surrender of general Winchester and the left wing of the American army—Gross mis-statements of the Americans corrected—Return of colonel Proctor to Sandwich—Augmentation of the American right wing, under general Harrison—His entrenchment at Fort-Meigs—Arrival of colonel Proctor from Amherstburg—Colonel Dudley's attack upon the British batteries—Defeat and capture of the Americans—Colonel Proctor's reduced force—His return to Sandwich.

WE must now transport the reader from the confines of the St. Lawrence to the strait connecting Lakes Erie and Huron, the scene of general Hull's early discomfiture. No sooner had intelligence of that event reached Washington, than the renewal of the north-western army, and the recovery of the surrendered territory, became one of the first objects of the American government. A report, industriously spread, that the inhabitants of Michigan " were now governed by an authority too rigorous to be compatible with those notions of liberty inspired by the genius of their own constitution, and were awaiting the expected succour from their friends, with the deepest anxiety,"* hastened the collection of a new army, which soon outnumbered the old. A brigade of Ohio volunteers, a second of Virginians, and a third of Kentuckians, also 2000 Pennsylvanian volunteers, and the 17th United States' regiment, were, by the early part of September, in full march from different points towards the Miami rapids, the place which had been assigned as the general rendezvous.

This army was afterwards divided into two wings; and the command of one given to major-general Harrison; of the other to major-general Winchester. By way of *fleshing* the troops, they were sent against the numerous tribes of Indians scattered over the uncultivated parts of the north-western country. The demi-barbarous Kentuckians, in particular, pillaged the provision grounds, and destroyed the towns and their inhabitants, with relentless fury.

Notwithstanding the apparent squeamishness

* Sketches of the War, p. 54.

of the United States' government, about accepting the aid of the *savages*, we are told of " arrangements having been made between general Harrison and the executive government, which authorized him to employ them;"* and accordingly, the services of the renowned chief Logan, and of 700 warriors, were accepted, but merely in consequence, it is carefully added, " of their desire of being taken into the service."—This happened in the early part of September, 1812; yet Mr. Madison's speech to congress, dated on the 4th of the succeeding November, and in which he notices the accumulating force under brigadier-general Harrison in the north-west, contains the following charge against the British:—" A distinguishing feature in the operations which preceded and followed this adverse event," (general Hull's surrender,) " is the use made by the enemy of the merciless savages under their influence. Whilst the benevolent policy of the United States invariably recommended peace, and promoted civilization,† among that wretched portion of the human race, and was making exertions to dissuade them from taking either side in the war, the enemy has not scrupled to call to his aid their ruthless ferocity, armed with the horrors of those instruments of carnage and torture, which are known to spare neither age nor sex."

* Sketches of the War, p. 58. † See p. 63.

Immediately after the capture of Detroit and the Michigan territory, colonel Proctor, pursuant to directions he had received from major-general Brock, prepared to send captain Muir, with a detachment of troops and Indians, to reduce Fort-Wayne, on the Ohio frontier; and which was then garrisoned by not more than 70 men. But the colonel received from general Brock, by the orders of sir George Prevost, the notification of the fatal armistice concluded with general Dearborn. The former communicated, at the same time, sir George's wish, that, although the armistice did not extend to general Hull's late command, it should be acted upon by colonel Proctor; who was also instructed to refrain from every hostile act, and to restrain the Indians by every means in his power. This apparent want of vigor on our part sent many of the Indians, highly dissatisfied, to their homes; and enabled the Americans to strengthen the whole of their north-western frontier, till then completely exposed; as well as to forward to their different posts ample supplies of stores and provisions.

After relieving Fort-Wayne from the hostile attacks of some Indians led by the Prophet, (Tecumseh's brother,) or, as it is falsely said, " of the allied British and Indians," major-general Harrison determined to make the Indians feel those effects of the war, which their repeated cruelties had provoked; and to convince them that the American troops were not so contemptible and degraded, as the Indians might conclude them to be, from the surrender of the late commander-in-chief on the same station."* The major-general, therefore, divided his force into scouting parties; and despatched them, under active and zealous officers, to massacre, burn, and destroy, the Indians and their towns. Through a sickening detail of several pages of Mr. Thomson's book, the destruction of numerous towns is pompously displayed, but the editor possessed too patriotic a spirit to attempt to describe the slaughter committed by his enlightened countrymen among those oppressed tenants of the woods,—" the wretched people," whose " civilization" the United States' government was so anxious to " promote."

The spirit of party is often a valuable friend to the cause of truth. While the democrats labored at glossing over, the federalists employed equal industry in rummaging every dusty corner for materials that might expose, the odious measures of the government. That they sometimes succeeded, appears by the following extract, taken from an old newspaper, published at Pittsburg, in the United States:

* Sketches of the War, p. 57.

"*Pittsburg*, May 17, 1791.

"We, the subscribers, encouraged by a large subscription, do propose to pay 100 dollars for every hostile Indian scalp, with both ears, if it be taken between this date and the 15th day of June next, by an inhabitant of Allegany-county."

   "GEORGE WALLIS,
   "ROBERT ELLIOTT,
   "WILLIAM AMBERSON,
   "ADAMSON TAUNHILL,
   "WILLIAM WILKINS, junior,
   "JOHN IRVINE."

Lest the world should imagine that a period of 21 years had wrought any other than a nominal improvement in the civilization of the American people, a general officer of the United States, employed against the Indians at the first of the war, inadvertently writes to a friend:—"The western militia always carry into battle a tomahawk and scalping knife, and are as dexterous in the use of them as any copper-coloured warriors of the forest. Eight hundred tomahawks have been furnished by the war-department to the north-western army."—Nay, the battle of Brownstown afforded ample proofs that this was actually the case.*

The preceding account illustrates a passage in one of our three histories.—" The Ken-

* See p. 66.

tuckians," says Mr. Thomson, " were held in great dread by most of the Indian warriors, and the expression of ' *Kentucky too much*,' has not unfrequently accompanied their orders to retreat, in the form of justification."* We can now understand what is meant, when Mr. O'Connor extols the *prowess* of the " veterans of Kentucky," and when Mr. Madison boasts of " the benevolent policy" of the United States.

Major-general Harrison, like his brother-generals to the northward, expressed a resolution of quartering for the winter in one of the Canadian garrisons. His more immediate object was the recovery of Detroit. To effect that, and the capture of Amherstburg†, abundance of ammunition, of ordnance and ordnance stores, and of provisions, had been ordered to Sandusky, the general's head-quarters. The two wings of his army had each taken a separate course through the Michigan territory; and were to concentrate at Presqu' Isle, preparatory to the combined attack upon Detroit. On the morning of the 17th of January, general Winchester, commanding the left wing, sent forward to Presqu' Isle, at the *alleged* solicitation of the inhabitants of Frenchtown, two detachments of troops, consisting, by one American account, of 11 companies of regulars, by another, of 800 men,‡ under

* Sketches of the War, p. 57.
† See p. 48.   ‡ Hist. of the United States, Vol. III. p. 211.

the command of lieutenant-colonel Lewis. On the morning of the 18th, the two detachments united at Presqu' Isle; whence colonel Lewis marched in the direction of Frenchtown, where, he states that he understood, "an advanced party of the British and Indians, amounting to about 500," were encamped.

At three o'clock in the afternoon of the 18th, colonel Lewis's force, encountered, in the neighbourhood of Frenchtown, well-posted behind some fences, 30 of the Essex militia, under the command of major Reynolds of that corps; assisted by a 3-pounder, to the use of which a bombardier of the royal artillery, who was also present, had trained three of the militia. A band of 200 Indians (Pottawattamies) accompanied the militia-force. After a desperate resistance, in which, says one American editor, major Reynolds and his men several times intrepidly attempted to break the American line, the militia and Indians, without losing their gun, or any more of their party, than one militia-man and three Indians killed, retreated to Brownstown, 18 miles from the scene of action. The Americans state their own loss at 12 killed, and 55 wounded; a satisfactory proof that, notwithstanding their superior numbers, they had no great reason to boast.

The American commander encamped upon the ground abandoned by major Reynolds; and immediately prepared to maintain his position till he should be joined by general Winchester. That junction was effected on the 20th; "when," says Dr. Smith, (for which we heartily thank him,) " their united forces formed a division 1000 strong."*

On hearing of the Americans being in possession of Frenchtown, (a village about 26 miles from Detroit,) and that the junction of the two wings for the attack on Detroit might shortly take place, colonel Proctor moved forward to Brownstown, at which place he had directed his force to assemble. This force, consisting of 140 rank and file of the 41st, and royal Newfoundland regiments, a few men of the 10th veteran battalion, together with militia, Canadian sailors, and royal artillery, the latter having with them three 3-pounders and a $5\frac{1}{2}$ inch howitzer, did not amount to 500 white troops. To these were added about 450 Indians; not more. †

We have American authority for stating, that the force under brigadier-general Winchester amounted to 1000 men. These, according to general Harrison's letter, ‡ consisted of the greater part of colonel Wells's regiment of United States'

* Hist. of the United States, Vol. III. p. 211.

† Sir George Prevost says 600, but he had received no returns, when he wrote his despatch covering colonel Proctor's letter.

‡ App. No. 28.

infantry, of the 1st and 5th Kentucky regiments, and of colonel Allen's rifle regiment; and were, in truth, the flower of the north-western army. General Winchester, piqued at general Harrison's having been promoted over him, was anxious to engage, previously to any junction; the more so, as he had received certain information of the inferior number, and motley description, of colonel Proctor's force.

Colonel Proctor advanced from Brownstown on the 21st; and, at day-dawn on the 22d, attacked general Winchester at his encampment. The American right division, after a few rounds, retreated, and was almost wholly cut to pieces by the Indians, who had been stationed in the rear of the encampment. The left division, consisting, by one American account, of 650, and, by general Winchester's letter, of "about 400 men," was stationed behind a breastwork; against which the British 3-pounders produced little or no effect. Admitting the strength of general Winchester's left division to have been 500 men, a number less than the mean of the two American accounts, how ridiculous appears Mr. Thomson's description of this battle. "Three furious onsets were made upon it" (the left division) "by the British 41st, each of which was received with distinguished coolness, and each of which terminated in the repulse of the enemy. In the desperate resistance which was made to the charges of this *regiment*, 30 of its men were killed, and between 90 and 100 wounded."*

The American infantry and riflemen, advantageously posted as they were, proved excellent marksmen. Several of the British were shot, while stretched on the snow, disabled; others, although wounded, did not quit their ranks; others, again, returned to their duty, as soon as their wounds were dressed. Such gallantry, although "repulsed" so often, must conquer at last. The whole of the left division surrendered, colonel Proctor says, " at discretion ;"† but, according to general Winchester, " on condition of their being protected from the savages, being allowed to retain their private property, and having their side-arms returned to them."‡ Had this been the understanding, one may suppose that some writing would have been drawn up; but, indeed, general Winchester was not in a condition to dictate terms. Stripped to his shirt and trowsers, and suffering exceedingly from the cold, the American general was found by colonel Proctor, near to one of the Indian fires, in the possession of the Wyandot chief Roundhead. The Indian had decked himself out in the general's great and uniform coats, waistcoat, and hat; and was so pleased with his new dress,

* Sketches of the War. p. 103. † App. No. 24.
‡ App. No. 27.

that the British commanding officer had great difficulty in persuading him to make restitution.

The whole number of prisoners, including those brought in by the indians, amounted to 538.* Mr. Thomson states the killed and missing at 297; and general Harrison, in his letter dated two days after the battle, mentions that 30 of the fugitives had joined him. Thus we account for 115 more than Mr. Thomson's "750;" and there will be no difficulty in accounting for the whole of doctor Smith's "1000," if we make allowance for those of the flying right division that escaped to their homes, or were killed by the Indians in the woods, without being included in the returns. The only difficulty is, to reconcile so small a number as 1000 men with general Harrison's statement, that the greater part of one, and the whole of three regiments composed general Winchester's force.

The American official account is silent as to the strength of colonel Proctor's army, beyond that it was "greatly superior in numbers;" † but Mr. Thomson has found out that the British force amounted to 2100 men,‡ and doctor Smith has just saved himself from the charge of plagiarism, by lopping off the odd 100. There is no difficulty in discovering how Mr. Thomson

* App. No. 25. † Ibid No. 27.
‡ Sketches of the War, p. 104.

obtained his numbers. He gathered from sir George Prevost's letter, that colonel Proctor's combined force amounted to about 1100 men;* but, in his confusion, he did not, or in his zeal he would not, perceive, that the three companies, or, as he has it, the *whole*, of " the British 41st regiment," were included in that estimate. Knowing, therefore, that a full regiment generally contains 1000 men, this shrewd historian adds that number to the 1100, and produces his 2100. In his account of the British loss, Mr. Thomson is not so happy. He obtains from colonel Proctor's return,† " 24 killed, and 158 wounded ;" but has the hardihood to say, that the loss sustained by the " 41st regiment" is not included; and this, although the very returns he had in his hands numbered 15 of those gallant fellows among the killed, and 97 among the wounded. But Mr. Thomson has now the satisfaction of saying :—" I am more than borne out in my assertions by the highly respectable testimony of the reverend S. S. Smith, D. D. and LL. D. and other literary gentlemen." True it is, indeed, that the authors of the " History of the United States" say thus:—" The enemy acknowledged a severe loss on their side. Of the 41st *regiment*, which three times charged the picqueted detachment under major Madison, and which was repulsed as often, 150 were killed

---

* See p. 186, Note †. † App. No. 26.

and wounded."*—To rail at these Munchausen tale-writers, would be a useless and an endless task: suffice it that we pursue them through all their wiles and turns; and finally, drag them, like culprits, before the bar of the public.

The severity of colonel Proctor's loss had reduced his number of white troops below the number of prisoners taken. This and the momentary expectation of general Harrison's arrival with the right wing, determined the colonel to quit the scene of action on the same evening, and retire to Brownstown. On this occasion, a few of the wounded Americans were unavoidably left at Frenchtown, in charge of the Indian department, as their surest protection, until a carriage could be sent to convey them forward. Unfortunately, a false alarm, that general Harrison's force was approaching, caused the individuals stationed as a protection to the wounded Americans, to desert their charge; and some of the latter were, in consequence, killed by straggling Indians; but not by the main body, for that had followed the troops. It is upon this that the American "prints known to be friendly to the war"† have raised a superstructure of calumny and abuse against the British character. Vain were the efforts of the few federal or opposition editors to explain the nature of the case. We are declared to have aided and abetted the

* Hist. of the United States, Vol. III. p. 213.   † See p. 162.

Indians, in torturing and massacring defenceless Americans; and so well have the slanderers succeeded in their aims, that the bulk of the American people still believe it to have been the fact. Our three historians, with shameless depravity, have copied into their pages none but the most violent paragraphs upon the subject; and one of them actually ushers his lies into notice with : " The fidelity of history will not allow them to be magnified." * But, out of all " the solemn affirmations" called in aid of so serious a charge against us, one officer only, and he in the militia service, has been brought forward. Mr. Thomson tell us, frankly, that "colonel Elliot was an American by birth, a native of Maryland."† He is described to have " long been notorious for his activity in exciting the savages to arm themselves against his fellow-citizens;" † and, in the present instance, to have promised his protection to, and then basely deserted, a young class-mate, his countryman. Admitting that this was an act " of the most unparalleled atrocity," it was perpetrated by a native of the United States: how, therefore, can it apply to " British officers"?—Mr. O'Connor has acted more consistently. He describes colonel Elliott as " a British officer;" and, after stating the promise which the latter had made to his " old

* Sketches of the War, p. 104.
† Ibid. p. 106.

acquaintance," — not " countryman". Mr. O'Connor emphatically adds:—" These were the promises of the British;—let our countrymen see how they were fulfilled."*

It is but justice to general Winchester to mention that, when about to write his official letter, he expressed himself highly gratified with the attention which had been paid to him, his officers, and the prisoners generally, by the British. That not a word of this appears in the official letter, can be accounted for only, by the supposition, that the American government, for reasons of policy best known to itself, has suppressed the paragraph.

The author of the " History of the United States" is, as may be supposed, very severe in his remarks upon our " employing the ruthless savages as auxiliaries in war, against a Christian people;" but, in his assertion, that " the government of the United States rejected the proffered assistance of the Indians, the reverend gentleman is quite misinformed; for, we have already shewn that, nearly four months previous to the battle of the Raisin, a formidable Indian chief and his tribe served as the allies of the United States.† It was with the greatest reluctance that the Indian chiefs at the Raisin acquiesced in the surrender of the Americans; whose destruction they had determined upon. Nothing induced them

* Hist. of the War, p. 70.   † See p. 180.

to relent, but the probability of general Harrison's immediate arrival. That the Indians, in general, do entertain an "inveterate animosity towards the Americans," no one can doubt, who has read of the tribes, and of the towns, that, from time to time, have been massacred and burnt by the "Christian people," during their 33 years of sovereignty and independence; or, as the Indians would say, of usurpation of *their* name and territories.

After the battle colonel Proctor marched back to Detroit; and thence crossed to Sandwich, to await the further operations of general Harrison's division, which was still in the neighbourhood of Upper Sandusky. General Winchester's movement to Frenchtown, and the subsequent disaster attending it, were entirely subversive of general Harrison's plans, and rendered a new levy of troops indispensably necessary, towards fulfilling the important object in view. From Sandusky the American commander and his army advanced to the rapids of the Miami, accompanied by the whole of the artillery and stores. Here general Harrison commenced building a fort, afterwards called Fort-Meigs; and he also caused fortifications to be erected at Upper Sandusky, under the directions of an intelligent officer.

In the midst of these alleged precautionary measures for the protection of the troops and the defence of the territory, detached parties from the American army were frequently "indulged"* in short excursions, " none of which resulted in any material advantage." In one excursion, against a party of Indians at Presq' Isle, general Harrison himself commanded. The American historian has prudently drawn a veil over the *manner* in which his countrymen "indulged" themselves during these their " frequent" visits to the Indian villages. A great portion of general Harrison's troops were Kentuckians. They, above all, could appreciate the general's *indulgences*; and, having their passions heated almost to frenzy by what, they had *been told*, had occurred at the Raisin, these " Christian people" no doubt employed their tomahawks and scalping-knives in taking of their less cruel—because less cultivated—enemies, a full measure of retaliation.

Towards the end of March, colonel Proctor received intelligence, that general Harrison was in expectation of considerable reinforcements and supplies, and that, on their arrival, he intended to commence active operations against Detroit. Resolved to try the issue of a contest, before the enemy, already much superior in numbers, gained a fresh acquisition of strength, colonel Proctor embarked at Amherstburg, on the 23d of April, with 522 regular troops, in-

* Sketches of the War, p. 108.

cluding the staff and other officers; and 461 officers and privates of militia; total 983 men.* After some delay in ascending the Miami, owing chiefly to the heavy rains that prevailed, the troops, with their baggage, stores, guns, and ammunition, landed on the north-side of the river, in the course of the 28th; and soon afterwards pitched their tents, near the scite of the old Fort-Miami, distant about a mile and a half from Fort-Meigs, general Harrison's head-quarters. By this time an Indian force of about 1200 had attached itself to the British army.

Fort-Meigs was situate on a commanding eminence; mounted 18 guns, chiefly 18 and 12-pounders; and was supplied with every necessary munition of war. General Harrison had, since early in April, received intelligence, by two Frenchmen, of colonel Proctor's intended attack; and, therefore, "was every day erecting fortifications of different descriptions,"† to defeat his adversary's plans. The number of American troops in the fort it is not easy to ascertain; but we read of the 12th and 13th regiments, and of a body of Kentuckians, exclusive of general Greene Clay's brigade, in hourly expectation at the fort.

On the 1st of May, two 24, and three 12-pounders, one 8-inch howitzer, and two $5\frac{1}{2}$ inch mortars, were opened upon Fort-Meigs, from

* App. No. 30.   † Sketches of the War, p. 100.

the opposite bank of the river; but, although 260 shots fell during the day, no effect was produced, beyond killing one, and wounding seven, of general Harrison's men. On the 3d, a small battery, consisting of two 6-pounder field-pieces, and one of the $5\frac{1}{2}$ inch mortars, was constructed on the south-side of the river, in the rear of the American fort. Both British batteries continued an ineffectual fire till the morning of the 5th, when general Harrison ordered major-general Clay, then in sight from the fort, to land 800 men, or rank and file, on the opposite, or north side of the river, to storm the British batteries; while a sortie, with 350 rank and file, was to be made from the garrison, for the purpose of capturing the two 6-pounders and mortar, at which had been stationed the two flank companies of the 41st regiment, and two companies of militia, altogether, 260 rank and file; under the command of captain Bullock of the 41st. About 300 Indians had crossed the river with the regulars and militia.

The American storming party, consisting, by the American accounts, of 800 rank and file, landed from the boats, in which, assisted by the spring-flood, they had descended the river; and they " now resolutely marched up to the mouth" of the British guns, at which were stationed not more than 30 artillerymen and additional gunners from the 41st regiment; and these without small-arms. This, in the American version, is "putting the British regulars and Canadian militia to flight."* The American troops spiked the guns; and colonel Dudley, with about 400 men, marched, by a neighbouring wood-side, to attack the British camp, leaving the remainder of his party, under major Shelby, in charge of the captured batteries. Scarcely had colonel Dudley got out of sight, before up marched two battalion-companies of the 41st regiment, and one company of militia, in all, 180 rank and file; commanded by captain Muir of the 41st. These gallantly attacked the American troops near the batteries; recaptured the latter, at the point of the bayonet; and took as prisoners major Shelby, and 430 inferior officers and privates; making, with 57 officers and privates found dead on the spot, a force of 488 men. Although this was an effort on the part of the British, certainly as brilliant as it was successful, it is but fair to state that, except about one company, the American force consisted of newly-raised militia; or, as Mr. Thomson, by way of compliment, styles them, of " brave but indiscreet Kentuckians."

While all this was going on at the fatal batteries, colonel Dudley and his detachment were drawn into an ambuscade, by a body of Indians, stationed in the woods. Here fell the colonel,

* Sketches of the War, p. 111.

and the greater part of his men. About 150 effected their escape, and subsequently arrived at Fort-Meigs; and 42 appear, by the returns,* to have been delivered up to the British. It is surprising that the American historians, so minute on other occasions, should not have attempted to enumerate their acknowledged heavy loss in prisoners. We shall see that they have not been forgetful of the few they took from us, on the opposite side of the river.

This brings us to the sortie made by colonel Miller upon captain Bullock's small detachment. Mr. Thomson says: " He (colonel Miller) assaulted the whole line of their works, which was defended, as has since been ascertained, by 200 regulars, 150 militia, and 4 or 500 Indians; and, after several brilliant and intrepid charges, succeeded in driving the enemy from his principal batteries, and in spiking the cannon. He then returned to the fort with 42 prisoners, among whom were two lieutenants."†

Now, let us descend from figurative, to plain language. Colonel Miller's party consisted of a detachment of the 19th regiment, and some militia, amounting, at least, to " 350 men."† These, after a pretty smart struggle, aided by a few well-directed shots from a gun which the garrison had the day previous turned in that direction, succeeded in defeating captain Bul-

* App. No. 32.   † Sketches of the War, p. 112.

lock's two flank-companies of the 41st, and in taking possession of one of the 6-pounders,—described as "the enemy's principal batteries." After the Americans had performed this exploit, in which they captured two lieutenants, one serjeant, and 37 rank and file, they "spiked the cannon." While doing this, and not before, 300 Indians, and the two companies of militia who had been detached, joined the few retiring regulars. The men immediately re-advanced, and, in a twinkling, recaptured the monstrous "cannon." The tables were now turned; and colonel Miller and his men, after sustaining a severe loss in killed and wounded, precipitately fled under cover of their batteries. Not a word of this appears in Mr. Thomson: unless we are to imply as much, from the gentle phrase,— "He then returned to the fort." The remainder of general Clay's brigade, consisting of about 400 men, assailed a body of Indians in the wood, near to Fort-Meigs; and, says Mr. Thomson, "would have been also drawn into an ambush, had not general Harrison ordered a party of dragoons to sally out, and protect their retreat to the fort."*

The British loss, during these operations, amounted to no more than 14 killed, 47 wounded, and 40 missing, or prisoners. The American loss, as far as it could be ascertained by

* Sketches of the War, p. 112.

their own people, amounted to 81 killed, and 189 wounded, besides the prisoners. We must not omit here to mention, that the famed Indian warrior, Tecumseh, buried his tomahawk in the head of a Chippeway chief, whom he found actively engaged in massacring some of colonel Dudley's men. The Americans, as usual, greatly exaggerated the British force; of which not much more than half was actually engaged; the remainder being at the encampment. The Indians, according to their custom after success, retired to enjoy the plunder they had obtained from the captured boats. So that, of colonel Proctor's 1200 Indians, Tecumseh and about 20 chiefs were all that were present at the close of the battle: by which time, also, it appears, "half of the militia,"* having their corn to plant, had retired to their homes. Thus situated, colonel Proctor considered himself obliged to raise the siege of Fort-Meigs. After re-embarking his small force of regulars, and the whole of his ordnance and stores of every description, he returned to Sandwich; there to await the expected reinforcements from the Niagara frontier.

* App. No. 29.

CHAPTER VII.

*Critical situation of major-general Vincent's army
—American army sent against it—Lieutenant-
colonel Harvey's gallant proposal of a night-
attack—Its adoption and successful result—
Capture of the two American generals—Confusion and retreat of the American army—
Commodore Chauncey's return to Sackett's Harbor—Sir James Yeo's attack upon the Americans at their second encampment—Arrival of
the American army at Fort-George, and abandonment of the detached posts—Surrender of
colonel Bœrstler and 541 Americans to a subaltern's detachment of the 49th—Colonel Clark's
successful attack on Fort-Schlosner—Alliance
between the Americans and Indians—The latter's
declaration of war against the Canadas—Gross
misrepresentations of the Americans corrected—
British plan for saving American prisoners in
the hands of the Indians—Barbarous experiment made with British prisoners by the American major Chapin—Lieutenant-colonel Bisshopp's
successful attack on Black Rock—His untimely
fall—Capture of unarmed Canadians—Second
capture of York—Its defenceless state—Destruction of private property—American officers on
parole.*

WE must now return to major-general Vincent, whom we left encamped at Burlington

Heights, distant from Fort-George about 50 miles. The capture of York, and the American superiority on the lake, rendered the situation of this army extremely critical. The officers and men were in absolute want of those necessaries, which they had been compelled, either to leave behind at the evacuation of, or to destroy during the retreat from, Fort-George. Should the enemy approach in force too superior to justify a battle, the British were without the means of carrying away their few field-pieces, or even their wounded. Should, on the other hand, a battle offer the slightest chance of success, the quantity of ammunition, 90 rounds per gun, was too small to admit of perseverance in their efforts.

Determined to drive the British from their position, or, if resolved to fight, to ensure their capture, general Dearborn, on the 1st and 2d of June, despatched from Fort-George generals Chandler and Winder, with their two brigades of infantry, accompanied by colonel Burn and his dragoons, and by a strong detachment of artillery, having in charge eight or nine field-pieces, both heavy and light. On arriving, on the morning of the 5th, at the vicinity of Stoney Creek, and within about seven miles of the British encampment, the Americans pitched their tents, in order to make further preparations for attacking a force, of much less than half their numbers.

Lieutenant-colonel Harvey, at the head of a reconnoitring party, consisting of the light companies of the 8th and 49th regiments, advanced close to the enemy's encampment, and took an accurate view of his position. With a promptitude, as honourable to his gallantry as his judgment, the lieutenant-colonel suggested to major-general Vincent, in the strongest terms, a night-attack upon the American camp. He had planned the whole in his mind; and offered, in person, to lead the advance. The object was, to throw the enemy into confusion; and, if possible, compel him to abandon his intended attack upon the British army. It was certainly a desperate measure, but British soldiers were to make the attempt, and not to make it would bring down the same consequences as a failure,—the capture or destruction of general Vincent's force.

The night of the 5th of June, as if propitious to the undertaking, proved one of the darkest that had been known for many years. Owing to that very circumstance, as small a number as could well be employed, would, it was justly considered, co-operate with the best effect. The men had been kept under arms, awaiting an attack from the enemy, since early in the afternoon; and, at half-past eleven, as if merely to take up some new position accessory to the defence of the post, five companies of the 8th, and the whole of the 49th regiment, marched out of camp. The number was exactly "704 firelocks,"* or, which is the same thing, rank and file.

Let us now pause awhile, till we have fixed, as accurately as may be, the number and force of the American army. The only assistance we procure from the American accounts, are the names of the regiments and corps. These consisted of the 5th, 13th, 14th, 16th, 22d, and 23d regiments of infantry, divided into two brigades, of, according to the lowest returns in an American work, 1450 men each. We find 800 artillery mentioned as part of the Fort-George force: admitting half only of that number, some of which were acting as light troops, to have been detached on this occasion, and adding the 250 dragoons under colonel Burn, we have, for the force encamped at Stoney Creek, 3550 men; but a Boston paper of June 24, 1813, states the number at 4000. It becomes us, however, to be rather under, than over the mark; we will therefore fix the amount, in round numbers, at 3500 Americans; just,—without estimating the nine field-pieces,—five times the number of the British who, in the solemn stillness of the night, were fearlessly marching to attack them.

The advance of this determined band was led by lieutenant-colonel Harvey; and, at 2 o'clock,

* App. No. 33.

the British regulars, with fixed bayonets, rushed into the centre of the American camp. The 49th regiment, headed by major (now lieutenant-colonel) Plenderleath, charged some field-pieces; and one of the artillerymen was bayonetted in the very act of discharging a gun. A body of American infantry, stationed near the artillery, and composed, it is said, of the light troops and 25th regiment, fired a most destructive volley at the 49th; but, instead of repeating what might have changed the fate of the day, turned upon their heels and fled. On this occasion major Plenderleath's horse was shot under him, and himself severely wounded. Serjeant Fraser of the 49th, having captured brigadier-general Winder, now brought him as a prisoner to major Plenderleath. The latter mounted the American general's horse, and lost that, also, by a shot, almost immediately afterwards. Brigadier-general Chandler was taken, much bruised, under one of the guns. All this while, the five companies of the 8th regiment, under major (now lieutenant-colonel) Ogilvie, who so distinguished himself at Fort-George, were dealing destruction to the enemy's left flank, composed of the 5th, 23d, and 16th regiments.

The utmost confusion reigned in the American camp, and the troops were flying in every direction to the surrounding heights. The plan having fully succeeded, and it not being prudent to let the Americans discover what a small force had so put them to the rout, lest they should rally, and overwhelm their few opponents, the latter, just as day dawned, retired to their cantonments ; taking with them two brigadier-generals, one major, five captains, one lieutenant, and 116 non-commissioned officers and privates, of the American army ; also two out of four of the captured pieces of artillery, along with nine horses to draw them.*

Owing to the extreme darkness of the night, each side suffered from friends as well as foes. Our loss amounted to 23 killed, 136 wounded, and 55 missing ;† being almost a third of the party. The Americans admit a loss of 17 killed, and 38 wounded; but make their missing amount, in all, to 100, instead of 125. General Dearborn's letter states that " colonel Clark" was mortally wounded, and fell into their hands. This was not the case, but brigade-major Clerk was most dangerously wounded, and found on the ground by two stragglers, one a British, the other an American soldier. They carried him to a farm-house, where he had scarcely been put to bed, when an American guard arrived, and the officer inhumanly ordered major Clerk, bed and all, to be placed in a waggon, the jolting of which set his wounds bleeding afresh, and nearly terminated his life.

* App. No. 35. † Ib. No. 34.

One of the American accounts of the Stoney Creek business contains the following statement: " Captain Manners, of that regiment, (the 49th) was taken in his bed by lieutenant Riddle; who, from a principle of humanity, put him on his parole, on condition of his not serving the enemy, until he should be exc anged. An engagement which that officer violated, by appearing in arms against the American troops, immediat after the recovery of his health."* This is a serious charge against a brave officer, now living. Thus it is answered. Close to captain Manners, on the field, lay a ptain Mills, of the American army, still more severely wounded. The two officers agreed, and mutually pledged their honors, that, no matter by which party captured, they should be considered as exchanged, and at liberty to serve again. Lieutenant Riddle soon afterwards came up; and, although he could not stay to bring away even his friend, exacted a parole from captain Manners. When the American army subsequently fled, the two officers were found by the British. The instant captain ls recovered from is wounds, he was sent by a fla to the American lines; and captain M nners became, of course, exonerated from his parole. That an American editor should give insertion to any story, reflecting upon a British officer, is not at all strange. But

* Sketches of the War, p. 157.

it is so, that an American officer should have allowed three editions of Mr. Thomson's book to pass, every one containing so scandalous a paragraph.

The American official account describes the 704 regulars that performed this exploit at Stoney Creek, as " the whole of the British and Indian forces;"* although not an Indian moved with the troops, and those that had been left at the encampment did not exceed 20 or 30. This Indian story was just the thing for Mr. O'Connor. Accordingly, he says: "The army, on this occasion, has proved its firmness and bravery, by keeping its position in a night-attack, in which the yells of the Indians, mingled with the roaring of the cannon and musketry, were calculated to intimidate."† General Dearborn, next, pronounces " the enemy completely routed, and driven from the field;" although he admits that, " by some strange fatality," his two brigadiers were taken prisoners.* So boasted commodore Chauncey, when sir James Yeo captured two of his schooners.‡ It is to the very circumstance of the absence of the two commanding brigadiers, perhaps, that we may attribute the general's want of information on the subject. Who else, for instance, but some stupid corporal or drummer, could

* App. No. 36.   † Hist. of the War, p. 98.
‡ James's Nav. Occur. p. 298.

have told him, that they sent in a flag with a request " to bury their dead." So far from that having been the case, the Americans ran away and left their own dead to be buried by the British.

Really, the confusion that prevailed in the American camp, seems to have extended its influence to the heads of the American historians. One editor declares, that the British, when they attacked, had " no musket loaded," and turned the captured guns upon the encampment; when, in truth, the British did fire their muskets, but did not fire the captured guns; chiefly, in the latter case, because they had no artillerymen to manage them. " The dragoons charged upon, and completely routed them ;"* says one editor. " The squadron of dragoons remained formed and steady at their posts, but could not act on account of the darkness of the night, and the thickness of the adjacent woods ;"* says another. The last was the fact; at least, no dragoons were encountered or seen by any of our troops.

Although general Dearborn had killed major-general Vincent, Mr. Thomson declared he was only missing, and " discovered by his own people, in the course of the same day, almost famished, at the distance of four miles from the scene of action."† At all events, both of the

* Hist. of the War, p. 98.   † Sketches of the War, p. 136.

captured American generals dined with the British general on the day of the attack, and were sent forward to Montreal that same afternoon. Amidst all their confusion, the three American historians agree in this, that the American troops behaved in the bravest manner; and that the British, although " superior" in numbers, " fled in every direction."

After the British had retired, and when broad daylight enabled the Americans to see well around them, the latter returned to their camp; but only to destroy their blankets, carriages, provisions, spare arms, ammunition, &c. They then, " having given up the pursuit of the enemy,"* precipitately retreated, or " fell back," gently, no doubt,—because the roads were scarcely passable,—to Forty-mile Creek, about 11 miles in the rear of the field of battle. Mr. O'Connor says, a council of war decided that the army " ought to retire." Admitting the council was not long sitting, this was probably the case. At all events, when a reconnoitring party of the British arrived in sight of the field of battle, about eleven o'clock on the same morning, not an American soldier was to be seen, except the dead and the badly wounded. Several of the British wounded, and among them major Clerk and captain Manners, again found themselves in the midst of their

* Sketches of the War, p. 137.

friends. The state of want to which our troops had been reduced, was in a great measure relieved by the spoils of the deserted camp.

The American army re-encamped on a plane of a mile in width; its right flank on the lake, its left on the Forty-mile Creek, skirting the base of a perpendicular mountain. On the afternoon of the day of battle, a detachment, consisting of the 6th and 15th United States' regiments, and a park of artillery, under colonel James Miller, joined the army; as did, the next afternoon, generals Lewis and Boyd, the former of whom assumed the command. The army, at this time, must have amounted to upwards of 4000 men.

As soon as commodore Chauncey had ascertained that the British fleet was again in Kingston, he left the protection of his batteries at the head of the lake, and hastened to Sackett's Harbor; there to await the launching and final equipment of the ship General Pike. On the 3d of June sir James Yeo, with his squadron, on board of which he had some clothing and provisions, and about 280 of the 8th regiment, for major-general Vincent, sailed from Kingston, to co-operate with that officer; as well as, by intercepting the enemy's supplies, and otherwise annoying him, to provoke commodore Chauncey to re-appear on the lake.

At daylight on the morning of the 8th, sir

James found himself close to general Lewis's camp at the Forty-mile Creek. It being calm, the larger vessels could not get in, but the Beresford and Sidney Smith schooners, and one or two gun-boats, succeeded in approaching within range of the American batteries. Four pieces of artillery were brought down to the beach; and, in less than half an hour, a temporary furnace for heating shot was in operation.* The fire of the British vessels was then returned, the Americans say, " with full effect." They admit, however, that at noon on the day of sir James's appearance, the troops broke up their cantonments, and scampered off as fast as they could, having previously sent away a part of their camp-equipage and baggage in batteaux to Fort-George; but this hasty removal, say the historians, was owing to orders just received from general Dearborn. The batteaux put off. Twelve of them, with their contents, were captured by the Beresford, and the remaining seven were driven on shore and abandoned by their crews.

In compliance with the directions of major-general Vincent, sir James Yeo landed the detachment of the 8th, under major Evans, at the Forty-mile Creek, that it might join lieutenant-colonel Bisshopp, with the flank company of the 49th, and one battalion company of the 41st,

* Sketches of the War, p. 138.

which had arrived there from the heights. At about seven o'clock on the evening of the 8th, this advanced corps, numbering about 450 rank and file, entered the second deserted American camp, where the men found, generously spared to them out of the conflagration of stores, 500 standing tents, 140 barrels of flour, 100 stands of arms, besides a variety of other useful and necessary articles; also about 70 prisoners. Nothing of this appears in the American accounts. The British advance, being now so well provided, encamped upon the spot, to await the arrival of the main body.

Whether it was through the imbecility of the officers, or the fears of the men, the American troops, under general Lewis, fled in the utmost haste; having sustained a loss in killed, wounded, and missing, including desertions, (if we may trust the American newspapers,) of nearly 1000 men. So apprehensive, indeed, were they of being cut off, that, instead of proceeding to Fort-George by the direct route, they marched round by Queenstown. The accounts they brought to general Dearborn, of the number and prowess of the British, led to preparations for defending that post, and to an immediate concentration of the detachments from Chippeway and Fort-Erie; nor was Fort-George, with the strongly entrenched camp in its neighbourhood, although garrisoned by upwards of 5000 Americans, deemed a situation of perfect security: therefore, the bulk of the remaining baggage was sent across the river to Fort-Niagara. Thus, was the whole interior of the Upper Canada peninsula rescued from the ravages of an invading army, by a mere handful of British troops, ordered from their own camp at the bold suggestion, and led into the midst of the enemy's, by the judgment and intrepidity, of lieutenant-colonel Harvey.

Major-general Vincent, having been reinforced by the 104th regiment, had placed the advanced corps of his little army under the command of lieutenant-colonel Bisshopp; who, about the 22d of June, pushed forward detachments, to occupy the cross-roads at the Ten-mile Creek, and at the Beaver Dam. One of these detachments, consisting of a subaltern and 30 rank and file, of the 104th, occupied a stone-house near to the dam. To reconnoitre, and, if possible, to capture this force, lieutenant-colonel Bœrstler, with a detachment of infantry, cavalry, artillery, militia and volunteers, numbering 673 officers and men, was sent from Fort-George.

At eight o'clcock on the morning of the 24th, colonel Bœrstler and his party unexpectedly encountered, in the woods, a body of about 200 Indians led by captain Kerr. A skirmish ensued, which lasted upwards of two hours, when the American troops, dreading being led into an ambush, endeavoured to gain the wood leading towards Lundy's Lane; but were unexpectedly encountered by lieutenant-colonel Thomas Clark, at the head of 15 militia-men, accidentally passing in that direction. These immediately opened a fire, from the wood, upon colonel Bœrstler's army; and compelled it to halt upon the open space of ground, across which it had been retreating. Mr. Thomson, out of kindness to colonel Bœrstler, has denominated these 16 militia, "one company of the 104th regiment, and about 200 militia, in all 340 men;" and declares, that even this force was continually augmenting, and became, at last, greatly superior. The colonel must have thought so too; for he sent to Fort-George, a distance of 16 miles, for an immediate reinforcement.

During the retreat from the Indians, lieutenant Fitzgibbon of the 49th, having with him a small detachment, consisting of a subaltern and 46 rank and file, closed upon, and reconnoitred the American troops. He stationed his men on an eminence to the right of their position; and, receiving information of the expected reinforcement from Fort-George, resolved upon the bold measure of immediately summoning colonel Bœrstler to surrender. This, lieutenant Fitzgibbon immediately did, in the name of lieutenant-colonel De Haren. Mr. Thomson has exerted himself to save colonel Bœrstler's character on this occasion, by stating, that "lieutenant Fitzgibbon informed him, on the honor of a British soldier, that the regular force, commanded by lieutenant-colonel Bisshopp, was double that of the American, and that the Indians were at least 700 in number. Colonel Bœrstler," proceeds this editor, "trusting to the veracity of the officer, fearing the impracticability of escaping, and being unwilling to abandon his wounded, agreed to terms of capitulation."*

Just as these were drawing up, arrived major De Haren, who had been sent for by lieutenant Fitzgibbon; and who brought with him about 220 men, consisting of the light troops attached to the advanced detachment. The major put the finishing stroke to this admirable *ruse de guerre*, by affixing his name to the document surrendering lieutenant-colonel Bœrstler, along with one major, six captains, 13 lieutenants, one cornet, one surgeon, 25 serjeants, two drummers, and 462 rank and file, as prisoners of war; besides 30 militia, intended to have been released on parole: making a total of 542 men. At the same time were also surrendered, one 12 and one 6-pounder, two cars, and the colours of the 14th United States' regiment.† The amount of the American wounded in the affair with the Indians no where appears; but, referring to the number of men sent on the expedition, either the loss

* Sketches of the War, p. 151.   † App. No. 38.

must have been great, or several of the party had escaped previously to the surrender.

The complete success attending this exploit, seems to have greatly mortified our three historians; one of whom had already boasted of "the terrifying effects of lieutenant-colonel Bœrstler's lungs upon the British;" alluding to the affair near Frenchman's creek.* We cannot learn whether the American colonel did, or did not, open his throat upon lieutenant Fitzgibbon; but we require no stronger evidence than the former's "unaccountable"† surrender, to be assured of this fact,—that a Stentor's lungs and a Cæsar's heart do not always inhabit the same breast.

As the American editors are very loud in their railings against us, because major-general Vincent refused to ratify the last article of the capitulation; stipulating, that the militia and volunteers should be permitted to return to the United States on parole, this may require an explanation. In the first place, the stand of colours of a militia-regiment was found concealed about the person of one of major Chapin's volunteers. In the next, these were recognized as the identical men who, led by their " gallant commander," had recently been pillaging the houses and carrying off the horses, of the Canadian inhabitants in the neighbourhood. In several instances, the marauders had actually

* See p. 114.   † App. No. 40.

forced from the frames, and carried away, the poor people's window-sashes.

Early in July, major-general De Rottenburg, the late president of Lower Canada, succeeded major-general Sheaffe as president of the upper province; and, as such, took the command of the troops from the hands of major-general Vincent. Major-general De Rottenburg, with the main body of the centre-divison of the army of Upper Canada, took his station in the neighbourhood of the Twelve-mile Creek, which is distant about 11 miles from Fort-George. About this time general Dearborn, harrassed in mind and body, very properly resigned the command of the American northern army. General Lewis was next in succession; but, he having been ordered to Sackett's Harbor to assist commodore Chauncey in repairing the defences of that fortress, the command of Fort-George and its dependencies, as also of Fort-Niagara, devolved upon major-general Boyd.

As a proof to what a helpless state this numerous army of invasion had, by its fears, been reduced, lieutenant-colonel Thomas Clark, of the Canadian militia, during the night of the 4th of July, with 40 of his men, passed over in boats from Chippeway to Fort-Schlosser; surprised the American guard stationed there; made 15 prisoners; and brought away a considerable quantity of flour, salt pork, and other provisions;

also a brass 6-pounder, several stands of arms, some ball-cartridges, &c.

Early in the same month, the American government threw off the mask, and openly called to its aid, upon the Niagara, as it had before done upon the north-western frontier, " the ruthless ferocity of the merciless savages."* " The characteristic mildness of American manners" † here underwent a surprising change; for which every one of our three editors has invented, what he no doubt conceives, an adequate apology. Mr. O'Connor declares it was " the invasion of New York by the British" ‡ that gave rise to the measure; thus tacitly admitting, that general Hull's invasion of Upper Canada, for which he had been preparing long previous to the declaration of war, justified *our* employment of the Indians. Mr. Thomson says, it was done " by way of intimidating the British and Indians, and of preventing a recurrence of their barbarities:" § and he has taken care to be provided with a flagrant case in support of his position. The clergyman is of opinion, that the Indian modes of warfare are not so much the objects of terror, as of horror; and declares that our employment of the Indians " rendered it expedient for the Americans to incorporate in their armies, the same kind of force, in order to

---

* See p. 180.   † Hist. of the United States, Vol. III. p. 238.
‡ Hist. of the War, 106.   § Sketches of the War, p. 153.

counteract the habitual stratagems of the savages, and defeat their insidious hostilities."* But this "fair and candid apology for the procrastinated alliance" * equally existed previous to the 4th of November, 1812; at which time " the use made by the enemy of the merciless savages under their influence rendered it expedient" for Mr. Madison to declare, that he " was making exertions to *dissuade* them from taking either side in the war."† The fact is, the American government would have employed the Indians at the commencement of hostilities, could it have held out to them any reasonable hopes of conquest or plunder, sufficient to overbalance that " deadly animosity which they felt towards the Americans," for reasons best known to the latter. The capture of York, and the possession of the forts, George and Erie, gave an air of reality to the boastings of the American generals; and the " Six Nations of Indians," described as " the Mohawks, Oneidas, Onondagoes, Senecas, Cayugas, and Tuscororas," or rather, a few stragglers from some of these nations, were persuaded to declare war against the provinces of Upper and Lower Canada.

In justice to the Indian character, we are bound to mention that, when our wise statesmen, at the peace of 1783, stipulated, by treaty, to surrender to the Americans the whole of the

* Hist. of the United States, Vol. III. p. 238. † See p. 180.

Indian country, all the Mohawks, and a part of the other five nations, abandoned their possessions; and, faithful to that alliance with us which they have never violated, settled in Upper Canada.

Mr. O'Connor has kindly favored us with the following

"DECLARATION OF WAR,
BY THE SIX NATIONS OF INDIANS.

"We, the chiefs and councillors of the Six Nations of Indians, residing in the State of New York, do hereby proclaim to all the war-chiefs and warriors of the Six Nations, that war is declared on our part, against the provinces of Upper and Lower Canada. Therefore, we do hereby command and advise all the war-chiefs to call forth immediately the warriors under them, and put them in motion, to protect their rights and liberties, which our brethren, the Americans, are now defending.

"BY THE GRAND COUNCILLORS."

Those who are acquainted with the language used in an Indian *talk*, can have no difficulty in guesing at the authors of this important state-paper, signed "by the great councillors." We could wish that equal publicity had been given to "the special covenant," by which, says doctor Smith, "the warriors of the Six Nations bound themselves to abstain from that barbarity towards the wounded and the dead, so congenial with their national habits, and so revolting to our civilized ideas."

The above declaration, although without a date, " issued immediately after the invasion of the state by the British;" and the first invasion of New York, the state in question, occured, as the reader knows, on the 22d of February.* Supposing, however, that the fourth act of invasion, colonel Clark's affair at Schlosser, gave *immediate* rise to the declaration; it must have issued on the 5th of July; and, therefore, could not have been occasioned by a case of barbarity, that, according to the relater, took place three days afterwards. Having rectified this mistake of Mr. Thomson, we shall now proceed to investigate his details of the affair itself. He states that on the 8th of July, lieutenant Eldridge, of the 13th regiment, was ordered to the support of the American outposts, with a small detachment of 39 men; and that his impetuosity "led him into a thick wood, where a superior force of the British and Indians lay in ambush, and that, after an obstinate but fruitless struggle, his party were entirely defeated, five only out of the whole number escaping. All the prisoners, including the wounded, were then inhumanly murdered, and their persons treated in so barbarous a manner that the

* See p. 136.

most temperate recital of the enemy's conduct may, perhaps, scarcely obtain belief. The same enemy," proceeds Mr. Thomson, " who had long ago implored the mercy of the American officer to be extended to his British prisoners, now fell upon the defenceless captives of his party, and scalped their heads whilst they were yet alive, split open their sculls with their tomahawks, tore their hearts out of their bodies, and stabbed and otherwise mutilated them. Lieutenant Eldridge was supposed to have experienced the same treatment. The inhabitants of the neighbourhood having informed the garrison that he had been led, wounded, into the woods, between two Indians, a flag was sent out on the next day, to ascertain his fate ; which soon after returned with an answer, that lieutenant Eldridge, having killed one of the Indian chieftains, the warriors of his tribe had retaliated this supposed act of treachery, by putting him to instant death. But this reply was ascertained to have been a subterfuge of the enemy, to evade the necessity of accounting for a prisoner who was known to have been taken alive."*

We have given this statement at length, for the purpose of shewing to what a pitch of horrid falsehood the malignant feelings of an American historian can lead him. The reader will be gratified to know, that not a British individual was

* Sketches of the War, p. 153.

present when this American invading party was surprised. Even Mr. O'Connor, the zealous Mr. O'Connor, confirms the fact. He explicitly states, that the lieutenant " unexpectedly found himself surrounded in the wood by *Indians*, who opened a deadly fire upon his little corps."* The word " Britith" no where appears in the account; nor even the expression " the enemy," so artfully inserted in Mr. Thomson's statement. We can gather from the " answer" returned, that the American lieutenant, after he had surrendered, took an opportnnity to kill " one of the Indian chieftains ;" and, for that " act of treachery," was, very properly, put to " instant death." This is designated in Mr. Thomson's *Index* to a work purporting to give " Sketches of the late War between the United States and Great Britain,"—" *Massacre of lieutenant Eldridge.*" Doctor Smith's entire silence upon the subject, satisfies us of his having received from some of his friends, the most satisfactory assurances, that the British did not in any shape participate in Mr. Thomson's " too well authenticated" charge against them.

The real case, indeed, was this. Some medicine-stores, of which the British were in immediate want, having been, upon their retreat from Fort-George, concealed in a spot, now close to an American outpost, the Indian chief, Black

* Hist. of the War, p. 106.

Bird, volunteerd, with 150 warriors, to bring them to the British camp. While performing this important service, he encountered, and captured, lieutenant Eldridge and his party. No sooner had the American lieutenant surrendered, than he drew forth a concealed pistol, and shot one of the chiefs through the head. The officer's life fell a sacrifice to his treachery; nor, can we wonder, if few of his men escaped to tell the tale.

This is the proper place to put the reader in possession of a fact, that will show how the British officers felt and acted, in reference to the cruel manner in which the Indians were wont to treat their prisoners. A committee, at the head of which was major-general Vincent, sat early in 1813, to devise the best means of putting an end to such barbarities; and finally resolved to pay to the Indians 10 dollars for every American prisoner they brought in alive. This proceeding was afterwards sanctioned by the prince regent. In the meanwhile, the British officers generally carried about them a supply of dollars, to enable them to put in practice so laudable a plan. Some account of the resolution appeared in a Boston paper; but none of the numerous Americans, officers as well as privates, whose lives and persons were saved in consequence, seem to have communicated any particulars to the furbishers of their exploits.

"Of the influence of a cultivated people," says doctor Smith, "whose manners and religion the savages respect, to induce them to resign their inhuman treatment of their prisoners, major Chapin gave an instructive example, immediately after uniting his force with the warriors of the Six Nations. A corps, composed of volunteer militia, and of these Indians, had completely put to the rout a party of the enemy in the vicinity of Fort-George. In a council held before the conflict, (for all things among them must be done by common consent,) the Indians, by his advice, agreed among themselves, besides the obligation of their general treaty, which they recognized, that no one should scalp or tomahawk prisoners, or employ towards them any species of savage inhumanity. Accordingly, after the battle, sixteen wounded captives were committed solely to their management; when, governed by a sacred regard to their covenant, and the benevolent advice of their commander, they exhibited as great magnanimity towards their fallen enemy, as they had shown bravery against their warring foe in battle."*

What could have possessed this American editor, when he,—and he alone has,—promulgated this fact? So, 16 British captives, writhing under the anguish of their yet bleeding wounds, were, by the orders of an American officer,

* History of the United States, Vol. III. p. 239.

"committed solely to the management" of a party of hostile Indians; to determine, by way of experiment, whether those " ruthless savages," that " faithless and perfidious race," would listen to the " *advice*" of their civilized " brethren," and " impose any restraints upon their known habits of warfare ;" or, whether they would scalp and otherwise torture their 16 captives as might best serve to glut " their demoniac thirst of blood." Even could the forbearance of the Indians have been religiously relied on by the American officer, what right had he thus to sport with the feelings of his prisoners? —Happily, amidst all that has been invented by the hirelings of the American government, to rouse the passions of the people, and gain over on their side the good wishes of other nations, no British officer stands charged with a crime half so heinous as that recorded to have been committed by the American major Chapin.

Following up colonel Clarke's exploit, lieutenant-colonel Bisshopp, taking with him, early on the morning of the 11th July, 20 of the royal artillery, 40 of the 8th, or king's, 100 of the 41st, and 40 of the 49th regiments; also about 40 of the 2d and 3d Lincoln militia,* amounting, in the whole, to 240 men, crossed the Niagara, below Black Rock; and moved up with great rapidity to the attack of that post. Two

* App. No. 41.

hundred American militia who had been stationed there, immediately fled; and the British took possession of the batteries, upon which eight guns were mounted. Four of these, two 12, and two 6-pounders, the British spiked; and they brought away one 12, and two 9-pounders, 177 muskets, some ammunition-kegs, round and case shot,* a considerable quantity of army-clothing, and other stores; also about 180 barrels of provisions, and seven large batteaux and one scow, in which the stores and provisions were contained.† The British likewise burnt a large schooner, and the blockhouse and barracks in the navy-yard, as well as those in the great battery.‡ "While the main body," says the *Buffaloe Gazette* of July 13, "was employed in thus disposing of the public property, a party entered many houses in the village; but we have not ascertained that they committed any outrages on private property." None of the American historians have thought it worth their while to record this fact.

Unfortunately, our troops were allowed to remain on shore longer than was prudent. A strong reinforcement of American regulars, militia, and Indians, under general Porter, arrived; and poured a destructive fire upon the British, as they were retiring to their boats. In consequence of this, we lost 15 men killed; lieu-

* App. No. 43.   † Ibid. No. 44.   ‡ Ibid. No. 41.

tenant-colonel Bisshopp, captain Saunders, and a lieutenant of the 41st, also 15 other officers and men, wounded. The gallant lieutenant-colonel Bisshopp had received three wounds; and died shortly after he returned to the Canada side. He was a promising young officer; not more than 27 years of age; and of a most amiable private character. The American loss was three killed, and five wounded. All the boats got clear off; but the British were compelled to leave behind, eight of their killed, and about six of their wounded, including captain Saunders. " Our savage friends," says the Buffaloe editor, " expressed a desire to scalp the dead, but were prevented." Here, then, it required some stronger arguments than " the influence of a cultivated people," " the *advice* of an American officer," or " the obligation of their general treaty," to restrain the Indians from committing their usual barbarities. Doctor Smith, having, in imitation of his brother historians, omitted to notice this fact, has had no occasion to rack his brains for an explanation.

The new American ship General Pike being completely equipped, and manned with a numerous crew, about 120 of whom had recently arrived from the Constitution, and the remainder from other ships lying in the Atlantic ports, commodore Chauncey, on the 26th of July, again appeared on the lake. His fleet now

consisted of 14 vessels, of the united burthen of
2721 tons; mounting altogether 114 guns, and
manned with 1193 seamen.* At this time, sir
James Yeo, with his fleet, which was just one-
third inferior to Chauncey's,† was lying in
Kingston, and had its movements watched by
two of the American schooners, stationed off
Sackett's Harbor. Commodore Chauncey's first
object was the destruction of a depôt of stores
and provisions at Burlington Heights. For that
purpose, he took on board at Niagara "about 300
regulars,"‡ under lieutenant-colonel Scott, according to sir George Prevost, "an unexchanged
prisoner of war on his parole;"§ and, on the
morning of the 30th, landed the troops, along
with a party of sailors and marines. But major
Maule's detachment, which amounted to no more
than 150 rank and file, was voted to consist of
" from 6 to 800 regulars, strongly intrenched,
and defended by about eight pieces of cannon;¶
and commodore Chauncey re-embarked his men
and the troops, as soon as they had made prisoners of some of the unarmed inhabitants of the
neighbourhood.

Commodore Chauncey was informed by the
prisoners, that the whole of the regulars stationed at York had, since the preceding even-

* James's Naval Occurrences, p. 298. † Ibid. p 297.
‡ Sketches of the War, p. 155. § App. No. 45.
¶ Hist. of the War, p. 110.

ing, marched to reinforce major Maule. This intelligence, coupled with his knowledge that the York militia were still bound by the parole which had been exacted of them by himself and general Dearborn, about three months previous,* determined the commodore to pay a second visit to York. The public was not supposed to know these facts; and, considering the small number of troops engaged in the enterprise, a successful attack upon the "capital of Upper Canada" would read well in the newspapers, and give additional *eclât* to the measures of the government.

Accordingly, about four o'clock on the afternoon of the 31st, the two ships, Pike and Madison, and the brig Oneida, came to anchor off York; while the nine schooners, with the troops under colonel Scott, reinforced by the marines of the fleet, stood into the harbor, and disembarked the whole at the garrison, as was expected, "without opposition."† The Americans then marched boldly into the town; of which, it being utterly defenceless for the reason already given, they took quiet possession. They opened the goal, liberated the prisoners, and, among them, three soldiers confined for felony. They then proceeded to the hospital, and parolled the few men that could not be removed. The store-houses of some inhabit-

* See p. 149.   † Hist. of the War, p. 111.

MAJOR GEN.^L WINFIELD SCOTT.

of the United States Army.

Engraved for the Analectic Magazine Published by M. Thomas.
Entered according to Act of Congress 25 Octr 1814.

ants, called "public store-houses,"* were next entered; and "several hundred barrels of flour and provisions" taken therefrom. About 11 o'clock on the same evening, the Americans, with their booty, returned to their vessels. On the next morning, Sunday, they again landed; and three armed boats went a short way up the Don in search of public stores. By evening, having captured or destroyed "five pieces of cannon, eleven boats, and a quantity of shot, shells, and other stores,"† the American troops and marines re-embarked; and the fleet made sail for Niagara.

Breaking parole is a serious charge to prefer against a national officer; one, especially, so high in rank as a lieutenant-colonel. All lists of prisoners, made, paroled, or exchanged, must necessarily be transmitted to the commander-in-chief; and sir George had, on the 13th of November, 1812, by one of his aides de camp, entered into an agreement with major-general Dearborn, relative to prisoners of war: in which agreement it was particularly stipulated,— "That prisoners on parole, of either party, should perform no military service whatever."‡ Even without this agreement, every officer, before he receives his parole, engages his honor, not to bear arms directly or *indirectly*, until

* Hist. of the War, p. 111. † Ibid.
‡ Wilkinson's Mem. Vol. III. p. 197.

regularly exchanged. The following is a copy of the parole signed by lieutenant George Reab, along with some other American officers, on the 19th of November, 1812.

"*Quebec.*

" We promise, on honor, not to bear arms, directly or indirectly, against his Britannic majesty, or his allies, during the present war, until we are regularly exchanged. We, likewise, engage, that the undermentioned non-commissioners and privates, soldiers in the service of the United States, who are permitted to accompany us, shall conform to the same conditions."*

To the doughty quarrel between Mr. President Madison and general James Wilkinson of the American army, we are indebted for some most important disclosures relative to paroled prisoners. The general very candidly tells us, that lieutenant George Reab, a witness examined on the part of the prosecution at the general's court-martial, held at Troy in the state of New York, in February, 1814, deposed on oath, " That on the 24th of December, 1813, while a prisoner on parole, he received from colonel Larned, an order to repair to Greenbush, in the following words:

" I am directed by the secretary of war, to

*'Wilkinson's Mem. Vol. III. p. 197.

call in all the American prisoners of war, on parole, at or near this vicinity, to their post, and that the officers join them for drilling, &c. You will, therefore, repair to the cantonments at Greenbush, without loss of time."

Lieutenant Reab further deposed, that he repaired to Greenbush in pursuance of the order, and made no objections to doing duty: that on general Wilkinson's arrival at Waterford, in the ensuing January, lieutenant Reab called upon him, and exhibited the order received from lieutenant-colonel Larned: that general Wilkinson thought the order very improper, and afterwards issued the following order, dated Waterford, January 18th, 1814:

"A military officer is bound to obey promptly, and without hesitation, every order he may receive, which does not affect his honor; but this precious inheritance must never be voluntarily forfeited, nor should any earthly power wrest it from him. It follows that, when an officer is made prisoner, and released on his parole of honor, not to bear arms against the enemy, no professional duties can be imposed on him, while he continues in that condition; and, under such circumstances, every military man will justify him for disobedience."*

Such are the principles upon which Mr. Madison conducted the late war!—Lieutenant-colonel

* Wilkinson's Memoirs, Vol. III. p. 93.

Scott, although, perhaps, not one of those American officers who, like lieutenant Reab, "made no objections to doing duty," in compliance with the shameful order of his government, did certainly give his parole at Queenstown, and yet subsequently appeared in arms, both at Fort-George and at York. It has, by British officers, been stated, that it was done in the belief that he had been virtually exchanged. Colonel (now major-general) Scott has been represented as a brave officer. To merit that character, he must be an honorable man; and would not, surely, have again unsheathed his sword, had he not felt himself justified in doing so. We take pleasure in mentioning, that lieutenant Carr, of the United States' army, also a prisoner at Queenstown, "declined obeying the order to perform duty, on the ground, that it was contrary to his parole."*—This meritorious act being, as it would appear, an excepted case, enhances its value; and it ought to operate as a lesson to that government, which could thus stab the reputation of its officers, to faciltate the means of conquest.

* Wilkinson's Mem. Vol. III. p. 93.

CHAPTER VIII.

Description of Lake Champlain—Gross error in the boundary line—Garrison at Isle aux Noix—Want of a naval force—Early naval preparations of the Americans—Capture of two American armed cutters—Expedition to Plattsburg, Swanton, and Champlain-town—American calumnies refuted—Appearance of the British off Burlington—Commodore Macdonough's cautious behaviour—Sudden reduction of the British naval force on this lake—Immediate advance of the American flotilla—Capture of a gun-boat and batteaux on the St. Lawrence—Rival fleets on Lake Ontario—Sickness of the British and American troops on the Niagara-frontier—Demonstration upon Fort-George—Contemplated expedition against Montreal—Preparations for it—Alarm of the garrison at Fort-George—American settlers—Departure of the expedition from Fort-George—Its difficulties, and arrival at the point of rendezvous—Contemporary movement of the British at the head of the lake.

NEW scenes of border-warfare carry us to one of the North-American lakes, of which we have hitherto given no description. Lake Champlain divides the north-east part of the state of New York from that of Vermont. It is about 80 miles in length, 18 miles in its broadest, and little more than one mile in its narrowest part: its mean width is about six miles. At the north-end its waters are discharged by the Richlieu, a river about 50 miles long, into the St. Lawrence; but the navigation is completely obstructed by shoals and rapids.

Lake Champlain belongs to the United States; the line of demarcation, owing to the ignorance or pusilanimity of the British commissioners employed in 1783, intersecting the Richlieu, at the distance of several miles down its course from the lake. The Canadians are, therefore, not only shut out from the lake, but from all water-communication with their own territory bordering on Missisqui Bay, formed by a tongue of land to the eastward. This they fully experienced, during the continuance of the several embargoes that preceded the war; when the American gun-boats, stationed at the foot of the lake, prevented the rafts of timber from being floated out of the bay, for passage down the river. And, in March, 1814, the Americans had in contemplation to establish, on Rouse's-point, at the entrance of the Richlieu, a heavy battery; that would have commanded the river, and blockaded the flotilla which we *then* thought of constructing for service on the lake.

The only military post possessed by the British in the neighbourhood of Lake Champlain is Isle aux Noix, a small island, containing only 85 acres, situate on the Richlieu; distant about 10 miles from the boundary line, and about 40, across the country, from Montreal. On Isle aux Noix are two or three well-constructed forts; besides several block-houses at the different assailable points. The garrison, in the summer of 1813, consisted of detachments of the 13th and 100th regiments, recently arrived from Quebec, and a small party of royal artillery, under the temporary command of major Taylor of the 100th.* The only British armed vessels at this port were three gun-boats, which had been built at Quebec, by the orders of the late governor, sir James Craig, and transported over land to St. John's, a town on the Richlieu, about eight miles below Isle aux Noix.

The Americans, with their usual foresight, had, soon after the commencement of the war, armed and equipped some vessels for the service of Lake Champlain. On the morning of the 1st of June, two sloops, or cutters, manned from the American ships on the seaboard, and commanded by lieutenant Sidney Smith, formerly of the Chesapeake frigate, entered the Richlieu, and crossed the line, to display themselves to the British at Isle aux Noix. The instant the

* App. No. 46.

headmost vessel was seen from the garrison, major Taylor ordered under weigh the three gun-boats, each having on board, besides her Canadian crew, three artillery-gunners. Soon afterwards the second American vessel came in sight; and the gun-boats commenced firing. To aid them in an attack against so very superior a force, major Taylor left the island in two batteaux and two row-boats; and ordered their crews, consisting of a small detachment of troops, to land on each side of the river, and fire on the enemy, then within the range of musketry. After a spirited action of three hours and a half, in which we had three men wounded; one severely by a grape-shot,* and the Americans one man killed, and eight men wounded, the two United States' sloops, Growler and Eagle, manned with 50 men each, all of whom, except the killed man, were taken prisoners; and armed, between them, with two Columbiad† 18-pounders, 10 long 6-pounders, and 10 18-pound carronades, total 22 guns,‡ fell into the hands of the three Canadian gun-boats, and their assistants on shore.

These sloops were a most valuable acquisition to us, and their loss occasioned a proportionate mortification to the Americans. We can, therefore, spare the latter the consolation they

* App. No. 46.   † James's Naval Occurrences, p. 5.
‡ App. No. 47.

derived from the bombastic accounts given of their capture. One editor says, it was effected by a detachment of the enemy, and "a number of gun-boats;" leaving the reader to fix, either 10, or 50, according to the temperature of his patriotism. Another editor declares, that "four other gun-boats" came to the assistance of the first; but, like a zealous naval writer, denies that the military contributed any thing to the capture; thus:—"They, (the two sloops,) however, continued an incessant and heavy fire; and kept the enemy on shore at such a respectable distance, that their fire had no effect."*—What defence these vessels were capable of making may be gathered, not only from their weight of metal and number of men, as already described, but from their formidable state of equipment, as exhibited in the "Return of ordnance, ammunition, and ordnance stores," subjoined to major Taylor's letter.† Neither of these 11-gun sloops carried more than 50 men, nor exceeded 110 tons; yet each of them had on board more cutlasses, and more axes and boarding-pikes, than a British 18-gun brig, of 121 men, and 385 tons.

The fortunate possession of these sloops, named, at first, the Broke and Shannon, but subsequently altered to the Chubb and Finch,

* Naval Monument, p. 256. † App. No. 47.
‡ James's Naval Occurr. p. 276.

suggested the idea of sending against the American ports on the borders of Lake Champlain a combined naval and military expedition. No seamen being at this time at Isle aux Noix, and none to be spared from Lake Ontario, the commander of H. M. brig Wasp, then lying at Quebec, gallantly volunteered, with himself and crew, to man the two sloops and gun-boats, and try to provoke commodore Macdonough, at the head of his very superior naval force, to a struggle for the ascendancy on the lake.

For the purpose of carrying into effect the intended operations along the shores, about 1000 officers and men, of the 13th and 100th regiments, under the command of lieutenant-colonel Murray, inspecting field-officer of militia, embarked at Isle aux Noix on the 29th of July, in the Broke, Shannon, three gun-boats, and about 40 batteaux provided for the purpose. The flotilla arrived, on the next day, at the American town of Plattsburg; where the troops landed, and, after frightening away, by their looks, about 400 militia, proceeded to fulfil the object of their mission. They burnt the state-arsenal, Pike's encampment, several block-houses, the extensive barracks at Saranac, (three miles off,) capable of containing 4000 troops, and every building belonging to the United States between the latter place and Plattsburg. After performing this laborious task, the troops re-embarked; carrying away with them a quantity of naval stores, shot, and equipments for a large number of batteaux. An Albany (United States) writer states the value of the public buildings destroyed at Plattsburg at 33,300 dollars. A party of the British next proceeded to Swanton, Vermont, near the head of Missisqui Bay: there they also destroyed the barracks and public stores, as well as several batteaux lying at the wharf; and then re-embarked.

Ere we accompany the expedition to its next point of landing, it behoves us to get rid of those calumnies which the American editors have heaped upon the British troops for their alleged ill-conduct at Plattsburg. Mr. Thomson contents himself with the general charge, as applicable to all the visited towns, of our " committing every species of depredation upon the property of the inhabitants."* Mr. O'Connor, aware of his forte, is far more explicit. He says: " The destruction of private property was not limited to such as they could eat, drink, and carry away, but furniture, which could not be of any use to the plunderers, was wantonly destroyed;—tables, bureaus, clocks, desks, cupboards, and crockery, were cut and broken to pieces, and thrown about the houses: books and writings were torn to pieces,

* History of the War, p. 156.

and scattered about the streets."* This industrious gentleman next charges us with excesses, " enormous, cruel, and wanton, in a high degree:"* rape and ravishment follow; and then we are dismissed with the honorable epithets of " faithless ruffians, unprincipled invaders."*

Of all the editors of " prints known to be friendly to the war,"† Mr. O'Connor, assuredly, deserves to be the best rewarded by the American government. If he is not already provided for, we do most strongly recommend him to the president's notice. But for an accidental glance at an American newspaper, as we suppose, *not* " friendly to the war," we should have been puzzled to produce any answer to so serious a charge, beyond, founded on the positive assertions of the officers employed, the most unqualified negation. Of two writers from Burlington, distant 24 miles only from Plattsburg, one says: " We have not heard of any private property being destroyed, and our accounts are to a late hour last night;"‡ the other says: " They have done no injury to private property."‡

On the 3d of August a detachment of the 100th regiment, under the command of captain Elliot, landed at Champlain-town, where the British destroyed two block-houses, and the

* History of the War. p. 134. † See p. 162.
‡ Boston Paper, Aug. 6, 1813.

commissary's stores. This was done without opposition, as no troops were in the village, and the inhabitants remained quiet. On the day previous captain Everard, with his own sloop, the Broke, the Shannon, captain Pring, and one gun-boat,* had proceeded off Burlington, an American post-town to the southward of the lake, distant 24 miles from Plattsburg. Mr. O'Connor says, the British fired into the town for some time, but that no considerable damage was done; also, that they, on the same evening, proceeded to Shelburne, four or five miles south of Burlington, where they burnt a sloop, having on board about 400 barrels of flour. After admitting that "the United States' troops at Burlington, under command of major-general Hampton, consisted of about 4000 men,"† Mr. O'Connor gravely tells us, that the general's "limited force did not justify his detaching any part of his troops;" and, as if to hit the poor general still harder, adds, "the marauding enemy wisely retired, before reinforcements could have arrived."†

By way of apologizing for British vessels being allowed thus to traverse, in active hostility, a lake belonging wholly to the United States, Mr. O'Connor says: "Commodore Macdonough had not a sufficient number of seamen to man his

* App. No. 49.   † History of the War, p. 135.

sloops, and would be highly reprehensible had he been defeated in an attempt to recover the ascendancy."* ' That commodore Macdonough had, however, no scarcity of seamen to complain of, may be inferred from the previous statements on the subject in the American newspapers; the easy transit from New York to Burlington, where the commodore's vessels lay; † and, above all, from the fact of his having sent, to cruize on the lake, when he had no enemy to fear, two of his flotilla so plentifully, if not lavishly, supplied with " seamen." Captain Everard, on the forenoon of the 2d, appeared close off commodore Macdonough's position, and observed two sloops, similar in size and force to those he had with him, " ready for sea," and another, somewhat larger, taking in her guns; also two gun-boats lying under the protection of 10 guns, mounted on a bank 100 feet high; two scows mounting one gun each, as floating batteries, and several field-pieces on the shore. Without the sloop that was equipping, the commodore had one gun-boat and two scows more than his one-armed adversary; ‡ who, after approaching as near to the batteries as was safe,

* Hist. of the War, p. 133.

† Burlington is 150 miles from Albany; thence, down the Hudson, it is 160 miles (performed by the steam-boats in 36 hours) to New York.

‡ Captain Everard had lost an arm, and is since dead.

stood out; and, not doubting he should provoke the American commodore to get under weigh, captured and destroyed four American vessels under his very nose. Vain were those gallant efforts. Too much risk would attend an encounter; and American caution was not to be entrapped.

After a diligent search for some better excuse for commodore Macdonough's forbearance, than was furnished by Mr. O'Connor, we find one, consisting of *three* words only, copied into all the American histories of the late war that have passed through our hands. These three magical words are—" sloops of war ;"* by which we are to understand, that the two late American sloops, or cutters, " Eagle and Growler,"† did, in a few days after they got into our possession, become metamorphosed into the size, force, and appearance of " two large sloops of war ;"‡ and commodore Macdonough actually finds it convenient, at a subsequent day, to confess himself the victim of the same delusion.§

Foiled in his hopes, and not willing to remain where his services would languish for want of a competitor, captain Everard returned, with his crew, to Quebec; leaving, in charge of the " two

* Sketches of the War, p. 165; and Hist. of the War, p. 133.
† Hist. of the War, p. 133.
‡ Nav. Hist. of the United States, Vol. I. p. 232.
§ James's Nav. Occur. p. 420.

large sloops of war" and three gun-boats at Isle aux Noix, captain Pring and about 18 seamen. Judging of what a small British naval force at this station might have done, from what it did do, who can refrain from wishing that the Wasp brig had been broken up at Quebec; or any other means devised, so as to have retained captain Everard and his gallant ship's company upon Lake Champlain?

Scarcely had commodore Macdonough been apprized of the final departure of his troublesome visitor, than, with his vessels all of a sudden fully manned, he sallied forth from his strong position, and swaggered across the lake. Had this important event been communicated to the public in a blustering newspaper-paragraph, no one, except an American, would have given it a second thought. But, above all things, who could expect it would have been made the subject of an official letter? For the honor of the cloth, we will suppose, that commodore Macdonough was ordered, by the war department, to dress up a story,* that should calm the fears of the inhabitants around the lake, as well as enable major-general Hampton to keep his soldiers within their ranks, preparatory to the great expedition on foot. We observe the word " advantage," as addressed to captain Pring's mighty force at Isle aux Noix. When the reader

* Appendix, No. 50.

knows that, three weeks previous to the date of this most important official document, commodore Macdonough had under his command four sloops, such as *he* would call " sloops of war," two gun-boats, and six scows, mounting altogether "48 guns,"* he will have no difficulty in deciding which party had an " advantage" to boast of.

Quitting, for busier scenes in the west, the waters of Lake Champlain, our course up the St. Lawrence is arrested by a little affair, for which the most cursory notice would have sufficed, had not the American editors, in compliment to their home-readers, conferred upon it a few embellishments of their own. On the 15th or 16th of July, two boats from commodore Chauncey's fleet at Sackett's Harbor, each armed with a 16-pounder,† and manned with 50 sailors, besides 20 soldiers furnished for the occasion by general Lewis, were sent to cruize in the St. Lawrence. On the following day they succeeded in capturing a British gun-boat of the second class; carrying, by one American account, "a 6-pound carronade," and by another " a 24-pounder," along with her convoy, fifteen batteaux, laden with 230 barrels of pork, 300 bags of pilot-bread, and some ammunition; and bound from Montreal to Kingston. The prisoners taken, consisting chiefly of Canadian boatmen, are stated to have amounted to 67.†

* Nav. Hist. of the U. S. Vol. I. p. 233.   † Nav. Mon. p. 262.

As soon as intelligence of this event reached Kingston, three gun-boats, commanded by lieutenant Scott, R. N. with a detachment of the 100th regiment, under captain Martin, proceeded to intercept the American party, together with the captured gun-boat and batteaux. Lieutenant Scott, having ascertained that they had gone into Goose Creek, on the American side of the river, pushed for that place; but the evening being too far advanced, it became necessary to defer the intended attack till the next morning. During the night the British were reinforced by another gun-boat, and a detachment of the 41st regiment under major Frend. This officer now assumed the command; and, at three o'clock, proceeded up the creek, in the hope of gaining the enemy's position by dawn of day. But it was soon discovered, that the Americans had removed higher up the creek, where the channel became so narrow that the gun-boats could not use their oars, nor turn so as to bring their guns to bear upon the banks. Their further progress up the creek was obstructed by large trees felled across the stream. In the attempt to remove these impediments, the British were fired upon from the two American sloops, and from a gun in a log-fort which the enemy had erected on the left bank, as well as from musketry fired out of a thick wood, on the same side of the creek;

the whole rendering the enemy's position a very strong one.

A detachment of troops had been landed on the right bank; whence it was found impracticable to reach the enemy's position. These troops immediately returned, and embarked in the sternmost boats, to cross over to the left bank; but, from the swampy nature of the soil, no fit place for landing could be found. The leading boat being exposed to a heavy and galling fire, and having so many of her crew wounded, as to check the fire of her gun, the only one that could be brought to bear on the enemy, the troops, led by lieutenant Fawcett, leaped into the water; and, carrying their arms and ammunition over their heads, succeeded in gaining the land. Here they drove the Americans, and compelled them, with precipitation, to seek shelter within a log entrenchment; but their encreasing numbers, the natural strength of their position, and the impracticability of any co-operation by the gun-boats, induced major Frend to order the re-embarkation of the troops. The British lost one gunner, and three soldiers of the 41st, killed; a midshipman, 12 soldiers, and four seamen, wounded; together with captain Milnes, one of sir George Prevost's aides de camp, who had just arrived from head-quarters to procure intelligence of the expedition. The American loss is no where mentioned; not even by Mr.

O'Connor; who has the effrontery, however, to declare, that the British loss, in " killed alone, was from 40 to 60."

Pursuing the thread of our military narrative, we again arrive at the western end of Lake Ontario. Since our departure thence, early in July, the naval operations on this lake have assumed a more imposing aspect; and, although we can refer to nothing decisive, commodore Chauncey's *losing* " victories," and sir James Yeo's *gaining* " defeats," (so amply detailed in our naval volume,*) cannot fail to interest the novice in American history. Major-general Wilkinson, in a letter to the American secretary of war, written about this time, bestows upon the British naval commander an epithet, than which, even in the opinion of well-informed Americans, none can be found more appropriate to himself and his friend the commodore. " If," says the general, " sir James Yeo comes out, I shall have the pleasure to see Chauncey give the *vapouring dog* a sound drubbing."†

Since the latter end of July major-general De Rottenburg had removed his army still nearer to Fort-George; and now held his head-quarters at the village of St. David, about seven miles distant. His advance posts occupied a position not four miles from the American entrenchment.

* James's Nav. Occurr. p. 297.
† Wilkinson's Mem. Vol. III. App. No. 29.

About this time that debilitating malady, the fever and ague, shewed itself in the British camp, where the number of troops, altogether, was far too inconsiderable, to admit of any, the slightest reduction. In some measure to counterbalance this, the proximity of the Americans to the river, their crowded state, and constant fears of attack, subjected them, also, to the ravages of sickness. According to an official return of regular troops at Fort-George and Niagara, towards the end of July, the aggregate number attached to the station was between 6 and 7000. Of these about 1100 were sick, and about 1600 absent, either on furlough or detached services; leaving, fit for duty, "3835 men." Admit about 300 of these to have been stationed at the opposite fort of Niagara; and there were, under major-general Boyd's command, at Fort-George, and the entrenched camp outside, full 3500 effective regular troops; while we had, threatening them on all sides, fewer than 2100 rank and file; including a numerous list of sick.

During the month of August, a few immaterial affairs of piquets occurred, in which both sides sustained some slight losses; and wherein, also, according to Mr. Thomson, "the character of the American arms was not in the least diminished."* About the 20th sir George Prevost arrived at the British encampment; and deter-

* Sketches of the War, p. 158.

mined to try the effect of a demonstration upon Fort-George. Accordingly, at day-break, on the 24th, a sudden attack was made by the British advanced troops upon all the piquets stationed in front of the American entrenchments. After a smart fire, the Americans, except about 50 or 60, got safe back to their works; carrying with them a captain of the 49th and 10 privates, whose ardor had led them too far in advance.

Mr. Thomson tells us, that the British forces gained possession of the town of Newark, and skirted the woods opposite Fort-George, within gun-shot of the American camp; also that brigadier-general Williams, who had a few days before arrived at that post, advanced from the works with his brigade; but, after a trifling skirmish was ordered back by general Boyd, and the troops were directed to act only on the defensive. "The British," proceeds Mr. Thomson, "soon after retired to their entrenchments, then about two miles distant. The capture of captain Fitzgerald and his men, was the only loss which the enemy is known to have sustained."* On the contrary, general Boyd found out, that we left " about 15 dead on the different grounds;" and, far from admitting a defeat, or noticing our re-possession of Newark, pompously concludes his despatch: " His force is withdrawn, out of our reach, into his strong holds."

* Sketches of the War, p. 158.

About this time major-general Wilkinson arrived at Sackett's Harbor, to take the command of the troops upon the American northern frontier; having under his immediate command at the harbor 2829 rank and file, and upon the whole line, 14,832 officers and men, of the regular army.* His direction were, to attack Kingston; if successful there, or if unlooked-for difficulties should render an attack unadvisable, he was to make a similar attempt upon Montreal: towards both of which objects commodore Chauncey was to lend his powerful co-operation. Soon after the general's arrival at Sackett's Harbor, he submitted the views of his government to a council of his officers; who, after mature consideration, determined as follows:—
"To rendezvous the whole of the troops on the lake in this vicinity, and in co-operation with our squadron, to make a bold feint upon Kingston; slip down the St. Lawrence; lock up the enemy in our rear to starve or surrender, or oblige him to follow us without artillery, baggage, or provisions, or eventually to lay down his arms; to sweep the St. Lawrence of armed craft; and, in concert with the division of major-general Hampton, to take Montreal."†

While general Wilkinson was at Sackett's Harbor, disciplining his troops and maturing his plans, he received information of the

* Wilkinson's Mem. Vol. III. p. 346.   † Ibid App. No. 1.

departure of both sir George and sir James from Kingston; leaving there a force of only " 1500 regulars, and 500 militia." In a letter to the secretary of war, he declares he would make a real attack on that post, could he " have mustered 3000 combatants, with transports to bear them." This is a specimen of that caution, which contributed, more than our few troops and weak batteries, to the salvation of the Canadas. Acting upon the same principle in his contemplated attack upon Montreal, the general hoped, by making feints to the westward, and by practising other " military deceptions," to reduce the number of his opponents within Mr. Secretary Armstrong's advised proportion.*

In the hot pursuit of his plans of subjugation, the general arrived at Fort-George on the 4th of September. Here he met with an unexpected check, in the sickness of a part of the troops, and the deficiency of transports to convey them to the point of rendezvous. He was still further delayed, by " the equivocal relation and unsettled superiority of the adverse squadrons;" for which he had to thank, not less the *vapouring* behaviour of his friend the commodore, than the bold measures and masterly manœuvres of his friend's opponent.

Early in September sir George returned to

* See p. 133.

Kingston, leaving major-general De Rottenburg in command of the troops before Fort-George. By this time, sickness had committed dreadful ravages among both officers and men. Intelligence of that event soon reached the American government; and, when the secretary of war was required to sanction the opinion given by a council held at Fort-George, on the 20th of September, that the works ought to be razed, and the place abandoned, he returned for answer, that Fort-George might be maintained; adding: " If the enemy's sick list amounts to 1400 out of 3000, they can undertake nothing with effect."* He then informs the general, of a proposition for raising, on the Niagara line, before the 1st of October, a volunteer-force of 1200 men, " exclusive of Indians," who, " with a train of artillery," says he, " are to be authorized to invade the enemy's territory." He further informs him, that a reinforcement of militia-forces will be sent, to replace the regulars destined for the expedition.

Towards the end of September a deserter from us went into Fort-George, with, as the best passport he could carry, the following note, addressed to a " Major V. Huych, 13th regiment."—" Every movement of the army is either an immediate attack or retreat: about 2270 strong." This piece of intelligence was penned

* Wilkinson's Mem. Vol. III. App. No. 32.

by an American settler, named Hopkins; afterwards hung, for this and other traitorous acts, or, as his countryman goodnaturedly says, "for his attachment to the United States."* This reminds us of the memorial presented to congress, at the conclusion of the war, by general Porter, on behalf of Abraham Markle, Gideon Frisbie, and their associates, survivors of the corps of Canadian volunteers," praying for a tract of land, in size proportionate to their several losses, &c.—An American writer from Washington has taken great pains to enforce the claims of this " generous, brave, and enterprising corps of men, raised," says he, " by the gallant, and ever-to-be-lamented colonel Willcocks, whose every impulse was in unison with the noblest feelings of humanity."† This "ever-to-be-lamented" traitor was a native of Ireland, and had been a member of the provincial assembly.

Mr. Secretary Armstrong's account of the British sick before Fort-George was not at all over-rated; although his account of the British force evidently was. The latter, fit for duty, amounted, towards the end of September, to about 2290 rank and file. On the other hand, we find the American force at Fort-George and Niagara, on the 19th of the same month,

* Wilkinson's Mem. Vol. III. p. 398.
† Col. Journal, Vol. I. p. 97.

stated at 4587 officers and men, including 1165 sick.* Deducting the latter, also the odd hundreds to allow for the garrison at Fort-Niagara, there were at Fort-George 3000 effective American regulars. At the time of the alarm created by Mr. Hopkins's billet, and which occurred ten days subsequent to the date of the above returns, (since which, the health of the men had been gradually amending,*) two columns of troops, one commanded by major-general Wilkinson, the other by major-general Boyd, actually marched out of the camp, and formed in its front and rear. What an opportunity was here for deciding the fate of Upper Canada!—Fortunately for the upper, and perhaps for the lower, province too, there existed, on an island about 200 miles down the St. Lawrence, a *will o' th' wisp*, that captivated the senses of these tyro-warriors; and, after dragging them, against wind, rain, and snow,† through the whole length of an angry lake, down foaming rapids, and amidst showers of " teazing" bullets, cast them on shore, jaded in body and broken in spirit, the reproach of their country, and the laughing-stock of those whose soil they were hastening to invade.

The commencing particulars of this "ill-fated" expedition we shall now proceed to detail. It should first be mentioned, that the

* Wilkinson's Mem. Vol. III. p. 281.   † Ibid, p. 289.

original plan had been altered to the actual capture of Kingston and Prescott, previous to the main attack upon Montreal. The knapsacks of the troops filled with "winter-clothing," transports at the beach waiting to receive, and a powerful fleet in sight on the lake ready to protect them; also, the long-expected 1500 New York militia arrived in the fort to assist the 23d regiment, about 600 strong, in repelling an attack, the first embarkation took place on the 28th of September; but, scarcely had the expedition proceeded ten miles beyond Niagara-point, when that "vapouring dog" sir James shewed himself, and led the commodore a sad dance.* Without waiting till the two fleets (as presently happened) "went out of sight," the troops hurried back as fast as oars and sails could drive them. It was upon their return, that the two generals made the demonstration which we have already noticed.

On the 1st of October the commodore returned to Niagara; and, having promised general Wilkinson, by letter, that he would do his best " to keep the enemy in check in this part of the lake, or effect his destruction," the troops were allowed to re-embark. Bad weather drove many of the boats into Twelve-mile Creek. The expedition again moved forward; and, after buffeting with a severe storm, in which several of the boats

* James's Naval Occurrences, p. 301.

were wrecked, arrived, about noon, on the 7th, at Oswego. Here the gale detained the expedition till the 13th; when it again appeared on the lake, and, after suffering from cold, wind, and rain, reached Henderson's Bay, in the neighbourhood of Sackett's Harbor. Leaving the American soldiers to dry their cloaths, and ponder upon the perils they are doomed to encounter, we hasten back to see what effect this sudden movement of the enemy produced upon the British army stationed before Fort-George.

At no loss to divine that some point on the St. Lawrence was to be the devoted spot, major-general De Rottenburg, on the 2d of October, commenced his march for Kingston, with the 104th and 49th regiments; the latter of which, as a proof how the whole division was still suffering from sickness, could muster, fit for duty, no more than 16, out of about 50, commissioned officers. Unfortunately, the two flank companies of De Watteville's regiment, proceeding from York on the same destination, by water-carriage, fell into the hands of commodore Chauncey. Major-general Vincent now resumed the command of the British troops upon the Niagara; where we will leave him, for the present, to attend to major-general Proctor and his little army, in their proceedings along the north-western frontier.

CHAPTER IX.

Advance of major-general Proctor—Augmentation of the American north-western army—Description of Fort-Stephenson—Gallant assault upon it—American masked battery—Defeat of the British—Major-general Proctor's return to Sandwich—Arrival of the remainder of the 1st battalion 41st regiment—Accumulated number of Indians—Scarcity of provisions on the Detroit frontier—Wretched state of captain Barclay's fleet—Effects of its capture upon the right division—Hardships endured by the troops—General Harrison's newly-raised army—Its entry into Amherstburg, and pursuit of major-general Proctor up the Thames—Losses of the British on the retreat—Their defeat near the Moravian village—Remarks on sir George Prevost's general order—Escape of major-general Proctor—Loss of territory arising from the defeat of the British—American rejoicings—Death and character of Tecumseh—Anecdotes respecting him—Description of the scalping-operation—Barbarities committed upon Tecumseh's body—American disrespect to a flag of truce—Imprisonment of British officers along with convicts.

MAJOR-GENERAL Proctor, having been reinforced with nearly the whole of the remaining effective strength of the 41st regiment, as well as rejoined by the Indians who had abandoned him, for a while, after the battle of the Miami,* advanced from Sandwich, on the 20th of July, for the purpose of recommencing hostilities against the American north-western army. In the mean while, the American goverment, still acting upon the principle, that " nothing ought, if possible, to be left to chance," had almost drained of resources the hitherto prolific western states; so that major-general Harrison, assisted by commodore Perry and his formidable fleet, might be able to finish the campaign in this quarter, in time to be one in the scramble for laurels among his brother-generals to the eastward.

The American head-quarters were at Seneca-town, near to Sandusky Bay on Lake Erie. Fort-Meigs, already so strong, had its works placed in a still more vigorous state of defence; and a fort had since been constructed on the west-side of Sandusky river, about 40 miles from its mouth, and 10 from the general's head-quarters. It stood on a rising ground, commanding the river to the east; having a plane to the north and south, and a wood to the west. The body of the fort was about 100 yards in length, and 50 in breadth; surrounded, outside of all, by a row of strong pickets, 12 feet over

* See p. 201.

ground; each picket armed at the top with a *bayonet*.* Next to, and against this formidable picket was an embankment, forming the side of a dry ditch, 12 feet wide, by seven feet deep; then a second embankment, or glacis. A strong bastion and two block-houses completely enfiladed the ditch. Within the fort were the hospital, military and commissary's store-houses, magazine, &c. As far as we can collect from the American accounts, the fort mounted but one 6-pounder; and that in a masked battery at the north-western angle. The number of troops composing the garrison cannot exactly be ascertained. One American account states, that the *effective* force did not amount to 160 men, or rank and file.

Major-general Proctor, when he landed near the mouth of Sandusky river, on the 1st of August, had, it is admitted, no other white troops with him than the 41st regiment. An American editor says, that the major-general, previous to his appearance on the Sandusky, had detached " Tecumseh, with 2000 warriors, and a few regulars, to make a diversion favorable to the attack upon Fort-Stephenson;"† and yet the same editor states major-general Proctor's force before that fort, on the evening of the 1st, at " 500 regulars, and 700 Indians."† Of the latter there were but 200; and they, as was

* Hist. of the War, p. 131. † Sketches of the War, p. 161.

generally their custom when the object of assault was a fortified place, withdrew to a ravine, out of gun-shot, almost immediately that the action commenced. Of regulars, there were two lieutenant-colonels, four captains, seven subalterns, (one a lieutenant of artillery,) eight staff, 22 serjeants, seven drummers, and 341 rank and file, including 23 artillerymen; making a total of 391 officers, non-commissioned officers, and privates.

On the morning of the 2d the British opened their artillery, consisting of two light 6-pounders, and two $5\frac{1}{2}$ inch howitzers, upon the fort; but without producing the slightest impression; and the different American accounts, as we are glad to see, concur in stating, that the fort "was not at all injured" by the fire directed against it. Under an impression that the garrison did not exceed 50 or 60 men, the fort was ordered to be stormed. Lieutenant-colonel Short, at the head of 180 rank and file, immediately advanced towards the north-west angle; while about 160 rank and file, under lieutenant-colonel Warburton, passed round through the woods skirting the western side of the fort, to its south side. After sustaining a heavy fire of musketry from the American troops, lieutenant-colonel Short approached to the stockade; and, with some difficulty, succeeded in getting over the pickets. The instant this gallant officer reached the ditch, he ordered his men to follow, and assault the works with the utmost vigor. The masked 6-pounder, which had been previously pointed to rake the ditch, and loaded " with a double charge of leaden slugs," was now fired at the British column, " the front of which was only 30 feet distant from the piece." A volley of musketry was fired at the same instant; and repeated in quick succession. This dreadful and, as to the battery, unexpected discharge killed lieutenant-colonel Short, and several of his brave followers; and wounded a great many more. Still undaunted, the men of the 41st, headed by another officer, advanced again to carry the masked 6-pounder; from which another discharge of " leaden slugs," aided by other vollies of musketry, was directed against them, and cleared the " fatal ditch" a second time. It was in vain to contend further; and the British retired, with as many of their wounded as they could carry away.

Lieutenant-colonel Warburton's party, having a circuit to make, did not arrive at its position till the first assault was nearly over. After a volley or two, in which the British sustained some slight loss, the troops at this point, also, were ordered to retire. The loss sustained by both divisions amounted to 26 killed, 29 wounded and missing, and 41 wounded (most of them slightly) and brought away; total 96. The

Americans state their loss at one killed, and seven wounded. Considering the way in which they were sheltered, and the circumstances of the attack altogether, no greater loss could have been expected.

The American editors seem determined to drag the Indians, in spite of their confirmed, and, to an American, well-known habits, within the limits of the " fatal ditch." " The Indians," says Mr. Thomson, " were enraged and mortified at this unparalleled defeat; and, *carrying their dead and wounded from the field*, they indignantly followed the British regulars to the shipping."* " It is a fact worthy of observation," says Mr. O'Connor, " that not one Indian was found among the dead, although it is known that from 3 to 400 were present."† A brave enemy would have found something to praise in the efforts of colonel Short and his men, in this their " *unparalleled* defeat;" but all is forgotten in the lavish encomiums bestowed upon major Croghan and the band of " heroes," who " compelled an army," says an American editor, " much more than 10 times superior,"* to relinquish the attack.

Major-general Proctor returned to Sandwich, accompanied by an hourly accumulating number of Indians; who, having deserted their hunting-grounds to follow the British, naturally

† Hist. of the War, p. 131.   * Sketches of the War, p. 163.

looked to the latter for supplies. Unfortunately, the store-houses along the Detroit had been nearly emptied of their contents already, to feed our importunate allies; neither would it have been prudent to order them back to their woods, nor even to impose upon them any restraints; when general Harrison had, for the last two months, been endeavouring, by means of a numerous body of spies, to sow distrust among the chiefs, and gain over them and their tribes as allies to the Americans.

The remainder of the 41st regiment had long been expected at Amherstburg from Fort-George, a distance of about 270 miles. A few companies did move forward in May; but, by the time the men had marched 90 miles, which, owing to the bad state of the roads, could not be performed in fewer than eight days, they were ordered back, to assist in defending Fort-George, then threatened with an attack. As soon as the centre-division of the army, under major-general De Rottenburg, had been reinforced by the 1st battalion of the royal Scots, the detachment of the 41st marched to Long-point, on Lake Erie; there to embark, along with the force already under major-general Proctor's command, on board captain Barclay's fleet, for the purpose of attacking Presq' Isle; where two large American brigs of war were building, and several schooners lying at anchor. The British were to have been joined by a numerous body of Indians; but who declined co-operating, until Fort-Stephenson should be reduced, as they could then move, with less apprehension of danger, along the south-shore of the lake. The assault had, as we have seen, been attempted without the reinforcement, and failed. On the very next day, commodore Perry appeared on Lake Erie, with eight vessels of war, including the two newly launched brigs; and captain Barclay, with his small command, was compelled to retire to Amherstburg, till the new ship that was building should be ready for the lake.

The reinforcement from Niagara had augmented major-general Proctor's force to 868 officers, non-commissioned officers, and privates, of the 41st regiment, 30 of the royal artillery, the same number of the royal veteran battalion and Newfoundland regiment, eight artillery-drivers, and about 50 provincial cavalry; making a total of 986 men; of whom between 1 and 200 were upon the sick-list.

So many men made a sensible reduction in the small quantity of provisions that remained in the store-houses on the Detroit frontier; and, to encrease the evil, the Indians kept flocking to Amherstburg, in such multitudes, that, by the 8th or 9th of September, upwards of 3500 warriors had attached themselves to general Proctor's division. One hope remained. Every exertion was making at Amherstburg to complete the new ship; which, when added to the others, and the whole equipped with stores, and manned with seamen, daily expected from Lake Ontario, might re-open the lake-communication.

Neither guns, stores, nor seamen came; beyond as many of the latter as augmented captain Barclay's number to 50. The new ship was launched, and the exigence became hourly more pressing. There remained no alternative but to strip the forts of their guns, and get them fitted, as far as was possible, to the ports of the Detroit.* This botching business ended, the four other vessels were deprived of a part of their already scanty stores, to enable the Detroit to move from her anchorage; or, when she met the enemy, to make use of her lumbering guns. By way of helping to man this " superior British fleet," major-general Proctor spared, in addition to the detachment of his army already on board, one lieutenant, three serjeants, and 148 rank and file from the 41st regiment.

Driven, as it were, out of port, captain Barclay, on the evening of the 9th of September, sailed forth upon the lake, to endeavour at clearing it from his vigilant, well-provided, and almost doubly superior foe. The meeting of

* The guns (24-pounder carronades) intended for this ship did not arrive at Burlington Heights from Kingston, till after she was captured.

the two fleets on the following morning; the sudden fatal change of wind; the gallant behaviour of the Detroit; the surrender to her of the American flag-ship, the St. Lawrence; the re-hoisting of the latter's colours; the renewal of the combat, and surrender of the British; the damages and loss of the two squadrons; their comparative strength in guns, men, and size; the extravagant boastings of the Americans, and their gross distortion of every feature in the action; are all fully, and, as we trust, correctly detailed in our naval volume.*

This was a sad blow upon the right division. As hope fled, despair found its way into the British camp. The situation of the men, it must be owned, was deplorable in the extreme. They had long been suffering, not only from a scarcity of provisions, but a scarcity of money. Few of them had received any pay for the last six months: to some, indeed, nine month's arrears were due. Winter, a Canadian winter, was fast approaching; and scarcely any of the soldiers had blankets, and all were without great coats. The severe privations which they had endured in the last, were therefore likely to be augmented rather than diminished, in the succeeding winter. In addition to all this, the commander of the forces appeared unmindful of their arduous exertions; and that, parti-

* James's Nav. Occur. p. 283.

cularly, in a description of service, to which neither their arms, clothing, nor discipline had adapted them. Not to gain credit for what they did, was, indeed, the lot of all the British troops employed against the Americans; chiefly, because the latter, ranking beneath them as soldiers, invariably got applause when they gained a victory over, or stood their ground against, two-thirds of their own number.

What movements commodore Perry's victory caused, on the part of major-general Harrison, we shall now proceed to detail. Satisfied that he should soon be able, not only to recover the surrendered territory, but to dissipate or destroy the British force in this quarter, the American general hastened to claim from governor Meigs a portion of 15,000 volunteers, just arrived from the state of Ohio.* Reinforced here, he received a fresh accession of strength in the arrival, on the 17th of September, of the governor of Kentucky, Isaac Sheby, "with 4000 well mounted volunteers."* The works on the Miami and Sandusky were abandoned, and their garrisons added to the already overwhelming army. On the 21st of September general Harrison, with the bulk of his troops, proceeded in boats to an island about 20 miles from Amherstburg, called the Eastern Sister; having despatched the remainder, consisting of colonel Johnson's mounted

* Sketches of the War, p. 169.

regiment, by land, to Detroit. On the 27th the American fleet, "composed of 16 vessels of war, and upwards of 100 boats," received on board general Harrison's divison, and landed it, on the afternoon of the same day, at a point three miles below Amherstburg; whence the troops marched forward to that village.

The full amount of the British white force on the Detroit having already been given, it now remains for us to shew, if we can, what was the number of American troops, with which general Harrison so sanguinely expected to " overthrow general Proctor's army." This does not appear, either in general Harrison's letter,* or in any of the American accounts, minute as they are in other less important particulars. Perhaps, by putting together such items of numbers as, in the general plan of concealment, may have escaped the notice of the different editors, we shall get within one or two thousands of the number of troops that landed below Amherstburg, as doctor Smith tells us, " without opposition." We find the 17th, 19th, 24th, 26th, 27th, and 28th regiments of infantry, named. Admitting every one of these to have been reduced to 250 men, the whole would give 1500. " Part of colonel Ball's regiment of dragoons" has been stated at 240; then there was a full rifle-regiment, say 450 strong; also major Wood's detachment

* App. No. 52.

of artillery, certainly not less than 150. Next come " major Suggett's three spy companies," 160 more; also " five brigades of Kentucky volunteers, averaging," according to general Harrison, " 500 men;"* but Mr. Thomson had before told us, that the volunteers from Kentucky, under governor Shelby, amounted to " 4000," and those well-mounted."† We shall be contented, however, with the smaller number; which, without proceeding further in our inquiry, gives a force of 5000 men. As these had but 17 miles to proceed by water, and that in the finest of weather, 2395 tons of shipping,‡ (without reckoning the 16th vessel,) along with " boats," afforded them ample room.

On arriving at Amherstburg the Americans found it abandoned by its garrison, and the fort and public buildings in ruins. To put the worst possible construction upon the retreat of the 800 British from this place, Mr. Thomson has not scrupled to state, that " the guns of the batteries had been previously sunk;" although he knew the latter were then on board commodore Perry's prize, the Detroit. After leaving, in possession of Amherstburg, colonel Smith's rifle regiment; general Harrison moved forward to Sandwich,§ attended in his course along the

* App. No. 52. † Sketches of the War, p. 168.
‡ James's Nav. Occurr. p. 293. § See p. 48.

side of the river, by the American brigs Niagara and Caledonia, and three of the schooners; armed between them with 30 heavy guns. At Sandwich general Harrison received authentic information of the small regular force which major-general Proctor had with him; also, that the Indians had been, and still were, abandoning him by hundreds at a time. This welcome news enabled the major-general, on the 29th, to leave a portion of his force, under lieutenant-colonel Ball, at Sandwich, and to send another portion, under brigadier-general M'Arthur, across to the opposite town of Detroit; especially as the general expected, and was the next day joined by, " colonel R. M. Johnson's regiment," consisting of " upwards of 1000 horsemen."*

Major-general Proctor had retreated towards the mouth of the river Thames, and made a temporary stand at a place called Dalson's, distant about 56 miles from Detroit. On the 2d of October the American army left Sandwich in close pursuit. Of what number that army, since a part had been detached, consisted, puzzles all calculation. Major-general Harrison speaks, in rather an obscure way, of general M'Arthur's force consisting of only " about 700 effectives;" but we have seen an account, bearing every mark of authenticity, which fixes brigadier-general M'Arthur's force at 100 artillery, and 1600

* Sketches of the War, p. 173.

infantry. The force with which the American general left Sandwich, is stated in the American official account at " about 3500 men." In another part of his letter, the major-general states his number of men at " something above 3000." On the other hand, the same account from which we extracted brigadier-general M'Arthur's force, gives what purports to be a list of the different corps and detachments of American troops that moved up the Thames, in pursuit of major-general Proctor; numbering altogether 6200 men. As, however, in a case of this kind, we have pledged ourselves to consider each party to be the best authority for its own numbers, major-general Harrison's force shall be fixed at no more than he himself admits, 3500 men. With this army, and two 6-pounders, the major-general, on the evening of the 2d, encamped at Riscum, about 26 miles from Sandwich.

Early on the morning of the 3d he resumed his march, accompanied by general Cass and commodore Perry, as his additional aides de camp. On arriving at the second bridge across a branch of the Thames, the American general succeeded in capturing a lieutenant and 11 rank and file of major-general Proctor's provincial dragoons. After proceeding a short way further up the Thames, the American general left his three gun-boats in charge of 150 infantry; and "determined to trust to fortune and the bravery of his troops," for effecting the further passage of the rivers. On the morning of the 4th, the American army again proceeded on its route; and, on reaching Chatham, distant about 17 miles from Lake St. Clair, found its progress obstructed by a deep and unfordable creek, the bridge of which had been partially destroyed by some Indians, who now made their appearance, and fired on the advanced guard. The major-general, "believing that the whole force of the enemy was there," halted his army, formed it in order of battle, and brought up his pieces of artillery. A few shot from the 6-pounders drove away the Indians; and the army repaired, and crossed the bridge. The American loss on this occasion amounted to two killed, and three or four wounded. Mr. Thomson states 13 as the loss, in killed only, of the Indians; or, as his term is, of " the enemy." On the same evening three of general Proctor's boats, loaded with ordnance-stores, were taken; as also " two 24-pounders, with their carriages," or, as Mr. Thomson has it, " several pieces of cannon."*

On the morning of the 5th, the pursuit of the British was eagerly renewed; and, before nine o'clock, two gun-boats and several batteaux were captured. With these boats and batteaux, and some Indian canoes, the American army was

* Sketches of the War, p. 171.

enabled, at 12 o'clock at noon, to cross over to the left bank of the Thames. About 12 miles above this ford, and two and a half from the Moravian town, major-general Proctor had drawn up his troops, to resist, if possible, the further advance of the American army. The amount of the British force we are fortunately enabled to state with accuracy. There were present, under arms, of the 41st regiment, (including 30 additional gunners,) one lieutenant-colonel, six captains, 10 lieutenants, three ensigns, two staff, 26 serjeants, four drummers, and 356 rank and file, total 408; among whom were one serjeant, and 26 rank and file, taken from the hospital on that very morning. There were also, 38 provincial dragoons. The artillery numbered six pieces, 3 and 6-pounders, and were worked by 30 of the royal artillery, assisted by the additional gunners from the 41st. So that the whole effective strength of the right division, on the morning of the 5th of October, amounted to 476 men. The remaining part of the right division was thus disposed of. The gun-boats and batteaux had on board, just previous to their capture, one captain, nine serjeants, 10 drummers, and 124 rank and file of the 41st; along with the 30 men of the royal veteran battalion and Newfoundland regiment. The hospital at the Moravian village contained 101 officers and privates; and those that attended them, and were on duty with the baggage, amounted to 63 officers and privates, all of the 41st regiment. Adding to this amount such of the eight artillery-drivers as had not been captured, and allowing for a few desertions, we account at once for the 834 officers and privates, composing major-general Proctor's force, when he commenced his retreat. Of his 3500 Indians, 500 only remained; and they were led by the brave and faithful Tecumseh.

The 356 rank and file of the 41st regiment were formed at open files, in a beach forest, without any clearing. The line crossed the York road, its left resting on the river, its right on the thicker part of the wood. On this point the troops joined the Indian warriors; who, forming an obtuse angle to the front, were the better able to get into the enemy's rear, the Indian's favorite system of action. At the back of the Indians, and about 300 yards from the river, was a miry swamp. A 6-pounder enfiladed the only road by which the Americans could advance in any order. The provincial dragoons were stationed a little in the rear of the infantry. This position was considered an excellent one; as the enemy, however numerous his force, could not turn the flanks of the British, or present a more extended front than theirs. The remaining five pieces of artillery were stationed upon some heights, a little to the north-eastward of the Moravian town, and consequently upwards of two miles from the field of battle; in order to guard a ford of the river, and, if necessary, cover the British retreat.

General Harrison has given us a very full description of the manner in which he arranged his force upon this occasion. Three brigades of volunteer-infantry, under the command of major-general Henry, were drawn up in three lines, having their right upon the road, and their left upon the swamp. The whole of general Desha's division, consisting of two brigades, was formed, *en potence*, upon the left of the first, or Trotter's brigade. " The American backwoodsmen," says the general, in his despatch, " ride better in the woods than any other people. A musket or rifle is no impediment, they being accustomed to carry them on horseback from their earliest youth." Consequently, colonel Johnson drew up his mounted regiment in close column, having its right at the distance of 50 yards from the road, and its left upon the swamp. His directions were, to charge at full speed, as soon as the enemy delivered his fire; and the general rightly conjectured that " the enemy would be quite unprepared for the shock, and could not resist it." Colonel Paul's regulars occupied the space between the road and the river, ready to seize " the enemy's artillery;" the quantity of which brought into action, is very cunningly left by the general to inference. Along the bank of the river were stationed " some 10 or 12 friendly Indians." An American account states, that " nearly 300 Indians" were, at this time, attached to general Harrison's army. Before we commence upon the attack, let us place before the reader, in one view, the force of the contending parties. The Americans had, by their own admission, and meaning " privates," or rank and file, 1200 cavalry, 1950 infantry, " some 10 or 12," or, let us say, 150 Indians, and two 6-pounders. The British had 38 cavalry, 356 infantry, 500 Indians, and one 6-pounder. We have no more to do with the remnant of the British force stationed beyond the Moravian town, than we have with the 400 men of the 27th United States' regiment, that were hastening to share the honors of the day.

The British gave the first fire; from which the horses of the front column recoiled. After the delivery of the second fire, the " brilliant charge" took effect. " In a few moments," says Mr. Thomson, " the enemy's line was pierced by upward of 1000 horsemen, who, dashing through the British regulars with irresistible speed, either trampled under foot, or cut down, every soldier who opposed them; and, having killed and wounded upwards of 50 at one charge, instantly formed in their rear, and repeated the attack. Such was the panic," proceeds the

American editor, " which pervaded the whole line of the enemy, that an order which had been issued to fix bayonets, was not attempted to be executed."*

The Indian warrors, led by the undaunted Tecumseh, rushed upon the enemy's front line of infantry, and " for a moment," says the general, " made some impression upon it." It was not, in short, till the infantry was reinforced by the whole of governor Shelby's, and a part of colonel Johnson's regiment; nor, till the fall of their lamented chief, and upwards of 30 of their warriors, that the brave foresters retired from the field of battle. Had the men of the 41st regiment at all emulated the Indians, the fate of the day might have been changed; or, did the enemy's great numerical superiority render that an improbable event, the American general would not, in the very paragraph in which he admits that he contended with an inferiority of force, have dared to claim for his troops " the palm of superior bravery." *His* troops possessed the peculiar privilege of not having their character affected by any similar conduct on their part; nay, not even, had they submitted to an equal, instead of a seven-fold force.

The British lost, in killed 12, in wounded 22, and in prisoners, including the wounded, 601.† Of these, 477 were taken on the day of the

* Sketches of the War, p. 173. † App. No. 52.

surrender; the remainder, previously and subsequently. Mr. Thomson, still regardless about contradicting the official accounts of his own generals, says:—" The enemy lost, in regulars alone, upwards of 90 killed, and about the same number wounded."* The Indians lost 33 killed, exclusive of such as fell during the retreat: their loss in wounded does not appear. The Americans admit a loss of 12 killed, and 17 wounded.

The censure passed upon the right division of the Canadian army, by the commander-in-chief, was certainly of unparalleled severity. Yet, who but must admire the valorous spirit that breathes through the general order of the 24th of November, promulgating sir George's indignation? Who could believe that this document was penned by the same hand that, six months previous, dragged away the British troops from the possession of Sackett's Harbor?†—The ardor which, as sir George himself admits, and every one else knows, had, till the fatal 5th of October, distinguished the 41st regiment, affords a strong belief it was not cowardice that made that corps surrender so tamely,—no matter to what superiority of force. The privations the troops had undergone, and the marked neglect which had been shewn at head-quarters to the representations of their commander, had probably possessed them with an idea, that any

* Sketches of the War, p. 175.   † See p. 163.

change would be an improvement in their condition.

Major-general Proctor, with some officers of his staff, and a part of his provincial cavalry, retreated towards the river *Grande;* after having his baggage and private papers captured by a squadron of dragoons, which major-general Harrison had sent in pursuit of him. Sir George's letter,* (the only one published,) as well as his general order, mentions that the Indians harrassed the American army on its retreat to Detroit. So far was this from being the case, that not a tomahawk was lifted after the day on which the British surrendered; and many of the Indians actually accompanied major-general Proctor on his route to Ancaster. In preference to pushing after the latter, major-general Harrison, on the day succeeding his easy victory, destroyed the Moravian town. This fact, owing, probably, to some political reason, does not appear in the official letter; although the latter bears date three days after the conflagration. But Mr. Thomson, in the fulness of his patriotism, cannot refrain from announcing the event to the public.† The Moravian town, or rather its site, is distant about 35 miles from the mouth of the Thames; and was under the superintendence of missionaries from the society of Moravian United

---

* App. No. 51. † Sketches of the War, p. 176.

Brethren, who maintained a chapel there. On the 9th of October major-general Harrison retired upon Detroit; and, on the 17th, major-general Proctor had concentrated at Ancaster, on the river *Grande*, not far from Burlington Heights, 204 rank and file of the right division; of whom more than half had escaped after having been captured.

The defeat of the British at the battle of the Thames was highly advantageous to the American cause. Not only was the whole territory of Michigan, except the fort of Michilimacinac, restored to the United States, but the western district of the upper province became a conquered country. Nor was it the least misfortune, that we lost the services of the whole of the north-western Indians, except 2 or 300 that subsequently joined the centre-division of the army. The American editors boast that general Harrison, before he left Detroit for Buffaloe, made peace with upwards of 3000 warriors. The reader now sees the fatal consequences; first, of not having, in the winter of 1812, destroyed the two or three schooners which were equipping at Buffaloe by lieutenant Elliott;* secondly, of not having, in the spring of 1813, secured the possession of Sackett's Harbor;† thirdly, of not having, in the summer of the same year, captured or destroyed

* See p. 83.   † See p. 174.

the whole American fleet, as it lay, unmanned, in Presq' Isle harbor;* and lastly, of not having sent a supply of guns, stores, and men, to captain Barclay at Amherstburg, so as to have enabled him to meet and conquer that same American fleet, whose growth and maturity had thus been so shamefully promoted.

The American public made no distinction, apparently, between the important consequences that ensued from general Harrison's capture of " a British regular *army*," and the merits of the victory itself. By adding some circumstances, and concealing others, the historian was able to convert the thing into what he pleased; but who could have imagined, that every town in the republic would illuminate, and every church ring a merry peal, on the occasion? Such was actually the case. All this to be sure, might have been a political measure, or, as general Wilkinson calls it, " a military deception,"† to render the war popular; but no sober-minded American could, one may suppose, see any reason to exult, because 3500 of his countrymen had conquered 4 or 500 British, and the same number of Indians. A Mr. Cheeves, however, member for South-Carolina, and one of the 98 " yeas" that declared the war, uttered, in the middle of a very long speech to congress " on the conduct of the war," the following sentence:

* See p. 268.   † See p. 162.

—" The victory of Harrison was such as would have secured to a Roman general, in the best days of the republic, the honors of a triumph."*—The American editor has not followed up the period with " *(hear, hear,)*" or introduced any remarks of his own, either in ridicule or surprise of the orator's modesty.

Let us now ascend in the scale of human beings, from a " member of congress" to a " savage,"—from Mr. Cheeves to the late Indian warrior Tecumseh. It seems extraordinary that general Harrison should have omitted to mention, in his letter, the death of a chief, whose fall contributed so largely to break down the Indian spirit, and to give peace and security to the whole north-western frontier of the United States. Tecumseh, although he had received a musket-ball in the left arm, was still seeking the hottest of the fire, when he encountered colonel R. M. Johnson, member of congress for Kentucky. Just as the chief, having discharged his rifle, was rushing forward with his tomahawk, he received a ball in the head from the colonel's pistol. Thus fell the Indian warrior Tecumseh, in the 44th year of his age. He was of the Shawanæ tribe; five feet ten inches high; and, with more than the usual stoutness, possessed all the agility and perseverance, of the Indian character. His carriage was dignified; his eye

* Burdick's Pol. and Hist. Regr. p. 147.

penetrating; his countenance, which, even in death, betrayed the indications of a lofty spirit, rather of the sterner cast. Had he not possessed a certain austerity of manners, he could never have controlled the wayward passions of those who followed him to battle. He was of a silent habit; but, when his eloquence became roused into action by the re-iterated encroachments of the Americans, his strong intellect could supply him with a flow of oratory, that enabled him, as he governed in the field, so to prescribe in the council. Those who consider that, in all territorial questions, the ablest diplomatists of the United States are sent to negotiate with the Indians, will readily appreciate the loss sustained by the latter in the death of their champion.

The Indians, in general, are full as fond as other savages, of the gaudy decoration of their persons; but Tecumseh was an exception. Cloaths and other valuable articles of spoil had often been his; yet he invariably wore a deer-skin coat and pantaloons. He had frequently levied subsidies to, comparatively, a large amount; yet he preserved little or nothing for himself. It was not wealth, but glory, that was Tecumseh's ruling passion. Fatal day! when the " Christian people" first penetrated the forests, to teach the arts of " civilization" to the poor Indian. Till then, water had been his only beverage; and himself and his race possessed all the vigor of hardy savages. Now, no Indian opens his lips to the stream that ripples by his wig-wam, while he has a rag of cloaths on his back, wherewith to purchase rum; and he and his squaw and his children wallow through the day, in beastly drunkenness. Instead of the sturdy warrior, with a head to plan, and an arm to execute, vengeance upon the oppressors of his country, we behold the puny besotted wretch, squatting on his hams, ready to barter his country, his children, or himself, for a few gulps of that deleterious compound, which, far more than the arms of the United States, is hastening to extinguish all traces of his name and character. Tecumseh, himself, in early life, had been addicted to intemperance; but no sooner did his judgment decide against, than his resolution enabled him to quit, so vile a habit. Beyond one or two glasses of wine, he never afterwards indulged.

"By whom are the savages led?" was the question, for many years, during the wars between the Americans and Indians. The name—"Tecumseh!" was itself a host on the side of the latter; and the warrior chief, while he signalized himself in all, came off victorious in most, of the many actions in which he had fought and bled. The American editors, superadded to a national dislike to the Indians, have some special reasons, which we shall develope presently, for blackening the character of Tecumseh. They say, that he neither gave nor accepted quarter. His inveterate hatred to the Americans, considering them, as he did, to have robbed his forefathers of their territory, renders such a proceeding, in a savage, not improbable. European history, even of modern date, informs us, that the civilized soldier can go into battle with a similar determination. Mr. Thomson says of Tecumseh, that, "when he undertook an expedition, accompanied by his tribe, he would relinquish to them the spoil, though he would never yield the priviledge of destroying the victim."* And yet, it was from an American publication, that we extracted the account of Tecumseh's killing a brother-chief, because the latter wanted to massacre an American prisoner.† This trait in Tecumseh's character is corroborated by all the British officers who have served with him. That it did not, however, proceed from any good-will towards the Americans, was made known, in an extraordinary manner, at the taking of Detroit. After the surrender of the American troops, general Brock desired, Tecumseh, not to allow the Indians under him to ill-treat the prisoners. Tecumseh promptly replied: "I despise them too much to meddle with them." Nor is there a

* Sketches of the War, p. 176. † See p. 201.

single act of violence charged to the Indians on that occasion. As a proper contrast to this, an American editor, describing a battle between general Jackson and the Creek Indians, in March, 1814, says: " Of about 1000 Creeks only 10 of the men are supposed to have escaped with life: 16 of the Creeks, who had hid themselves, were killed the morning after the battle. The American commander said, in his despatch, that he was ' *determined to exterminate*' the tribe; of course," proceeds the editor, " no quarter was given, except to a few women and children."*

Few officers in the United States' service were so able to command in the field, as this famed Indian chief. He was an excellent judge of position; and not only knew, but could point out, the localities of the whole country through which he had passed. To what extent he had travelled over the western part of the American continent, may be conceived from the well-known fact, that he visited the Creek Indians, in the hopes of prevailing on them to unite with their northern brethren, in efforts to regain their country as far as the banks of the Ohio. His facility of communicating the information he had acquired, was thus displayed before a concourse of spectators. Previously to general Brock's crossing over to Detroit, he

* Burdick's Pol. and Hist. Reg. p. 186.

asked Tecumseh what sort of a country he should have to pass through, in case of his proceeding further. Tecumseh, taking a roll of elm-bark, and extending it on the ground by means of four stones, drew forth his scalping-knife, and, with the point, presently etched upon the bark a plan of the country, its hills, woods, rivers, morasses, and roads; a plan which, if not as neat, was, for the purpose required, fully as intelligible, as if Arrowsmith himself had prepared it. Pleased with this unexpected talent in Tecumseh, also with his having, by his characteristic boldness, induced the Indians, not of his immediate party, to cross the Detroit, prior to the embarkation of the regulars and militia, general Brock, as soon as the business was over, publicly took off his sash, and placed it round the body of the chief. Tecumseh received the honor with evident gratification; but was, the next day, seen without his sash. General Brock, fearing something had displeased the Indian, sent his interpreter for an explanation. The latter soon returned with an account, that Tecumseh, not wishing to wear such a mark of distinction, when an older, and, as he said, abler, warrior than himself was present, had transferred the sash to the Wyandot chief Round-head.* Such a man was the unlettered "savage" Tecumseh;

* See p. 188.

and such a man have the Indians for ever lost. He has left a son; who, when his father fell, was about 17 years old, and fought by his side. The prince regent, in 1814, out of respect to the memory of the old, sent out as a present to the young Tecumseh, a handsome sword. Unfortunately, however, for the Indian cause and country, faint are the prospects, that Tecumseh, the son, will ever equal, in wisdom or prowess, Tecumseh, the father.

According to Mr. Thomson, 120 Indians were killed at the battle of the Thames. General Harrison numbers 33 only. No *wounded* are mentioned by either. While the affair with the Creeks is fresh in our minds, what are we to infer from this?—However, let us proceed. Full two-thirds of general Harrison's army, at the battle of the Thames, were Kentuckians. As every soldier wore a scalping-knife as part of his accoutrements, and was extremely "dexterous in the use of it;"* as the *live* Kentuckians bore to the *dead* Indians (taking Mr. Thomson's estimate) fully as 20 to one; and as one head could conveniently afford but one scalp, we can picture to ourselves what a scramble there must have been for the trophies. For the European reader's edification, we will endeavour at describing the manner in which the operation of scalping is performed. A circular incision,

* See p. 183.

of about three inches or more, in diameter, according to the length of the hair, is made upon the crown of the head. The foot of the operator is then placed on the neck or body of the victim, and the *scalp*, or tuft of skin and hair, torn from the scull by strength of arm. In case the hair is so short as not to admit of being grasped by the hand, the operator, first with his knife turning up one edge of the circle, applies his teeth to the part ; and, by that means, quite as effectually disengages the *scalp*. In order to preserve the precious relict, it is then stretched and dried upon a small osier hoop. The western Indians invariably crop their hair, almost as close as if it were shorn ; to retaliate upon their enemies, probably, by drawing some of their teeth. As captain M'Culloch's prisoner* was a western Indian, we were, therefore, wrong in supposing, that the American officer practised any refinement in the art of *scalping*.

The body of Tecumseh was recognised, not only by the British officers who were prisoners, but by commodor Perry, and several American officers. An American writer (from the spot, it would appear) says :—" There was a kind of ferocious pleasure, if I may be allowed the expression, in contemplating the contour of his features, which was majestic, even in death."†—Poor chief! the *majesty* of his features

* See p. 62.   † Burdick's Pol. and Hist. Reg. p. 84.

could no longer, now he was dead, awe the Kentuckians; and that majesty was, by their merciless scalping-knives, soon converted into hideousness. Had the " ferocious pleasure" of Americans required no further gratification than Tecumseh's scalp, custom might have been their excuse. The possessor of this valuable trophy would not, it may be supposed, part with a hair of it. Were the other Kentuckians, then, to march home empty-handed?—Ingenuity offered a partial remedy. One, more dexterous than the rest, proceeded to *flay* the chief's body; then, cutting the skin in narrow slips, of 10 or 12 inches long, produced, at once, a supply of *razor-straps* for the more " ferocious" of his brethren. We know that the editor of the United States' government-paper, the " National Intelligencer," not many months ago,* flew into a violent rage, because some anonimous writer here had mentioned the circumstance. How will the American government bear to hear the fact thus solemnly repeated, accompanied by the declaration, that some of the British officers witnessed the transaction, and are ready to testify to the truth of it?—But, have we not *American* testimony in support of the charge?—The same writer who was so struck with the *majesty* in Tecumseh's countenance, and who, of course, would, by every means in

* Aug. 21, 1817.

his power, soften down an account that reflected so high dishonor upon his countrymen, says thus:—" Some of the Kentuckians disgraced themselves by committing indignities on his dead body. He was scalped, and *otherwise disfigured.*" *

Considering the importance of Tecumseh's death to the American cause, it is difficult to account for general Harrison's omission to notice it; unless we suppose, that the general did transmit the account, but so blended with the " indignities" committed upon the chief's person, that the American secretary at war, finding a difficulty in garbling, suppressed altogether, that paragraph of the letter. This is strengthened by the circumstance of the *flaying* ceremony having been the topic of conversation in the United States, very soon after the receipt of the official letter, and of the private ones forwarded by the same express. † We now discover why the American editors wished to prejudice the public mind against the character of Tecumseh. One of the three editors has been both artful and graceless enough, to lavish encomiums upon the *humanity* of the " volunteers of Kentucky." These are his words :—" History can record to their honor that, not merely professing to be

* Burdick's Pol. and Hist. Reg. p. 84.
† The Author heard it spoken of in Philadelphia, about the middle of October.

Christian people, they gave a high example of Christian virtues. For evil they returned not evil. For cruelty they returned mercy and protection."*—Had we taken up Dr. Smith's book, for the first time, we should have pronounced this an excellent piece of irony.

On the day succeeding the battle of the Thames, major-general Proctor sent captain Le Breton, of the Newfoundland regiment, with a flag, to general Harrison, requesting "that humane treatment might be extended to the British prisoners."† Contrary to the laws of war, however, the American general detained the British officer, and sent no reply to major-general Proctor's letter. Soon afterwards, general Harrison wrote a very insolent letter to major-general Vincent, on the subject of major-general Proctor's application; enclosing letters from some of the British officers, in which the latter mentioned, that they were kindly treated by the Americans. General Harrison, in his letter to general Vincent, avows a knowledge of the contents of these enclosures. The impression once made, was not easily to be effaced. The British officers soon saw through the trick ; soon began to repent that, urged by premature gratitude, they had so grossly deceived themselves, their friends, and the public.

* History of the United States, Vol. III. p. 258.
† Sketches of the War, p. 176.

On the 22d of October general Harrison, after garrisoning Detroit, Sandwich, and Amherstburg, and discharging the principal part of his Kentucky and Ohio volunteers, embarked, with his disposable regular force, on board commodore Perry's fleet, to join, agreeably to the orders of his government, the troops on the Niagara frontier. About the same time, the commissioned and non-commissioned officers, and privates, of major-general Proctor's late army, were transported, by water, from Detroit, to the portage on Lake Erie, distant 45 miles; and thence marched to Franklin-town, distant 129 miles. Here they embarked in boats, and proceeded 100 miles down the Scioto to Chillicothe; at which place some of the non-commissioned officers and privates were detained. The remainder of the British prisoners again proceeded by the Scioto, to Cincinnati on the Ohio. Here and at Newport-town, a military depôt, half a mile across the river, was detained a second detachment, comprehending nearly all that were left, of the non-commissioned officers and privates. The small remnant, consisting almost wholly of commissioned officers, proceeded to the ultimate point of destination, Frankfort, in Kentucky; just 612 miles from Detroit, and about the same distance from the nearest Atlantic port.

Here, at Frankfort, Kentucky, were " colonels

Evans, Warburton, and Baubee, and majors Muir and Chambers,"* and other British commissioned officers, thrown into prison.—Into what prison? The Penitentiary, along with 40 convicts, condemned for murder, rape, forgery, coining, burglary, horse-stealing, &c.— Lest the reader should doubt this, he will, in the Appendix, find, furnished by the keeper of the prison, a list of the convicts, their crimes, and sentences.† Comments are unnecessary. Yet, general Sheaffe did not behave thus to the American officers who surrendered at the battle of Queenstown.‡ Many will be surprised that this mode of incarcerating British officers of rank and distinction, taken in honorable war, should be realized—not at *Verdun* in France, but—at Kentucky, in the United States: the land of *liberty*, where, among other advantages, a man may compound for " shooting his wife"† by a four years' imprisonment, but, for " horse-stealing,"† he runs the chance of remaining in confinement six years longer!—Leaving our poor countrymen to ruminate over their misfortunes, in the midst of company so *respectable*, we hasten to beguile the reader, with the busy scenes of hostility still carrying on in the neighbourhood of Lake Ontario.

* Sketches of the War, p. 173.
† App. No. 53.   ‡ See p. 101.

CHAPTER X.

Progress of the expedition from Sackett's Harbor—Its rendezvous at Grenadier Island—Montreal decided upon as the point of attack—Feint upon Kingston—Cannonade by British vessels upon the encampment at French Creek—General Hampton's advance from Burlington, to form the proposed junction—Battle of Chateaugay—Defeat of general Hampton's army—Its retreat across the lines—Further progress of the expedition—General Wilkinson's proclamation to the Canadians—Attack on Matilda—Council of war at the White House—Landing of the American troops—Skirmish at Hoop-pole Creek—Departure of the British corps of observation from Kingston—Its arrival at Fort-Wellington, and its disembarkation at Point Iroquois—Mutual cannonade between the rival gun-boats—Battle of Chrystler's—Retreat of the Americans—Pursuit by the British—Council of war at Barnharts—Sudden termination of the expedition—Remarks on the causes of its failure—Loyalty of the Lower Canada militia—General Wilkinson's new projects—His abandonment of his position at the French Mills—Destruction of his boats, and retreat to Plattsburg—Colonel Scott's incursion to Malone.

THE grand, or *Wilkinsonian* expedition again claims our attention; and we will endeavour at a faint description (for faint it must be) of the perils, both of the weather and of the enemy, which it encountered by the way: not omitting the catastrophe that gave a turn to its destination, as sudden as it was unexpected.

Grenadier Island,* distant 18 miles from Sackett's Harbor, had, owing to its contiguity to the St. Lawrence, been chosen for the point of rendezvous. As soon as commodore Chauncey could place his squadron, so as to prevent the army from being " enterprised on by the enemy on an island," the division of troops previously stationed at Sackett's Harbor, as well as that which, part by water and part by land, had arrived there from Henderson's Bay and Sandy Creek, pushed off, in high spirits, for Grenadier Island. Again the wind roared, and again the rain pelted; but the expedition did arrive, in " scattered fragments," between the 17th and 24th of October. The army, when fully assembled, consisted of four brigades, or 12 regiments, of infantry, a corps of reserve, a strong rifle regiment, two regiments of dragoons, and three regiments of artillery, to which were attached 38 field-pieces, exclusive of about 20 pieces of battering cannon, mortars, howitzers, &c. From the American official returns we gather, that this force amounted to 8826 " non-commissioned officers and privates."

* See Plate II.

During the early part of the month, in a correspondence that took place between general Wilkinson and commodore Chauncey, the former states, that sir James Yeo, with his fleet, is in Kingston, and asks the commodore if it would be in his power to co-operate with his squadron in making the attack. The commodore replies, —" This squadron is now, and always has been, ready to co-operate with the army in any enterprise against the enemy, where it could be done with effect." Mr. Secretary Armstrong, who, in order to invigorate the movements of the army, had been at Sackett's Harbor since early in the preceding month, appears to have taken his determination from the above chilling "*where it could be done with effect;*" for, on the 16th of October, he writes to major-general Hampton thus:—" Advices from the Bay of Cante state, that he (the enemy) is coming down to Kingston, and that his sick and convalescents, to the number of 1200, had already arrived there. He will bring with him about 1500 effectives; and, thanks to the storm, and our snail-like movements down the lake, they will be there before we can reach it. The manœuvre intended is lost, so far as regards Kingston. What we now do against that place, must be done by hard blows at some risk."*

These " hard blows" which 8826 American,

* Wilkinson's Mem. Vol. III. p. 361.

might receive from 1500 British troops, saved Kingston. " Montreal is the safer and greater object," says the soft-hearted secretary, " the weaker place, and you will find there the smaller force to encounter."* To ensure a still " smaller force" at Montreal, the next place of halt for the expedition was to be French Creek,† emptying itself directly opposite to the point at which an army, destined for Kingston, might be supposed to land. The expedition, consisting now of about 300 large boats and scows, exclusive of schooners, sloops, and gigs; and protected by 12 heavy gun-boats, arrived at the creek, between the 26th of October and 3d of November. As a precaution against any sudden attack, four " large battering 18-pounders, and two $5\frac{1}{2}$ inch howitzers," had been put in scows, ready-mounted, accompanied by every requisite for heating a furnace on shore.

The " violent wind and snow-storms" that had been so long raging, ceased on the 1st; but, on the evening of the 3d, the genius of the Canadas resumed her annoyance, in the shape of " two brigs, two schooners, and several gun-boats;" which, as if to expose to ridicule the American commodore's assurance, that he was " in a situation to watch both channels," had got out of Kingston, and descended one of them, time enough to cannonade the army at its

* Wilkinson's Mem. Vol. III. p. 448.   † See Plates II. and III.

encampment, by the creek side. Three of the American 18-pounders, and some field-pieces, were presently mounted on a flat rock; and a furnace was constructed. The British vessels, however, sustained little or no damage; but, early the next morning, were compelled to retire, by the sudden appearance of the hostile fleet.

Surprising as it may be, the above 8826 American troops, with their 58 guns and howitzers, formed a part only of the force that was destined to the attack of Montreal; although there were " no fortifications at that city, or in advance of it," and only " 200 sailors and 400 marines, with the militia, numbers unknown;" but there were, to be sure, " 2500 regular troops expected daily from Quebec."* General Hampton, therefore, with the American northern army, consisting of an " effective regular force of 4053" rank and file, and " about 1500 militia," had been ordered to advance from Burlington, Vermont, and to form a junction with general Wilkinson at St. Regis. As some little obstructions had, unknown to the commander-in-chief, interfered to prevent this co-operation of the northern army, we shall leave the different generals at French Creek, arranging the flags of their brigades, while we attend to the movements of general Hampton.

The American secretary at war, in the same

* Wilkinson's Memoirs, Vol. III. ; his App. No. 24.

letter in which he appears to feel, by anticipation, the "hard blows"* preparing for his countrymen at Kingston, says thus to major-general Hampton:—" In the case of an immediate descent of the St. Lawrence, the army will make its way to Isle Perrot,† whence we shall immediately open a communication with you. Under these circumstances, you will approach the mouth of the Chateaugay, or other point which shall favor our junction, and hold the enemy in check." The major-general immediately set about obeying his orders; and the first point of halt at which his army, on its route from Burlington, excites any interest, is Chateaugay Four Corners, a small settlement, distant five miles from the national boundary-line, and about 45 from the now proposed point of junction. Here it arrived on or about the 8th of October. General Hampton's force has been stated at "7000 infantry, and 200 cavalry;"‡ but we have no American authority for supposing that the latter exceeded 180, or the former 5520, making a total of 5700 men; accompanied by 10 pieces of cannon. This army, except the small militia force attached to it, was the same that, with general Dearborn at its head, paraded across the lines and back to Plattsburg, in the autumn of 1812.§ During the twelvemonth that had since

* See p. 308.   † About 46 miles from Montreal.
‡ App. No. 54.   § See p. 129.

elapsed, the men had been drilled under an officer, major-general Izard, who had served one or two campaigns in the French army. The troops were all in uniform, well clothed and equipped: in short, general Hampton commanded, if not the most numerous, certainly the most effective, regular army, which the United States were able to send into the field during the late war.

Having made arrangements that should ensure a communication with general Wilkinson, so soon as he had passed Ogdensburg, general Hampton moved forward from Four Corners on the 21st of October. On the same evening the advance, under major-general Izard, came suddenly upon 10 Indians, who had squatted down to take their meal. It is seldom that Indians are surprised, but they were in this instance. One was shot, the remainder fled. This the American editors call " driving in the British piquets." On the evening of the 22d the main body of the American army encamped at Sears's, distant from Chateaugay about 25 miles. The engineers had been compelled to cut a road for the artillery; and, with great labour and difficulty, had dragged it thus far on the march.

The British advanced corps stationed near the frontiers, was commanded by lieutenant-colonel De Saluberry, of the Canadian fencibles, and consisted of the two flank companies of that corps, four companies of voltiguers, and six flank companies of embodied militia and Chateaugay chasseurs, placed under the immediate orders of lieutenant-colonel Macdonell, late of the Glengarry's, and who so distinguished himself at Ogdensburg.* The whole of this force did not exceed 800 rank and file. There were also at the post 172 Indians, under captain Lamotte. No sooner was it known that the American army had crossed the lines, than lieutenant-colonel De Saluberry commenced operations to check its advance. Having selected a position on the north-west side of the Chateaugay river, along which runs the road by which general Hampton would be compelled to pass to Isle Perrot, the lieutenant-colonel caused trees to be felled, and placed as temporary breast-works on the banks of four deep ditches, or ravines, which, issuing from a thick wood, crossed the road, and were distant from each other about 220 yards.

In order that the enemy's artillery might not be brought to bear upon these hastily-constructed breast-works, lieutenant-colonel De Saluberry sent forward, to a spot about a mile and a half in advance of his first, or outer line, a party of axe-men to destroy the bridges, and, with the fragments and fallen trees, to *abattis*,

* See p. 136.

or obstruct the road. That the working party sent on this service might not be molested by the enemy's skirmishers, it was accompanied by two subaltern's detachments of voltigeurs. An American editor, in his account of this "succession of breastworks," says that the rear-most one "was well supplied with ordnance."* On the contrary, not a gun was mounted there; and the nearest guns were two 6-pounders, stationed about seven miles off.

On the night of the 25th colonel Purdy, at the head of the first brigade of the American army, forded the Chateaugay river, and marched down the right bank, for the purpose of flanking the British position, while major-general Izard, with the second brigade, should attack it in front. It was not, however, till the next morning, at 10 o'clock, that the American troops appeared in sight of the working party on the left bank. The two picquets, after exchanging a few shots, retired to the *abattis;* whither the firing had brought lieutenant colonel De Saluberry, with a small force, which he instantly drew up in line; placing, in extended order, captain Fergusson's company, of the Canadian fencibles, flanked by 22 Indians, on the right and centre; and, on the left, extending to the river, captain Jean Baptiste Duchenay's company of voltigeurs. The third, or captain

* Sketches of the War, p. 187.

Jucherau Duchesnay's company of voltigeurs, along with about 60 of the Beauharnois militia, was thrown back, *en potence;* on the left side of the *abattis*; so as to flank the approach of colonel Purdy's brigade against the few Beauharnois militia, stationed on the right bank of the river. The little band of Canadians, thus assembled on the front line, amounted to no more than 240 rank and file. The remainder of colonel De Saluberry's force, exclusive of a few Beauharnois militia on the right bank, was under lieutenant-colonel Macdonell's command, and distributed, as a reserve, behind the different breastworks; the outermost of which was upwards of a mile in the rear of the *abattis*, now about to be attacked.

Soon after the lieutenant-colonel had made his disposition, general Hampton's second brigade of infantry, along with some cavalry, advanced across the plane in front of the *abattis*. The Canadians commenced firing, and continued it with such effect, as to check the forward movement of the enemy; who, after remaining motionless for some time, wheeled to the left into line, and then opened upon the Canadians a spirited fire, which presently drove the skirmishers, stationed near to the left, behind the front edge of the *abattis*. The Americans, although they did not occupy one foot of the *abattis*, nor lieutenant-colonel De Saluberry retire one inch from the ground on which he had been standing, celebrated this partial retiring as a retreat. They were not a little surprised, however, to hear their huzzas repeated by the Canadians, accompanied by a noise ten times more terrific than even "colonel Bœrstler's Stentorian voice," By way of animating his little band, when thus momentarily pressed, colonel De Saluberry ordered the bugleman to sound the advance. This was heard by lieutenant-colonel Macdonnell, who, thinking the colonel was in want of support, caused his own bugles to answer; and immediately advanced with two of his companies. He, at the same time, sent 10 or 12 buglemen into the adjoining woods, with orders to separate, and blow with all their might. This little *ruse de guerre* led the Americans to believe, that they had more thousands than hundreds to contend with, and deterred them from even attempting to penetrate the *abattis*. They contented themselves with a long-shot warfare, in which, from the nature of the defences, they were almost the only sufferers.

On the opposite, or right bank of the river, colonel Purdy's brigade, although neither *abattis* nor breastworks interfered to oppose its advance, had fared no better than major-general Izard's. After overpowering about 60 of the Beauharnois militia, under captain Bruyere, the Americans fired across the river at the left of lieutenant-colonel De Saluberry's line; and received a prompt fire in return from the left of captain I. Baptiste Duchesnay's, and the right of captain Jucherau Duchesnay's companies of voltigeurs. Lieutenant-colonel Macdonnell, previous to his advance to the front line, had sent across the river, at the ford, by way of supporting the Beauharnois militia, captain Daly's company of militia, numbering 70 men. The latter, taking with him such of the Beauharnois men as had rallied, advanced along the river-bank; where he unexpectedly encountered a part of the enemy, emerging, in great force, from the wood. Captain Daly's men, as they had been taught by lieutenant-colonel Macdonnell, fired a volley, kneeling. The return-volley was fired by tenfold numbers, and, but for that precaution, would have destroyed nearly the whole of captain Daly's command. As it was, he received a severe wound; and, with his men, several of whom were wounded, and himself a second time, was compelled to retreat. The Americans, in their pursuit, had to pass opposite to the voltigeurs who had been stationed *en potence;* and to which point colonel De Saluberry had just arrived from the front line. Here the enemy's shouts of victory were suddenly stopped by a heavy and well-directed fire from the companies *en potence.* This threw the American troops into the greatest confusion, and drove them, with precipitation, into the woods from which they had just advanced.

It adds to the value of this gallant morning's work, which was achieved by less than 400 rank and file, that the British, or rather the Canadian, loss amounted to only two killed, 16 wounded, and four missing: three of the latter were, in the official return,* included by mistake among the *killed*. After the firing had ceased against the British, it by no means ceased altogether; for, no sooner did darkness come on, than the American troops, stationed in the wood on the opposite, or right bank of the river, commenced a most destructive fire upon each other; and continued it during the greater part of the night. Just as day dawned, about 20 Americans, mistaking some of the Canadian militia on the left bank for their own people, were compelled by them to surrender. In the course of that day, upwards of 90 bodies and graves were found by our people, on the right bank; also a large quantity of muskets, drums, knapsacks, provisions, &c. Every thing, in short, indicated the confusion into which the Americans had been thrown just previous to their retreat. On the 28th a party of the Beauharnois militia destroyed some newly erected bridges, within a mile of the enemy's camp. On the same evening the Indians, under captain La Motte, proceeded

* App. No. 16.

through the woods, and came up with the enemy's rear guard. Here a slight skirmish ensued, in which the Americans lost one killed, and seven wounded. On the next day general Hampton's army broke up its second encampment, and was on the high road to Four Corners. On this day, or the day previous, captain Debartzch, of the militia, was sent to the American head-quarters with a flag. When he stated the number and description of troops by which general Hampton had been opposed, the latter, scarcely able to keep his temper, insisted that the British force amounted to 7000 men. On being assured of the contrary, he asked,— "What, then, made the woods ring so with bugles?"—Captain Debartzch explained this; but it was, apparently, to no purpose.

The American historian who undertakes to narrate the battle of Chateaugay, has certainly no enviable task to perform. One editor brings himself through pretty well, by not stating his own force at all, and then designating ours as "a considerable force of British regulars, well supplied with ordnance." He names several American officers who "were particularly distinguished;" and assures us, as he did at the battle of Stoney Creek,* that the army retreated "on the advice of a council."† Mr. O'Connor

* See p. 211.   † Sketches of the War, p. 188.

sets all shame at defiance, and declares boldly, that " the whole American force engaged did not exceed 225 men, on the side where the greatest force of the enemy were opposed; the other regiments did not arrive until the moment when the enemy were *retiring*, and were only formed, and in line, but took no part in the engagement."* In another place he says: " The hardships the American army had endured, the continual rains that were falling, and the obstructions" (over which any soldier might have jumped) " in front, would have damped the ardor of troops less disposed to disregard all sufferings and perils in pursuit of glory, and in the service of their country; but, on the contrary, partaking largely of the spirit which inspired their commander in chief, every individual seemed uncommonly emulous of the enterprise." Mr. O'Connor afterwards lets us into the secret of what kind of " spirit" it was which the troops derived from their commander's example. He quotes a part of colonel Purdy's despatch, wherein the latter says: " I have, in common with other officers, been induced to believe, that he (general Hampton) was under the influence of a too free use of spirituous liquors."* The editor of an American newspaper, the " Albany Register," compliments

* Hist. of the War, p. 138.

" the brave Hampton, and his Spartan band," for their performances at Chateaugay ; and this without meaning it as a joke.

From these amusing details we turn to the solemn asseverations of American officers engaged in the action. Colonel William King, of the 3d rifle regiment, part of general Hampton's force, and who had been despatched with the intelligence to major-general Wilkinson, informed the latter, that general Hampton's army had been defeated by a party of about 300 men ; adding that, although he could not speak with precision of the number opposed to the Americans, the latter certainly had to contend with a very inferior force, and that the best troops, or those upon the right bank, behaved in the most rascally manner.*

It is an additional satisfaction, to find it stated, in the same American work, that the force under major-general Hampton, was at least 5500 men. This battle was, indeed, sadly bungled by the Americans. Had colonel Purdy's men pushed boldly forwards to the ford at which captain Daly crossed, they would have got into the rear of colonel De Saluberry's position, and compelled his small force to surrender. They had nothing to fear from reinforcements ; for no British regulars were within 20 miles of the spot ; and even they were not put in motion to support

* Wilkinson's Mem. Vol. III. p. 74, 129.

colonel De Saluberry. The miscarriage originated partly, no doubt, in the ignorance or treachery of the guide employed by the American general. We have sought in vain through doctor Smith's book for any account of the Chateaugay battle; and yet the cant-phrase of all these " literary gentlemen" who take upon themselves to write " history," is, to be " studiously impartial."

One circumstance in the statement given of the British force by Messrs. Thomson and O'Connor, had almost escaped us. By way of adding to the difficulties, against which the American troops had to combat, these editors will insist, that the " British regulars" within the breast-works were " commanded by sir George Prevost in person;" founding their assertions on the official letter: and yet the more positive of the two declares the same official letter to be quite "improbable, and wide from the truth."* The fact is, sir George Prevost, having been visiting some posts in the neighbourhood, did arrive at the inner breast-work, just as the action ended. He received colonel De Saluberry's report; and, after bestowing praise upon him and his little party, left the spot. If sir George could employ a substitute to write the official letter of a defeat, in which he, unfortunately, commanded, † what

* History of the War. p. 140.   † See p. 172.

difficulty is there in supposing, that he could himself write the official letter of a victory, in which he, fortunately, did not command?

Not feeling himself safe at the Four Corners, general Hampton, on the 11th of November, broke up his encampment, and retreated through Morris-town and Chazee, to Plattsburg; taking with him only five, out of 45, days' provisions. Now let us return to the expedition. Commodore Chauncey having driven the " teazing" British vessels from the bay opposite French Creek, the guns and troops were re-embarked; and, on the morning of the 5th of November, this expedition which was to capture or *blow-up* Montreal, floated down the stream, " wind light, but favorable"; weather pleasant," and, at midnight, arrived at a place called Hoag's, four miles below Morrisville, and about 40 from French Creek. At this point the water-procession halted, preparatory to passing Fort-Wellington, distant six miles further. The general here drew up, agreeably to established custom, a proclamation, addressed to the inhabitants of the country he was about to conquer.* For its brevity, no less than its moderation, it far surpasses any thing of the sort hitherto promulgated by an American general. On the following day, the 7th, the powder and ammunition were landed, and placed in eight waggons;

* App. No. 57.

and the troops, except enough to man the boats strongly, were also landed. As soon as it was quite dark, the boats, keeping close on the Ogdensburg side, and muffling their oars, passed Fort-Wellington, with little or no injury; and, in order to re-embark the troops and ammunition, halted again, opposite to the Red Mill, 14 miles below Ogdensburg.

On the afternoon of the 7th, colonel Macomb was ordered to land on the Canadian side, with " about 1200 men," for the purpose of driving the British from the prominent points of the river, and particularly from *Fort*-Matilda, where the river is little more than 500 yards wide. Observing some people on the shore, the colonel landed his men " under the fire of the enemy," whom *he* rated at " about 200 militia and Indians, and 100 regulars;"* but captain John Biddle, who was also present, says :—" They (the boats) were fired at by some militia, perhaps 50 or 60."† The colonel says :—" One officer of the regular forces was taken."* Captain Biddle, in qualification of this, says :—" We took prisoner captain Green, of the commissary's department." During the march of the American troops from the point of landing to Matilda, distant one mile below, " two platoons, being unable to distinguish, in consequence of the darkness, *fired at each other.*" On arriving at *Fort-*

* Wilkinson's Mem. Vol. III. p. 169.   † Ibid. p. 303.

Matilda, there was nothing there, says the American captain," which indicated that it had been hastily abandoned. There was no artillery there. No artillery or munitions of war were found."* The American colonel says:—" Here (at Fort-Matilda) we *expected* the enemy would make a stand; but they ran off, leaving *eight* or *ten* muskets,"† whether with or without locks no where appears; and the colonel actually deposes, (for all this is on oath,) that " there was, at Matilda, every indication of a *large force*."†

On the forenoon of the 8th the boats arrived, and halted, at the White House, opposite to Matilda. At this point the dragoons were carried across, from the American side, in the artillery scows. While the expedition rested here, general Wilkinson, having just been advised, " by a confidential intelligencer direct from Montreal, employed and paid by colonel Swift of the engineers," that the British had, " at Cornwall 400 regular troops, at the *Coteau du Lac*, an island opposite, 1000, and at the Cedars 2 or 300," ‡ summoned a council of his principal officers; to whom he stated his force at " 7000 non-commissioned officers and privates," and declared he looked forward to the junction with general Hampton at St. Regis. The small

*Wilkinson's Mem. Vol. III. p. 305.   † Ibid. p. 162.
‡ Ibid. p. 449.

force at Montreal and its immediate neighbourhood* was also stated; when four of the general officers decided to "proceed to attack Montreal, the object of the expedition;" the remaining two qualified their assent with—" because we know of no other alternative." The only part of this document that surprises us, is the reduced amount of the American force. We can conceive that some loss had ensued from sickness, desertion, and other casualties, but not equal to the difference between 8826, and 7000, non-commissioned officers and privates. We must suppose that the general had begun to be less sanguine in his expectations; and that he stated the force at his immediate disposal somewhat below the truth, in order to induce the council to adopt the safer proceeding.

In the afternoon of the 9th of November the flotilla arrived at Williamsburg, on the Canadian shore, near Chrystler's field. From this place colonel Bissel was sent down the river, with about 400 men, to reconnoitre a small island, upon which some Canadian militia-men were supposed to be stationed, and brigadier-general Brown was ordered to land on the Canadian side, with his own brigade, the *elite* corps, and a detachment of artillery, amounting in all to " from 2300 to 2500 men,"† and drive the British troops, if any should be discovered, from

* See p. 304.   † Wilkinson's Mem. Vol. III. p. 83.

the shore; down which he was to march, to Barnhart's, a distance of about 20 miles. At the same time, in order to lighten the boats, so that they might descend, with less danger, a long and violent *rapid*, called the Long Saut, brigadier-general Boyd was ordered to land with "all the well men of the other brigades," excepting a sufficient number to navigate the boats; in order to prevent the British on the rear from making an advantageous attack; and, if attacked, general Boyd was " to turn about and beat them."* The American commander-in-chief further ordered that, " in case of an attack in force, beyond all expectation,"* the two brigades were to form a junction.

Colonel Bissel, with his detachment of infantry and artillery, protected by four gun-boats, landed on the island near the foot of the dreaded *rapid*, and was told by some females, that " the enemy *had been* there." Brigadier-general Brown, on the morning of the 10th, advanced on his march along the Canada-shore, and arrived about noon in the neighbourhood of Hoop-pole Creek, distant from Chrystler's farm about 12, and from the village of Cornwall,† on the St. Lawrence, about seven miles. At the latter place was stationed captain Dennis of the 49th, with one serjeant, and one rank and file of that regiment, 300 militia belonging to the counties of

* Wilkinson's Mem. Vol. III. p. 151.   † See Plate II.

Dundass and Glengarry, and 28 Indians. The instant this active officer was apprized of general Brown's approach, he, with his small force, sallied forth to endeavour at checking his advance. He first destroyed the bridge across the creek, and then so distributed his men in a thick wood bordering on the opposite bank, that their fire distracted the American troops, and caused them to suppose they had a numerous enemy to contend with. Although " some rounds of grape-shot were fired,"* no loss was sustained on our part. The Americans admit a loss of several men killed, and one officer, lieutenant Corry, of the 25th regiment, wounded. This trifling skirmish, and the breaking up of the bridges, delayed general Brown's march, upwards of three hours; thereby enabling captain Dennis, not only to carry off all the stores that had been deposited at Cornwall, but to save from capture 12 batteaux that were proceeding to Kingston. One of general Brown's officers states captain Dennis's force at " 4 or 500 Scotch militia and Indians." Another officer will insist, it was "*colonel* Dennis of the regular army," with 800 men. Most of the other officers say, 1500 men, besides Indians. So many troops, under the command of a *captain*, would look suspicious: therefore, those who had raised the men, found no difficulty in promoting the officer.

* Wilkinson's Mem. Vol. III. p. 301.

These " 1500 men" were " teazing" the general in front, and a like number were " hanging on and disturbing" his rear. Having reduced the former full three-fourths, we shall now proceed to give an account of what the latter consisted. As soon as the departure of the expedition from French Creek had pointed out its real destination, major-general De Rottenburg, who had just arrived from Queenstown with the 49th regiment, made preparations to harass its rear. On the 4th of November the two flank-companies of that regiment were pushed on to Fort-Wellington. The disposable force now at Kingston amounted to eight very weak companies of the 49th, and nine equally weak companies of the 2d battalion of the 89th, under lieutenant-colonel Morrison ; who, on the morning of the 7th, taking with him, besides the remains of those regiments, a small detachment of artillery and artillery-drivers, having in charge two 6-pounders, the whole amounting to about 560 rank and file, embarked on board the Beresford and Sir Sidney Smith schooners, seven gun-boats, and a quantity of batteaux, manned from the vessels of the fleet, and commanded by captain Mulcaster, R.N. This distinguished officer, bidding defiance to commodore Chauncey's annihilating threats, stood out of the harbor, with his flotilla, and dropped down the St. Lawrence to Fort-

Wellington. Of this, general Wilkinson had certainly reason to complain; because commodore Chauncey, only three days previous, had promised him that, in case sir James should detach any of his force down the north channel, he would send a sufficient force down to oppose him. Lieutenant-colonel Pearson had resumed the command of Fort-Wellington;* and, on the 8th, joined his force, consisting of the two flank-companies of the 49th, of detachments of the Canadian fencibles and voltigeurs, of militia-artillery, with a 6-pounder, and of half a dozen provincial dragoons, in all, about 240 rank and file, to the division under lieutenant-colonel Morrison. The two schooners, drawing too much water, were here substituted for batteax; and the whole, within a few hours, were again advancing towards an enemy, whose numerical force was nearly ten-times superior.

On the 9th lieutenant-colonel Morrison, with his corps of observation, landed at Point Iroquois, on the Canadian side of the St. Lawrence, and distant from Fort-Wellington 13 miles. In the course of this day the Indians had a slight skirmish with general Brown's piquet, in which the American major Forsythe and one of his men were wounded. On the 10th the British encountered, at Weaver's-point, in Williamsburg, general Boyd's advanced corps;

* See p. 135.

but, after a few rounds from the 6-pounders, the Americans retired. At noon on that day captain Mulcaster got sight of the American gun-boats, and drove six of them behind a point, near to which a part of the American army, protected by a battery of two 18-pounders, was stationed. Considering the smallness of captain Mulcaster's force, and the impracticability of his retreating up the river, it required all the skill, as well as gallantry, of that officer to carry on his manœuvres with safety. On the morning of the 11th the British gun-boats " continued to scratch "* poor general Wilkinson; and were again cannonaded in return, not only by the American gun-boats, eight in number; (four having been detached,) but by the 18-pounder battery on shore.

Colonel Morrison's British, and general Boyd's American, detachments of troops being now very near to each other, we will endeavour to shew their relative strength. The British force, including 342 of the 49th regiment, amounted to 800 rank and file ;† besides lieutenant Anderson and about 30 Indians, who had accompanied the detachment from Kingston. General Wilkinson, in his *amended* official letter,‡ has contrived to swell this force to " 1800 regulars, 300 militia, and 40 Indians, total 2170 ;" and, in a note to his massy " Memoirs," written long subsequently

* App. No. 59.   † Ibid. No. 58.   ‡ Ibid. No. 60.

to that letter, the American general actually ventures to state thus:—" The enemy shewed 2500 men in ' battalia', on the 11th, and this force was beaten back, by 1700 of our undisciplined troops, upon a reserve of 700 men; making the whole strength of the enemy 3200 men."* Yet colonel Walbach, who was in the action, and " had a fair view of the enemy," swore, at the general's court-martial, that he supposed " the whole, regulars, Indians, and militia, to have been between 11 and 1200."† And as a further proof that general Wilkinson had been grossly misinformed, major-generals Lewis, Boyd, Covington, and Swartwout, all " concurred in opinion," that the British force which appeared on the plane, " on the afternoon of the 10th, amounted to about 500, and was not sufficient to prevent the advance of the American troops."‡

Having settled the point, as to the amount of the British force present at Chrystler's on the 11th of November, our next task is to fix that of the Americans. General Wilkinson, in his first letter, declares that general Boyd's " force engaged did not exceed 1800 men." In his second letter, the general corrects his omission of a force of 600 men, under lieutenant-colonel Upham. How are we to reconcile this state-

* Wilkinson's Mem. Vol. III. p. 65.   † Ibid. p. 151.
‡ Ibid. p. 123.

ment of general Boyd's force, with that contained in the note to the general's book, already quoted; or, both those statements, with the following new assertion: " The force under general Boyd, which engaged the enemy at Chrystler's, *was superior to him.*"?* Consequently, it ought to have exceeded " 3200 men:" which was not the case. Major-general Boyd had six pieces of artillery; two, in the first instance; and four that were brought up along with colonel Upham's reinforcement.† As to the quality of general Boyd's detachment, we may gather that from general Wilkinson himself. " To lighten the batteaux," says the general, in his address to the court-martial, " and save the army from insult, brigadier-general Boyd was ordered to land with a *select detachment.*"‡ It was only three days previous that general Wilkinson stated his effective force at " 7000 non-commissioned officers and privates."§ General Brown's detachment is stated not to have exceeded 2500 men; colonel Macomb's, for the daring service at *Fort*-Matilda, 1200 men; and colonel Bissell's, with which he boldly landed upon a deserted island near the long Saut, 400 men. Admitting neither of these detachments to have re-joined, this would leave 2900 men for the force under general Boyd, and for the few

* Wilkinson's Mem. Vol. III. p. 451.   † Ibid. p. 152.
‡ Ibid. p 490.   § See p. 303.

troops stationed on board the flotilla, to assist the crews in navigating the rapids. That no other of the 2900 remaining troops were absent from the field at Chrystler's, we have the best of evidence, that of general Wilkinson himself. After he has said: " I directed 600 men, under lieutenant-colonel Upham, and major Malcolm to reinforce brigadier-general Boyd," he adds,— " and ordered every man capable of bearing arms, who could be spared from the boats, to sustain the troops engaged."*—However, the disparity between lieutenant-colonel Morrison and major-general Boyd is already so great, that we can cede to the latter a deduction equal to half the amount of the former's force; and yet leave on the American side a " select detachment" of 2500 infantry, dragoons, and artillery; supported by six field-pieces.

No sooner did general Boyd, whose force was at this time believed by the British commander to amount to " between 3 and 4000 men," evince a disposition for battle, than the latter undauntingly drew up,—to borrow an American phrase—" his Spartan band,"† in order to indulge his adversary. Having, on his march by Chrystler's farm, selected a position, the lieutenant-colonel formed his men in the open fields, upon a front of about 700 yards. The flank companies of the 49th and the detachment of the

* Wilkinson's Mem. Vol. III. p. 491.   † See p. 299.

Canadian fencibles, with a 6-pounder, were posted on the right, a little advanced on the road that passed the farm-house. Still further to the right, and resting on the river, were three companies of the 89th, under captain Barnes, formed *en échelon;* accompanied by the second 6-pounder. The remnants of the 49th and 89th regiments, thrown more to the rear, with the third 6-pounder, formed the main body and reserve; extending to a pine wood on the left. This wood was occupied by the detachment of Canadian voltigeurs under major Herriot, and by lieutenant Anderson and his 30 Indians; both parties having stationed themselves somewhat in advance.

The American army was drawn up in three columns; and four out of the six pieces of artillery were planted so as to enfilade the British right. At about two o'clock the British skirmishers were attacked by the American 21st regiment, of 632 rank and file,* under colonel Ripley, assisted by the artillery; and were driven in upon the main body. Mr. Thomson, so famous in battle-narrative, thus describes colonel Ripley's exploit: " Upon entering the open field, he discovered the British advance, consisting of the 49th and Glengarry† regiments. With these he immediately commenced an action, in

* Wilkinson's Mem. vol. III. p. 126.
† Not a man of the Glengarry's was in the field.

which he twice charged these united regiments, either of which being more than equal to the 21st, and drove them over the ravines and fences by which Chrystler's field was intersected; when they fell upon their main body."*

At about half past two the action became general. The whole of general Swartwout's brigade, of which the 21st formed part, attempted to turn the British left; but was repulsed by the remnants of the 49th and 89th regiments, of united, not more than 415 rank and file. These two corps now moved resolutely forward, firing occasionally by platoons. In the meanwhile, general Covington's brigade, supported by four pieces of artillery, had assaulted the British right. The 49th and 89th, immediately took ground in that direction, *en échelon*, and formed in line under a heavy but irregular fire from the enemy, who was drawn up within half-musket shot distance. A repetition of the steady platoon-firing, which so disconcerted the other, now threw into confusion this brigade. The 200 men of the 49th then proceeded to charge one of the American guns, but were restrained, in consequence of a charge made upon the right by a body of American dragoons, under adjutant-general Walbach; who would have had it in their power to attack the 49th in the rear. But the dragoons were so warmly

* Sketches of the War, p. 184.

received by captain Barnes's three companies of the 89th, and the 6-pounder, that they quickly retreated. The 89th companies, following up their advantage, rapidly charged upon, and captured, the 6-pounder posted opposite to theirs. By this time major-general Covington had received a mortal wound, " which threw his brigade into confusion."* In spite of the arrival of colonel Upham's reinforcement, and of a supply of ammunition, the American troops gradually lost ground; till, at about half-past four, they gave way at all points. Their light infantry attempted to cover their retreat, but was driven away by a judicious movement on the part of lieutenant-colonel Pearson. The detachment for the night, under the command of lieutenant-colonel Plenderleath, occupied the ground from which the enemy had been driven. Had the 19th light dragoons been attached to colonel Morrison's force, the Americans might have been immediately pursued, and a great number of them taken prisoners. But the great disparity of numbers forbad a night-pursuit by infantry; especially as the enemy had the means of reinforcing himself, so as to have encreased his superiority to a height that must have given him success.

Hitherto the battles between the British and American troops had been chiefly *bush-fighting*

* Sketches of the War, p. 184.

skirmishes. Now they met in an open champaign, where there was no shelter for the American riflemen, nor *rests* for their pieces. All was conducted, as general Wilkinson says, " in open space and fair combat." So steady was the firing, and so prompt and regular the movements, of colonel Morrison's little corps, that, on their part, it resembled a field-day, rather than a destructive battle. Their opponents, although three-fold in number, fell before the superior tactics,—not to say, as, in a similar case, an American writer would, superior bravery, of the British regulars. The American troops, besides their want of discipline and inexperience, had difficulties to contend with, none of which are mentioned in the American accounts of the battle. They had been under arms all the previous night, during an incessant rain; and had to march to the attack over ploughed ground, almost knee-deep in mud. This was certainly discouraging to men, of whom we do not think quite so highly as general Wilkinson has made a British officer declare he did, in the expression :—" Your troops, sir, are the *bravest men I have ever seen.*"*

The loss of the British on this occasion amounted to one captain, (captain Nairne of the 49th,) two drummers, and 19 rank and file killed; one lieutenant-colonel, one captain,

* Wilkinson's Mem. Vol. III. p. 65.

nine subalterns, six serjeants, 131 rank and file, wounded; and nine rank and file, and three Indians, missing; total 182.—This is one more than appears in the returns; because lieutenant-colonel Plenderleath, having been struck in the thigh by a grape-shot, as he thought slightly, did not report himself; but, in a day or two afterwards, he experienced much uneasiness from his wound. Lieutenant-colonel Pearson, and captain Davis of the quarter-master-general's department, each had a horse shot under him. According to general Wilkinson's second official letter, some one had been *hoaxing* him, with an account, " that the enemy's loss exceeded 500 killed and wounded." For the American loss in killed and wounded, we want no higher authority than the general's first letter. By that it appears that 102 were killed, and 237 wounded; total 339. Not a word is said about the missing, or prisoners; although, besides the 100 and upwards in our possession, more were hourly bringing in, at the date of colonel Morrison's despatch.

Mr. O'Connor favors us with the conclusion of major-general Boyd's report. The general, to whose epistolary qualifications at least we are no strangers,* admits that " the result of this action was not so brilliant and decisive" as he could have wished; and has the assurance to

* See p. 254.

say: " The enemy were superior to us in numbers, and greatly superior in position, and supported by seven or eight heavy gun-boats." The first of these assertions needs no answer; the second may be true; and, as to the third, it may be replied to by the question,—What had become of the 12 gun-boats attached to the American flotilla? Mr. Boyd actually terminates his farcical letter with,—" When all these circumstances are recollected, perhaps this day may be thought to have added some reputation to the American arms."* After this we can scarcely be surprised at any inconsistencies in the official account of general Wilkinson; who, lying on his sick pallet, had to contrive a letter as well as he could, out of the statements brought to him; among which he, no doubt, very cheerfully inserted, that " the front of the enemy was at first forced back more than a mile," and that " they never regained the ground they lost." Colonel Morrison's main body never lost an inch of ground: on the contrary, it advanced upon the American line, or how could it have captured the piece of artillery, and the more than 100 prisoners? Having contributed nothing to fight, the general endeavours to argue, us out of the victory. He appears to have thought that colonel Morrison, with his 800 men, was purposely sent, not merely to

* Hist. of the War, p. 144.

watch the movements, and try to cut off a part, but to surround and capture the whole, of the 8000 men, whom he, the general, was conducting in such haste to Montreal. It is admitted, on all sides, that colonel Morrison did not do this. Had he made the attempt, he would have laid himself open to the charge which the general so strongly urges against his own troops, in the words—" In the American service, temerity is too often taken for bravery, &c."* That colonel Morrison, however, by his splendid victory (for we insist upon calling it so) at Chrystler's, did not only " retard," but mainly contribute to break up, the *wild-goose* expedition of messieurs Armstrong, Wilkinson, and company, no reasonable man can doubt.

Major-general Boyd, with all his swaggering, considered himself as the beaten party; or why, when general Wilkinson, through his aide de camp, colonel Pinkney, inquired of him, " Whether he (general Boyd) could maintain himself on the bank that night," did he reply, " that he *could not*"?† The same officer deposes, that general Wilkinson exclaimed against the boats putting off from the Canadian shore, and attempted to stop the movement; remarking,—as a proof how rightly he *then* judged,—" that the enemy would say we had run away, and claim a victory."† Mr. Thomson's account is an echo

* See p. 92.   † Wilkinson's Mem. Vol. III. p. 311.

of general Wilkinson's letter, enriched with some observations of his own. " An impartial examination of the result," urges the historian, " will lead to the conclusion, that it was a drawn battle; or that, if any advantage occurred to either party, they were decidedly gained by the Americans."* This is saying, with Ralpho,—

> " For those that save themselves and fly,
> Go halves, at least, i' th' victory."

But the general's admission of the severe loss he had sustained, renders only partially applicable the next couplet:

> " And sometimes, when the loss is small,
> And danger great, they challenge all."

Mr. O'Connor, in his account, is more than usually eloquent. "This battle," he says, " was contested with a courage and obstinacy, that perhaps had no parallel. To witness undisciplined troops, and unexperienced officers, substituting courage and patriotism, in place of military knowledge, and thus opposed for three hours to a regular army, was a sight on which the guardian angel of America must have looked with exulting gratification. Amidst a shower of musketry, and *shrapnel*-shells, the brave Americans, insensible to fear, dashed into the ranks of the enemy, whose position was strengthened by ravines and thickets. The enemy retired

* Sketches of the War, p. 185.

for more than a mile before the resolute and repeated charges. The brigade, first engaged, had expended its ammunition, and was compelled to retire, in order to procure a supply. This movement so disconcerted the line, as to render it expedient for another brigade to retire. The artillery, owing to the nature of the ground, could not be brought up until after this event. The fire of the artillery was very destructive to the enemy; but when directed to retire, in passing a deep ravine, one piece was lost, but not till after the fall of its gallant leader, lieutenant Smith, and most of his men. The whole of the line was re-formed on the borders of those woods from which the enemy had first been driven; when night coming on, and the storm continuing, and the object of attack having been fully accomplished, the troops were directed to return to the ground near the flotilla; which movement was executed in good order, and without any interruption from the enemy."* Doctor Smith, having the advantage of gleaning from both his brother historians, could not possibly miss incorporating into his account, Mr. O'Connor's ingenious story about the piece of artillery sticking in the ravine while the troops were retiring. "The enemy," adds the doctor, " having seized the abandoned piece of ordnance, claimed it as a trophy of

* Hist. of the War, p. 142.

victory."* Nor has he omitted our "500 in killed and wounded;" assuring his readers, that "there cannot be a doubt of the enemy's defeat." As both Mr. O'Connor and doctor Smith admit that the Americans "retired," and got clear off; yet claim for them the victory, what is this but friend Ralpho's argument:—

> "For those who run from th' enemy,
> Engage them equally to fly;
> And, when the fight becomes a chace,
> Those win the day that win the race."?

On the evening of the day of battle, the American infantry embarked in their boats. Their progress "in the descent" of the St. Lawrence, is very laconically expressed in the diary of the American captain Paige. Here are the words: "11th.—Battle; embark, and sail down the river about four miles; land on the American shore;"† we may add,—to be out of harm's way. The next day the American troops re-embarked, and proceeded, at a furious rate down the rapids, to Barnhart's, near to Cornwall. At this point major-general Brown's, and the other detachments joined. Soon afterwards arrived colonel Atkinson, inspector-general of the division under major-general Hampton, with a letter from the latter to general Wilkinson, dated at Four Corners, November 8. In

* History of the United States, Vol. III. p. 264.
† Wilkinson's Memoirs, Vol. III. p. 289.

this letter general Hampton suggests a point of junction, preferable, in his opinion, to St. Regis; and, after stating how the roads are *abattied* and obstructed, even by Champlain and Cognawago, which is the route he proposes to take, subjoins this consolotary assurance: " But, by the employment of pack-horses, if I am not overpowered, I hope to be able to prevent your starving."

Since the first appearance of day-light, on the morning of the 12th, colonel Morrison, with his victorious troops, now reduced by their loss at Chrystler's to about 620 rank and file, had proceeded down the Canadian shore, still further to annoy the invading foe. Scarcely had colonel Atkinson, on the afternoon of the same day, delivered his letter to the almost distracted general, than information came, that the " teazing" enemy was again within a few hour's march of the American encampment. A council was instantly summoned; which, imitating in point of despatch that assembled near Stoney Creek,* soon gave it as their *unanimous* opinion, " That the attack on Montreal should be abandoned for the present season, and the army near Cornwall be immediately crossed to the American shore, for taking up winter quarters."† Accordingly, on the breaking up of the council, the dragoons and the artillery-horses passed over to

* See p. 211.   † Hist. of the War, p. 144.

the American side of the river; and proceeded to French Mills, a settlement so called, situate upon the right bank of the river Salmon, close to where it intersects the national boundary line.

An army of upwards of 6000 men, with an immense quantity of artillery, would necessarily occupy a considerable time in embarking. There was, therefore, no occasion for the general to say: " I remained on the Canadian shore till the next day."* If, indeed, he and his troops are entitled to any praise for their exertions during the progress of their voyage from Fort-George, it was when the whole of them contrived to huddle on board their vessels at Barnhart's; to descend the St. Lawrence, 15 miles, to the mouth of the Salmon river; to ascend that stream, seven miles, to French Mills; and there to disembark,—all in the course of one day. That this actually took place, we have American evidence to show. Captain Paige's journal concludes with the two following items:—" 12th, Sail to Cornwall."—" 13th, to French Mills." Very shortly after the Americans had quitted Cornwall, colonel Morrison, in order to observe what would be their next movement, transferred thither his head-quarters. Previously to his arrival at Cornwall, this enterprising officer had detached a force to the American village of Hamilton, on the St. Lawrence; which force

* App. No. 59.

seized and secured, to be held in safety till sent for, a considerable quantity of property, lately belonging to merchants of Kingston.* Another detachment brought away from Ogdensburg a 13-inch iron, and a 10-inch brass mortar, with their stores, and a large supply of provisions; all which had been deposited there, in confident security, by general Wilkinson's orders.

As soon as the American general had despatched the dragoons to Utica, he set a portion of his troops to felling trees, and constructing block-houses and *abattis*, lest colonel Morrison, or the British at Coteau du Lac, should, with their small force, cross over to attack him. This sudden change from offensive to defensive measures, on the part of general Wilkinson, produced a corresponding effect upon the minds of the Canadians; whose well-founded alarm had now given place to a feeling bordering on contempt.

Before we proceed further, we will submit a few remarks upon the causes that led to the failure of an expedition, whose magnitude, in the eyes of all but of those engaged in it, appeared quite disproportionate to the object for which it had been so expensively, and so boastingly got up.

General Wilkinson lays much of the blame at the door of Mr. Secretary Armstrong; first, for having played a double part between general

* App. Nos. 55. and 56.

Hampton and him; next, for having deceived him as to the real point of attack, and as to commodore Chauncey's capabilty to prevent his being pursued and "scratched" by captain Mulcaster's gun-boats, as well as by the force landed out of them at Chrystler's; but, above all, as to the disposition of the Canadians, along whose shores the voyage to Montreal must necessarily be undertaken. One of the secretary's letters, dated "Antwerp, 27th of October, 1813," contains this paragraph:—"Three days ago, he (the enemy) called out a regiment of militia, which produced but 15 men, 14 of whom deserted during the first night of their service." From this, general Wilkinson very naturally expected, that the people would, the instant they read his proclamation, throw themselves, by hundreds, upon American protection. How he was deceived may be gathered from his own words. " The enemy," says the general, in his official letter, " deserve credit for their zeal and intelligence, which the active universal hostility of the male inhabitants of the country enabled them to employ to the greatest advantage." This is certainly a high compliment, if not to the foresight and penetration of the American secretary, at least to the loyalty and devotion of the inhabitants of the Canadas. Among the causes of delay in the early movements of the expedition, we are pleased to see a prominent one stated in " the masterly manœuvres of the British squadron, under sir James Yeo;"*—a proof that the latter's " vapouring" was more substantial than the general, when he reproached him with that epithet, had reason to expect.

It was certainly a surprise to many, that the American government should have expected to succeed in amalgamating two such characters as Hampton and Wilkinson; men whose political tenets were, and always had been, diametrically opposite; and that in a country, too, where party-rancor rises to the highest pitch; often making *Montagues* and *Capulets* of families that would otherwise live in the bonds of harmony and good fellowship.

From the moment the expedition had departed from French Creek, the real point of attack was no longer doubtful. What occasion was there for detaching 1200 men to capture a commissary and six muskets; or 400, with a show of gun-boats, to alarm " some females"? It is true, 800 British troops followed general Wilkinson's rear; and, when attacked by, conquered in style, 2500 American troops. Why did not the latter rally the next morning, and, as Mr. Secretary Armstrong himself says, " destroy or disperse" this puny British force? The American troops having escaped, however, and got safe to

* Wilkinson's Mem. Vol. III. p. 378.

Cornwall, three-fourths of the distance from Fort-George to Montreal, what obstacle arose to prevent the expedition from proceeding, along the remaining 80 miles, to an honorable, as, considering the force employed, it must have been successful, termination?—What! without general Hampton's co-operation?— Had not general Wilkinson already with him 6000 troops; and did he not state, in substance, to his council on the 8th,* and repeat to the secretary at war on the 15th, of November, two days after he had been at French Mills, that there were no fortifications at Montreal, and that " the British garrison consisted solely of 400 marines and 200 sailors, which had been sent up from Quebec"?† The secret, then, of the failure of the attack upon Montreal, if chargeable exclusively to the commander of the expedition, may be summed up in the words applied by an American editor to a British commanding officer; — "the predominance of his apprehension over his bravery and fore-sight."‡ — If the blame lay upon the troops, it was because they were deficient in those qualities which awed and conquered them at Chrystler's; and which alone can lead to glorious results, or, particularly where high expectations have been formed, save the parties concerned from public derision.

* See p. 175. † Hist. of the War, p. 145.
‡ See p. 175.

Intelligence of the expedition's having passed Fort-Wellington had reached Montreal early on the morning of the 9th. The militia-force of the country was instantly assembled, and stationed to the best advantage for defending the city. Much credit is due to the Canadians, for the promptitude with which they obeyed the call to repel the invaders. From the state of the weather, and the known rapidity of the current, it was expected that the enemy would be almost at the messenger's heels. On the 13th, after waiting so long in suspense, arrived the joyful tidings of colonel Morrison's victory; and, on the 18th, the militia, in excellent spirits, commenced their march homewards.

Exclusive of colonel Morrison's force at Cornwall, the chief part of the 103d regiment, under colonel Scott, was stationed at Coteau du Lac. Had the whole of this force, in conjunction with captain Mulcaster's flotilla, proceeded up the Salmon river, before general Wilkinson began to fortify his quarters, the disheartened condition of his troops would have rendered their numerical superiority of no avail; and resulted, at least, in the capture or destruction of the river-craft and gun-boats. This enterprise was actually contemplated; but, no orders for its execution arriving from head-quarters, was afterwards abandoned. According to an American official return, the effective troops at French Mills, on the 1st of December, amounted to " 4482 non-commissioned officers and privates ;"* and colonels Morrison and Scott could have brought into the field about 1750: consequently, in reference to the affair at Chrystler's, the disparity was not very alarming.

The restless spirit of the American general could not allow many days to elapse, without his projecting another expedition against some " defenceless" point of our Canadian possessions. For the re-establishment of his health he had fixed his head-quarters at Malone, a village about 15 miles south of French Mills; and, on the 7th of December, he forwarded to the secretary at war a plan of Isle aux Noix, with the fortifications, drawn up from the information of a deserter who left that post in July. The general considered that " the capture of the place might be easily accomplished in the course of the winter from Plattsburg."† We are not told what reply the American secretary at war made to this proposition; but presume it was a negative, as the general comes forward, on the 7th of January, with another plan, of much greater magnitude. " I propose," says this indefatigable schemer, " to march, on the 3d or 4th of next month, a column of 2000 men from Chateaugay, and the same from Platts-

* Wilkinson's Mem. Vol. III. p. 376.
† Ibid. his App. No. 43.

burg, with the appropriate attirail, and the necessary sleighs for transport: the first to move by the route of general Hampton, to sweep the enemy to the St. Lawrence, then to turn to the right, and march for St. Pierre, while the second will march by the route of Hemmersford and La Tortue to form a junction at St. Pierre; from which point the united corps will proceed against the posts of St. Philip, L'Acadie, and St. John, and having beaten, routed, or captured the detachments at these defenceless cantonments, shall be governed by circumstances, whether to occupy their quarters and hold the country, and reduce the Isle aux Noix, or return to our cantonments. Simultaneous with these movements, 4000 men from the French Mills will cross the St. Lawrence, attack Cornwall, capture or route the corps of the enemy's regular troops in that vicinity, disperse the militia, fortify and hold possession of the village, and then effectually cut off the intercourse between the two provinces."*

This "*contre-coup*" which was to "reach to the bone of the enemy,"* the general himself, in five days afterwards, declares to be unfeasible; although he had built his hopes of taking Cornwall upon the knowledge that the 49th regiment had, since the middle of December, been detached to Montreal. In his next letter to the

* Wilkinson's Mem. Vol. III. his App. No. 48.

secretary at war, he complains sadly of the difficulty of subsisting the troops. "In this situation," says he " instead of advancing on the enemy, we are in danger of being compelled to retrograde for subsistence; and, as it would almost destroy the troops to erect second cantonments at this inclement season, with the approbation of government, I will endeavour to find quarters for them in Prescott and Kingston, which I consider practicable to a corps of hardihood and resolution, aided by the facility of movement to be derived from sleds. Charge me not with caprice for thus suddenly varying my plan of operations; since it is caused by posterior information, which presents an insuperable obstacle to the execution of the project submitted in my despatch of the 7th instant. The object now presented had not escaped my mind, but it was opposed by my repugnance to give ground to the enemy, and to sacrifice our boats, the infallible consequence of its execution. Should the president sanction the plan now proposed, I shall remove the sick, the convalescent, and every article of useless baggage, together with the artillery and munitions of war, for which I shall have no occasion, to Plattsburg; shall destroy our boats, and break up the cantonments at the French Mills and Chateaugay; and, whilst I keep the enemy in expectation that these precautions are preparatory to the attack of their posts and cantonments in my vicinity, I shall detach 1000 selected men, to steal a march, and take Prescott by surprise or storm; whither I shall follow that detachment, with the main body, a few hours after it marches; and, having every thing in readiness for the movement, by its rapidity, and the feints of some light parties, I shall prevent the enemy from penetrating my real design, until I have gained my first point."

In another part of his book the general favors us with " an accurate plan and description" of the post, whose capture he designed to be his " first point." " Prescott," says he, " is a quadrangle of sod-work, without a single flanking angle, or exterior obstruction of any kind, with its battery pointed to the river, which the post was originally intended to command; and to serve, at the same time, as an *entrépôt* between Montreal and Kingston: a block-house had been erected for the interior defence, but the roof was flat, and could have been gained without difficulty from the parapet. Such a place, without a fraising, ditch, palisades, or abattis, garrisoned by only 200 or 250 men, its utmost strength, could have made little opposition to columns of 500 select men marching simultaneously upon each of its faces." After having achieved this exploit, Kingston, it was considered, would fall with ease; and " Montreal might be taken in the spring." For carrying his plans into execution, the general declares he can march from his present quarters " 5500 men;" having, according to the American journals, just received a reinforcement of regulars from Sackett's Harbor. He expects to be joined by 2000 more regulars from the same place, and by an equal number of volunteers or militia; making a total of 9500 men. " If successful," says this wordy warrior, " we shall destroy the squadron of the enemy at Kingston; kill and capture, eventually, 4000 of his best troops; recover what we have lost; save much blood and treasure to the nation; and conquer a province."*—The secretary, far less sanguine, saw too much " chance"† in the issue of this enterprise; and, on the 20th, four days after the date, and scarcely as many hours after the receipt, of general Wilkinson's letter, directs him to abandon his position, to detach general Brown with 2000 men and a competent proportion of the field and battering cannon, to Sackett's Harbor, and to fall back with the residue of his force, stores, and baggage, to Plattsburg.

On the night of the 12th of February, general Wilkinson gave orders to burn his 300 river-craft and 12 gun-boats, all of which were frozen up; and then his huts, block-houses, and bar-

* Wilkinson's Mem. Vol. I. p. 624. † See p. 133.

racks, which had been erected at great labor and expense. His battering cannon and field-artillery he succeeded in getting away; also a part of the stores and provisions. The detachment which had been ordered to Sackett's Harbor proceeded thither; and the remainder of the troops, with the general at their head, made a rapid retreat upon Plattsburg and Burlington. Previously to the enemy's complete evacuation of his position, colonel Scott, of the 103d regiment, with small detachments from that corps, the 89th, and the Canadian fencibles, and a piquet of light cavalry, from Coteau du Lac and Cornwall, amounting, in all, to about 1100 rank and file, passed over the ice from the latter place to Salmon river, and arrived in time to press upon general Wilkinson's rear-guard, and to capture about 100 sleigh-loads of stores and provisions. Colonel Scott and his party then proceeded, without the slightest opposition, to Malone; thence to Madrid, and within a few miles of Plattsburg; and returned, by the route of Four Corners, with the loss of about 200 men by desertion, to his post at Coteau du Lac.

Mr. Thomson has magnified our force, upon this occasion, to " 2000 regulars;" although he must have seen, in the public prints, that the 49th regiment had arrived at Montreal, since the 18th of December. This editor declares we " pillaged the property of individuals;" carried off, not 100 sleigh-loads, but "several barrels," of provisions; and that colonel Scott, on "hearing of the approach of the American troops, retreated in great confusion."* Had the American troops travelled somewhat more slowly, a second opportunity would have been afforded them, of trying their boasted "hardihood and resolution" before a small corps of British; and the signal for battle would have at once dispelled from the minds of the latter all thoughts of desertion. But the American commander reserved his men, perhaps, to carry into effect some ulterior plan of annoyance, less subject to "hard blows" in its progress, or to "chance" in its result, than any of the numerous plans he had already been projecting.

* Sketches of the War, p. 256.

APPENDIX.

No. 1.

From captain Roberts to the adjutant-general.

Sir,   Fort-Michilimacinac, July 17, 1812.

On the 15th instant I received letters, by express, from major-general Brock, with orders to adopt the most prudent measures either for offence or defence, which circumstances might point out; and having received intelligence from the best information, that large reinforcements were expected to be thrown into this garrison, with the thorough conviction that my situation at St. Joseph's was totally indefensible, I determened to lose no time in making the meditated attack on this fort.

On the 16th, at 10 o'clock in the morning, I embarked my few men, with about 180 Canadians, and two iron 6-pounders. The boats arrived without the smallest accident at the port of rendezvous, at three o'clock the following morning; by the exertions of the Canadians, one of the guns was brought up a height commanding the garrison, and ready to act about 10 o'clock. A summons was then sent in; a copy of the capitulation which followed I have the honor to enclose. At 12 o'clock the American colours were hauled down, and those of his majesty were hoisted. A committee has been appointed to examine into the state of the public stores.

Enclosed also are the returns of the ordnance and military stores found in the fort, and the strength of the garrison. The greatest praise is due to every individual employed in the expedition; to my own officers I am indebted, in particular, for their active assistance in carrying all my orders into effect.

I have the honor to be, &c.

CHAS. ROBERTS, Capt. Com.

The adjutant-gen. &c. &c. &c.

****

No. 2.

American capitulation.

Heights above Fort-Michilimacinac, July 17, 1812.

Capitulation agreed upon between captain Charles Roberts, commanding his Britannic majesty's forces, on the one part, and lieutenant Hanks, commanding the forces of the United States of America, on the other.

Article I. The fort of Michilimacinac shall immediately be surrendered to the British forces.

Art. II. The garrison shall march out with the honors of war, lay down their arms, and become prisoners of war, and shall be sent to the United States of America by his Britannic majesty, not to serve this war until regularly exchanged; and for the due performance of this article the officers pledge their word and honor.

Art. III. All the merchant vessels in the harbor, with their respective cargoes, shall be in possession of their respective owners.

Art. IV. Private property shall be held sacred as far as in my power.

Art. V. All citizens of the United States, who shall not take the oath of allegiance to his Britannic majesty, shall depart with their property from the island, in one month from the date hereof.

CHARLES ROBERTS, captain, commanding his Britannic majesty's troops.

Lieut. HANKS, commanding the forces of the United States at Fort-Michilimacinac.

APPENDIX. 355

Return of the garrison of Fort-Michilimacinac.

Two first-lieutenants, one surgeon's mate, three serjeants, four corporals, five musicians, six artificers, 39 privates, one private sick.—Total 61.

Return of ordnance taken in Fort-Michilimacinac.

Two brass $5\frac{1}{2}$ inch howitzers, two brass 6-pounders on garrison carriages, one brass 3-pounder on a garrison carriage, two iron 9-pounders on garrison carriages.

With a considerable proportion of ammunition and ordnance stores.

ALEX. PILMOUR, military conductor of stores.

No. 3.

From lieutenant Hanks to general Hull.

SIR, Detroit, August 14th, 1812

I take the earliest opportunity to acquaint your excellency, of the surrender of the garrison of Michilimacinac under my command, to his Britannic majesty's forces under the command of captain Charles Roberts, on the 17th ultimo. On the 16th I was informed that several nations of Indians then at St. Joseph's, and a British detachment, distant 45 miles, intended to make an immediate attack on Michilimacinac; I accordingly despatched captain Daurman to St. Joseph's to watch the Indians; he embarked about sun-set and met the British forces within 10 or 15 miles of the island, by whom he was made prisoner, and put on his parole of honor. He was landed on the island at day-break, with positive orders to give no intelligence whatever; he was also instructed to take the inhabitants of the village, indiscriminately, to a place on the west side of the island, where their persons and property would be protected by a British guard; but, should they go to the fort, they would be subject to a general massacre by the savages, which would be inevitable if the garrison fired a gun. This information I received from Dr. Day, who was passing through the village, when every person was flying for refuge to the enemy. Immediately on being informed of the approach of the enemy, I placed ammunition, &c. in the block-houses, ordered every gun to be charged, and every preparation for action. About nine o'clock, I could discover that the enemy were in possession of the heights that commanded the fort, and one piece of artillery directed to the most defenceless part of the garrison. The Indians at this time were to be seen at the edge of the woods. At half-past 11 o'clock, the enemy sent in a flag of truce, demanding a surrender of the fort and island to his Britannic majesty's forces. This, sir, was the first information I had of the declaration of war; I had however anticipated it, and was as well prepared to meet such an event, as I possibly could have been with the force under my command, amounting to 57 effective men, including officers.

I have the honor to be, &c.

Gen. Hull. ———— HANKS.

No. 4.

General Hull's proclamation.

By William Hull, brigadier-general and commander of the North-western army of the United States;

A PROCLAMATION.

Inhabitants of Canada,

After 30 years of peace and prosperity, the United States have been driven to arms. The injuries and aggressions, the insults and indignities of Great Britain, have once more left them no alternative but manly resistance, or unconditional submission. The army under my command has invaded your

APPENDIX. 357

country; the standard of the United States now waves over the territory of Canada. To the peaceable unoffending inhabitants, it brings neither danger nor difficulty. I come to find enemies, not to make them. I come to protect, not to injure you.

Separated by an immense ocean, and an extensive wilderness, from Great Britain, you have no participation in her councils, no interest in her conduct.

You have felt her tyranny; you have seen her injustice; but I do not ask you to avenge the one, or to redress the other. The United States are sufficiently powerful to afford every security, consistent with their rights and your expectations. I tender you the invaluable blessing of civil, political, and religious liberty, and their necessary result, individual and general prosperity; that liberty which gave decision to our councils, and energy to our conduct, in a struggle for independence, which conducted us safely and triumphantly through the stormy period of the revolution—the liberty which has raised us to an elevated rank among the nations of the world, and which afforded us a greater measure of peace and security, of wealth and improvement than ever fell to the lot of any people. In the name of my country, and the authority of government, I promise you protection to you persons, property, and rights: remain at your homes; pursue your peaceful and customary avocations; raise not your hands against your brethren. Many of your fathers fought for the freedom and independence we now enjoy. Being children, therefore, of the same family with us, and heirs of the same heritage, the arrival of an army of friends must be hailed by you with a cordial welcome. You will be emancipated from tyranny and oppression, and restored to the dignified station of freedom. Had I any doubt of eventual success, I might ask your assistance; but I do not. I come prepared for every contingency—I have a force which will break down all opposition, and that force is but the vanguard of a much greater. If contrary to your own interests, and the just expectations of my country, you should take part in the approaching contest, you will be considered and treated as enemies; and the horrors and calamities of war will stalk before you. If the barbarous and savage policy of Great Britain be pursued, and the savages are let loose to murder our citizens, and butcher our women and children, this war will be a war of extermination. The first stroke of the tomahawk—the first attempt with the scalping-knife, will be the signal of one indiscriminate scene of desolation. No white man found fighting by the side of an indian, will be taken prisoner—instant death will be his lot. If the dictates of reason, duty, justice, and humanity, cannot prevent the employment of a force which respects no rights, and knows no wrong, it will be prevented by a severe and relentless system of retaliation. I doubt not your courage and firmness—I will not doubt your attachment to liberty. If you tender your services voluntarily, they will be accepted readily. The United States offer you peace, liberty, and security. Your choice lies between these and war, slavery and destruction. Choose then; but choose wisely; and may he who knows the justice of our cause, and who holds in his hand the fate of nations, guide you to a result the most compatible with your rights and interests, your peace and happiness.

By the general,

A. P. HULL.

Captain of the 3d United States' regiment of infantry, and aide de camp. Head-quarters, Sandwich, July 12, 1812.

WILLIAM HULL.

No. 5.

Major-general Broke's proclamation, in answer.

The unprovoked declaration of war by the United States of America, against the United Kingdom of Great Britain and Ireland, and its dependencies, has been followed by the actual

APPENDIX.

invasion of this province, in a remote frontier of the western districts, by a detachment of the United States.

The officer commanding that detachment has thought proper to invite his majesty's subjects, not merely to a quiet and unresisting submission, but insults them with a call to seek voluntarily the protection of his government.

Without condescending to repeat the illiberal epithets bestowed, in this appeal of the American commander to the people of Upper Canada, on the administration of his majesty, every inhabitant of the province is desired to seek the confutation of such indecent slander in the review of his own particular circumstances. Where is the Canadian subject who can truly affirm to himself, that he has been injured by the government, in his person, his property, or his liberty? Where is to be found, in any part of the world, a growth so rapid in prosperity and wealth, as this colony exhibits? Settled, not 30 years, by a band of veterans, exiled from their former possessions on account of their loyalty, not a descendant of these brave people is to be found, who, under the fostering liberality of their sovereign, has not acquired a property and means of enjoyment superior to what were possessed by their ancestors.

This unequalled prosperity would not have been attained by the utmost liberality of the government, or the persevering industry of the people, had not the maritime power of the mother country secured to its colonists a safe access to every market, where the produce of their labour was in request.

The unavoidable and immediate consequences of a separation from Great Britain must be the loss of this inestimable advantage; and what is offered you in exchange? To become a territory of the United States, and share with them that exclusion from the ocean which the policy of their government enforces; you are not even flattered with a participation of their boasted independence; and it is but too obvious that, once estranged from the powerful protection of the United Kingdom, you must be re-annexed to the dominion of France, from which the provinces of Canada were wrested by the arms of Great Britain, at a vast expense of blood and treasure, from no other motive than to relieve her ungrateful children from the oppression of a cruel neighbour. This restitution of Canada to the empire of France, was the stipulated reward for the aid afforded to the revolted colonies, now the United States; the debt is still due, and there can be no doubt but the pledge has been renewed as a consideration for commercial advantages, or rather for an expected relaxation in the tyranny of France over the commercial world. Are you prepared, inhabitants of Canada, to become willing subjects, or rather slaves, to the despot who rules the nations of Europe with a rod of iron? If not, arise in a body, exert your energies, co-operate cordially with the king's regular force to repel the invader, and do not give cause to your children, when groaning under the oppression of a foreign master, to reproach you with having so easily parted with the richest inheritance of this earth—a participation in the name, character, and freedom, of Britons; the same spirit of justice, which will make every reasonable allowance for the unsuccessful efforts of zeal and loyalty, will not fail to punish the defalcation of principle. Every Canadian freeholder is, by deliberate choice, bound by the most solemn oaths to defend the monarchy, as well as his own property; to shrink from that engagement is a treason not to be forgiven. Let no man suppose that if, in this unexpected struggle, his majesty's arms should be compelled to yield to an overwhelming force, that the province will be eventually abandoned; the endeared relation of its first settlers, the intrinsic value of its commerce, and the pretensions of its powerful rival to repossess the Canadas, are pledges that no peace will be established between the United States and Great Britain and Ireland, of which the restoration of those provinces does not make the most prominent condition.

Be not dismayed at the unjustifiable threat of the commander of the enemy's forces, to refuse quarter, should an Indian appear in the ranks. The brave bands of natives which inhabit this colony, were, like his majesty's subjects, punished for their zeal and fidelity, by the loss of their possessions in the late colonies, and rewarded by his majesty with lands of superior value in this province.

The faith of the British government has never yet been violated—they feel that the sod they inherit is to them and their posterity protected from the base arts, so frequently devised to over-reach their sympathy. By what new principle are they to be prohibited from defending their property? If their warfare, from being different to that of the white people, is more terrific to the enemy, let him retrace his steps. They seek him not; and cannot expect to find women and children in an invading army. But they are men, and have equal rights with all other men to defend themselves and their property when invaded, more especially when they find in the enemy's camp a ferocious and mortal foe, using the same warfare which the American commander affects to reprobate.

This inconsistent and unjustifiable threat of refusing quarter, for such a cause as being found in arms with a brother-sufferer, in defence of invaded rights, must be exercised with the certain assurance of retaliation, not only in the limited operations of war in this part of the king's dominions, but in every quarter of the globe; for the national character of Britain is not less distinguished for humanity than retributive justice, which will consider the execution of the threat as deliberate murder, for which every subject of the offending power shall make expiation.

ISAAC BROCK, major-gen. and president.

Head-quarters, Fort-George, July 22, 1812.

By order of his honor the president,
J. B. GLEGG, captain and aide de camp.

No. 6.

From major-general Brock to sir George Prevost.

Sir, H. Q. Detroit, Aug. 17.

I have had the honor of informing your excellency, that the enemy effected his passage across the Detroit river on the 12th ult. without opposition; and that, after establishing himself at Sandwich, he had ravaged the country as far as the Moravian town. Some skirmishes occurred between the troops under lieut.-col. St. George and the enemy, upon the river Canard, which uniformly terminated in his being repulsed with loss. I judged it proper to detach a force down the river Thames, capable of acting in conjunction with the garrison of Amherstburg offensively, but captain Chambers, whom I had appointed to direct this detachment, experienced difficulties that frustrated my intentions. The intelligence received from that quarter admitting of no delay, colonel Proctor was directed to assume the command, and his force was soon after increased, with sixty rank and file of the 41st regiment.

In the mean time, the most strenuous measures were adopted to counteract the machinations of the evil-disposed, and I soon experienced the gratification of receiving voluntary offers of service from that portion of the embodied militia the most easily collected. In the attainment of this important point, gentlemen of the first character and influence shewed an example highly creditable to them; and I cannot, on this occasion, avoid mentioning the essential assistance I derived from John M'Donell, esq. his majesty's attorney-general, who, from the beginning of the war, has honored me with his services as my provincial aide de camp A sufficiency of boats being collected at Long Point for the conveyance of 300 men, the embarkation took place on the 8th instant, and in five days we arrived in safety at Amherstburg.

I found that the judicious arrangement which had been adopted immediately upon the arrival of colonel Proctor, had

APPENDIX. 363

compelled the enemy to retreat, and take shelter under the guns of his fort, : that officer commenced operations, by sending strong detachments across the river, with a view of cutting off the enemy's communication with his service.

This produced two smart skirmishes on the 5th and 9th inst. in which the enemy's loss was considerable, whilst ours amounted to three killed, and 13 wounded; amongst the latter, I have particularly to regret captain Muir and lieutenant Sutherland, of the 41st regiment: the former an officer of great experience, and both ardent in his majesty's service. Batteries had likewise been commenced opposite Fort-Detroit, for one 18-pounder, two 12, and two $5\frac{1}{2}$ inch mortars; all of which opened on the evening of the 15th, (having previously summoned brigadier-gen. Hull to surrender,) and although opposed by a well-directed fire from seven 24-pounders, such was their construction, under the able direction of captain Dixon, of the royal engineers, that no injury was sustained from its effect.

The force at my disposal being collected in the course of the 15th in the neighbourhood of Sandwich, the embarkation took place a little after day-light on the following morning, and the able arrangements of lieutenant Dewar, of the quarter-master-general's department, the whole was, in a short time, landed without the smallest confusion at Spring Well, a good position, three miles west of Detroit. The Indians, who had in the mean time effected their landing two miles below, moved forward and occupied the woods, about a mile and a half on our left.

The force, which I instantly directed to march against the enemy, consisted of 30 royal artillery, 250 41st regiment, 50 royal Newfoundland regiment, 400 militia, and about 600 Indians, to which were attached three 6-pounders and two 3-pounders. The service of lieutenant Troughton, commanding the royal artillery, an active and intelligent officer, being required in the field, the direction of the batteries was intrusted to captain Hall, and the marine department, and I cannot withhold my entire approbation of their conduct on this occasion.

APPENDIX.

I crossed the river, with an intention of waiting in a strong position the effect of our force upon the enemy's camp, and in hopes of compelling him to meet us in the field; but receiving information upon landing, that colonel M'Arthur, an officer of high reputation, had left the garrison three days before with a detachment of 500 men, and hearing, soon afterwards, that his cavalry had been seen that morning three miles in our rear, I decided on an immediate attack. Accordingly, the troops advanced to within one mile of the fort, and having ascertained that the enemy had taken little or no precaution towards the land-side, I resolved on an assault, whilst the Indians penetrated his camp. Brigadier-gen. Hull, however, prevented this movement, by proposing a cessation of hostilities, for the purpose of preparing terms of capitulation. Lieutenant-col. John M'Donell and captain Glegg were accordingly deputed by me on this mission, and returned within an hour with the conditions, which I have the honor herewith to transmit. Certain considerations afterwards induced me to agree to the two supplementary articles.

The force thus surrendered to his majesty's arms, cannot be estimated at less than 2500 men. In this estimate, colonel M'Arthur's detachment is included, as he surrendered, agreeably to the terms of capitulation, in the course of the evening, with the exception of 200 men, whom he left escorting a valuable convoy at some little distance in his rear; but there can be no doubt the officer commanding will consider himself equally bound by the capitulation.

The enemy's aggregate force was divided into two troops of cavalry; one company of artillery engineers; the 4th United States' regiment; detachments of the 1st and 3d United States' regiments, volunteers; three regiments of the Ohio militia; one regiment of the Michigan territory.

Thirty-three pieces of brass and iron ordnance have already been secured.

When this contest commenced, many of the Indian nations were engaged in the active warfare with the United States, notwithstanding the constant endeavours of this government to dissuade them from it. Some of the principal chiefs happened to be at Amherstburgh, trying to procure a supply of arms and ammunition, which for years had been withheld, agreeably to the instructions received from sir James Craig, and since repeated by your excellency.

From that moment they took a most active part, and appeared foremost on every occasion; they were led yesterday by colonel Elliot and captain M'Kie, and nothing could exceed their order and steadiness. A few prisoners were taken by them, during the advance, whom they treated with every humanity; and it affords me much pleasure in assuring your excellency, that such was their forbearance and attention to what was required of them, that the enemy sustained no other loss in men than what was occasioned by the fire of our batteries.

The high sense I entertain of the abilities and judgment of lieut.-col. Myers, induced me to appoint him to the important command at Niagara; it was with reluctance I deprived myself of his assistance, but I had no other expedient; his duties, as head of the quarter-master-general's department, were performed to my satisfaction by lieut.-colonel Nichol, quarter-master-general of the militia.

Captain Glegg, my aide-de-camp, will have the honor of delivering this despatch to your excellency; he is charged with the colours taken at the capture of Fort-Detroit, and those of the 4th United States' regiment.

Captain Glegg is capable of giving your excellency every information respecting the state of this province, and I shall esteem myself highly indebted to your excellency to afford him that protection, to which his merit and length of service give him a powerful claim.

I have the honor to be, &c.

ISAAC BROCK, maj.-gen.

P. S. I have the honor to enclose a copy of a proclamation which I issued immediately on taking possession of this country.

I should have mentioned in the body of my despatch the capture of the Adams; she is a fine vessel, and recently repaired, but without arms.

No. 7.

Capitulation of Fort-Detroit.

Camp at Detroit, Aug. 16, 1812.

Capitulation for the surrender of Fort-Detroit, entered into between maj.-gen. Brock, commanding his Britannic majesty's forces, on the one part, and brigadier-gen. Hull, commanding the north-western army of the United States on the other part.

Article I. Fort-Detroit, with all the troops, regulars as well as militia, will be immediately surrendered to the British forces under the command of maj.-gen. Brock, and will be considered as prisoners of war, with the exception of such of the militia of the Michigan territory, who have not joined the army.

Art. II. All public stores, arms, and all public documents, including every thing else of a public nature, will be immediately given up.

Art. III. Private persons, and property of every description will be respected.

Art. IV. His excellency, brigadier-general Hull, having expressed a desire that a detachment from the state of Ohio, on its way to join his army, as well as one sent from Fort-Detroit, under the command of colonel M'Arthur, should be included in the capitulation, it is accordingly agreed to. It is, however, to be understood, that such part of the Ohio militia as have not joined the army, will be permitted to return to their homes, on condition that they will not serve during the war; their arms will be delivered up, if belonging to the public.

Art. V. The garrison will march out at the hour of 12 this

APPENDIX. 367

day, and the British forces will take immediate possession of the fort.

    J. MACDONELL, lieut.-col. militia, P. A. D. C.
    J. B. GLEGG, major, A. D. C.
    JAMES MIETER, lieut.-col. 5th U. S. infantry.
    E. BRUSH, col. commanding 1st regiment of Michigan militia.

Approved—W. HULL, brig.-gen. commanding the N. W. army.

Approved—ISAAC BROCK, major-general.

An article supplementary to the articles of capitulation, concluded at Detroit, the 16th of August, 1812.

It is agreed that the officers and soldiers of Ohio militia and volunteers shall be permitted to proceed to their respective homes, on this condition, that they do not serve during the present war, unless they are exchanged.

    W. HULL, brig.-gen. commanding U. S. N. W. army.
    ISAAC BROCK, maj.-gen.

An article in addition to the supplementary article of capitulation, concluded at Detroit, the 16th August, 1812.

It is further agreed that the officers and soldiers of the Michigan militia and volunteers, under the command of major Weatherall, shall be placed on the same principles as the Ohio militia and volunteers are placed by the supplementary article, of the 16th instant.

    W. HULL, brig.-gen. commanding the N. W. army U. S.
    ISAAC BROCK, maj.-gen.

Return of the ordnance taken in the fort and batteries at Detroit, August 16th, 1812.

Iron Ordnance—nine 24-pounders, eight 12-pounders, five 9-pounders. Brass ordnance—three 6-pounders, two 4-poun-

ders, one 3-pounder, one 8-inch howitzer, one 3½-inch ditto.—
Total of ordnance taken—33.

FELIX TROUGHTON, lieut.-col. royal artillery.

N. B. No time to take an inventory of ordnance stores, &c. and no return could be procured from the American officer.

No. 8.

Proclamation by Isaac Brock, Esq. major-general commanding his majesty's forces in the province of Upper Canada, &c.

Whereas the territory of Michigan was this day, by capitulation, ceded to the arms of his Britannic majesty, without any other condition than the protection of private property, and wishing to give an early proof of the moderation and justice of his majesty's government, I do hereby announce to all the inhabitants of the said territory, that the laws heretofore in existence shall continue in force until his majesty's pleasure be known, or so long as the peace and safety of the said territory will admit thereof; and I do hereby also declare and make known to the said inhabitants, that they shall be protected in the full exercise and employment of their religion, of which all persons both civil and military will take notice, and govern themselves accordingly.

All persons having in their possession, or having any knowsedge of, any public property, shall forthwith deliver in the same, or give notice thereof to the officer commanding, or lieutenant colonel Nichol, who are duly authorised to receive and give proper receipts for the same.

Officers of militia will be held responsible, that all arms in the possession of militia-men be immediately given up, and all individuals whatever who have in their possession arms of any kind, will give them up without delay.

Given under my hand at Detroit, this 16th day of August, 1812, and in the 52d year of his majesty's reign.

ISAAC BROCK, maj.-gen.

No. 9.

From brigadier-general Hull to the American secretary at war.

Fort-George, August 26, 1812.

SIR,

Enclosed are the articles of capitulation, by which the fort of Detroit has been surrendered to major-general Brock, commanding his Britannic majesty's forces in Upper Canada, and by which the troops have become prisoners of war. My situation at present forbids me from detailing the particular causes which have led to this unfortunate event. I will, however, generally observe, that after the surrender of Michilimackinac, almost every tribe and nation of Indians, excepting a part of the Miamis and Delawares, north from beyond Lake Superior, west from beyond the Mississippi, south from the Ohio and Wabash, and east from every part of Upper Canada, and from all the intermediate country, joined in open hostility, under the British standard, against the army I commanded, contrary to the most solemn assurances of a large portion of them to remain neutral: even the Ottawa chiefs from Arbecrotch, who formed the delegation to Washington the last summer, in whose friendship I know you had great confidence, are among the hostile tribes, and several of them distinguished leaders. Among the vast number of chiefs who led the hostile bands, Tecumseh, Marpot, Logan, Walk-in-the-water, Split-log, &c. are considered the principals. This numerous assemblage of savages, under the entire influence and direction of the British commander, enabled him totally to obstruct the only communication which I had with my country. This communication had been opened from the settlements in the state of Ohio, 200 miles through a wilderness, by the fatigues of the army, which I had marched to the frontier on the river Detroit. The body of the lake being commanded by the British armed ships, and the shores and rivers by gun-boats, the army was totally deprived of all communication by water. On this extensive road it depended for transportation of provisions, military stores, medicine, cloathing, and every other supply, on pack horses—all its operations were successful until its arrival at Detroit, and in a few days it passed into the enemy's country, and all opposition seemed to fall before it.— One month it remained in possession of this country, and was fed from its resources. In different directions, detachments penetrated 60 miles in the settled part of the province, and the inhabitants seemed satisfied with the change of situation which appeared to be taking place. The militia from Amherstburg were daily deserting, and the whole country, then under the control of the army, asked for protection. The Indians generally, in the first instance, appeared to be neutralized, and determined to take no part in the contest. The fort of Amherstburg was 18 miles below my encampment. Not a single cannon or mortar was on wheels suitable to carry before that place. I consulted my officers whether it was expedient to make an attempt on it with the bayonet alone, without cannon to make a break in the first instance. The council I called was of the opinion it was not. The greatest industry was exerted in making preparation, and it was not until the 7th of August that two 24-pounders, and three howitzers, were prepared. It was then my intention to have proceeded on the enterprise. While the operations of the army were delayed by these preparations, the clouds of adversity had been for some time, and seemed still thickly to be, gathering around me. The surrender of Michilimacinac opened the northern hive of

Indians, and they were swarming down in every direction. Reinforcements from Niagara had arrived at Amherstburg, under the command of colonel Proctor. The desertion of the militia ceased. Besides the reinforcements that came by water, I received information of a very considerable force under the command of major Chambers, on the river Le Trench, with four field-pieces; and collecting the militia on his route, evidently destined for Amherstburg. And, in addition to this combination and increase of force, contrary to all my expectations, the Wyandotes, Chippeways, Ottawas, Pottawatamies, Munsees, Delawares, &c. with whom I had the most friendly intercourse, at once passed over to Amherstburg, and accepted the tomahawk and scalping-knife. There being now a vast number of Indians at the British post, they were sent to the river Huron, Brownstown, and Maguago to intercept my communication.—To open this communication, I detached major Vanhorn, of the Ohio volunteers, with 200 men, to proceed as far as the river Raisin, under an expectation he would meet captain Brush, with 150 men, volunteers from the state of Ohio, and a quantity of provision for the army. An ambuscade was formed at Brownstown, and major Vanhorn's detachment defeated, and returned to camp, without effecting the object of the expedition.

In my letter of the 7th instant, you have the particulars of that transaction with a return of the killed and wounded. Under this sudden and unexpected change of things, and having received an express from general Hall, commanding opposite the British shore on the Niagara-river, by which it appeared that there was no prospect of any co-operation from that quarter, and the two senior officers of the artillery having stated to me an opinion that it would be extremely difficult, if not impossible, to pass Turkey-river, and river Aux Canards, with 24-pounders, and that they could not be transported by water, as the Queen Charlotte, which carried 18 24-pounders, lay in the river Detroit above the mouth of the river Aux Canards; and that it appeared indispensibly necessary to open the communication to the river Raisin and the Miami, I found myself compelled to suspend the operation against Amherstburg, and concentrate the main force of the army at Detroit. Fully intending at that time, after the communication was opened, to re-cross the river, and pursue the object at Amherstburg, and strongly desirous of continuing protection to a very large number of inhabitants of Upper Canada, who had voluntarily accepted it under my proclamation, I established a fortress on the banks of the river, a little below Detroit, calculated for a garrison of 300 men. On the evening of the 7th, and morning of the 8th instant, the army, excepting the garrison of 250 infantry, and a corps of artillerists, all under the command of major Denny of the Ohio volunteers, re-crossed the river and encamped at Detroit. In pursuance of the object of opening the communication, on which I considered the existence of the army depending, a detachment of 600 men, under the command of lieutenant-colonel Miller, was immediately ordered. For a particular account of the proceedings of this detachment, and the memorable battle which was fought at Maguago which reflects the highest honor on the American arms, I refer you to my letter of the 31st August instant, a duplicate of which is enclosed, marked G.* Nothing, however, but honor was acquired by this victory; and, it is a painful consideration, that the blood of 75 gallant men, could only open the communication as far as the points of their bayonets extended. The necessary care of the sick and wounded, and a very severe storm of rain, rendered their return to camp indispensibly necessary for their own comfort. Captain Brush with his small detachment, and the provisions being still at the river Raisin, in a situation to be destroyed by the savages, on the 13th instant, in the evening, I permitted colonels M'Arthur and Cass to select from their regiment 400 of their most effective men, and proceed by an upper route through the woods, which I had sent an express to captain Brush to take, and had directed the militia of the river Raisin to accompany him as a reinforcement.

* Not published.

APPENDIX. 373

The force of the enemy continually increasing, and the necessity of opening the communication, and acting on the defensive, becoming more apparent, I had, previous to detaching colonels M'Arthur and Cass on the 11th instant, evacuated and destoyed the fort on the opposite bank. On the 13th, in the evening, general Brock arrived at Amherstburg, about the hour colonels M'Arthur and Cass marched, of which at that time I had received no information. On the 15th I received a summons from him to surrender Fort-Detroit, of which the paper marked A is a copy.* My answer is marked B* At this time I received no information from colonels M'Arthur and Cass. An express was immediately sent, strongly escorted, with orders for them to return. On the 15th, as soon as general Brock received my letter, his batteries opened on the town and fort, and continued until evening. In the evening, all the British ships of war came nearly as far up the river as Sandwich, three miles below Detroit. At day-light, on the 16th, (at which time I had received no information from colonels M'Arthur and Cass, my expresses, sent the evening before, and in the night, having been prevented from passing by numerous bodies of Indians,) the cannonade re-commenced, and in a short time I received information, that the British army, and Indians, were landing below the Spring wells, under the cover of their ships of war.

At this time the whole effective force at my disposal at Detroit did not exceed 800 men. Being new troops, and unaccustomed to a camp life; having performed a laborious march; having been engaged in a number of battles and skirmishes, in which many had fallen, and more had received wounds, in addition to which a large number being sick, and unprovided with medicine, and the comforts necessary for their situation, are the general causes by which the strength of the army was thus reduced. The fort at this time was filled with women, children, and the old and decrepit people of the town and country; they were unsafe in the town, as it was entirely

* Not published.

open and exposed to the enemy's batteries. Back of the fort, above or below it, there was no safety for them on account of the Indians. In the first instance, the enemy's fire was principally directed against our batteries, towards the close, it was directed against the fort alone, and almost every shot and shell had their effect.

It now became necessary either to fight the enemy in the field; collect the whole force in the fort; or propose terms of capitulation. I could not have carried into the field more than 600 men, and left an adequate force in the fort. There were landed at that time of the enemy a regular force of much more than that number, and twice the number of Indians. Considering this great inequality of force, I did not think it expedient to adopt the first measure: the second must have been attended with a great sacrifice of blood, and no possible advantage, because the contest could not have been sustained more than a day for want of powder, and but a very few days for the want of provisions. In addition to this, colonels M'Arthur and Cass would have been in a most hazardous situation. I feared nothing but the last alternative —I have dared to adopt it—I well know the high responsibility of the measure, and I take the whole of it on myself—it was dictated by a sense of duty, and a full conviction of its expediency. The bands of savages which had then joined the British force, were numerous beyond any former example. Their numbers have since increased, and the history of the barbarians of the north of Europe does not furnish examples of more greedy violence than these savages have exhibited. A large portion of the brave and gallant officers and men I command, would cheerfully have contested until the last cartridge had been expended, and the bayonets worn to the sockets. I could not consent to the useless sacrifice of such brave men, when I knew it was impossible for me to sustain my situation. It was impossible, in the nature of things, that an army could have been furnished with the necessary supplies of provisions, military stores, cloathing and comfort for the

APPENDIX. 375

sick, on pack-horses, through a wilderness of 200 miles, filled with hostile savages. It was impossible, sir, that this little army, worn down by fatigue, by sickness, by wounds, and deaths, could have supported itself not only against the collected force of all the northern nations of Indians; but against the united strength of Upper Canada, whose population consists of more than 20 times the number contained in the territory of Michigan, aided by the principal part of the regular forces of the province, and the wealth and influence of the north-west and other trading establishments among the Indians, which have in their employment and under their entire control more than 2000 white men. Before I close this despatch, it is a duty I owe my respectable associates in command, colonels M'Arthur, Findley, Cass, and lieutenant-colonel Miller, to express my obligations to them for the prompt and judicious manner they have performed their respective duties. If aught has taken place during the campaign, which is honorable to the army, these officers are entitled to a large share of it. If the last act should be disapproved, no part of the censure belongs to them. I have likewise to express my obligation to general Taylor, who has performed the duty of quarter-master-general, for his great exertions in procuring every thing in his department, which it was possible to furnish, for the convenience of the army; likewise to brigade-major Jessop, for the correct and punctual manner in which he has discharged his duty; and to the army generally for their exertion and the zeal they have manifested for the public interest. The death of Dr. Foster soon after he arrived at Detroit, was a severe misfortune to the army; it was increased by the capture of the Chichaga packet, by which the medicine and hospital stores were lost. He was commencing the best arrangements in the department of which he was the principal, with the very small means he possessed. I was likewise deprived of the necessary services of captain Partridge by sickness, the only officer of the corps of engineers attached to the army. All the officers and men have gone to their respective homes, excepting the 4th United States' regiment, and a small part of the 1st, and captain Dyson's company of artillery. Captain Dyson's company was left at Amherstburg, and the others are with me prisoners; they amount to about 340. I have only to solicit an investigation of my conduct, as early as my situation and the nature of things will admit; and to add the further request that the government will not be unmindful of my associates in captivity, and of the families of those brave men who have fallen in the contest. I have the honor to be, very respectfully, your most obedient servant,

W. HULL, Brig.-Gen.
Commanding the north-western army of the United States.

Hon. W. Eustis, secretary of
   the department of war.

No. 10.

From major-general Sheaffe to sir G. Prevost.

SIR,   Fort-George, Oct. 13, 1812.

I have the honor of informing your excellency, that the enemy made an attack, with considerable force, this morning, before day-light, on the position of Queenstown. On receiving intelligence of it, major-general Brock immediately proceeded to that post; and, I am excessively grieved in having to add, that he fell whilst gallantly cheering his troops to an exertion for maintaining it. With him the position was lost: but the enemy was not allowed to retain it long, reinforcements having been sent up from this post, composed of regular troops, militia, and Indians, a movement was made to turn his left, while some artillery, under the able direction of captain Holcroft, supported by a body of infantry, engaged his attention in front. This operation was aided too by the judicious position which Norton, and the Indians with him, had taken on the woody brow of the high ground above Queenstown. A

APPENDIX. 377

communication being thus opened with Chippeway, a junction was formed with succours that had been ordered from that post. The enemy was then attacked, and after a short but spirited conflict, was completely defeated. I had the satisfaction of receiving the sword of their commander, brigadier-general Wadsworth, on the field of battle, and many officers, with 900 men, were made prisoners, and more may yet be expected. A stand of colours, and one 6-pounder, were also taken. The action did not terminate till nearly three o'clock in the afternoon, and their loss, in killed and wounded, must have been considerable. Ours, I believe to have been comparatively small in numbers: no officer was killed besides major-general Brock, one of the most gallant and zealous officers in his majesty's service, whose loss cannot be too much deplored, and lieutenant-colonel Macdonnell, provincial aide de camp, whose gallantry and merit render him worthy of his chief.

Captains Dennis and Williams, commanding the flank-companies of the 49th regiment, who were stationed at Queenstown, were wounded, bravely contending at the head of their men against superior numbers; but I am glad to have it in my power to add, that captain Dennis fortunately was able to keep the field, though it was with pain and difficulty; and captain Williams's wound is not likely long to deprive me of his services.

I am particularly indebted to captain Holcroft of the royal artillery, for his judicious and skilful co-operation with the guns and howitzers under his immediate superintendance; their well-directed fire contributed materially to the fortunate result of the day.

Captain Derenzy of the 41st regiment, brought up the reinforcement of that corps from Fort-George, and captain Bullock led that of the same regiment from Chippeway: and under their commands those detachments acquitted themselves in such a manner, as to sustain the reputation which the 41st regiment had already acquired in the vicinity of Detroit.

Major-general Brock, soon after his arrival at Queenstown,

had sent down orders for battering the American Fort-Niagara. Brigade-major Evans, who was left in charge of Fort-George, directed the operations against it with so much effect, as to silence its fires, and to force the troops to abandon it; and by his prudent precautions, he prevented mischief of a most serious nature, which otherwise might have been effected, the enemy having used heated shot in firing at Fort-George. In these services he was most effectually aided by colonel Claus, (who remained in the fort at my desire,) and by captain Vigoreaux, of the royal engineers. Brigade-major Evans also mentions the conduct of captains Powell and Cameron, of the militia-artillery, in terms of commendation.

Lieutenant Crowther, of the 41st regiment, had charge of two 3-pounders that had accompanied the movement of our little corps, and they were employed with good effect.

Captain Glegg, of the 49th regiment, aide-de-camp to our lamented friend and general, afforded me most essential assistance; and I found the services of lieutenant Fowler of the 41st regiment, assistant-deputy-quarter-master-general, very useful. I derived much aid, too, from the activity and intelligence of lieutenant Kerr, of the Glengarry fencibles, whom I employed in communicating with the Indians and other flanking-parties.

I was unfortunately deprived of the aid of the experience and ability of lieutenant-colonel Myers, deputy quarter-master-general, who had been sent up to Fort-Erie a few days before on duty, which detained him there.

Lieutenant-colonels Butler and Clark of the militia; and captains Hatt, Durand, Rowe, Applegarth, James, Crooks, Cooper, Robert Hamilton, M'Ewen, and Duncan Cameron; and lieutenants Richardson and Thomas Butler, commanding flank-companies of the Lincoln and York militia, led their men into action with great spirit. Major Merritt, commanding the Niagara dragoons, accompanied me, and gave much assistance, with part of his corps. Captain A. Hamilton, belonging to it was disabled from riding, and attached himself to the guns under captain Holcroft, who speaks highly of his activity and usefulness. I beg leave to add, that volunteers Shaw, Thomson and Jarvis, attached to the flank companies of the 49th regiment, conducted themselves with great spirit; the first having been wounded, and the last having been taken prisoner. I beg leave to recommend these young men to your excellency's notice. Norton is wounded, but not badly; he and the Indians particularly distinguished themselves, and I have very great satisfaction in assuring your excellency, that the spirit and good conduct of his majesty's troops, of the militia, and of the other provincial corps, were eminently conspicuous on this occasion.

I have not been able to ascertain yet the number of troops, or of those of the enemy engaged; ours, I believe, did not exceed the number of the prisoners we have taken; and their advance, which effected a landing, probably amounted to 13 or 1400 men.

I shall do myself the honor of transmitting to your excellency further details, when I shall have received the several reports of the occurrences which did not pass under my own observation, with the return of the casualties, and those of the killed and wounded, and of the ordnance taken.

I have the honor to be, &c.
(Signed) R. H. SHEAFFE. maj.-gen.
To his excellency sir George Prevost, bart. &c.

No. 11.

From general Van Rensselaer, to the American secretary of war.

Head-quarters, Lewistown, October 14th, 1812.

SIR,

As the movements of this army under my command, since I had last the honor to address you on the 8th, have been of a very important character, producing consequences serious to many individuals; establishing facts actually connected with the interest of the service and the safety of the army; and as I stand prominently responsible for some of these consequences, I beg leave to explain to you, sir, and through you to my country, the situation and circumstances in which I have had to act, and the reasons and motives which governed me; and if the result is not all that might have been wished, it is such that, when the whole ground shall be viewed, I shall cheerfully submit myself to the judgment of my country.

In my letter of the 8th instant, I apprised you that the crisis in this campaign was rapidly advancing; and that (to repeat the same) " the blow must be soon struck, or all the toil and expense of the campaign will go for nothing, for the whole will be tinged with dishonor."

Under such impressions, I had, on the 5th instant, written to brigadier-generel Smyth, of the United States forces; requesting an interview with him, major-general Hall, and the commandants of regiments, for the purpose of conferring upon the subject of future operations. I wrote major-general Hall to the same purport. On the 11th had received no answer from general Smyth: but in a note to me of the 10th, general Hall mentioned that general Smyth had not yet then agreed upon any day for the consultation.

In the mean time, the partial success of lieutenant Elliott at Black Rock (of which, however, I have received no official information) began to excite a strong disposition in the troops to act. This was expressed to me through various channels, in the shape of an alternative; that they must have orders to act, or at all hazards they would go home. I forbear here commenting upon the obvious consequences, to me personally, of longer withholding my orders under such circumstances.

I had a conference with ——, as to the possibility of getting some person to pass over into Canada, and obtain correct information. On the morning of the 4th, he wrote to me that he had procured the man, who bore his letter to go over.

Instructions were given him: he passed over, and obtained such information as warranted an immediate attack. This was confidently communicated to several of my first officers, and produced great zeal to act; more especially as it might have a controlling effect upon the movement at Detroit, where it was supposed that general Brock had gone with all the force he dared to spare from the Niagara frontier. The best preparations in my power, were therefore made to dislodge the enemy from the heights of Queenstown, and possess ourselves of the village; where the troops might be sheltered from the distressing inclemency of the weather.

Lieutenant-colonel Fleming's flying artillery, and a detachment of regular troops under his command, were ordered to be up in season from Fort Niagara. Orders were also sent general Smyth, to send down from Buffaloe, such detachment of his brigade as existing circumstances in that vicinity might warrant. The attack was to be made at 3 o'clock, on the morning of the 11th, by crossing over in boats from the old ferry opposite the heights. To avoid any embarrassment in crossing the river, (which is here a sheet of violent eddies,) experienced boatmen were procured, to take the boats, from the landing below to the place of embarkation. Lieutenant Sim was considered the man of the greatest skill for this service; he went a-head, and, in the extreme darkness, passed the intended place far up the river; and there, in a most extraordinary manner, fastened his boat to the shore, and abandoned the detachment. In this front boat he had carried nearly all the oars, which were prepared for the boats. In this agonizing dilemma stood officers and men, whose ardor had not been cooled by exposure, through the night, to one of the most tremendous north-east storms, which continued unabated for 28 hours, and deluged the whole camp. Colonel Van Rensselaer was to have commanded the detachment.

After this result, I had hoped that the patience of the troops would have continued, until I could submit the plan suggested in my letter of the 8th, that I might act under, and in conformity to, the opinion which might be then expressed. But my hope was idle; the previously excited ardor seemed to have gained new heat from the late miscarriage; the brave men were mortified to stop short of their object, and the timid thought laurels half won by the attempt.

On the morning of the 12th, such was the pressure upon me from all quarters, that I became satisfied that my refusal to act might involve me in suspicion, and the service in disgrace.

Lieutenant-colonel Christie, who had just arrived at the Four-mile Creek, and had, late in the night of the 1st, contemplated an attack, gallantly offered me his own and his men's services: but he got my permission too late. He now again came forward, had a conference with colonel Van Rensselaer, and begged that he might have the honor of a command in the expedition. The arrangement was made. Colonel Van Rensselaer was to command one column of 300 militia; and lieutenant-colonel Christie a column of the same number of regular troops.

Every precaution was now adopted as to boats, and the most confidential and experienced men to manage them. At an early hour in the night, lieutenant-colonel Christie marched his detachment by the rear road from Niagara to the camp. At 7 in the evening, lieutenant-colonel Stranahan's regiment moved from Niagara falls: at 8 o'clock, Mead's, and at 9, lieutenant-colonel Bland's regiment marched from the same place. All were in camp in good season. Agreeably to my orders issued upon this occasion, the two columns were to pass over together; as soon as the heights should be carried, lieutenant-colonel Fenwick's flying artillery was to pass over; then major Mullany's detachment of regulars; and the other troops to follow in order.

Colonel Van Rensselaer, with great presence of mind, ordered his officers to proceed with rapidity, and storm the fort. This service was gallantly performed, and the enemy driven down the hill in every direction. Soon after this, both parties were considerably reinforced, and the conflict was renewed in various places. Many of the enemy took shelter behind a stone guardhouse, where a piece of ordnance was now briskly served. I ordered the fire of our battery to be directed upon the guardhouse; and it was so effectually done, that with eight or ten shot the fire was silenced. The enemy then retreated behind a large stone house; but in a short time the route became general, and the enemy's fire was silenced, except from a one-gun battery, so far down the river as to be out of the reach of our heavy ordnance; and our light pieces could not silence it. A number of boats now passed over unannoyed, except by the one unsilenced gun. For sometime after I passed over, the victory appeared complete: but in expectation of further attacks, I was taking measures for fortifying my camp immediately; the direction of this service I committed to lieutenant Totten, of the engineers. But very soon the enemy were reinforced, by a detachment of several hundred Indians from Chippeway; they commenced a furious attack; but were promptly met and routed by the rifle and bayonet. By this time I perceived my troops were embarking very slowly. I passed immediately over to accelerate their movements; but, to my utter astonishment, I found that, at the very moment when complete victory was in our hands, the ardor of the unengaged troops had entirely subsided. I rode in all directions; urged the men by every consideration to pass over, but in vain. Lieutenant-col. Bloom, who had been wounded in action, returned, mounted his horse, and rode through the camp; as did also judge Peck, who happened to be here, exhorting the companies to proceed—but all in vain.

At this time a large reinforcement from Fort-George was discovered coming up the river. As the battery on the hill was considered an important check against their ascending the heights, measures were immediately taken to send them a fresh supply of ammunition, as I learnt there were only left 20 shot for the 18-pounders. The reinforcements, however, obliqued to the right from the road, and formed a junction with the Indians, in the rear of the heights. Finding, to my infinite mortification, that no reinforcement would pass over; seeing that another severe conflict must soon commence; and knowing that the brave men at the heights were quite exhausted, and nearly out of ammunition; all I could do, was to send them a fresh supply of cartridges. At this critical moment I despatched a note to general Wadsworth, acquainting him with our situation: leaving the course to be pursued much to his own judgment; with assurance that if he thought best to retreat, I would endeavour to send as many boats as I could command, and cover his retreat by every fire I could safely make. But the boats were dispersed; many of the boatmen had fled, panic struck; and but few got off. My note, however, could but little more than have reached general W. about 4 o'clock, when a most severe and obstinate conflict commenced, and continued for about half an hour, with a tremendous fire of cannon, flying artillery, and musketry. The enemy succeeded in re-possessing their battery, and gaining advantage on every side; the brave men who had gained the victory, being exhausted of strength and ammunition, and grieved at the unpardonable neglect of their fellow soldiers, gave up the conflict.

I can only add, that the victory was really won; but lost for the want of a small reinforcement; one-third part of the idle men might have saved all.

I have the honor to be, &c.

STEPHEN VAN RENSSELAER.

Hon. William Eustis, secretary of war.

No. 12.

From captain Wool to colonel Van Rensselaer.

Dear sir,   Buffaloe, Oct. 23, 1812.

I have the honour to communicate to you the circumstances attending the storming of Queenstown battery, on the 13th inst.;

APPENDIX.

with those which happened previously you are already well acquainted.

In pursuance of your order, we proceeded round the point and ascended the rocks, which brought us partly in rear of the battery. We took it without much resistance. I immediately formed the troops in rear of the battery, and fronting the village, when I observed general Brock with his troops formed, consisting of four companies of the 49th regiment, and a few militia, marching for our left flank. I immediately detached a party of 150 men, to take possession of the heights above Queenstown battery, and to hold general Brock in check; but in consequence of his superior force they retreated. I sent a reinforcement; notwithstanding which, the enemy drove us to the edge of the bank: when, with the greatest exertions, we brought the troops to a stand, and ordered the officers to bring their men to a charge as soon as the ammunition was expended, which was executed with some confusion, and in a few moments the enemy retreated. We pursued them to the edge of the heights, when colonel M'Donald had his horse shot from under him, and himself was mortally wounded. In the interim, general Brock, in attempting to rally his forces, was killed, when the enemy dispersed in every direction. As soon as it was practicable, I formed the troops in a line on the heights fronting the village, and immediately detached flanking parties, which consisted of captain Machesney of the 6th regiment, lieutenant Smith, and ensign Grosvenor, with a small detachment of riflemen, who had that moment arrived; at the same time, I ordered lieutenant Ganesvoort and lieutenant Randolph, with a detachment of artillery, to drill out an 18-pounder which had been previously spiked, and if possible to bring it to bear upon the village. The wounded and prisoners I ordered to be collected, and sent to the guard-house. About this time, which was about three or four o'clock in the afternoon, lieutenant-col. Christie arrived, and took the command. He ordered me across the river to get my wounds dressed. I remained a short time. Our flanking parties had been driven in by the Indians;

but general Wadsworth and other officers arriving, we had a short skirmish with them, and they retreated, and I crossed the river.

The officers engaged in storming the battery, were captains Wool and Ogilvie; lieutenants Kearney, Hugouin, Carr, and Simmons, of the 43d regiment; lieutenants Ganesvoort and Randolph of the light artillery, and major Lush of the militia.

I recommend to your particular notice lieutenants Randolph, Carr, and Kearney, for their brave conduct exhibited during the whole of the action.

I have the honour to be,
Your most obedient humble servant,
JOHN E. WOOL, capt. 13th regt. inf.

Colonel S. Van Ransselaer.

No. 13.

From lieutenant-col. Bisshopp to Major-gen. Sheaffe.

Frenchman's Creek, near Fort-Erie,
Dec. 1, 1812.

Sir,

I have the honor to inform you, that, on the morning of the 28th ultimo, between 4 and 5 o'clock, a firing was heard at Chippeway, on the right of the line under my command. I proceeded instantly in that direction, having given orders for captain Kerby, of the militia artillery, with a light 6-pounder, captain Saunders's detachment of the 41st regiment, and captain Hamilton's company of the 2d Lincoln militia, to march, under the command of lieutenant-col. Clark, to reinforce the right. On my arrival within six miles of Fort-Erie, I overtook major Hatt, of the 5th Lincoln regiment, with the militia under his command, intending to march to oppose the enemy: a detachment of the 49th regiment, and the light company of the 41st regiment, under the command of lieutenant M'Intyre, having retreated to this position.

APPENDIX. 387

Major Ormsby informs me, that, about 2 o'clock in the morning, the enemy, consisting of about 400 men, many of whom were sailors, effected a landing at the Red House, opposite the quarters of lieutenant Lamont, 49th regiment, and succeeded in gaining possession of the batteries, after having been most gallantly and warmly opposed by lieutenant King, of the royal artillery, commanding two field-pieces, and lieutenant Lamont, with a party, consisting of about 30 men only; the remainder of his detachment being stationed at the two batteries on his right. Both these officers were severely wounded : the former taken prisoner. Captain Bostwick, commanding the Norfolk militia, stationed at the ferry, on hearing the report of musketry, immediately ordered the men under his command to form, and march to the point of attack : after having exchanged a few rounds with the enemy, and finding he was of superior force, he retired. Lieutenant Bryson, of the militia-artillery, finding the enemy gaining possession of the batteries, and being unable to defend himself against such a superior force, immediately spiked the 24-pounder in the half-moon battery, prior to its falling into the hands of the enemy. The sentries at Fort-Erie hearing a firing in the direction of the batteries, major Ormsby marched at 2 o'clock, with the detachment of the 49th regiment, consisting of 80 men, to meet the enemy, and to support the batteries; leaving captain Whelan, according to directions I had before given in case of an attack, to defend that fortress. Major Ormsby advanced towards the batteries, by the back-road, to support lieutenant Lamont; but having met with lieutenant Bryson, of the militia-artillery, who informed him that the enemy were in possession of the batteries, and it being then dark, he changed his direction, and moved to the right along the front road, below the batteries, with a view of falling in with some part of lieutenant Lamont's detachment, and likewise another party on the left, consisting of 35 men, stationed opposite to the end of Squaw Island, commanded by lieutenant Bartley; but who, it appears, had moved from thence, early in the morning, to the left, where the enemy had likewise landed their troops, opposite to this place.

Lieutenant Bartley attacked the enemy, consisting of about 250 men, and kept up a fire upon the boats for about 15 or 20 minutes, when he observed a party coming towards him, which he took to be our militia; but, finding them to be a party of the enemy, and a number of his men being killed, wounded, or missing, he retired, crossing Frenchman's Creek at the mill; a little above which he joined major Ormsby, having only 16 or 17 men left. Major Ormsby, whose detachment continued their march to Frenchman's creek, was fired on from a house above the bridge by a party of the enemy; and having returned their fire with two or three rounds from his detachment, he succeeded in passing the bridge, although partly destroyed by the enemy. He here halted, to ascertain the force opposed to him; but as it still continued very dark, he could neither see the enemy, nor discover his movements. He then proceeded about a mile further on the road downward, where he was joined by lieutenant M'Intyre, of the light infantry, 41st regiment, and remained there until day-light; when I arrived, and immediately advanced with the whole of the force here concentrated under major Ormsby, and major Hatt of the 5th Lincoln militia, having under his command the different companies of militia on this line, consisting of about 300 men, towards this place, with a light 6-pounder, where we took captain King, of the United States' Infantry, and about 80 rank and file, prisoners. The enemy, at this time, were crossing the river with a considerable numer of boats, having about 30 men in each, making towards the land. I ordered the 6-pounder to open upon them, which was ably directed by bombardier Jackson, of the royal artillery, and acted with much execution. I formed the line on the bank, major Ormsby and the 49th being on the right. After a few rounds from our musketry the enemy retired to the American shore, behind Squaw Island, having sustained considerable loss. The Indian warriors, under major Given, having heard the report of our fire, immediately joined us: I then marched with the light company of the 41st to ascertain the number and position of the enemy in our front, in which movement I received the greatest assistance from major Given, and the Indians under his command. The enemy had dismounted the guns, and left the batteries: I ordered the line to advance, and took up a position in their rear, waiting his further operations. I had been joined by lieutenant-col. Clark, and his detachment, from Chippeway. Captain Whelan still continued in Fort-Erie, and had not been attacked during the absence of major Ormsby and his detachment. The enemy kept up a strong fire on our lines from their batteries till one o'lock; when a flag of truce came over to summon Fort-Erie, and to demand the surrender of that fort to the American army. A copy of general Smyth's letter accompanies this despatch. I sent captain Fitzgerald of the 49th regiment with my answer, which was—"that the troops under my command being sufficient to repulse any attack from the enemy; and having received reinforcements from below, I should not agree to his request." The 6-pounder taken by the enemy in the morning, as likewise the 3-pounders, were found without having sustained the least injury. Great credit is due to captain Kerby and his artillery, for their exertions in getting up the guns on the batteries; which, by the morning of the 30th, we succeeded in, and have been ever since in expectation of an attack, but which the enemy do not think proper to make. To captain Kerby, lieutenants Bryson and Hall of the militia-artillery, and bombardier Jackson of the royal artillery, the greatest credit is due; as well as to lieutenant-col. Nichol, quartermaster-general of militia, and lieutenant Bernard, acting staff-adjutant. I have also derived the greatest assistance from lieutenant-col. Clark, commanding the militia; major Ormsby, commanding a detachment of the 49th regiment; and major Hatt, of the 5th Lincoln militia, and all officers in command of corps and companies under my orders. The Norfolk militia, under captain Bostwick, gave a strong proof of the valor which has uniformly distinguished the militia of this country, when called into action. I must likewise mention the names of captain Whelan, of the Newfoundland regiment; captains Chambers and Saunders, of the 41st; captain Fitzgerald, 49th; and captain Hamilton, of the 2d Lincoln militia, who first apprized me of the enemy's movement.

I enclose a list of the killed, wounded, and missing. I have not been able to ascertain the loss of the enemy; but, from the numbers left on the field, and the boats that were sunk, it must have been very great.

I have the honor to be, &c.

CECIL BISSHOPP, lieut.-col. commanding.

Return of killed, wounded, and missing, of the following corps of the division of the army serving in Upper Canada, under the command of major-general Sheaffe, in an affair with the enemy on the 21st and 28th Nov. 1812.

21st November.—Royal artillery;—1 rank and file, wounded.
49th foot; 1 rank and file, killed.
28th November.—Royal artillery;—1 rank and file, killed; 1 lieutenant, 1 rank and file, wounded.
49th foot;—12 rank and file, killed; 1 lieutenant, 3 serjeants, 22 rank and file, wounded; 3 drummers, 21 rank and file, missing.
Militia artillery;—1 serjeant, wounded.
1st regiment, Norfolk militia;—1 serjeant, killed; 1 captain, 1 lieutenant, 8 rank and file, wounded; 2 rank and file, missing.
2d regiment, Norfolk militia;—1 rank and file, killed; 7 rank and file wounded; 4 rank and file missing.

Total loss;—14 rank and file, (line,) 1 serjeant, 1 rank and file, (militia,) killed; 2 lieutenants, 3 serjeants, 24 rank and file, (line,) 1 captain, 1 lieutenant, 1 serjeant, 15 rank and file, (militia,) wounded; 3 drummers, 21 rank and file, (line,) 11 rank and file, (militia,) missing.

General total; 1 serjeant, 16 rank and file, killed; 1 captain, 3 lieutenants, 4 serjeants, 39 rank and file, wounded; 3 drummers, 32 rank and file, missing.

APPENDIX. 391

Officers wounded.

Royal artillery—Lieutenant King, severely, and taken prisoner.

49th foot—Lieutenant Lamont, severely.

1st Norfolk militia—Captain Bostwick, slightly; lieutenant Byerson, severely.

THOMAS EVANS, major of brigade.
To major-general Sheaffe,
&c. &c. &c.

No. 14.

General Smyth's Proclamation.

To the men of New York.

For many years you have seen your country oppressed with numerous wrongs. Your government, although above all others, devoted to peace, have been forced to draw the sword, and rely for redress of injuries on the valor of the American people.

That valor has been conspicuous. But the nation has been unfortunate in the selection of some of those who directed it. One army has been disgracefully surrendered and lost. Another has been sacrificed by a precipitate attempt to pass it over at the strongest point of the enemy's lines, with most incompetent means. The cause of these miscarriages is apparent. The commanders were popular men, "destitute alike of theory and experience" in the art of war.

In a few days the troops under my command will plant the American standard in Canada. They are men accustomed to obedience, silence, and steadiness. They will conquer or they will die.

Will you stand with your arms folded, and look on this

interesting struggle? Are you not related to the men who fought at Bennington and Saratoga? Has the race degenerated? Or have you, under the baneful influence of contending factions, forgotten your country? Must I turn from you, and ask the men of the six nations to support the government of the United States? Shall I imitate the officers of the British king, and suffer our ungathered laurels to be tarnished with ruthless deeds? Shame, where is thy blush! No. Where I command, the vanquished and the peaceful man, the child, the maid, and the matron shall be secure from wrong. If we conquer, we will " conquer but to save."

Men of New York!

The present is the hour of renown. Have you not a wish for fame? Would you not choose in future times to be named as one of those, who, imitating the heroes whom Montgomery led, have, in spite of the seasons, visited the tomb of the chief, and conquered the country where he lies? Yes. You desire your share of fame. Then seize the present moment: if you do not, you will regret it; and say, " the valiant have bled in vain; the friends of my country fell,—and I was not there."

Advance, then, to our aid. I will wait for you a few days. I cannot give you the day of my departure. But come on. Come in companies, half companies, pairs, or singly. I will organize you for a short tour. Ride to this place, if the distance is far, and send back your horses. But remember, that every man who accompanies us, places himself under my command, and shall submit to the salutary restraints of discipline.

ALEX. SMYTH, brig.-gen.

Camp, near Buffaloe, Nov. 10, 1812.

No. 15.

From brigadier-general Smyth, to lieutenant-colonel Bisshopp.

SIR,

As you have seen a part of the hourly encreasing force under my command, I propose to you the surrender of Fort-Erie, to spare the effusion of blood. I take the opporunity to assure you, that the devastation you have witnessed has been committed by sailors not under my authority, and against my will.

Very respectfully,
Your most obedient,
ALEXANDER SMYTH, brig.-gen.

Colonel Bisshopp, commanding the
    British army, Fort-Erie.
November 5th, 1812.

No. 16.

From major Macdonnell, to sir G. Prevost.

Prescott, February 23, 1813

SIR,

I have the honor to acquaint you, for the information of his excellency the commander of the forces, that, in consequence of the commands of his excellency to retaliate, under favorable circumstances, upon the enemy, for his late wanton aggressions on this frontier, I this morning, about 7 o'clock, crossed the river St. Lawrence upon the ice, and attacked and carried, after a little more than an hour's action, his position in and near the opposite town of Ogdenburg, taking eleven pieces of cannon, and all his ordnance, marine, commissariat, and quarter-master-general's stores, four officers and 70 prisoners, and burning two armed schooners, and two large gun-boats, and both his barracks.

My force consisted of about 480 regulars and militia, and was divided into two columns: the right commanded by captain Jenkins, of the Glengarry light infantry fencibles, was composed of his own flank company, and about 70 militia; and, from the state of the ice, and the enemy's position in the old French fort, was directed to check his left, and interrupt his retreat, whilst I moved on with the left column, consisting of 120 of the king's regiment, 40 of the royal Newfoundland corps, and about 200 militia, towards his position in the town, where he had posted his heavy field artillery. The depth of the snow in some degree retarded the advance of both columns, and exposed them, particularly the right, to a heavy cross fire from the batteries of the enemy, for a longer period than I had expected; but pushing on rapidly after the batteries began to open upon us, the left column soon gained the right bank of the river, under the direct fire of his artillery and line of musketry, posted on an eminence near the shore; moving on rapidly, my advance, consisting of the royal Newfoundland and some select militia, I turned his right with the detachment of the king's regiment, and after a few discharges from his artillery, took them with the bayonet, and drove his infantry through the town; some escaping across the Black river into the fort, but the majority fled to the woods, or sought refuge in the houses, from whence they kept such a galling fire, that it was necessary to dislodge them with our field-pieces, which now came up from the bank of the river, where they had stuck, on landing, in the deep snow.

Having gained the high ground on the brink of the Black river, opposite the fort, I prepared to carry it by storm; but the men being quite exhausted, I procured time for them to recover breath, by sending in a summons, requiring an unconditional surrender. During these transactions, captain Jenkins had gallantly led on his column, and had been exposed to a heavy fire of seven guns, which he bravely attempted to take with the bayonet, though covered with 200 of the enemy's best troops: advancing as rapidly as the deep snow, and the exhausted state (in consequence) of his men, would admit, he ordered a charge, and had not proceeded many paces, when his left arm was broken to pieces by a grape-shot; but still undauntedly running on with his men, he almost immediately afterwards was deprived of the use of his right arm, by a discharge of case-shot; still heroically disregarding all personal consideration, he nobly ran on, cheering his men, to the assault, till, exhausted by pain and loss of blood, he became unable to move; his company gallantly continued the charge under lieutenant M'Auley; but the reserve of the militia not being able to keep up with them, they were compelled, by the great superiority of the enemy, to give way, leaving a few on a commanding position, and a few of the most advanced, in the enemy's possession, nearly about the time that I gained the height above mentioned. The enemy hesitating to surrender, I instantly carried his eastern battery, and by it silenced another, which now opened again; and ordering on the advance the detachment of the king's, and the Highland company of militia, under captain Eustace, of the king's regiment, he gallantly rushed into the fort; but the enemy retreating by the opposite entrance, escaped into the woods, which I should have effectually prevented, if my Indian warriors had returned sooner from a detached service, on which they had that morning been employed.

I cannot close this statement without expressing my admiration of the gallantry and self-devotion of captain Jenkins, who had lost one arm, and is in danger of losing the other. I must also report the intrepidity of captain Lefievre, of the Newfoundland regiment, who had the immediate charge of the militia under colonel Fraser; of captain Eustace, and the other officers of the king's regiment; and particularly of lieutenant Ridge, of that corps, who very gallantly led on the advance; and of lieutenant M'Auley, and ensign M'Donnell, of the Glengarry regiment; as also lieutenant Gangueben, of the royal engineers;

and of ensign M'Kay, of the Glengarry light-infantry; and of ensign Kerr, of the militia, each of whom had charge of a field-piece; and of lieutenant Impey, of the militia, who has lost a leg. I was also well supported by colonel Fraser and the other officers and men of the militia, who emulated the conspicuous bravery of all the troops of the line. I inclose a list of killed and wounded. The enemy had 500 men under arms, and must have sustained a considerable loss.

I have the honor to be, &c.

G. MACDONNELL, major, Glengarry light-infantry, lieutenant-colonel, commanding in the eastern district of Upper Canada.

Sir G. Prevost, &c.

Return of the killed and wounded in the action of the 22d of February, 1813.

Royal artilley ;—2 rank and file, killed.

8th; (or king's regiment;)—1 serjeant, killed; 1 subaltern, 12 rank and file, wounded.

Glengarry light-infantry ;—2 rank and file, killed; 1 captain, 1 subaltern, 3 serjeants, 9 rank and file, wounded.

Total loss;—1 serjeant, 7 rank and file, killed; 1 field-officer, 2 captains, 5 subalterns, 4 serjeants, 40 rank and file, wounded.

Names of officers wounded.

8th; (or king's regiment;) —Ensign Powell.

Glengarry regiment ;—Lieutenant-colonel Macdonnell, captain Jenkins, and ensign M'Kay.

Militia;—Captain M'Donnell, and lieutenants Impey, M'Lean, and M'Dound.

EDWARD BAYNES,
Adjutant-general, North America.

APPENDIX. 397

No. 17.

From major-general Sheaffe to sir G. Prevost.

Sir, Kingston, May 5th, 1813.

I did myself the honor of writing to your excellency, on my route from York, to communicate the mortifying intelligence that the enemy had obtained possession of that place on the 27th of April. I shall now give your excellency a further detail of that event.

In the evening of the 26th, information was received that many vessels had been seen to the eastward. Very early the next morning, they were discovered lying-to, not far from the harbor: after some time had elapsed, they made sail, and to the number of 16, of various descriptions, anchored off the shore, some distance to the westward. Boats full of troops were immediately seen assembling near their commodore's ship, under cover of whose fire, and that of other vessels, and aided by the wind, they soon effected a landing, in spite of a spirited opposition from major Givens, and about 40 Indians. A company of Glengarry light-infantry, which had been ordered to support them, was, by some mistake, (not in the smallest degree imputable to its commander,) led in another direction, and came late into action. The other troops, consisting of two companies of the 8th, (or king's regiment,) and about a company of the royal Newfoundland regiment, with some militia, encountered the enemy in a thick wood. Captain M'Neal, of the king's regiment, was killed while gallantly leading his company, which suffered severely. The troops, at length, fell back; they rallied several times, but could not maintain the contest against the greatly superior and increasing numbers of the enemy. They retired under cover of our batteries, which were engaged with some of the enemy's vessels that had moved nigher to the harbor. By some unfortunate accident the magazine at the western battery, blew up, and killed and wounded a considerable number of men, and crippled the battery. It became too evident that our numbers and means of defence were inadequate to the task of maintaining possession of York against the vast superiority of force brought against it. The troops were withdrawn towards the town, and were finally ordered to retreat on the road to Kingston; the powder-magazine was blown up, and the new ship and the naval-stores destroyed. Lieutenant-colonel Chervett and major Allan, of the militia, residents in the town, were instructed to treat with the American commanders for terms: a statement of those agreed on with major-general Dearborn and commodore Chauncey, is transmitted to your excellency, with returns of the killed and wounded, &c. The accounts of the number of the enemy vary from 1890 to 3000. We had about 600, including militia and dock-yardmen. The quality of these troops was of so superior a description, and their general disposition so good, that under less unfavorable circumstances, I should have felt confident of success, in spite of the desparity of numbers. As it was, the contest, which commenced between six and seven o'clock, was maintained for nearly eight hours.

When we had proceeded some miles from York, we met the light-company of the king's regiment, on its route for Fort-George: it retired with us and covered the retreat, which was effected without molestation from the enemy.

I have the honor to be, &c.
R. H. SHEAFFE, major-general.

His excellency sir George Prevost, &c.

Return of killed, wounded, prisoners, and missing, of the troops engaged at York, under the command of sir Roger Hall Sheaffe, on the 27th ultimo.

Kingston, May 10th, 1813.

Royal artillery;—3 gunners, killed; 1 driver, wounded and prisoner; 1 bombardier, 3 gunners, prisoners; 1 gunner, missing.

8th; (or king's regiment;)—1 captain, 1 serjeant-major, 3

APPENDIX. 399

serjeants, 40 rank and file, killed; 2 serjeants, 21 rank and file, wounded; 1 serjeant, 25 rank and file, wounded and prisoners; 2 rank and file, prisoners; 1 rank and file, missing.

Newfoundland regiment;—1 serjeant, 1 drummer, 10 rank and file, killed; 1 drummer, 6 rank and file, wounded; 1 lieutenant, 3 serjeants, 1 drummer, 8 rank and file, wounded and prisoners; 2 rank and file, prisoners; 2 rank and file, missing.

Glengarry light infantry;—2 rank and file, killed; 1 ensign, 3 rank and file, wounded; 3 rank and file, missing.

49th regiment;—3 rank and file, wounded and prisoners; 2 rank and file prisoners (these two men were in the hospital at the time of the action).

Total;—1 captain, 1 serjeant-major, 4 serjeants, 1 drummer, 52 rank and file, 3 gunners, killed; 1 ensign, 2 serjeants, 1 drummer, 30 rank and file, wounded; 1 lieutenant 4 serjeants, 1 drummer, 36 rank and file, 1 driver, wounded and prisoners; 6 rank and file, 1 bombardier, 3 gunners, prisoners; 6 rank and file, 1 gunner, missing.

Names of officers killed and wounded.

Killed;—8th *(or king's regiment);* captain M'Neal;—volunteer D. Macleane, clerk of the house of assembly.

Wounded;—*Royal Newfoundland regiment*; Lieutenant D. Koven, prisoner.

Glengarry light infantry;—Ensign Robins, slightly.

General staff;—Captain Loring, 104th regiment, slightly.

Incorporated militia;—Captain Jarvis, volunteer; —— Hartney, barrack-master.

RICHARD LEONARD,
Acting deputy-assistant-adjutant-general.

EDWD. BAYNES.
Adjutant-general, North America.

No. 18.

Capitulation of York.

Terms of the capitulation entered into on the 27th of April, 1813, for the surrender of the town of York, in Upper Canada, to the army and navy of the United States, under the command of major-gen. Dearborn and commodore Chauncey.

That the troops, regular and militia, at this post, and the naval officers and seamen, shall be surrendered prisoners of war; the troops, regular and militia, to ground their arms immediately on the parade, and the naval officers and seamen be immediately surrendered on the parade.

That all public stores, naval and military, shall be immediately given up to the commanding officers of the army and navy of the United States.

That all private property shall be guaranteed to the citizens of the town of York.

That the papers belonging to the civil officers shall be retained by them.

That such surgeons as may be procured to attend the wounded of the British regular and Canadian militia, shall not be considered as prisoners of war.

That one lieutenant colonel, one major, 13 captains, nine lieutenants, 11 ensigns, one quarter-master, and one deputy adjutant-general of the militia; *viz.*

Lieutenant-col. Chervet; major Wm. Allan; captains, John Willson, John Button, Peter Robinson, John Arnold, James Fenwick, James Mustard, Duncan Cameron, David Thomson, John Robinson, Samuel Ridout, Thomas Hamilton, John Burn, Wm. Jarvie, Lieutenants John Shultz, George Mustard, Barnet Vanderburgh, Robert Stanton, Gorge Ridout, William Jarvis, Edward M'Mahon, J. Mahon, J. Wilson, E. Playter; ensigns Andrew Thompson, A. Smalley, Donald M'Arthur, William Smith, Andrew Mercer,

APPENDIX. 401

James Chevcet, George Kuck, Edward Thompson, Charles Dennison, George Dennison, D'Arcy Boulton; quarter-master Charles Baynes; 19 serjeants; four corporals; 204 rank and file; of the field-train department, William Dunbar; of the provincial army, one captain, one lieutenant, two midshipmen, one clerk; *viz.*

Captain Francis Grauvreau; lieutenant Green; John Ridout, John Paupre, midshipmen; James Longsden, clerk; one boatswain; 15 naval artificers; of his majesty's regular troops, one lieutenant; *viz.* lieutenant De Koven; one serjeant-major; and of the royal artillery, one bombardier and three gunners, shall be surrendered prisoners of war, and accounted for in the exchange of prisoners between the United States and Great Britain. -

>G. C. MITCHELL, lieut.-col. 3d artillery, U. S. A.
>
>SAM. S. CONNER, major, and A. D. C. to major-gen. Dearborn.
>
>WM. KING, major U. S. infantry.
>
>JESSE D. ELLIOTT, lieutenant U. S. navy.
>
>WM. CHERVET, lieutenant-col. 3d. regiment York militia.
>
>WM. ALLAN, major 3d regiment York militia.
>
>F. GAUVRAU, lieut. marine department.

York, April 28, 1813.

The foregoing agreement, or terms of capitulation, is approved by us,

>WILLIAM DEARBORN, major-gen.
>ISAAC CHAUNCEY, commodore.

No. 19.

From major-gen. Dearborn to the American secretary of war.

Head-quarters, York, capital of Upper Canada,
Sir, April 28, 1813.

After a detention of some days by adverse winds, we arrived at this place yesterday morning, and at 8 o'clock commenced landing the troops about three miles westward from the town, and one and a half from the enemy's works. The wind was high, and in an unfavorable direction for the boats, which prevented the landing of the troops at a clear field, the site of the ancient French fort, Toronto. It prevented, also, many of the armed vessels from taking positions which would have most effectually covered our landing; but every thing that could be done was effected.

The riflemen under major Forsythe first landed, under a heavy fire from the Indians, and other troops. General Sheaffe commanded in person. He had collected his whole force in the woods, near the point were the wind compelled our troops to land. His force consisted of 700 regulars and militia, and 100 Indians. Major Forsythe was supported as promptly as possible; but the contest was sharp and severe for near half an hour, and the enemy were repulsed by a number far inferior to theirs. As soon as general Pike landed with 7 or 800 men, and the remainder of the troops were pushing for the shore, the enemy retreated to their works. Our troops were now formed on the ground originally intended for their landing, marched through a thick wood, and after carrying one battery by assault, were moving in columns towards the main work; when within 60 rods of this, a tremendous explosion took place, from a magazine previously prepared, and which blew out such an immense quantity of stone, as most seriously to injure our troops. I have not yet been able to collect a return of the killed and

and wounded; but our loss will, I fear, exceed 100, and among these I have to lament the loss of that brave and excellent officer, Brigadier-gen. Pike, who received a contusion from a large stone, which terminated his valuable life in a few hours. His loss will be severely felt.

Previously to this explosion, the enemy had retired into the town, excepting a party of regulars, to the number of 40, who did not escape the effects of the shock, and were destroyed.

General Sheaffe moved off with the regular troops, and left directions with the commanding-officer of the militia to make the best terms he could. In the mean time, all further resistance on the part of the enemy ceased, and the outlines of a capitulation were agreed on.

As soon as I learned that general Pike had been wounded, I went on shore. To the general I had been induced to confide the immediate attack, from a knowledge that it was his wish, and that he would have felt mortified had it not been given to him.

Every movement was under my view. The troops acted with great firmness, and deserve much applause, particularly those first engaged, and under circumstances which would have tried the steadiness of veterans.

Our loss in the morning, and in carrying the first battery, was not great, perhaps 40 or 50 killed and wounded, and of them a full proportion of officers.

Notwithstanding the enemy's advantage in position and numbers in the commencement of the action, their loss was greater than ours, especially in officers. It was with great exertion that the small vessels of the fleet could work into the harbour against a gale of wind; but as soon as they got a proper position, a tremendous cannonade opened upon the enemy's batteries, and was kept up against them until they were carried or blown up, and had no doubt, a powerful effect upon the enemy.

I am under the greatest obligations to commodore Chauncey, for his able and indefatigable exertions in every possible manner which could give facility and effect to the expedition. He is equally estimable for sound judgment, bravery, and industry. The government could not have made a more fortunate selection.

Unfortunately, the enemy's armed ship prince Regent left this place for Kingston a few days before we arrived. A large ship on the stocks, and nearly planked up, and much naval stores, were set fire to by the enemy soon after the explosion of the magazine. A considerable quantity of military stores and provisions remain, but no vessel fit for use.

We have not the means of transporting prisoners, and must of course leave them on parole.

I hope we shall so far complete what is necessary to be done here, as to be able to sail to-morrow for Niagara, whither I send this by a small vessel, with notice to general Lewis of our approach.

I have the honor to be, &c.

HENRY DEARBORN.

Hon. gen. J. Armstrong, secretary
of war, Washington.

No. 20.

From commodore Chauncey to the American secretary of the navy.

U. S. ship Madison, at anchor off York,
Sir, April 28th, 1813.

Agreeably to your instructions and arrangements made with major-gen. Dearborn, I took on board the squadron under my command, the general and suite, and about 1700 troops, and left Sackett's Harbor on the 25th instant for this place. We arrived here yesterday morning, and took a position about one mile to the southward and westward of the enemy's principal fort, and as near the shore as we could with safety to the vessels.

APPENDIX.

The place fixed upon by the major-general and myself, for landing the troops, was the site of the old French fort Toronto.

The debarkation commenced about 8 o'clock A.M. and was completed about 10. The wind blowing heavy from the eastward, the boats fell to leeward of the position fixed upon, and were, in consequence, exposed to a galling fire from the enemy, who had taken a position in a thick wood, near where the first troops landed; however, the cool intrepidity of the officers and men overcame every obstacle. Their attack upon the enemy was so vigorous that he fled in every direction, leaving a great many of his killed and wounded upon the field. As soon as the troops were landed, I directed the schooners to take a position near the fort, in order that the attack upon the enemy by the army and navy might be simultaneous. The schooners were obliged to beat up to their position, which they did in a very handsome order, under a very heavy fire from the enemy's batteries, and took a position within about 600 yards of their principal fort, and opened a heavy cannonade upon the enemy, which did great execution, and very much contributed to their final destruction; the troops, as soon as landed, were formed under the immediate orders of brigadier-general Pike, who led in a most gallant manner the attack upon the forts, and after having carried two redoubts on his approach to the principal work, the enemy (having previously laid a train) blew up his magazine, which, in its effects upon our troops, were dreadful, having killed and wounded a great many; and among the former, the ever to be lamented brigadier-general Pike, who fell at the head of his column, by a contusion received by a heavy stone from the magazine. His death at this time is much to be regretted, as he had the perfect confidence of the major-general; and his known activity, zeal, and experience, makes his loss a national one.

In consequence of the fall of general Pike, the command of the troops for a time devolved upon colonel Pierce, who soon after took possession of the town. At about 2 P.M. the American flag was substituted for the British, and at 4, our troops were in quiet possession of the town. As soon as general Dearborn learnt the situation of general Pike, he landed, and assumed the command. I have the honor of enclosing a copy of the capitulation that was entered into and approved of by general Dearborn and myself.

The enemy set fire to some of his principal stores, containing large quantities of naval and military stores, as well as a large ship on the stocks, nearly finished. The only vessel found here, was the Duke of Gloucester undergoing repairs. The Prince Regent left here on the 24th for Kingston. We have not yet had a return made of the naval and military stores; consequently cannot form a correct idea of the quantity, but have made arrangements to have all taken on board that we can receive; the rest will be destroyed.

I have to regret the death of midshipmen Thompson and Hatfield, and of several seamen killed—the exact number I do not know, as the returns from the different vessels have not yet been received.

From the judicious arrangements made by general Dearborn, I presume that the public stores will be disposed of, so that the troops will be ready to re-embark to-morrow, and proceed to execute other objects of the expedition the first fair wind.

I cannot speak in too much praise of the cool intrepidity of the officers and men generally, under my command; and I feel myself particularly indebted to the officers commanding vessels, for their zeal in seconding my views.

I have the honor to be, very respectfully,
Your most obedient servant,
ISAAC CHAUNCEY.

To the hon. the secretary of the navy.

(Terms of capitulation as before.)

APPENDIX.

No. 21.

From brigadier-general Vincent to sir G. Prevost.

SIR,   Forty-mile Creek, May 28, 1813.

I have the honor to inform your excellency, that yesterday morning, about day-break, the enemy again opened his batteries upon Fort-George: the fire not being immediately returned, it ceased for some time. About 4 o'clock A.M. a combination of circumstances led to a belief that an invasion was meditated. The morning being exceedingly hazy, neither his means nor his intention could be ascertained, until, the mist clearing away at intervals, the enemy's fleet, consisting of 14 or 15 vessels, was discovered under way, standing towards the light-house, in an extended line of more than two miles, covering from 90 to 100 large boats and scows, each containing an average of 50 or 60 men. Though at this time no doubt could be entertained of the enemy's intention, his points of attack could only be conjectured. Having again commenced a heavy fire from his fort, line of batteries, and shipping, it became necessary to withdraw all the guards and piquets stationed along the coast, between the fort and light-house, and a landing was effected at the Two-mile Creek, about half a mile below the latter-place. The party of troops and Indians stationed at this point, after opposing the enemy, and annoying him as long as possible, were obliged to fall back, and the fire from the shipping so completely enfiladed and scowered the plains, that it became impossible to approach the beach. As the day dawned, the enemy's plan was clearly developed, and every effort to oppose his landing having failed, I lost not a moment in concentrating my force between the town of Fort-George and the enemy, there awaiting his approach. This movement was admirably covered by the Glengarry light infantry, joined by a detachment of the royal Newfoundland regiment and militia, which commenced skirmishing with the enemy's riflemen, who were advancing through the brushwood. The enemy having perfect command of the beach, he quickly landed from 3 to 4000 men, with several pieces of artillery, and this force was instantly seen advancing in three solid columns, along the lake bank, his right covered by a large body of riflemen, and his left and front by the fire of the shipping, and batteries in their fort. As our light troops fell back upon the main body, which was moved forwards to their support, they were gallantly sustained by the 8th (king's) regiment, commanded by major Ogilvie, the whole being under the immediate direction of colonel Myers, acting quarter-master-general, who had charge of the right wing. In the execution of this important duty, gallantry, zeal, and decision, were eminently conspicuous; and I lament to report that I was deprived of the services of colonel Myers, who, having received three wounds, was obliged to quit the field. Lieutenant-colonel Harvey, the deputy adjutant-general, whose activity and gallantry had been displayed the whole morning, succeeded colonel Myers, and brought up the right division, consisting of the 49th regiment, and some militia.

The light artillery under major Holcroft were already in position, awaiting the enemy's advance on the plain. At this moment the very inferior force under my command, had experienced a severe loss in officers and men; yet nothing could exceed the ardor and gallantry of the troops, who shewed the most marked devotion in the service of their king and country, and appeared regardless of the consequence of the unequal contest. Being on the spot, and seeing that the force under my command was opposed with ten-fold numbers, who were rapidly advancing under cover of their shipping and batteries, from which our positions were immediately seen, and exposed to a tremendous fire of shot and shells, I decided on retiring my little force to a position which I hoped might be less assailable by the heavy ordnance of the enemy, and from which a retreat would be left open, in the event of that measure becoming necessary. Here, after awaiting the approach of the enemy for about half an hour, I received authentic information, that his force, consisting of from 4 to 5000 men, had re-formed his columns, and was making an effort to turn my right flank. At this critical juncture not a moment was to be lost, and sensible that every effort had been made, by the officers and men under my command, to maintain the post of Fort-George, I could not consider myself justified in continuing so unequal a contest, the issue of which promised no advantage to the interests of his majesty's service. Having given orders for the fort to be evacuated, the guns to be spiked, and the ammunition destroyed, the troops under my command were put in motion, and marched across the country in a line parallel to the Niagara river, towards the position near the Beaver Dam, beyond Queenstown Mountain, at which place I had the honor of reporting to your excellency that a depôt of provisions and ammunition had been formed some time since. The rear-guard of the army reached that position during the night, and we were soon afterwards joined by lieutenant-colonel Bisshopp, with all the detachment from Chippeway to Fort-Erie. The light, and one battalion company of the 8th, (king's,) joined us about the same time, as did captain Barclay, with a detachment of the royal navy.

Having assembled my whole force the following morning, which did not exceed 1600 men, I continued my march towards the head of the lake, where it is my intention to take up a position, and shall endeavour to maintain it, until I may be honored with your excellency's instructions, which I shall feel most anxious to receive. I beg leave to suggest the great importance that exists for a communication being opened with me, through the medium of the fleet. The anchorage under Mrs. Brandt's house is perfectly good and very safe. I believe your excellency need not be informed, that in the event of it becoming necessary that I should fall back upon York, the assistance of shipping would be requisite for the transport of my artillery. I cannot conclude this long communication, without expressing a well-merited tribute of approbation to the gallantry and assiduity of every officer of the staff, and indeed of every individual composing my little army;—every one most zealously discharged the duties of his respective station. The struggle on the 27th continued from three to four hours; and, I lament to add, it was attended with very severe loss.

I have the honor to enclose a list of the killed, wounded, and missing, with as much accuracy as the nature of existing circumstances will admit. Many of the missing, I hope, will be found to be only stragglers, and will soon rejoin their corps. I shall reach the head of the lake to-morrow evening. Hitherto the enemy has not attempted to interrupt my movements. Information reached me this morning, through an authentic channel, that he has pushed on 3000 infantry, and a considerable body of cavalry, towards Queenstown. His whole force is stated to amount to nearly 10000 men.

I send this despatch by Mr. Mathison, who acted as a volunteer on the 27th; and I am happy to inform your excellency, that his conduct was very honorable to his character, and merits my marked approbation. Ammunition will be wanting by the first vessel. Captain Milnes has been kind enough to remain with me until my next despatch.

I have the honor to be, &c.
JOHN VINCENT, brig.-gen.

His excellency lieutenant-general
sir George Prevost, &c. &c. &c.

>Return of killed, wounded, and missing, of his majesty's troops in action with the enemy at Fort-George, May the 27th, 1813.

General staff;—1 wounded.

Royal artillery;—1 rank and file killed; 1 rank and file wounded.

8th; (or king's regiment;)—1 lieutenant killed; 1 major, 3 lieutenants, 1 ensign, wounded; 11 serjeants, 4 drummers, 181 rank and file, missing.

41st regiment;—3 rank and file wounded and missing.

APPENDIX.

49*th regiment;*—2 rank and file killed; 2 rank and file wounded; 4 drummers, 28 rank and file, wounded and missing.

Left in hospitals, and wounded on former occasions, 16 rank and file, not included.

Glengarry regiment;—1 captain, 1 ensign, 1 serjeant, 24 rank and file, killed; 1 captain, 1 lieutenant, 1 ensign, 3 serjeants, 20 rank and file, wounded; 1 lieutenant, 2 serjeants, 23 rank and file, wounded and missing.

Royal Newfoundland regiment;—21 rank and file, killed; 1 captain, 1 lieutenant, 1 serjeant, 6 rank and file, wounded; 5 rank and file wounded and missing.

Total;—1 captain, 1 lieutenant, 1 ensign, 1 serjeant, 48 rank and file, killed; 1 general-staff, 1 major, 2 captains, 5 lieutenants, 2 ensigns, 4 serjeants, 29 rank and file, wounded; 1 lieutenant, 13 serjeants, 8 drummers, 240 rank and file, wounded and missing.

Names of officers killed and wounded.

Killed;—8*th; (or king's regiment;)*—Lieutenant James Drummie;

Glengarry regiment;—Captain Liddle, ensign M'Lean.

Wounded;—Colonel Myers, acting quarter-master-general, severely, not dangerously.

8*th regiment;*—Major Edward Cotton, lieutenant I. W. Lloyd, severely, and prisoner; lieutenants Mortimer, M'Mahon, and Horace Noel; ensign Richard Nicholson, severely, and prisoner.

Glengarry regiment;—Captain Roxburgh, lieutenant Kerr, ensign Kerr.

Royal Newfoundland regiment;—Captain Winter, lieutenant Stewart.

EDWARD BAYNES,
Adjutant-general, North America.

No. 22.

From major-general Dearborn to the American secretary at war.

Sir,

Head-quarters, Fort-George,
Upper Canada, May 27.

The light-troops under the command of colonel Scott and major Forsythe, landed this morning, at nine o'clock. Major-general Lewis's division, with colonel Porter's command of light-artillery, supported them. General Boyd's brigade landed immediately after the light troops, and generals Chandler and Winder followed it in quick succession. The landing was warmly and obstinately disputed by the British forces; but the coolness and intrepidity of our troops soon compelled them to give ground in every direction. General Chandler, with the reserve, (composed of his brigade and colonel Macomb's artillery,) covered the whole. Commodore Chauncey had made the most judicious arrangement for silencing the enemy's batteries near the point of landing. The army is under the greatest obligations to that able naval commander for his co-operation in all its important movements, and especially in its operations this day. Our batteries succeeded in rendering Fort-George untenable; and when the enemy had been beaten from his positions, and I found it necessary to re-enter it, after firing a few guns, and setting fire to the magazines, which soon exploded, he moved off rapidly by different routes. Our light troops pursued them several miles. The troops having been under arms from one o'clock in the morning, were too much exhausted for any further pusuit. We are now in possession of Fort-George and its immediate dependencies; to-morrow we shall proceed on. The behaviour of our troops, both officers and men, entitles them to the highest praise; and the difference of our loss with that of the enemy, when we consider the advantages his position afforded him, is astonishing. We had 17 killed, and 45 wounded. The enemy had 90 killed, and 160 wounded, of the regular troops. We have taken 100 prisoners, exclusive of the wounded. Colonel Myers, of the 49th, was wounded, and taken prisoner. Of ours only one commissioned officer was killed, lieutenant Hobart, of the light-artillery.

  I have the honor to be, sir,
    With great consideration and respect,
      Your most obedient servant,
Hon. gen. John Armstrong,   H. DEARBORN.
 secretary at war.

No. 23.

From adjutant-general Baynes to sir G. Prevost.

Sir,   Kingston, May 30th, 1813.

I have the honor to report to your excellency, that in conformity to an arranged plan of operations with commodore sir James Yeo, the fleet of boats assembled a-stern of his ship, at 10 o'clock on the night of the 28th instant, with the troops placed under my command, and led by a gun-boat, under the direction of captain Mulcaster, royal navy, proceeded towards Sackett's Harbor, in the order prescribed to the troops, in case the detachment was obliged to march in column; viz. the grenadier company, 100th, with one section of the royal Scots, two companies of the 8th, (or king's,) four of the 104th, two of the Canadian voltigeurs, two 6-pounders, with their gunners, and a company of Glengarry light-infantry, were embarked on board a light schooner, which was proposed to be towed, under the direction of officers of the navy, so as to insure the guns being landed in time to support the advance of the troops. Although the night was dark, with rain, the boats assembled in the vicinity of Sackett's Harbor, by one o'clock, in compact and regular order; and in this position it was intended to remain until the day broke, in the hope of effecting a landing before the enemy could be prepared to line the woods with troops, which surround the coast; but, unfortunately, a strong current drifted the boats considerably, while the darkness of the night, and ignorance of the coast, prevented them from recovering their proper station until the day dawned, when the whole pulled for the point of debarkation.

It was my intention to have landed in the cove formed by Horse Island, but, on approaching it, we discovered that the enemy were fully prepared, by a very heavy fire of musketry from the surrounding woods, which were filled with infantry supported by a field-piece. I directed the boats to pull round to the other side of the island, where a landing was effected in good order and with little loss, although executed in the face of a corps, formed with a field-piece in the wood, and under the enfilade of a heavy gun of the enemy's principal battery. The advance was led by the grenadiers of the 100th regiment, with undaunted gallantry, which no obstacle could arrest. A narrow causeway, in many places under water, not more than four feet wide, and about 400 paces in length, which connected the island with the main land, was occupied by the enemy, in great force, with a 6-pounder. It was forced, and carried in the most spirited manner, and the gun taken before a second discharge could be made from it; a tumbril, with a few rounds of ammunition, was found; but, unfortunately, the artillerymen were still behind, the schooner not having been able to get up in time, and the troops were exposed to so heavy and galling a fire from a numerous, but almost invisible foe, as to render it impossible to halt for the artillery to come up. At this spot two paths led in opposite directions round the hill; I directed colonel Young, of the king's regiment, with half of the detachment, to penetrate by the left; and major Drummond, of the 104th, to force the path by the right, which proved to be more open, and was less occupied by the enemy. On the left the wood was very thick, and was most obstinately maintained by the enemy.

The gun-boats which had covered our landing, afforded material aid, by firing into the woods; but the American soldier, secure behind a tree, was only to be dislodged by the bayonet. The spirited advance of a section produced the flight of hundreds. From this observation all firing was directed to cease, and the detachment being formed in as regular order as the nature of the ground would admit, pushed forward through the wood upon the enemy, who, although greatly superior in numbers, and supported by field-pieces, and a heavy fire from their fort, fled with precipitation to their block-house and fort, abandoning one of their guns. The division under colonel Young was joined in the charge, by that under major Drummond, which was executed with such spirit and promptness, that many of the enemy fell in their enclosed barracks, which were set on fire by our troops;—at this point the further energies of the troops became unavailing. Their block-house and stockaded battery could not be carried by assault, nor reduced by field-pieces, had we been provided with them; the fire of the gun-boats proved inefficient to attain that end: light and adverse winds continued, and our larger vessels were still far off. The enemy turned the heavy ordnance of the battery to the interior defence of his post. He had set fire to the store-houses in the vicinity of the fort.

Seeing no object within our reach to attain, that could compensate for the loss we were momentarily sustaining from the heavy fire of the enemy's cannon, I directed the troops to take up the position on the crest of the hill we had charged from. From this position we were ordered to re-embark, which was performed at our leisure, and in perfect order, the enemy not presuming to shew a single soldier without the limits of his fortress. Your excellency having been a witness of the zeal and ardent courage of every soldier in the field, it is unnecessary in me to assure your excellency, that but one sentiment animated every breast, that of discharging to the utmost of their power their duty to their king and country.—But one sentiment of regret and mortification prevailed, on being obliged to quit a beaten enemy, whom a small band of British soldiers had driven before them for three hours, through a country abounding in strong positions of defence, but not offering a single spot of cleared ground favorable for the operations of disciplined troops, without having fully accomplished the duty we were ordered to perform.

The two divisions of the detachment were ably commanded by colonel Young, of the king's, and major Drummond, of the 104th. The detachment of the king's under major Evans, nobly sustained the high and established character of that distinguished corps; and captain Burke availed himself of the ample field afforded him in leading the advance, to display the intrepidity of British grenadiers.

The detachment of the 104th regiment, under major Moodie, captain M'Pherson's company of Glengarry light-infantry, and two companies of Canadian voltigeurs, commanded by major Hammot, all of them levies of the British provinces of North America, evinced most striking proofs of their loyalty, steadiness, and courage. The detachment of the royal Newfoundland regiment behaved with great gallantry. Your excellency will lament the loss of that active and intelligent officer, captain Gray, acting deputy-quarter-master-general, who fell close to the enemy's work, while reconnoitring it, in the hope to discover some opening to favor an assault. Commodore sir James Yeo conducted the fleet of boats in the attack, and, accompanying the advance of the troops, directed the co-operation of the gun-boats. I feel most grateful for your excellency's kind consideration, in allowing your aides de camp majors Coote and Fulton, to accompany me in the field, and to these officers for the able assistance they afforded me.

I have the honor to be, &c.

EDWARD BAYNES,

Col. Glengarry light-infanty, commanding.

To his excellency lieutenant-general
sir George Prevost, Bart. &c. &c. &c.

APPENDIX. 417

Return of the killed, wounded, and missing, in an attack on Sackett's Harbor, on the 29th of May, 1813.

General staff;—1 killed.

Royal artillery;—2 gunners, wounded.

Royal Scots;—2 rank and file, killed; 1 rank and file, wounded and missing; 4 rank and file, wounded.

8th; (or king's regiment;)—5 rank and file, killed; 2 captains, 1 ensign, 7 rank and file, wounded and missing; 1 major, 2 lieutenants, 3 serjeants, 60 rank and file, wounded.

100th regiment;—1 serjeant, 5 rank and file, killed; 3 rank and file, wounded and missing; 1 drummer, 19 rank and file, wounded.

104th regiment;—2 serjeant, 20 rank and file, killed; 1 rank and file, wounded and missing; 2 majors, 2 captains, 3 lieutenants, 3 serjeants, 1 drummer, 57 rank and file, wounded.

Royal Newfoundland regiment;—4 rank and file, killed; 1 rank and file, wounded and missing; 13 rank and file, wounded.

Glengarry light-infantry;—6 rank and file, killed; 1 captain, 1 ensign, 1 serjeant, 17 rank and file, wounded.

Canadian voltigeurs;—2 rank and file, killed; 2 rank and file, wounded.

Total;—1 general staff, 3 serjeants, 44 rank and file, killed; 3 majors, 3 captains, 5 lieutenants, 1 ensign, 7 serjeants, 2 drummers, 172 rank and file, 2 gunners, wounded; 2 captains, 1 ensign, 13 rank and file, wounded and missing.

Names of officers killed and wounded.

Killed;—Captain A. Gray, acting deputy-quarter-master-general.

Wounded; 8th; (or king's regiment;)—Major Evans, slightly; captain Blackmore, dangerously; captain Tythe, severely; lieutenant Nutall; (since dead;) lieutenant Lowry; ensign Greig, prisoner.

VOL. I.   E E

418   APPENDIX.

104*th regiment ;*—majors Drummond and Moody, slightly; captain Leonard, severely; captain Shore, slightly; lieutenants Rainford, Moore, and Delancey.

Glengarry light infantry ;—Captain M'Pherson, severely; ensign Mathewson, slightly.

      EDWARD BAYNES,
       Adjt. Gen. North America.

***

No. 24.

From colonel Proctor to major-general Sheaffe.

S<small>IR</small>,   Sandwich, January 25th, 1813.

In my last despatch I acquainted you, that the enemy was in the Michigan territory, marching upon Detroit, and that I therefore deemed it necessary that he should be attacked without delay, with all and every description of force within my reach. Early in the morning, on the 19th, I was informed of his being in possession of Frenchtown, on the river Raisin, 26 miles from Detroit, after experiencing every resistance that major Reynolds, of the Essex militia, had it in his power to make, with a 3-pounder, well served and directed by bombardier Kitson, of the royal artillery, and the militia, three of whom he had well trained to the use of it. The retreat of the gun was covered by a brave band of Indians, who made the enemy pay dear for what he obtained. This party, composed of militia and Indians, with the gun, fell back, 18 miles to Brown's town, the settlement of the brave Wyandots, where I directed my force to assemble. On the 21st instant, I advanced 12 miles to Swan Creek, from whence we marched to the enemy, and attacked him at break of day, on the 22d instant; and after suffering, for our numbers, a considerable loss, the enemy's force posted in houses and enclosures, and which, from dread of falling into the hands of the Indians, they most obstinately defended, at length surrendered at discretion; the other part of their force, in attempting to retreat by the way they came,

APPENDIX. 419

were, I believe, all, or with very few exceptions, killed by the Indians. Brigadier-general Winchester was taken in the pursuit, by the Wyandot chief Roundhead, who afterwards surrendered him to me.

You will perceive that I have lost no time; indeed, it was necessary to be prompt in my movements, as the enemy would have been joined by major-general Harrison in a few days. The troops, the marine, and the militia, displayed great bravery, and behaved uncommonly well. Where so much zeal and spirit were manifested, it would be unjust to attempt to particularize any: I cannot, however, refrain from mentioning lieutenant-colonel St. George, who received four wounds in a gallant attempt to occupy a building which was favorably situated for annoying the enemy; together with ensign Kerr, of the Newfoundland regiment, who, I fear, is very dangerously wounded. The zeal and courage of the Indian department were never more conspicuous than on this occasion, and the Indian warriors fought with their usual bravery. I am much indebted to the different departments, the troops having been well and timely supplied with every requisite the district could afford.

I have fortunately not been deprived of the services of lieutenant Troughton, of the royal artillery, and acting in the quarter-master-general's department, although he was wounded, to whose zealous and unwearied exertions I am greatly indebted, as well as to the whole of the royal artillery for their conduct in this affair.

I enclose a list of the killed and wounded, and cannot but lament that there are so many of both; but of the latter, I am happy to say, a large proportion of them will return to their duty, and most of them in a short time: I also enclose a return of the arms and ammunition which have been taken, as well as of the prisoners, whom you will perceive to be equal to my utmost force, exclusive of the Indians.

It is reported that a party, consisting of 100 men, bringing 500 hogs to general Winchester's force, has been completely cut off by the Indians, and the convoy taken. Lieutenant M'Lean, my acting brigade-major, whose gallantry and exertions were conspicuous on the 22d instant, is the bearer of this despatch, and will be able to afford you every information respecting our situation.

I have the honor to be, &c.
HENRY PROCTOR, colonel.

To major-general Sheaffe, &c. &c. &c.
    Fort-George.

No. 25.

Return of prisoners taken after the action at Riviere au Raisin, on the 22d day of January, 1813.

1 brigadier-general; 1 colonel; 1 major; 9 captains; 6 lieutenants; 10 ensigns; 1 brigade-major; 1 adjutant; 1 quarter-master; 2 surgeons; 27 serjeants; 435 rank and file. Total—495.

N. B. The Indians have brought in and delivered up several prisoners since the above return was taken; they continue to do so this morning, so that this return is not perfectly correct, nor can a correct one be procured until they arrive at Sandwich.

FELIX TROUGHTON, R. A.
Act. dep. assist. quarter-master-gen.

No. 26.

Return of the killed and wounded in the action at Riviere au Raisin, 22d January, 1813.

Royal artillery ;—1 serjeant, 1 gunner, killed; 1 lieutenant, 1 corporal, 1 bombardier, 5 gunners, wounded.

10th royal veteran battalion ;—2 privates, wounded.

APPENDIX.

41st foot ;—15 privates, killed ; 1 captain, 1 lieutenant, 3 serjeants, 1 corporal, 91 privates, wounded.

Royal Newfoundland regiment ;—1 private, killed; 1 ensign, 1 serjeant, 3 corporals, 13 privates, wounded.

Marine department ;—1 seaman, killed; 2 lieutenants, 1 midshipman, 1 gunner, 12 seamen, wounded.

1st Essex militia ;—2 privates, killed ; 1 captain, 2 lieutenants, 2 serjeants, 7 privates, wounded.

2d Essex militia ;—3 privates, killed ; 1 ensign, 3 privates, wounded.

Staff ;—1 lieutenant-colonel, wounded.

Total ;—1 serjeant, 1 gunner, 21 privates, 1 seaman, killed ; 1 lieutenant-colonel, 2 captains, 6 lieutenants, 2 ensigns, 1 midshipman, 6 serjeants, 5 corporals, 1 bombardier, 6 gunners, 116 privates, 12 seamen, wounded.

General Total ;—24 killed ; 158 wounded.

Names of the officers wounded.

Royal artillery ;—Lieutenant Troughton.

41st foot ;—Captain Tallon and lieutenant Clemow.

Royal Newfoundland regiment ;—Ensign Kerr.

Marine department ;—Lieutenants Rolette and Irvine, and midshipman Richardson.

1st Essex militia ;—Captain Mills, and lieutenants M'Cormic and Gordon.

2d ditto ;—Claude Garvin.

Staff ;—Colonel St. George.

FELIX TROUGHTON, Lt. R. A.
Act. dep. asst.-quarter-master.-gen.

APPENDIX.

No. 27.

From brigadier-general Winchester to the American secretary of war.

Sir, Malden, January 28th, 1813.

A detachment from the left wing of the north-western Army under my command, at Frenchtown, on the river Raisin, was attacked on the 23d instant, by a force greatly superior in numbers, aided by several pieces of artillery. The action commenced at the dawn of day: the piquet-guards were driven in, and a heavy fire opened upon the whole line, by which part thereof was thrown into disorder; and being ordered to form on more advantageous ground, I found the enemy doubling our left flank with force and rapidity.

A destructive fire was sustained for some time; at length, borne down by numbers, the few of us that remained with the party retired from the lines, submitted. The remainder of our force, in number about 400, continued to defend themselves with great gallantry, in an unequal contest against small-arms and artillery, until I was brought in as a prisoner to that part of the field occupied by the enemy.

At this latter place, I understood that our troops were defending themselves in a state of desperation; and I was informed by the commanding-officer of the enemy, that he would afford them an opportunity of surrendering themselves prisoners of war; to which I acceded. I was the more ready to make the surrender, from being assured, that unless done quickly, the buildings adjacent would be immediately set on fire, and that no responsibility would be taken for the conduct of the savages, who were then assembled in great numbers.

In this critical situation, being desirous to preserve the lives of a number of our brave fellows who still held out, I sent a flag to them, and agreed with the commanding-officer of the enemy, that they should be surrendered prisoners of war, on

APPENDIX.

condition of their being protected from the savages, and being allowed to retain their private property, and having their sidearms returned to them. It is impossible for me to ascertain, with certainty, the loss we have sustained in this action, from the impracticability of knowing the number who have made their escape.

Thirty-five officers, and about 487 non-commissioned officers, and privates, are prisoners of war. A list of the names of officers is herewith enclosed to you. Our loss in killed is considerable.

However unfortunate may seem the affair of yesterday, I am flattered by the belief, that no material error is chargeable upon myself, and that still less censure deserved by the troops I had the honor of commanding.

With the exception of that portion of our force which was thrown into disorder, no troops have ever behaved with more determined intrepidity.

I have the honor to be, with high respect,
Your obedient servant,
JAMES WINCHESTER,
Hon. secretary at war.   Brig.-gen. U. S. army.

Here follows a list of the officers taken;

General Winchester; colonel Lewis; major Madison; captains Overton, Hightower, Ballard, Cholier, James Kelly, Hamilton, Williams, Sabrie, and Bledsoe; lieutenants Gerrard, M'Cella; adjutant Keen; Q. M. Holden, Rule M'Guire, Ganard, Moore, and Higgins; ensigns Comstock, Butler, T. Chin, Flarron, Nash, Botts, Munday, Herson, Nash; Mooring, Fleet, and Caldwell; surgeon Todd.—Total, 36.

The Indians have still a few prisoners in their possession, which I have reason to hope will be given up to colonel Proctor, at Sandwich.

JAMES WINCHESTER, brig.-gen.

No. 28.

From major-general Harrison, to governor Shelby.

Camp on Carrying Rock, 15 miles from
the Rapids, January 24, 1813.

My dear Sir,

I send colonel Wells to you, to communicate the particulars (as far as we are acquainted with them) of an event that will overwhelm your mind with grief, and fill your whole state with mourning.

The greater part of colonel Wells's regiment, United States' infantry, and the 1st and 5th regiments Kentucky infantry, and Allen's rifle regiment, under the immediate orders of general Winchester have been cut to pieces by the enemy, or taken prisoners. Great as the calamity is, I still hope that, as far as it relates to the objects of the campaign, it is not irreparable. As soon as I was informed of the attack upon general Winchester, about 12 o'clock on the 22d instant, I set out, to overtake the detachment of Kentucky's troops, that I had sent that morning to reinforce him, and I directed the only regiment that I had with me to follow. I overtook major Robb's detachment at the distance of 6 miles; but before the troops in the rear could get up, certain information was received of general Winchester's total defeat.

A council of war was called, and it was the unanimous opinion of the generals Payne and Perkins, and all the field officers, that there was no motive that could authorize an advance but that of attacking the enemy, and that success was not to be expected after a forced march of 40 miles against an enemy superior in number, and well provided with artillery. Strong detachments of the most active men were, however, sent forward on all the roads, to assist and bring in such of our men as had escaped. The whole number that reached our camp does not exceed 30, amongst whom were major M'Clannahan and captain Claves.

Having a large train of heavy artillery, and stores coming on this road from W. Sandusky, under an escort of four companies, it was thought advisable to fall back to this place, for the purpose of securing them. A part of it arrived last evening, and the rest is within 30 miles. As soon as it arrives, and a reinforcement of three regiments from the Virginia and Pennsylvania brigades, I shall again advance, and give the enemy an opportunity of measuring their strength with us once more.

Colonel Wells will communicate some circumstances, which, while they afflict and surprise, will convince you that Kentucky has lost none of her reputation for valor, for which she is famed. The detachment to the river Raisin was made without my knowledge or consent, and in direct opposition to my plans. Having been made, however, I did every thing in my power to reinforce them, and a force exceeding by 300 men that which general Winchester deemed necessary, was on its way to join him, and a fine battalion within 14 miles of its destination.

After the success of colonel Lewis, I was in great hopes that the post could be maintained. Colonel Wells will communicate my future views to you, much better than I can do in writing at this time.

I am, dear Sir, &c.
W. H. HARRISON.

His excellency governor Shelby.

No. 29.

From brigadier-general Proctor to sir G. Prevost.

Sir, Sandwich, May 14th, 1813.

From the circumstances of the war, I have judged it expedient to make a direct report to your excellency of the operations and present state in this district.

APPENDIX.

In the expectation of being able to reach the enemy, who had taken post near the foot of the Rapids of the Miami, before the reinforcements and supplies could arrive, for which only he waited to commence active operations against us, I determined to attack him without delay, and with every means in my power; but from the necessary preparations, and some untoward circumstances, it was not in my power to reach him within three weeks of the period I had proposed, and at which he might have been captured or destroyed. From the incessant and heavy rains we experienced, and during which our batteries were constructed, it was not until the morning of the 1st instant, the fifth day after our arrival at the mouth of the river, 12 miles from the enemy, that our batteries could be opened.

The enemy, who occupied several acres of commanding ground, strongly defended by block-houses, and the batteries well furnished with ordnance, had, during our approach, so completely entrenched and covered himself, as to render unavailing every effort of our artillery, though well served, and in batteries most judiciously placed and constructed, under the able direction of captain Dixon, of the royal engineers, of whose ability and unwearied zeal, shewn particularly on this occasion, I cannot speak too highly.

Though the attack has not answered fully the purpose intended, I have the satisfaction to inform your excellency of the fortunate result of an attack of the enemy, aided by a sally of most of their garrison, made on the morning of the 5th instant, by a reinforcement, which descended the river a considerable distance in a very short time, consisting of two corps, Dudley's and Roswell's, amounting to 1300 men, under the command of brigadier-general Green Clay. The attack was very sudden, and on both sides of the river. The enemy were for a few minutes in the possession of our batteries, and took some prisoners. After a severe contest, though not of long continuance, the enemy gave way; and, except the body of those who sallied from the fort, must have been mostly killed or taken.

APPENDIX. 427

In this decisive affair, the officers and men of the 41st regiment, who charged and routed the enemy near the batteries, well maintained the long established reputation of the corps. Where all deserve praise, it is difficult to distinguish. Captain Muir, an old officer, who had seen much service, had the good fortune to be in the immediate command of these brave men. Besides my obligations to captain Chambers, for his unwearied exertions preparatory to, and on the expedition, as deputy assistant quartermaster-general, I have to notice his gallant conduct in attacking the enemy near the batteries, at the point of the bayonet; a service in which he was well supported by lieutenants Bullock and Clements of the 41st, and lieutenant Le Breton, of the Royal Newfoundland regiment. The courage and activity displayed through the whole scene of action by the Indian chiefs and warriors, contributed largely to our success. I have not been able to ascertain the amount of prisoners in the possession of the Indians. I have sent off, agreeable to agreement, nearly 500 prisoners to the river Huron, near Sandusky.

I have proposed an exchange, which is referred to the American government.

I could not ascertain the amount of the enemy's loss in killed, from the extent of the scene of action, and mostly in the woods. I conceive his loss in killed and prisoners to have been between 1000 and 1200 men. These unfortunate people were not volunteers, and complete Kentucky's quota. If the enemy had been permitted to receive his reinforcements and supplies undisturbed, I should have had, at this critical juncture, to contend with him for Detroit, or perhaps on this shore.

I had not the option of retaining my situation on the Miami. Half of the militia had left us. I received a deputation from the chiefs, counselling me to return, as they could not prevent their people, as was their custom after any battle of consequence, returning to their villages with their wounded, their prisoners and plunder, of which they had taken a considerable quantity in the boats of the enemy.

Before the ordinance could be drawn from the batteries, I was left with Tecumseh, and less than 20 chiefs and warriors; a circumstance which strongly proves that, under present circumstances at least, our Indian force is not a disposable one, or permanent, though occasionally a most powerful aid. I have, however, brought off all the ordnance; and, indeed, have not left any thing behind; part of the ordnance is embarked under the fire of the enemy.

The service on which we were employed has been, though short a very severe one; and too much praise cannot be given to both officers and men, for the cheerfulness with which, on every occasion, they met the service. To lieutenant-col. Warburton I feel many obligations, for the aid he zealously afforded me on every occasion. From my brigade-major, lieutenant M'Lean, I received the same zealous assistance as on former occasions. To captain Mockler, royal Newfoundland regiment, who acted as my aide-de-camp, I am much indebted for the assistance afforded me.

Lieutenant Le Breton, of the Newfoundland regiment, assistant-engineer, by his unwearied exertions, rendered essential service; as did lieutenant Gardiner, of the 41st regiment, from his science in artillery. The royal artillery, in the laborious duties they performed, displayed their usual unwearied zeal, and were well assisted by the royal Newfoundland, (under lieutenant Garden,) as additional gunners. The laborious duties which the marine, under commodore Hall, have performed, have been most cheerfully met, and the most essential service rendered.

I have the honor to send an embarkation return of the force that served under my command at the Miami, exclusive of the Indians, who may be stated at 1200.

I also enclose a return of our killed, wounded, and prisoners, who have, however, been exchanged.

I had taken upon me to give the rank of major to the six captains of the line, as militia were employed on the same service with them; some of them are old officers; all of them deserving; any mark of your excellency's approbation of them would be extremely grateful to me.

I beg leave to mention the four volunteers of the 41st regt. Wilkinson, Richardson, Laing, and Proctor, as worthy of promotion.

I have the honor to be, &c.
HENRY PROCTOR,
Brigadier-general commanding.

I beg to acknowledge the indefatigable exertions of the commissariat.

HENRY PROCTOR.

To his excellency, lieutenant-general
Sir G. Prevost, Bart. &c. &c.

No. 30.

Embarkation-return of the western army commanded by brigadier-gen. Proctor, on an expedition to the Miamis.

Amherstburg, April 23d, 1813.

General staff;—1 general, 1 lieutenant-col. 1 deputy-assistant-quarter-master-general, 1 brigade-major, 1 staff-adjutant.

Royal artillery;—1 lieutenant, 1 serjeant, 1 surgeon, 27 rank and file.

Royal engineers;—1 captain.

10th veteran battalion;—5.

41st regiment;—3 captains, 7 lieutenants, 1 assistant-surgeon, 22 serjeants, 6 drummers and bugles, 374 rank and file.

Royal Newfoundland regiment;—1 captain, 2 lieutenants, 3 serjeants, 2 drummers, 55 rank and file.

Commissariat;—1 deputy-assistant-commissary-general, 1 assistant to ditto, 1 issuer.

Field train;—1 clerk of stores, 1 conductor.

Militia;—1 major, 12 captains, 11 lieutenants, 8 ensigns, 1 adjutant, 22 serjeants, 406 rank and file.

PETER L. CHAMBERS, major,
captain 41st regt. D. A. Q. master-general.

No. 31.

Return of killed, wounded, missing, and prisoners, of the army under the command of brigadier-general Proctor at the battle fought at the Miamis, May 5th, 1813.

Royal artillery;—1 serjeant, 1 rank and file, wounded; 2 rank and file, prisoners.

41st regiment;—11 rank and file, killed; 1 lieutenant, 3 serjeants, 35 rank and file, wounded; 2 lieutenants, 1 serjeant, 1 drummer, 33 rank and file, prisoners.

Royal Newfoundland regiment;—1 drummer, 2 rank and file, killed; 1 rank and file, wounded; 1 rank and file, prisoner.

Militia;—1 captain, 4 rank and file, wounded; 1 rank and file, prisoner.

Total ;—1 drummer, 13 rank and file, killed, 1 captain, 1 lieutenant, 4 serjeants, 41 rank and file, wounded; 2 lieutenants, 1 serjeant, 37 rank and file, prisoners.

Names of officers wounded and prisoners.

41st regiment;—Lieutenant Bullock, wounded on the 3d ult.; lieutenants M'Intire and Hales, prisoners.

Militia;—Captain Bandy, since deceased.

PETER CHAMBERS, major,
captain 41st.regt. D. A. Q. M.-gen.

APPENDIX.

No. 32.

Return of officers, non-commissioned officers, and privates, taken prisoners from the enemy on the 5th of May, 1813, at the battle fought at the Miamis.

United States' regulars;—1 captain, 21 rank and file.

10th and 13th detached Kentucky militia;—2 majors, 1 brigade-inspector, 8 captains, 9 lieutenants, 6 ensigns, 1 adjutant, 1 pay-master, 1 surgeon, 26 serjeants, 3 drummers, 373 rank and file.

Prisoners since delivered up by the Indians;—1 ensign, 1 assistant-surgeon, 12 rank and file.—Grand total, 467.

N. B. There are a number of prisoners not yet come in, who are in the possession of the Indians, but they are bringing them in daily.

PETER L. CHAMBERS, major,
captain 41st regiment D. A. Q. M.-gen.

May 17;—Since the above return, 28 prisoners have been given up by the Indians.

A. H. M'LEAN, B. M.

No. 33.

From brigadier-gen. Vincent to Sir G. Prevost.

Burlington-heights, head of Lake-Ontario,
SIR,   June 6th, 1813.

Having yesterday received information of the enemy having advanced from the Forty-mile Creek, with a force consisting of 3500 men, eight or nine field-pieces, and 250 cavalry, for the avowed purpose of attacking the division under my command in this position; and having soon afterwards received a report that he had passed the swamp, and driven in my advanced posts from Stony Creek and Brady's, lieutenant-col. Harvey, deputy-adjutant-general immediately went forward with the light companies of the king's, and 49th regiments; and having advanced close to, and accurately ascertained, the enemy's position, sent back to propose to me a night-attack on the camp.

The enemy's camp was distant about seven miles. About half past eleven I moved forward with five companies of the 8th, (or king's), and the 49th regiments, amounting together to only 704 firelocks; lieutenant-colonel Harvey, who conducted it with great regularity and judgment, gallantly led on the attack. The enemy was completely surprised, and driven from his camp, after having repeatedly formed in different bodies, and been as often charged by our brave troops, whose conduct, throughout this brilliant enterprise, was above all praise. The action terminated before day light, when three guns and one brass howitzer, with three tumbrils; two brigadier-generals, Chandler and Winder, first and second in command, and upwards of 100 officers, non-commissioned officers, and privates, remained in our hands.

Not conceiving it prudent to expose our small force to the view of the enemy, who, though routed, and dispersed, was still formidable as to numbers and position, he having fled to the surrounding heights, and having still four or five guns, the troops were put in motion at day-break and marched back to their cantonments. After we had retired, and it had become broad day, the enemy ventured to re-occupy his camp, only, however, for the purpose of destroying his incumbrances, such as blankets, carriages, provisions, spare arms, ammunition, &c.; after which, he commenced a precipitate retreat towards the Forty-mile Creek, where he effected a junction with a body of 2000 men, who were on their march from Niagara to reinforce him.

I cannot conclude this despatch without calling your excellency's attention to the following officers:—

APPENDIX. 433

To lieutenant-col. Harvey, the deputy-adjutant-general, my obligations are particularly due. From the first moment the enemy's approach was known, he watched his movements, and afforded me the earliest information. To him, indeed, I am indebted for the suggestion and plan of operations; nothing could be more clear than his arrangements, nor more completely successful in the result. The conduct of major Plenderleath, who commanded the 49th regt., was very conspicuous. By his decision and prompt efforts, the surprize of the enemy's camp was completed, and all his efforts to make a stand were rendered ineffectual by the bayonet, which overthrew all opposition. A party of the 49th, with major Plenderleath at their head, gallantly charged some of the enemy's field-pieces, and brought off two 6-pounders.

Major Ogilvie led on, in the most gallant manner, the five companies of the king's regiment; and whilst one half of that highly disciplined and distinguished corps supported the 49th regiment, the other part moved to the right, and attacked the enemy's left flank, which decided our midnight contest.

I have also received the greatest assistance from major Glegg, brigade-major to the forces, and beg leave to mention the names of captains M'Dowal and Milnes, your excellency's aides-de-camp, who accompanied me to the attack, and upon all occasions have volunteered their services. I have likewise to acknowledge the assistance of captain Chambers, of the 41st regiment, who had arrived some days before from Amherstburg; and Mr. Brook, pay-master of the 49th, who assisted me as acting aide-de-camp.

To Mr. Hackett, acting-staff-surgeon to this army, I feel particularly indebted, for his judicious arrangments, by which the wounded have received every attention, and are most of them likely to be restored to the service.

It would be an act of injustice, were I to admit assuring your excellency, that gallantry and discipline were never more conspicuous than during our late short service; and I feel the greatest satisfaction in assuring you, that every officer and individual seemed anxious to rival each other in his efforts to support the honor of his majesty's arms, and to maintain the high character of British troops.

I beg leave to refer your excellency to the inclosed reports for particulars respecting our loss, which, I regret, has been very severe.

I have the honor to be, &c.
JOHN VINCENT,
Brigadier-general.

His excellency sir Geo. Prevost, Bart. &c.

No. 34.

General return of killed, wounded, and missing, in action with the enemy near the head of Lake-Ontario, June 6th, 1813.

Staff;—1 fort-major, wounded.

8th; (*or king's regiment;*)—1 lieutenant, 2 serjeants, 7 rank and file, killed; 1 major, 2 captains, 2 lieutenants, 4 serjeants, 51 rank and file, wounded; 13 rank and file missing.

49th regiment;—1 serjeant, 12 rank and file, killed; 1 major, 3 captains, 1 ensign, 1 adjutant, 5 serjeants, 2 drummers, 62 rank and file, wounded; 3 serjeants, 39 rank and file, missing.

Total;—1 lieutenant, 3 serjeants, 19 rank and file, killed; 2 majors, 5 captains, 2 lieutenants, 1 ensign, 1 adjutant, 1 fort-major, 9 serjeants, 2 drummers, 113 rank and file, wounded; 3 serjeants, 52 rank and file, missing.

List of officers killed and wounded.

Killed;—*8th;* (*or king's regiment;*)—Lieut. Hooper.
Wounded;—*Staff;*—Fort-major Taylor, severely.
8th; (*or king's regiment;*)—Major Ogilvie and captain

APPENDIX. 435

Munday, severely, not dangerously; captain Goldrick, and lieutenants Weyland and Boyd, slightly.

49th regiment ;—Major Plenderleath, severely, not dangerously; brigade-major Clark, dangerously; brigade-major Dennis, and captain Manners, slightly; ensign Davy, dangerously; adjutant Stean, slightly.

J. HARVEY, deputy-adj.-gen.
EDWARD BAYNES, adj.-gen.

No. 35.

Return of American prisoners of war, captured near Stoney-Creek, in the action of the 6th instant.

Two brigadier-generals, 1 major, 5 captains, 1 lieutenant, 116 non-commissioned officers and privates.

J. HARVEY, deputy-adj.-gen.
EDWARD BAYNES, adj.-gen.

Return of ordnance, &c. &c. captured from the Americans by a division of the troops under the command of brigadier-general Vincent, in action on the 6th of June, 1813, at the head of Lake-Ontario.

Ordnance ;—3 iron 6-pounders, 1 brass $5\frac{1}{2}$ inch howitzer.

Carriages ;—1 limber 6-pounder, 1 tumbril, with 6-pounder ammunition, complete.

Harness ;—4 sets thill, 4 sets trace.

Horses ;—9 artillery.

WILLIAM HOLCROFT, major,
commanding royal artillery.

N. B. Two of the above 6-pounders were spiked and left on the ground, in consequence of the impossibility of removing them.

No. 36.

Major-general Dearborn to the American secretary at war.

SIR, Head-quarters, Fort-George, June 6th.
I have received an express from the head of the Lake this evening, with intelligence that our troops, commanded by brigadier-general Chandler, were attacked at 2 o'clock this morning, by the whole of the British and Indian forces; and by some strange fatality, though our loss was but small, (not exceeding 30,) and the enemy completely routed and driven from the field, both brigadier Chandler and Winder were taken prisoners. They had advanced to ascertain the situation of a company of artillery when the attack commenced. General Vincent is reported to be among the killed of the enemy. Col. Clark was mortally wounded, and fell into our hands, with 60 prisoners of the 49th British regiment. The whole loss of the enemy is 250. They sent in a flag, with a request to bury their dead. General Lewis, accompanied by brigadier-general Boyd, goes on to take the command of the advanced troops.

I have the honor to be, &c.
HENRY DEARBORN.

Hon. general John Armstrong,
    secretary at war.

No. 37.

From lieutenant Fitzgibbon to major De Haren.

SIR, Township of Louth, June 24th, 1813.
At De Coris, this morning, about 7 o'clock, I received information that about 1000 of the enemy, with two guns, were advancing towards me, from St. David's. I soon after heard a firing of cannon and musketry, and in consequence rode in

advance two miles on the St. David's road. I discovered, by the firing, that the enemy was moving for the road on the mountain. I sent off cornet M'Kenney, to order out my detachment of the 49th, consisting of a subaltern and 46 rank and file, and closed upon the enemy, to reconnoitre. I discovered him on the mountain road, and took a position on an eminence to the right of it. My men arrived, and pushed on in front, to cut off his retreat, under a fire from his guns, which, however, did no execution. After examining his position, I was informed he expected reinforcements; I therefore decided upon summoning him to surrender. After the exchange of several positions, between lieutenant-colonel Bœrstler and myself, in the name of lieutenant-colonel De Haren, lieutenant-colonel Bœrstler agreed to surrender on the terms stated in the articles of capitulation. On my return to my men to send an officer to superintend the details of a surrender you returned.

I have the honor to be, &c.

J. FITZGIBBON, lieut. 49th foot.

To major De Haren, &c. &c.

No. 38.

Capitulation of Colonel Bœrstler and 541 Americans.

June 24th, 1813.

Particulars of the capitulation made between captain M'Dowell, on the part of lieutenant-colonel Bœrstler, of the United States' army, and major De Haren, of his Britannic majesty's Canadian regiment, on the part of lieutenant-colonel Bisshopp, commanding the advance of the British, respecting the force under the command of lieutenant-colonel Bœrstler.

Article I. That lieutenant-colonel Bœrstler, and the force under his command, shall surrender prisoners of war.

Art. II. That the officers shall retain their arms, horses, and baggage.

Art. III. That the non-commissioned officers and soldiers shall lay down their arms at the head of the British column, and shall become prisoners of war.

Art. IV. That the militia and volunteers, with lieutenant-colonel Bœrstler, shall be permitted to return to the United States on parole.

ANDREW M'DOWELL,
Captain United States' light artillery.

Acceded to and signed,   P. G. BŒRSTLER,
lieutenant-colonel,
commanding detachment
United States' army.
P. V. DE HAREN, major,
Canadian regiment.

No. 39.

Return of prisoners taken near Fort-George, June 24th, 1813.

Light dragoons ;—1 cornet, 1 serjeant, 19 rank and file.

Light artillery;—1 captain, 1 lieutenant, 2 serjeants, 31 rank and file.

6th regiment of infantry;—1 captain, 1 lieutenant, 3 serjeants, 54 rank and file.

14th ditto;—1 lieutenant-colonel, 3 captains, 11 lieutenants, 1 surgeon, 15 serjeants, 301 rank and file.

20th ditto;—1 major.

23d ditto;—1 captain, 4 serjeants, 2 drummers, 57 rank and file.

Total—1 lieutenant-colonel, 1 major, 6 captains, 13 lieutenants, 1 cornet, 1 surgeon, 25 serjeants, 2 drummers, 462 rank and file.

Thirty militia released on parole not included in this return.

APPENDIX. 439

Officers names and rank.

Light dragoons;—Cornet Bud.
Light artillery;—Captain M'Dowell; lieutenant Morris.
6th regiment infantry;—Captain M'Kenney; lieutenant Shell.
14th ditto;—Lieutenant-colonel Bœrstler; Captains M'Kenzie, Cumings, and Flemming; lieutenants Saunders, Amdell, Karney, Marshall, Waring, Mudd, Murdock, Goodwin, Clarke, Robinson, and Bundall; surgeon Young.
20th ditto;—Major Taylor.
23d ditto;—Captain Roach.

Return of ordnance, &c. taken.

One 12-pounder, 1 6-pounder, 2 cars, stand of colours of the 14th United States' regiment.

EDWARD BAYNES, adj.-gen.

The loss of the enemy supposed to be about 100 in killed and wounded.

No. 40.

From major-general Dearborn to the American secretary at war.

Head-quarters, Fort-George, June 28, 1813.

SIR,

I have the mortification of informing you of an unfortunate and unaccountable event which occurred yesterday. On the 23d, at evening, lieutenant-colonel Bœrstler, with 570 men, infantry, artillery, cavalry, and riflemen, in due proportion, was ordered to march by way of Queenstown, to a place called the Beaver Dams, on the high ground, about eight or nine miles from Queenstown, to attack and disperse a body of the enemy, collected there for the purpose of procuring provisions, and harassing those inhabitants who are considered friendly to the United States.

Their force was, from the most direct information, composed of one company of the 104th regiment, above 80 strong; from 150 to 200 militia, and from 50 to 60 Indians. At eight o'clock yesterday morning, when within about two miles of Beaver Dam, our detachment was attacked from an ambuscade, but soon drove the enemy some distance into the woods, and then retired to a clear field, and sent an express for a reinforcement, saying he would maintain his position until reinforced. A reinforcement of 300 men marched immediately, under the command of colonel Christie; but, on arriving at Queenstown, colonel Christie received authentic information that lieutenant-colonel Bœrstler, with his command, had surrendered to the enemy, and the reinforcement returned to the camp.

A man who belonged to a small corps of mounted volunteer riflemen, came in this morning, who states that the enemy surrounded our detachment in the woods, and towards 12 o'clock commenced a general attack—that our troops fought more than two hours, until the artillery had expended the whole of its ammunition, and then surrendered; and at the time of the surrender, the informant made his escape.

Why should it have been deemed proper to remain several hours in a position surrounded with woods, without either risking a decisive action, or effecting a retreat, remains to be accounted for, as well as the project of waiting for a reinforcement from a distance of 15 or 16 miles.

No information has been received of the killed or wounded. The enemy's fleet has again arrived in our neighbourhood.

With respect and esteem,
I am, sir, your's, &c.
HENRY DEARBORN.

Hon. John Armstrong, secretary at war.

No. 41.

From lieutenant-colonel Clark to lieutenant-colonel Harvey.

Sir, Chippeway, July 12, 1813.

I have the honor to report to you, for the information of major-general de Rottenburg, that the detachment under the command of lieutenant-colonel Bisshopp, consisting of a detachment of royal artillery, under lieutenant Armstrong, 40 of the king's regiment, under lieutenant Barstow, 100 of the 41st, under captain Saunders, 40 of the 49th, under lieutenant-Fitz-Gibbons, and about 40 of the 2d and 3d Lincoln militia, embarked at two o'clock on the morning of the 11th instant, to attack the enemy's batteries at Black Rock.

The detachment landed half an hour before day-light, without being perceived, and immediately proceeded to attack the batteries, which they carried with little opposition; the enemy heard the firing at their advanced posts, and immediately retreated with great precipitation to Buffaloe.

The block-houses, barracks, and navy-yard, with one large schooner, were burnt; and such of the public stores as could be got off were taken possession off, and carried across the river by the troops. Before the whole of the stores were taken away, the enemy advanced, having been reinforced by a considerable body of Indians, whom they posted in the woods on their flanks and in their advance; they were gallantly opposed by the whole of the troops; but finding the Indians could not be driven from the adjoining woods without our sustaining a very great loss, it was deemed prudent to retreat to the boats, and the troops re-crossed the river under a very heavy fire.

I am extremely sorry to add, lieutenant-colonel Bisshopp fell, severely wounded, on our retreat to the boats; fortunately the detachment did not suffer by it, every thing having been arranged and completed previous to his receiving his wounds.

Inclosed are the returns of the killed, wounded, and missing, with the exception of those of the 49th regiment and militia, which have not yet been received.

I have also inclosed the returns of the ordnance, and other stores captured.

I have the honor to be, &c.
THOMAS CLARK,
Lieut.-col. 2d Lincoln militia.

To lieutenant-col. Harvey,
  deputy adjutant-gen.

No. 42.

Return of killed, wounded, and missing, on the morning of the 11th instant.

July 13, 1813.

Staff;—1 inspecting field-officer, wounded.

8th regiment;—3 privates, killed; 1 captain 1 ensign, 1 serjeant, 10 privates, wounded; 4 privates, missing.

49th regiment;—4 privates, killed; 3 privates, wounded; 2 privates, missing.

Militia;—1 lieutenant-colonel, wounded.

Total—13 privates killed; 1 inspecting field-officer, 1 lieutenant-colonel, 1 captain, 1 ensign, 1 serjeant, 1 corporal, 19 privates, wounded; 6 privates missing.

Names of officers wounded.

Staff;—Lieutenant-colonel Bisshopp, inspecting field-officer, severely (not dangerously).

2d Lincoln militia;—Lieutenant-colonel Clark, slightly.

41st regiment;—Captain Saunders, severely, and prisoner; ensign Mompesson, slightly.

J. HARVEY, lieut.-col. D. A. gen.

No. 43.

Return of ordnance destroyed and captured from the enemy at Black Rock, July 12, 1813.

One iron 12-pounder, with garrison carriage; 1 iron

APPENDIX.

6-pounder, with garrison carriage; 1 brass 6-pounder, with travelling carriage; 1 brass 6-pounder, without travelling carriage.

Total—4; 177 English and French muskets, 1 3-pounder travelling carriage, 6 ammunition kegs, a small quantity of round and case shot, (quantity not yet known).

Taken and destroyed.

Two iron 12-pounders, 2 iron 9-pounders.

R. S. ARMSTRONG,
lieut.-col. royal artil.

No. 44.

Return of stores, &c. &c. captured at, and brought from, Black Rock, on the 14th July, 1813.

One hundred and twenty-three barrels of salt, 46 barrels of whiskey, 11 barrels of flour, 1 barrel of molasses, 1 barrel of tar, 2 large bales of blankets, (about 200,) 70 large blankets loose, 5 large casks of clothing; 3 cases, containing 396 soldiers' caps, 16 bars of iron, 1 bar of steel, 1 side of sole leather, 7 sides of upper leather, (some of them marked serjeant Fitzgerald, 41st regiment, and taken from Fort Erie, to be returned to the 41st regiment,) 7 large batteaux, 1 large scow.

THOMAS CLARK,
lieut.-col. 2d Lincoln militia.

No. 45.

From sir G. Prevost to earl Bathurst.

Head-quarters, Kingston,
My Lord,   Upper Canada, August 8th, 1813.

I have the honor to acquaint your lordship, that the enemy's fleet, of 12 sail, made its appearance off York on the 31st ultimo. The three square-rigged vessels, the Pike, Madison, and Oneida, came to anchor in the offing; but the schooners passed up the harbor, and landed several boats full of troops at the former garrison, and proceeded from thence to the town, of which they took possession. They opened the goal, liberated the prisoners, and took away three soldiers confined for felony: they then went to the hospitals, and parolled the few men that could not be removed. They next entered the store-houses of some of the inhabitants, seized their contents, chiefly flour, and the same being private property. Between 11 and 12 o'clock that night they returned on board their vessels. The next morning, Sunday, the 1st instant, the enemy again landed, and sent three armed boats up the river Don, in search of public stores, of which being disappointed, by sun-set both soldiers and sailors had evacuated the town, the small barrack wood-yard, and store-house, on Gibraltar Point, having been first set on fire by them; and at day-light the following morning the enemy's fleet sailed.

The plunder obtained by the enemy upon this predatory expedition has been indeed trifling, and the loss has altogether fallen upon individuals; the public stores of every description having been removed; and the only prisoners taken by them there being confined to felons and invalids in the hospital.

The troops which were landed were acting as marines, and appeared to be about 250 men; they were under the command of commodore Chauncey and lieutenant-colonel Scott, an unexchanged prisoner of war on his parole, both of whom landed with the troops. The town, upon the arrival of the enemy, was totally defenceless; the militia were still on their parole; and the principal gentlemen had retired, from an apprehension of being treated with the same severity used towards several of the inhabitants near Fort-George, who had been made prisoners, and sent to the United States. Lieutenant-colonel Battersby, of the Glengarry fencibles, with the detachment of light troops under his command, who had been stationed at York, was, upon the appearance of the enemy's

APPENDIX. 445

fleet off that place, on the 29th ult. ordered with his detachment and light artillery to proceed for the protection of the depôts formed on Burlington Heights, where he had joined major Maule's detachment of the 104th regiment, and concentrated his force on the following evening. The enemy had, during the course of that day, landed from the fleet 500 men, near Brandt's house, with an intention of storming the heights; but finding major Maule well prepared to receive them, and being informed of lieutenant-colonel Battersby's march, they re-embarked, and stood away for York.

My last accounts from major-general De Rottenburg are to the 3d instant, when the enemy's fleet had anchored off Niagara. I have received no tidings of our squadron under sir James Yeo, since its sailing from hence on the 31st ultimo.

I have the honor to be, &c.

GEORGE PREVOST.

Earl Bathurst, &c. &c. &c.

No. 46.

From major Taylor to major-general Stoven.

SIR, Isle aux Noix, June 3d, 1813.

In the absence of lieutenant-colonel Hamilton, I have the honor to acquaint you, that one of the enemy's armed vessels was discerned from the garrison, at half-past four o'clock this morning, when I judged it expedient to order the three gun-boats under weigh; and before they reached the point above the garrison, another vessel appeared in sight, when the gun-boats commenced firing. Observing the vessels to be near enough to the shore for musketry, I ordered the crews of two batteaux and row-boats (which I took with me from the garrison to act according to circumstances) to land on each side of the river, and take a position to rake the vessels; the firing was briskly kept up on both sides; the enemy with small-arms and grape-shot occasionally. Near the close of the action, an express came off to me in a canoe, with intelligence, that more armed vessels were approaching, and about 3000 men from the enemy's lines, by land. On this information, I returned to put the garrison in the best order for their reception, leaving directions with the gun-boats and parties, not to suffer their retreat to be cut off from it; and before I reached the garrison, the enemy's vessels struck their colours, after a well contested action of three hours and a half. They proved to be the United States' armed vessels Growler and Eagle, burthen from 90 to 100 tons, and carrying 11 guns each; between them, 12, 18, and 16-pounder carronades; completely equipped under the orders of the senior officer, of the Growler, captain Sidney Smith, with a complement of 50 men each. They had one man killed and eight wounded: we had only three men wounded, one of them severely from the enemy's grape-shot on the parties on shore. The alacrity of the garrison, on this occasion, calls forth my warmest approbation. Ensigns Dawson, Gibbons, and Humphreys, and acting quarter-master Pilkington, and crews, of the 100th (prince regent's) regiment, and lieutenant Lowe, of the marine department, with three gunners of the artillery to each boat, behaved with the greatest gallantry: I am particularly indebted to captain Gordon, of the royal artillery, and lieutenant Williams, with the parties of the 100th regiment, on shore, who materially contributed to the surrender of the enemy. The Growler is arrived at the garrison in good order, and is apparently a fine vessel, and the boats are employed in getting off the Eagle, which was run a-ground to prevent her sinking. I have hopes she will be saved, but in the meantime have had her dismantled, and her guns and stores brought to the garrison. Ensign Dawson, of the 100th regiment, a most intelligent officer, will have the honor of delivering you this.

I have the honor to be, &c.

GEORGE TAYLOR,
major of the 100th regt.

Major-general Stovin,
  commanding at Chambly.

APPENDIX.

Number of men killed, wounded, and prisoners on board the United States' armed vessels the Growler and Eagle, June 3d, 1813.

1 killed; 8 severely wounded; 91 prisoners.—Total 100.

No. 47.

Return of ordnance, ammunition, and ordnance-stores, taken on board the United States' armed vessels Eagle and Growler, on the morning of the 3d of June, 1813.

Iron ordnance;—2 short 18-pounders, 10 6-pounders, 10 18-pounder carronades.

Carriages, with breeching and tackles complete;—2 18-pounders, 10 6-pounders, 10 18-pounder carronades.

Tompions;—8 18-pounders;—12 6-pounders.

8 beds and coins, 69 muskets, 60 bayonets, 12 pistols, 43 cutlassess, 31 boarding-axes, 23 boarding-pikes, 61 pouches and belts, 20 side-belts.

Sponges and rammers;—9 18-pounder, 10 6-pounder.

Wadhooks and ladles;—7 18-pounder, and 8 6-pounder, 12 lint-stocks, 4 port-fire sticks, 3 handspikes, 166 18-pounder, 72 6-pounder fixed case-shot.

Empty cartridges;—100 18-pounder, 40 6-pounder.

Cartridges;—230 musket-balls.

1 whole barrel of powder.

Shot;—129 round 18-pounder, 180 round 6-pounder, 28 round 3-pounders, 20 case 18-pounder, 72 case 6-pounder, 83 grape 18-pounder, 3 grape 6-pounders.

Iron pintails for grape-shot;—36 18-pounder, 41 6-pounder.

14 tin tubes, 4 port-fires, 12lbs. slow-match, 9 powder-horns, 3 copper lanthorns, 12 tin lanthorns, 10 crow-bars, 1 pair of scissars, 1 claw-hammer.

FRED. GORDON, capt. R. A.

To major Taylor, commanding Isle aux Noix.

N. B. The ammunition and stores on board the armed vessel Eagle, being under water, no account has yet been taken of them.

No. 48.

From lieutenant-colonel Murray to major-general Sheaffe.

SIR,　　　　　　　Isle aux Noix, August 3d, 1813.

The land forces of the expedition that left the province on the 29th July, on an enterprise on Lake Champlain, returned this day, after having fully accomplished the objects proposed, and having carried every order into execution.

The enemy's arsenal and block-house, commissary-buildings, and stores at the position of Plattsburg, together with the extensive barracks at Saranac, capable of containing 4000 troops, were destroyed; some stores were brought off, particularly a quantity of naval-stores, shot, and equipments for a large number of batteaux. The barracks and stores at the position at Swanton, on Missisquoi Bay, together with several batteaux at the landing place, were destroyed.

A detachment has been sent to destroy the public buildings, barracks, block-houses, &c. at Champlaintown. Every assistance was rendered by the co-operation of captains Everard and Pring, royal navy, commanding his majesty's sloops of war Broke and Shannon.

I experienced very great benefit from the military knowledge of lieutenant-colonel Williams (13th regiment, second in command). I have to report, in the highest terms of approbation, the discipline, regularity, and cheerful conduct of the whole of the troops, and feel fully confident that, had an opportunity offered, their courage would have been equally conspicuous.

General Hampton has concentrated the whole of the regular forces in the vicinity of Lake Champlain, at Burlington, from the best information, said to be about 4500 regular troops, and a large body of militia. The militia force assembled for the defence of Plattsburg, disbanded on the appearance of the armament. The naval part of the expedition is still cruising on the lake. For any further information, I beg leave to refer

APPENDIX.

you to your aide de camp, captain Loring, the bearer of this despatch.

I have, &c.

J. MURRAY, lieut.-col.

To major-general sir R. H. Sheaffe,
Bart. &c. &c. &c.

No. 49.

From captain Everard to sir George Prevost.

His majesty's sloop Broke, Lake Champlain, August 3d, 1813.

SIR,

Major-general Glasgow has apprised your excellency of my repairing, with a party of officers and seamen, to man the sloops and gun-boats at Isle aux Noix, in consequence of your letter of the 4th ultimo, addressed to the senior officer of his majesty's ship at Quebec, stating it to be of great importance to the public service, that an attempt should be made to alarm the enemy on the Montreal-frontier, &c.; and agreeably to your wish that I should communicate any thing interesting that might occur, I have the honor to acquaint you, that the object for which the corps under the command of lieutenant-colonel Murray had been detached, having been fully accomplished, by the destruction of the enemy's block-house, arsenal, barracks, and public store-houses remaining on the west side of the lake beyond Plattsburg, I stood over to Burlington with the Shannon and one gun-boat, to observe the state of the enemy's force there, and to afford him an opportunity of deciding the naval superiority of the lake. We were close in, on the forenoon of the 2d, and found two sloops of about 100 tons burthen, one armed with 11 guns, the other 13, ready for sea, a third sloop, (somewhat larger,) fitting out, with guns on board, and two gun-schooners, lying under the protection of 10 guns,

450   APPENDIX.

mounted on a bank of 100 feet high, without a breast-work, two scows, mounting one gun each, as floating batteries, and several field-pieces on the shore. Having captured and destroyed four vessels, without any attempt on the part of the enemy's armed vessels to prevent it, and seeing no prospect of inducing him to quit his position, where it was impossible for us to attack him, I am now returning to execute my original orders.

I have the honor to be, &c.
THOMAS EVERARD,
commander of his majesty's sloop Wasp.

Lieut.-gen. sir G. Prevost, Bart.
   &c. &c. &c.

No. 50.

From commodore Macdonough to the American secretary of the navy.

United States' sloop President, near
Plattsburg, Sept. 9, 1813.

Sir,

I have the honor to inform you, that I arrived here yesterday from near the lines, having sailed from Burlington on the 6th instant, with an intention to fall in with the enemy, who were then near this place. Having proceeded to within a short distance of the lines, I received information that they were at anchor; soon after, they weighed and stood to the northward out of the lake—thus, if not acknowledging our ascendancy on the lake, evincing an unwillingness (although they had the advantage of situation, owing to the narrowness of the channel in which their galleys could work, when we should want room) to determine it.

I have the honor to be &c.
THOS. MACDONOUGH.

Hon. W. Jones, secretary of the navy.

APPENDIX. 451

No. 51.

From sir George Prevost to earl Bathurst.

Head-quarters, Montreal,
My lord, Oct 30th, 1813.

Since I had the honor of addressing your lordship in my despatch of the 22d of September last, I have received the enclosed communication from major-general Proctor. I have, however, been informed from the other quarters, that he commenced his retreat from Sandwich on the 24th of that month, having previously dismantled the posts of Amherstburg and Detroit, and totally destroyed the public buildings and stores of every description. That, on the 5th of October following, when within a few miles of a strong position, which it was his intention to take up at the Moravian village on the river Thames, he was attacked by so overwhelming a force, under major-gen. Harrison, that the small numbers he had with him, consisting of not more than 450 regular troops, were unable to withstand it, and consequently compelled to disperse; that he had afterwards rallied the remains of his division, and retired upon Ancaster, on the grand river, without being pursued by the enemy, and where he had collected the scattered remains of his force, amounting to about 200 men, and had with it subsequently reached Burlington-heights, the head quarters of major-general Vincent. Tecumseh, at the head of 1200 Indian warriors, accompanied our little army on its rear from Sandwich: and the prophet, as well as his brother Tecumseh were of the most essential service, in arresting the further progress of the Americans; but, as to the extent of our loss on this occasion, or the particulars of this disastrous affair, I am as yet ignorant; major-general Proctor having signified to major-general De Rottenburg, commanding in the upper province, that he had sent a flag of truce to general Harrison, to ascertain the fate of the officers and soldiers who were missing, and requesting his indulgence for a few days until its return, in order to make his official report.

I also understand, that the enemy, so far from attempting to improve the advantage they had gained, by pursuing our troops on their retreat to the Grand river, had retired to Sandwich, followed by Tecumseh and his warriors, who had much harassed them on their march. Five or 600 Indians, belonging to the right division, are reported to have joined the centre.

I regret to say, that I am still without any official account of captain Barclay's action on Lake-Erie, the result of which has led to our relinquishment of the Michigan territory, excepting Michilimacinac, and our abandonment of the post in Upper Canada beyond the Grand river.

I have the honor to be, &c.
GEORGE PREVOST.

Earl Bathurst, &c. &c.

No. 52.

From major.gen. Harrison to the American secretary at war.

SIR, Head-quarters, Detroit, Oct. 9th, 1813.

In my letter from Sandwich of the 30th ultimo, I did myself the honor to inform you, that I was preparing to pursue the enemy the following day. From various causes, however, I was unable to put the troops in motion until the morning of the 22nd inst., and then to take with me only about 140 of the regular troops—Johnson's mounted regiment, and such of governor Selby's volunteers as were fit for a rapid march, the whole amounting to about 3500 men. To general M'Arthur, (with about 700 effectives,) the protecting of this place and the sick was committed; general Cass's brigade, and the corps of lieutenant-col. Ball were left at Sandwich, with orders to

APPENDIX. 453

follow me as soon as the men received their knapsacks and blankets, which had been left on an island in Lake Erie.

The unavoidable delay at Sandwich was attended with no disadvantage to us. General Proctor had posted himself at Dalson's, on the right side of the Thames, (or Trench,) 56 miles from this place, which I was informed he intended to fortify, and wait to receive me. He must have believed, however, that I had no disposition to follow him, or that he had secured my continuance here, by the reports that were circulated that the Indians would attack and destroy this place upon the advance of the army, as he neglected the breaking up the bridges until the night of the 2d instant. On that night our army reached the river, which is 25 miles from Sandwich, and is one of four streams crossing our route, over all of which are bridges; and they being deep and muddy, are rendered unfordable for a considerable distance into the country. The bridge here was found entire; and in the morning I proceeded with Johnson's regiment to save, if possible, the others. At the second bridge, over a branch of the river Thames, we were fortunate enough to capture a lieutenant of dragoons and 11 privates, who had been sent by general Proctor to destroy them. From the prisoners, I learned that the third bridge was broken up, and that the enemy had no certain information of our advance. The bridge having been imperfectly destroyed, was soon repaired, and the army encamped at Drake's Farm, four miles below Dalson's.

The river Thames, along the banks of which our route lay, is a fine deep stream, navigable for vessels of a considerable burthen, after the passage of the bar at its mouth, over which there is six and a half feet water.

The baggage of the army was brought from Detroit in boats, protected by three gun-boats, which commodore Perry had furnished for the purpose, as well as to cover the passage of the army over the Thames, or the mouths of its tributary streams; the bank being low and the country generally open (Priaries) as far as Dalson's, these vessels were well calculated

for that purpose. Above Dalson's, however, the character of
the river and adjacent country is considerably changed. The
former, though still deep, is very narrow, and its banks high
and woody. The commodore and myself, therefore, agreed
upon the propriety of leaving the boats under the guard of 150
infantry ; and I determined to trust to fortune and the bravery
of my troops to effect the passage of the river. Below a place
called Chatham, and four miles above Dalson's, is the third unfordable branch of the Thames ; the bridge over its mouth had
been taken up by the Indians, as well as that at M'Gregor's
Mills, one mile above. Several hundred of the Indians remained to dispute our passage; and upon the arrival of the
advanced guard, commenced a heavy fire from the opposite
bank of the creek, as well as that of the river. Believing that the
whole force of the enemy was there, I halted the army, formed
in order of battle, and brought up our two 6-pounders to cover
the party that were ordered to cover the bridge. A few shot
from those pieces soon drove off the Indians, and enabled us in
two hours to repair the bridge and cross the troops. Colonel
Johnson's mounted regiment, being upon the right of the army,
had seized the remains of the bridge at the mills under a heavy
fire from the Indians. Our loss upon this occasion was two
killed, and three or four wounded ; that of the enemy was
ascertained to be consideraby greater. A house near the bridge,
containing a very considerable number of muskets had been set
on fire ; but it was extinguished by our troops, and the arms
saved. At the first farm above the bridge, we found one of the
enemy's vessels on fire, loaded with arms, ordnance, and other
valuable stores; and learned that they were a few miles a-head of
us, still on the right bank of the river, with a great body of Indians. At Bowles' Farm, four miles from the bridge, we
halted for the night, found two other vessels and a large dis-
tillery filled with ordnance, and other valuable stores, to an
immense amount, in flames ; it was impossible to put out the
fire ; two 24-pounders, with their carriages, were taken, and
a large quantity of ball and shells of various sizes. The army

APPENDIX. 455

was put in motion early on the morning of the 5th. I pushed on in advance with the mounted regiment, and requested governor Shelby to follow as expeditiously as possible with the infantry; the governor's zeal, and that of his men, enabled them to keep up with the cavalry, and by 9 o'clock we were at Arnold's mills, having taken, in the course of the morning, two gun-boats and several batteaux, loaded with provisions and ammunition.

A rapid stream of the river at Arnold's mills, affords the only fording to be met with for a considerable distance; but upon examination, it was found too deep for the infantry. Having, however, fortunately taken two or three boats, and some Indian canoes, on the spot, and obliging the horsemen to take a footman behind each, the whole were safely crossed by 12 o'clock. Eight miles from the crossing we passed a farm, where a part of the British troops had encamped the night before, under the command of colonel Warburton. The detachment with general Proctor was stationed near to, and fronting, the Moravian town, four miles higher up. Being now certainly near the enemy, I directed the advance of Johnson's regiment to accelerate their march for the purpose of procuring intelligence. The officer commanding it, in a short time, sent to inform me, that his progress was stopped by the enemy, who were formed across our line of march. One of the enemy's waggoners being also taken prisoner, from the information received from him, and my own observation, assisted by some of my officers, I soon ascertained enough of their position and order of battle, to determine that which it was proper for me to adopt.

I have the honour herewith to enclose you my general order of the 27th ult. prescribing the order of march and of battle, when the whole of the army should act together. But as the number and description of the troops had been essentially changed, since the issuing of the order, it became necessary to make a corresponding alteration in their disposition. From the place where our army was last halted, to the Moravian town, a distance of about three miles and a half, the road passes through a beach forest without any clearing, and for the first two miles near to the river. At from 2 to 300 yards from the river, a swamp extends parallel to it, throughout the whole distance. The intermediate ground is dry, and although the trees are tolerably thick, it is in many places clear of underbrush. Across this strip of land, their left *appuyed* upon the river, supported by artillery placed in the wood, their right in the swamp, covered by the whole of their Indian force, the British troops were drawn up.

The troops at my disposal consisted of about 120 regulars, of the 27th regiment, five brigades of Kentucky volunteer militia-infantry, under his excellency governor Shelby, averaging less than 500 men, and colonel Johnson's regiment of mounted infantry, making, in the whole, an aggregate something above 3000. No disposition of an army opposed to an Indian force can be safe, unless it is secured on the flanks, and in the rear. I had therefore no difficulty in arranging the infantry conformably to my general order of battle. General Trotter's brigade of 500 men formed the front line, his right upon the road, and his left upon the swamp. General King's brigade as a second line, 150 yards in the rear of Trotter's; and Child's brigade, as a corps of reserve, in the rear of it. These three brigades formed the command of major-general Henry; the whole of general Desha's division, consisting of two brigades, were formed *en potence* upon the left of Trotter.

Whilst I was engaged in forming the infantry, I had directed colonel Johnson's regiment, which was still in front, to form in two lines opposite to that of the enemy; and upon the advance of the infantry, to take ground to the left; and, forming upon that flank, to endeavor to turn the right of the Indians. A moment's reflection, however, convinced me, that from the thickness of the wood, and swampness of the ground, they would be unable to do any thing on horseback, and that there was no time to dismount them, and place their horses in security; I therefore determined to refuse my left to the Indians, and to break the British line, at once, by a charge of the mounted infantry: the measure was not sanctioned by any thing that I had seen or heard of, but I was fully convinced that it would succeed. The American back-woodsmen ride better in the woods than any other people. A musket or rifle is no impediment, they being accustomed to carry them on horseback from their earliest youth. I was persuaded, too, that the enemy would be quite unprepared for the shock, and that they could not resist it. Conformably to this idea, I directed the regiment to be drawn up in close column, with its right at the distance of 50 yards from the road, (that it might be in some measure protected by the trees from the artillery,) its left upon the swamp, and to charge at full speed as soon as the enemy delivered their fire. The few regular troops, under their colonel, (Paul,) occupied, in column of sections of four, the small space between the road and the river, for the purpose of seizing the enemy's artillery; and some 10 or 12 friendly Indians were directed to move under the bank. The crotchet formed by the front line and general Desha's division, was an important point. At that place the venerable governor of Kentucky was posted, who, at the age of 66, preserves all the vigor of youth, the ardent zeal which distinguished him in the revolutionary war, and the undaunted bravery which he maintained at King's Mountain. With my aide de camp the acting-assistant adjutant-general, captain Butler, my gallant friend commodore Perry, who did me the honor to serve as my volunteer aide de camp, and brigadier-general Cass, who having no command, tendered me his assistance, I placed myself at the head of the front line of infantry, to direct the movements of the cavalry, and to give them the necessary support. The army had moved on in this order but a short distance, when the mounted men received the fire of the British line, and were ordered to charge; the horses in the front of the column recoiled from the fire; another was given by the enemy, and our column at length getting into motion, broke through the enemy with an irresistible force. In one minute the contest in front was over, the British officers seeing no hopes of reducing their disordered ranks to order, and our mounted men wheeling upon them, and pouring in a destructive fire, immediately surrendered. It is certain that three only of our troops were wounded in the charge. Upon the left, however, the contest was more severe with the Indians. Colonel Johnson, who commanded on the flank of his regiment, received a most galling fire from them, which was returned with great effect. The Indians still further to the right advanced, and fell in with our front line of infantry, near its junction with Desha's division, and for a moment made some impression on it. His excellency governor Shelby, however, brought up a regiment to its support, and the enemy received a severe fire in front, and a part of Johnson's regiment having gained their rear, they retreated with precipitation. Their loss was very considerable in the action, and many were killed in their retreat.

I can give no satisfactory information of the number of Indians that were in action; but there must have been considerably upwards of 1000. From the documents in my possession, general Proctor's official letters, (all of which were taken,) and from the information of respectable inhabitants of this territory, the Indians kept in pay by the British were much more numerous than has been generally supposed. In a letter to general De Rottenburg, of the 27th ult. general Proctor speaks of having prevailed upon most of the Indians to accompany him. Of these it is certain that 50 or 60 Wyandot warriors abandoned him.*

The number of our troops was certainly greater than that of the enemy; but when it is recollected that they had chosen a position, that effectually secured their flank, which it was impossible for us to turn, and that we could not present to them a line more extended than their own, it will not be con-

---

* A British officer of high rank assured one of my aides de camp, that on the day of our landing, general Proctor had at his disposal upwards of 3000 Indian warriors, but asserted that the greater part had left him previous to the action.

sidered arrogant to claim for my troops the palm of superior bravery.

(Here follows an encomium upon the officers generally. *)

Major Wood, of the engineers, already distinguished at Fort-Meigs, attended the army with two 6-pounders. Having no use for them in action, he joined in the pursuit of the enemy, and with major Payne, of the mounted regiment, two of my aides de camp, Todd and Chambers, and three privates, continued it for several miles after the rest of the troops had halted, and made many prisoners.

I left the army before an official return of the prisoners, or that of the killed and wounded was made out. It was, however, ascertained that the former amounted to 601 regulars, including 25 officers. Our loss is 7 killed, and 22 wounded, 5 of whom have since died. Of the British troops, 12 were killed, and 22 wounded. The Indians suffered most, 33 of them having been found upon the ground, besides those killed on the retreat.

On the day of the action, six pieces of brass artillery were taken, and two iron 24-pounders the day before. Several others were discovered in the river, and can be easily procured. Of the brass pieces, three are the trophies of our revolutionary war; they were taken at Saratoga and York, and surrendered by general Hull. The number of small arms taken by us and destroyed by the enemy, must amount to upwards of 5000; most of them had been ours, and had been taken by the enemy at the surrender of Detroit, at the river Raisin, and colonel Dudley's defeat. I believe the enemy retain no other military trophy of their victories than the standard of the 4th regiment. They were not magnanimous enough to bring that of the 41st regiment into the field, or it would have been taken.

You have been informed, sir, of the conduct of the troops under my command in action. It gives me great pleasure to inform

* It is thus stated in the published account from which this was copied.

you, that they merit also the approbation of their country for their conduct, in submitting to the greatest privation with the utmost cheerfulness.

The infantry were entirely without tents, and for several days the whole army subsisted upon fresh beef, without either bread or salt.

I have the honor to be, &c.

W. H. HARRISON.

General John Armstrong,
    secretary of War.

P. S. General Proctor escaped by the fleetness of his horses, escorted by 40 dragoons, and a number of mounted Indians.

APPENDIX.
No. 53.

List of convicts confined in the same penitentiary at Frankfort, Kentucky, with the British officers taken prisoners 5th Oct. 1813, with a statement of their crimes, and the punishment sentenced them.

NAMES.	CRIMES.	SENTENCES. Years.
Samuel Moops,	A rape on a child, (castrated himself,)	17
George Williams,	A rape,	10
Daniel Caine,	A rape and murder,	6
William Coleman,	Murder, (called manslaughter,)	7
Newbury Man,	Ditto ditto,	6
John Cox,	Ditto ditto,	5
Preto Sharp,	Ditto ditto,	5
Samuel Bogan,	Ditto, (shooting his wife),	4
Thomas Pegget,	Ditto,	$3\frac{1}{2}$
Samuel Danby,	Ditto,	$3\frac{1}{2}$
James Moore,	Forgery,	4
William Mitchell,	Ditto and coining,	4
Samuel Smith,	Ditto,	4
William Whiteside,	Ditto,	2
James Long,	Ditto,	2
John Lee,	House-breaking and robbery,	2
John Rower,	Ditto,	2
David Ferguson,	Stealing 3 negroes and 3 horses,	$4\frac{3}{4}$
Joseph Jones,	Ditto 1 ditto ditto,	$2\frac{1}{2}$
William Taylor,	Ditto 1 ditto ditto,	$2\frac{1}{2}$
James Hanson,	Ditto 1 ditto ditto,	6
William Hannoy,	Ditto 1 negress,	2
George Fieldie,	Horse-stealing,	6
Alexander White,	Ditto,	10
Thomas Lofton,	Ditto,	$4\frac{1}{4}$
Daniel Dougherty,	Ditto,	$4\frac{1}{2}$
James Porter,	Ditto,	4
William Harding,	Ditto,	4
Ephraim Nowling,	Ditto,	4
John Oder,	Ditto,	4
John Brown,	Ditto,	4
Burgess Irvin,	Ditto,	4
Booth Sitrons,	Ditto,	4
Levi Dunn,	Ditto,	3
John M'Vey,	Ditto,	2
John Kelly,	Ditto,	2
Wm. H. Steer,	Stealing a bolt of cloth,	2
John Allwright,	Stealing clothes which were made up,	2
Jesse Burton,	Stealing a saddle,	2
Philip Jones,	Stealing a beef skin,	2

APPENDIX.

No. 54.

From sir George Prevost to earl Bathurst.

Head-quarters, Montreal, Oct. 30, 1813.

MY LORD,

On the 8th instant, I had the honor to report to your lordship that major-general Hampton had occupied, with a cosiderable force of regulars and militia, a position on the Chateauguay river, near the settlement of the Four Corners. Early on the 21st the American army crossed the line of separation between Lower Canada and the United States, surprised a small party of Indian warriors, and drove in a piquet of sedentary militia, posted at the junction of the Outard and Chateauguay rivers, where it encamped, and proceeded in establishing a road of communication with its last position, for the purpose of bringing forward its artillery. Major-general Hampton, having completed his arrangements on the 24th, commenced, on the following day, his operations against my advanced posts: at about 11 o'clock in the forenoon of the 26th, his cavalry and light troops were discovered advancing on both banks of the Chateauguay, by a detachment covering a working party of *habitans* employed in felling timber, for the purpose of constructing abattis. Lieutenant-colonel De Salaberry who had the command of the advanced piquets, composed of the light infantry company of the Canadian fencibles, and two companies of voltigeurs, on the north side of the river, made so excellent a disposition of his little band, that he checked the advance of the enemy's principal column, led by major-general Hampton in person, and accompanied by brigadier-general Izard; whilst the American light brigade, under colonel M'Carty, was in like manner repulsed in its progress on the south side of the river, by the spirited advance of the right flank-company of the third battalion of the embodied militia, under captain Daly, supported by captain Bruyers' company of Chateauguay chasseurs; captains Daly and Bruyers being both wounded, and their companies having sustained some loss, their position was immediately taken up by a flank-company of the first battalion of embodied militia; the enemy rallied and repeatedly returned to the attack, which terminated only with the day, in his complete disgrace and defeat; being foiled at all points by a handful of men, who by their determined bravery maintained their position, and screened from insult the working parties, who continued their labours unconcerned. Having fortunately arrived at the scene of action shortly after its commencement, I witnessed the conduct of the troops on this glorious occasion, and it was a great satisfaction to me to render on the spot that praise which had become so justly their due. I thanked major-general De Watteville for the wise measures taken by him for the defence of his position, the advance, and lieutenant-colonel De Saluberry, for the judgment displayed by him in the choice of his ground, and the bravery and skill with which he maintained it; I acknowledged the highest praise to belong to the officers and men engaged that morning, for their gallantry and steadiness, and I called upon all the troops in advance, as well for a continuance of that zeal, steadiness, and discipline, as for that patient endurance of hardships and privations which they have hitherto evinced; and I particularly noticed the able support lieutenant-colonel De Saluberry received from captain Fergusson, in command of the light company of the Canadian fencibles, and from captain J. B. Duchesnay and captain J. Duchesnay, and adjutant Hebder, of the voltigeurs, and also from adjutant O'Sullivan, of the sedentary militia, and from captain La Motte, belonging to the Indian warriors. Almost the whole of the British troops being pushed forward for the defence of Upper Canada, that of the lower province must depend, in a great degree, on the valor and continued exertions of its incorporated battalions and its sedentary militia, until the 70th regiment and the two battalions of marines, daily expected, arrive. It is, therefore, highly satisfactory to state to your lordship, that there appears a determination among all classes of his majesty's Canadian subjects, to persevere in a loyal and honorable line of conduct. By the report of prisoners taken from the enemy in the affair on the Chateauguay, the American force is stated at 7000 infantry, and 200 cavalry, with 10 field-pieces. The British advanced force, actually engaged, did not exceed 300. The enemy suffered severely from our fire, and from their own; some detached corps in the woods fired upon each other.

I have the honor to transmit to your lordship, a return of the killed and wounded on the 26th. I avail myself of this opportunity humbly to solicit from his royal highness the prince regent, as a mark of his gracious approbation of the conduct of the embodied battalion of the Canadian militia, five pairs of colours for the 1st, 2d, 3d, 4th, and 5th battalions.

I have the honor to be, &c.

GEORGE PREVOST.

Return of killed, wounded, and missing, of his majesty's forces, in the action with the enemy, in advance of Chateauguay, on the 26th Oct. 1813.

Canadian fencible infantry, light company;—3 rank and file, killed; 1 serjeant, 3 rank and file, wounded.

3d battalion embodied militia, flank-company;—2 rank and file, killed; 1 captain, 6 rank and file, wounded; 4 rank and file, missing.

Chateauguay Chasseurs;—1 captain, wounded.

Total;—5 rank and file, killed; 2 captains, 1 serjeant, 13 rank and file, wounded; 4 rank and file, missing.

Names of officers wounded.

3d battalion embodied militia;—Captain Daly, twice wounded, severely.

Chateauguay chasseurs;—Captain Bruyers, slightly.

EDWARD BAYNES, adjutant-general.

Right Hon. earl Bathurst,
&c. &c. &c.

APPENDIX.

No. 55.

From lieutenant-colonel Morrison to major-general De Rottenburg.

Williamsburg, Upper Canada, Nov. 11, 1813.

Sir,

I have the honor to inclose a copy of the agreement entered into by captain Mulcaster, of the royal navy, and myself, with two of the principal inhabitants of Hamilton, in the state of New York. Having understood, when passing that place, that public property was deposited there, and being informed by lieutenant-colonel Pearson, that his excellency the commander of the forces had directed a small force to act against that village, we considered it our duty, as we possessed the means, to fulfil the intentions of his excellency.; but not having sufficient conveyance, or time, to bring the property away, and as it appeared that it principally belonged to merchants at Kingston, we deemed the inclosed terms best to propose. I also inclose herewith a copy of major-general Wilkinson's proclamation.

J. W. MORRISON, lieut.-colonel,
89th, commanding corps of observation.

Major-general De Rottenburg.

No. 56.

American agreement to deliver up captured property.

We do hereby promise, on our respective words and honor, to deliver on the opposite side of the river, at the house of Jacob Wager, if a flag should be permitted to land, all the public property of the United States, if any should be found here; also all property belonging to his Britannic majesty's government, and the individuals thereof, now deposited in the house of Charles Richards. It being expressly understood that the property and persons of the inhabitants of the village have been spared in consideration of the preceeding arrangement. And we do hereby further pledge our honors, that the boats shall also be delivered, which belong either to the government of the United States, or to his Britannic majesty's government. And we do further admit, that on the non-compliance with these conditions, the village be subject to be destroyed.

     DAVID A. OGDEN.
     ALEX. RICHARDS.
     W. H. MULCASTER,
    Captain royal navy, commanding flotilla.
     J. W. MORRISON,
    Lieut.-colonel, 89th regt. commanding
        corps of observation.

Hamilton, Nov. 10, 1813.

No. 57.

Proclamation of James Wilkinson, major-general and commander-in-chief of an expedition against the Canadas, to the inhabitants thereof.

The army of the United States, which I have the honor to command, invaded this province to conquer, and not to destroy, to subdue the forces of his Britannic majesty, not to war against his unoffending subjects. Those, therefore, among you who remain quiet at home, should victory incline to the American standard, shall be protected in their persons and property; but those who are found in arms must necessarily be treated as avowed enemies. To menace is unmanly—to seduce dishonorable—yet it is just and humane to place these alternatives before you.

APPENDIX 467

Done at the head-quarters of the army of the United States, this 6th day of November, 1813, near Ogdensburg, on the river St. Lawrence.

JAS. WILKINSON.

By the general's command, W. Pinkney,
major and aide de camp.

No. 58.

From lieutenant-colonel Morrison to major-general De Rottenburg.

Chrystler's, Williamsburg, Upper Canada,
Nov. 12, 1813.

Sir,

I have the heartfelt gratification to report the brilliant and gallant conduct of the detachment from the centre-division of the army, as yesterday displayed in repulsing and defeating a division of the enemy's force, consisting of two brigades of infantry and a regiment of cavalry, amounting to between 3 and 4000 men, who moved forward, about two o'clock in the afternoon, from Chrystler's-point, and attacked our advance, which gradually fell back to the position selected for the detachment to occupy; the right resting on the river, and the left on a pine-wood, exhibiting a front of about 700 yards. The ground being open, the troops were thus disposed: the flank companies of the 49th regiment, the detachment of the Canadian fencibles, with one field-piece, under lieutenant-colonel Pearson, on the right, a little advanced on the road; three companies of the 89th regiment, under captain Barnes, with a gun, formed in echellon, with the advance on its left supporting it. The 49th and 89th, thrown more to the rear, with a gun, formed the main body and reserve, extending to the woods on the left, which were occupied by the voltigeurs, under major Herriot, and the Indians under lieutenant Anderson. At about half past two the action became general, when the enemy endeavoured, by moving forward a brigade from his right, to turn our left, but was repulsed by the 89th, forming *en potence* with the 49th, and both corps moving forward, occasionally firing by platoons. His efforts were next directed against our right, and to repulse this movement the 49th took ground in that direction in echellon, followed by the 89th; when within half-musket-shot the line was formed, under a heavy but irregular fire from the enemy. The 49th was then directed to charge the gun posted opposite to ours; but it became necessary, when within a short distance of it, to check the forward movement, in consequence of a charge from their cavalry on the right, lest they should wheel about, and fall upon their rear; but they were received in so gallant a manner by the companies of the 89th, under captain Barnes, and the well-directed fire of the artillery, that they quickly retreated, and by an immediate charge from those companies one gun was gained. The enemy immediately concentrated their force to check our advance, but such was the steady countenance, and well-directed fire of the troops and artillery, that at about half past four they gave way at all points from an exceeding strong position, endeavouring by their light infantry to cover their retreat, who were soon driven away by a judicious movement made by lieutenant-colonel Pearson. The detachment for the night occupied the ground from which the enemy had been driven, and are now moving in pursuit.

I regret to find our loss in killed and wounded has been so considerable; but trust a most essential service has been rendered to the country, as the whole of the enemy's infantry, after the action, precipitately retired to their own shores. It is now my grateful duty to point out to your honor the benefit the service has received from the ability, judgment, and active exertions of lieutenant-colonel Harvey, the deputy-adjutant-general, for sparing whom to accompany the detachment, I must again publicly express my acknowledgments. To the cordial co-operation and exertions of lieutenant-colonel Pearson, commanding the detachment from Prescott, lieutenant-colonel Plenderleath, of the 49th, major Clifford, of the 89th, major Herriott, of the voltigeurs, and captain Jackson, of the royal artillery, combined with the gallantry of the troops, our great success may be attributed. Every man did his duty, and I believe I cannot more strongly speak their merits than in mentioning, that our small force did not exceed 800 rank and file. To captains Davis and Skinner, of the quarter-master-general's department, I am under the greatest obligations for the assistance I have received from them; their zeal and activity has been unremitting. Lieutenant Hagerman, of the militia, has also, for his services, deserved my public acknowledgements, as has also lieutenant Anderson, of the Indian department. As the prisoners are hourly bringing in, I am unable to furnish your honor with a correct return of them, but upwards of 100 are in our possession; neither of the ordnance stores taken, as the whole have not yet been collected.

I have the honor to be, &c.
J. W. MORRISON,
lieut.-col. 89th, commanding
corps of observation.

To major-general de Rottenburg,
&c. &c. &c.

Return of killed, wounded, and missing.

Royal artillery;—2 rank and file, wounded.

Royal artillery drivers;—1 rank and file, wounded.

49th foot;—1 captain, 1 drummer, 5 rank and file, killed; 5 subalterns, 3 serjeants, 34 rank and file, wounded.

89th foot;—1 drummer, 4 rank and file, killed; 1 captain, 1 subaltern, 3 serjeants, 57 rank and file, wounded.

49th foot, flank company;—2 rank and file, killed; 1 subaltern, 11 rank and file, wounded; 6 rank and file, missing.

Canadian fencibles;—4 rank and file, killed; 2 subalterns, 14 rank and file, wounded.

Canadian voltigeurs;—4 rank and file, killed; 9 rank and file, wounded; 3 rank and file, missing.

Militia artillery;—1 rank and file, wounded.

Militia dragoons ;—1 rank and file, wounded.

Indians ;—1 warrior, wounded ; 3 warriors, missing.

Total—1 captain, 2 drummers, 19 rank and file, killed; 1 captain, 9 subalterns, 6 serjeants, 131 rank and file, wounded; 12 rank and file, missing.

Names of officers killed and wounded.

Killed ;—*49th foot ;*—Captain Nairne.

Wounded ;—*49th foot ;*—Lieutenant Jones, dangerously; lieutenant Bartley, severely, not dangerously; lieutenant Claus, left leg amputated; lieutenant Morton, severely, not dangerously; lieutenant Richmond, slightly.

89th foot ;—Captain Browne, severely, not dangerously; ensign Leaden, slightly.

49th foot :—*Flank company ;*—Lieutenant Holland, severely.

Canadian fencibles ;—Lieutenant Delorimiere, dangerously, since dead; ensign Armstrong, dangerously.

***

No. 59.

From major-general Wilkinson to the American secretary at war.

Head-quarters, French Mills, adjoining the province of Lower Canada,

Sir,   16th November, 1813.

I beg leave to refer you to the journal which accompanies this letter, for the particulars of the movements of the corps under my command, down to the St. Lawrence, and will endeavour to exert my enfeebled mind to detail to you the more striking and important incidents which have ensued since my departure from Grenadier island, at the foot of Lake-Ontario, on the 3d instant.

The corps of the enemy which followed me from Kingston, being on my rear, and in concert with a heavy galley and a few gun-boats, seemed determined to retard my progress. I was

APPENDIX. 471

tempted to halt, turn about, and put an end to his teazing: but alas! I was confined to my bed. Major-general Lewis was too ill for any active exertions; and above all, I did not dare to suffer myself to be diverted a single day from the prosecution of the views of government. I had written major-general Hampton on the 6th instant, by adjutant-general-colonel King, and had ordered him to form a junction with me on the St. Lawrence, which I expected would take place on the 9th or 10th. It would have been unpardonable, had I lost sight of this object an instant. I deemed it of vital importance to the issue of the campaign.

The enemy deserve credit for their zeal and intelligence, which the active universal hostility of the male inhabitants of the country enabled them to employ to the greatest advantage.

Thus, while menaced by a respectable force in the rear, the coast was lined with musketry in front, and at every critical pass of the river, which obliged me to march a detachment, and this impeded my progress.

On the evening of the 9th, the army halted a few miles from the head of Longue Saut. On the morning of the 10th, the enclosed order was issued. General Browne marched, agreeably to order, and at noon we were apprised, by the reports of his artillery, that he was engaged some distance below us. At the same time the enemy were observed in our rear, and their galley and gun-boats approached our flotilla, and opened a fire upon us, which obliged me to order a battery of 18-pounders to be planted, and a shot from it compelled the enemy's vessels to retire, together with their troops, after some firing between the advanced parties. By this time, in consequence of his disembarking and re-embarking the heavy guns, the day was so far spent, that our pilots did not dare to enter the Saut, (eight miles a continued rapid,) and therefore we fell down about two miles, and came to anchor for the night.

Early the next morning every thing was in readiness for motion, but having received no intelligence from general Brown, I was still delayed, as sound precaution required I should learn the result of his affair, before I committed the flotilla to the Saut.

At half past 10, A. M. an officer of dragoons arrived with a letter, in which the general informed me he had forced the enemy, and would reach the foot of the Saut early in the day. Orders were immediately given for the flotilla to sail, at which instant the enemy's gun-boats appeared, and began to throw shot among us. Information was at the same time brought me from brigadier-general Boyd, that the enemy's troops were advancing in column. I immediately gave orders to him to attack them. This report was soon contradicted. Their gun-boats, however, continued to scratch us, and a variety of reports of their movements and counter-movements were brought me in succession, which convinced me of their determination to hazard an attack, when it could be done to the greatest advantage; and I therefore resolved to anticipate them. Directions were accordingly sent by that distinguished officer colonel Swift, of the engineers, to brigadier-general Boyd, to throw down the detachments of his command, assigned to him in the order of the preceding day, and composed of men of his own, Covington's, and Swartwout's brigades, into three columns, to march upon the enemy, outflank them if possible, and take their artillery.

The action soon after commenced with the advanced body of the enemy, and became extreemely sharp and galling; and lasted, with occasional pauses, not sustained with great vivacity, in open space, and fair combat, for upwards of two hours and a half, the adverse lines alternately yielding and advancing. It is impossible to say with accuracy what was our number on the field, because it consisted of indefinite detachments, taken from the boats, to render safe the passage of the Saut.

General Covington and Swartwout voluntarily took part of the action, at the head of the detachments from their respective brigades, and exhibited the same courage that was displayed by brigadier-general Boyd, who happened to be the senior officer on the ground. Our force engaged might have reached 16 or

APPENDIX.

1700 men, but actually did not exceed 1800. That of the enemy was estimated from 1200 to 2000, but did not probably amount to more than 1500 or 1600; consisting, as I am informed, of detachments from the 49th, 84th, and 104th regiments of the line, with three companies of the Voltigeur and Glengarry corps, and the militia of the country, who are not included in the estimate.

It would be presumptuous in me to attempt to give you a detailed account of this affair, which certainly reflects high honor on the valor of the American soldiers, as no example can be produced of undisciplined men with inexperienced officers, of braving a fire of two hours and a half, without quitting the field; or yielding to their antagonists. But, Sir, the information I now give you is derived from officers in my confidence, who took active parts in the conflict; for, although I was enabled to order the attack, it was my hard fortune not to be able to lead the troops I commanded.

The disease with which I was assailed on the 2d of September, on my journey to Fort-George, having, with a few short intervals of convalescence, preyed on me ever since; and at the moment of this action I was confined to my bed, unable to sit on a horse, and to move ten paces without assistance. I must, however, be pardoned for trespassing on your time a few remarks in relation to this affair. The objects of the British and the American commanders were precisely opposed, the first being bound by the instructions of his government, and the most solemn obligations of duty, to precipitate his descent of the St. Lawrence by every practicable means, because this being effected, one of the greatest difficulties opposed to the American army would be surmounted; and the former, by duties equally imperious, to retard it, and if possible to prevent such a descent. He is to be accounted victorious who effected this purpose. The British commander having failed to gain either of the objects, can lay no claims to the honors of the day. The battle fluctuated, and the victory seemed at different times inclined to the contending corps. The front of the

APPENDIX.

enemy was at first forced back more than a mile, and though they never regained the ground they lost, their stand was permanent, and their charges resolute. Amidst these charges, and near the close of the contest, we lost a field-piece by the fall of the officer who was serving it with the same coolness as if he had been at parade, or at a review. This was lieutenant Smith, of the light artillery, who in point of merit stood conspicuous. The enemy having halted, and our troops having again formed in battalia, front to front, and the fire having ceased on both sides, we resumed our position on the bank of the river, and the infantry being much fatigued, the whole were re-embarked, and proceeded down the river without further annoyance from the enemy or their gun-boats, while the dragoons with five pieces of light artillery marched down the Canada shore without molestation.

It is due to his rank, merit, and services, that I should make particular mention of brigadier-general Covington, who received a mortal wound directly through his body, while animating his men, and leading them to the charge. He fell where he fought, at the head of his men, and survived but two days.

The next day the flotilla passed through the Saut, and joined that excellent officer, brigadier-gen. Brown, at Barnhart's, near Cornwall, where he had been instructed to take post and wait my arrival, and where I confidently expected to hear of major-general Hampton's arrival on the opposite shore.

But immediately after I had halted, col. Atkinson, inspector-general of the division under major-general Hampton, waited on me with a letter from that officer, in which, to my unspeakable mortification and surprize, he declined the junction ordered,—and informed me he was marching to Lake-Champlain, by way of co-operation in the proposed attack upon Montreal. This letter, together with a copy of that to which it is in answer, were immediately submitted to a council of war, composed of many general officers, and the colonel commanding the elite, the chief engineer, and adjutant-general, who immediately gave it as their opinion, that the attack on the Montreal should be abandoned for the present season, and the army near Cornwall be immediately crossed to the American shore, for taking up winter quarters, and that this place afforded an eligible position for such quarters. I acquiesced in this opinion, not from the shortness of the stock of provisions, (which had been reduced by the acts of God), because our meat had been increased five days, and our bread had been reduced only two days; and because we could, in case of extremity, have lived on the enemy, but because the loss of the division under major-general Hampton weakened my force too sensibly to justify the attempt.

In all my measures and movements of consequence I have taken the opinion of my general officers, which have been accordant with my own.

I remained on the Canadian shore till the next day, without seeing or hearing from the powerful force of the enemy in our neighbourhood, and the same day reached this position with the artillery and infantry.

The dragoons have been ordered to Utica and its vicinity, and I expect are 50 or 60 miles on the march. You have, under cover, a summary abstract of the killed and wounded in the affair of the 11th instant, which will soon be followed by a particular return; in which, a first regard will be paid to individual merit. The dead rest in honor, and the wounded bleed for their country, and deserve its gratitude. With respect,

I have the honor to be, sir,

Your obedient servant,

JAS. WILKINSON.

Here follows a statement of the killed and wounded;— *Killed*, 102.—*Wounded*, 237.

Hon. J. Armstrong, &c. &c. &c.

APPENDIX.

No. 60.

From general Wilkinson to the American secretary at war.

Sir,   Head-quarters, French Mills, Nov. 18, 1813.

I beg this may be considered as an appendage to my official communication respecting the action of the 11th instant.

I last evening received the enclosed information, the result of the examination of sundry prisoners taken on the field of battle, which justifies the opinion of the general officers who were in the engagement. This goes to prove, that although the imperious obligations of duty did not allow me sufficient time to rout the enemy, they were beaten; the accidental loss of one field-piece notwithstanding, after it had been discharged 15 or 20 times. I have also learned, from what has been considered good authority, but I will not vouch for the correctness of it, that the enemy's loss exceeded 500 killed and wounded.

The enclosed report will correct an error in my former communication, as it appears it was the 89th, and not the 84th, British regiment, which was engaged on the 11th. I beg leave to mention, in the action of the 11th, what, from my severe indisposition, I have omitted.

Having received information, late in the day, that the contest had become somewhat dubious, I ordered up a reserve of 600 men, whom I had ordered to stand by their arms, under lieutenant-col. Upham, who gallantly led them into action, which terminated a few minutes after their arrival on the ground. With great consideration and respect, I have the honor to be, &c.   JAMES WILKINSON.

Hon. John Armstrong, secretary at war.

Here follows a statement of the strength of the British forces, engaged in action of the 11th of Nov.—1800 regulars, 300 militia, 40 Indians.—Total, 2170; upwards of 1500 more than they were.

END OF VOL. I.

www.ingramcontent.com/pod-product-compliance
Lightning Source LLC
Chambersburg PA
CBHW061922220426
43662CB00012B/1777